ANGER

The Misunderstood Emotion

REVISED EDITION

Carol Tavris

A TOUCHSTONE BOOK
Published by Simon & Schuster Inc.
New York   London   Toronto   Sydney   Tokyo

Touchstone

First Touchstone Edition, 1984
Revised Touchstone Edition, 1989

TOUCHSTONE and colophon are registered trademarks
of Simon & Schuster Inc.

Designed by Irving Perkins Associates
Manufactured in the United States of America

1   3   5   7   9   10   8   6   4   2   Pbk.

Library of Congress Cataloging in Publication Data

Tavris, Carol
Anger: the misunderstood emotion / Carol Tavris.—Rev. ed.
p.   cm.
Bibliography: p.
Includes index.
1. Anger.   I. Title.
BF575.A5T38 1989   89-33129
152.4'7—dc20   CIP
ISBN 0-671-67523-0   Pbk.

Grateful acknowledgment is due the following for permission to reprint
previously published material:
Arnold Buss, for the irritability scale of the Buss-Durkee Inventory.
The New Yorker for material by Herbert Warren Wind. Copyright © 1981 by
Herbert Warren Wind, originally in *The New Yorker*.
Random House, Inc., for the excerpt from *Rolling Thunder* by D. Boyd.
Copyright © 1974 by Random House, Inc.
Redbook magazine, June 1979. Copyright © 1979 by The Redbook
Publishing Company.
John Wiley & Sons, Inc., for the excerpt from *After the Honeymoon*
by Daniel Wile. Copyright © 1988 by John Wiley & Sons, Inc.

For Ronan O'Casey

Anger is the emotion preeminently serviceable for the display of power.

—WALTER B. CANNON

[Anger] is a management vehicle.

—ALEXANDER HAIG

Contents

Preface to the Second Edition   11
Acknowledgments   15

Introduction: A Point of View   17

1. Rage and Reason—an Eternal Ambivalence   **27**
The Fallacy of the Swami's Snake   33
The Freudian Legacy   38
The Anger Business   42
The Use and Abuse of Anger   46

2. Uncivil Rites—the Cultural Rules of Anger   **48**
The Judicial Emotion   50
A Brief Madness   60
Manners, Emotions, and the American Way   65

3. The Anatomy of Anger   **70**
Emotions and the Brain   73
Temper and Temperament: The Genetic Ingredient   80
The Fuel of Anger   85
Thinking About Feeling   91
Biological Politics   95

4. Stress, Illness, and Your Heart—Myths of Suppressed Anger   **101**
Eating Disorders, Overweight, and Ulcers   104

Anger and Depression   107
The Stress Connection   112
Anger and Heart Disease   119
Considerations   125

5. "Getting It Out of Your System"—Myths of Expressed Anger   128
Myth #1: Aggression   131
Myth #2: Talking Out Anger   138
Myth #3: Tantrums   142
The Conditions of Catharsis   150

6. "Seeing Red"   161
Frustration   164
Noise   167
Crowds   170
Drivers and Dawdlers   173
Alcohol   177
Exercise and Sports   181
Considerations   191

7. Shouters, Sulkers, Grouches, and Scolds—Which Sex Has the Anger Problem?   193
The Stereotype Up Close   200
The Persistence of Myth   210
Two Cultures   216

8. The Marital Onion   220
The Onion Unpeeled   222
The Systems Solution   237
In Praise of Civility   247

9. A Rage for Justice   **251**
The Rationalizing Species   252
The Birth and Death of Anger   263
Temper of the Times   282

10. Rethinking Anger: Strategies for Living with Anger and Getting Beyond It   **286**
Chronic Anger   288
The Difficult Person   293
The Angry Divorce   299
The Aggressive Child   307
The Victim   313
Considerations   318

Further Reading   320
Notes   321
Bibliography   343
Index   369

Preface
to the Second Edition

It is a rare author who is given the chance for second thoughts about a book. But since this book was first published, several developments have occurred that made me want to get my hands back on it.

Although I was no stranger to anger the first time around, either in my personal life or in my experiences with the movement for women's rights over the last two decades, neither had I written this book to exorcise some personal angry demon. (I wrote it because I was angry, with a small *a*, at the destructive advice and commonplace notions about anger that I believe wreak much havoc in our society and our relationships.) Nevertheless, as it must to all of us, anger came home to roost on my doorstep. Two events in particular occurred to teach me viscerally what I had written about intellectually—the unnecessarily destructive power of anger. One was a family rift: not the usual quarrels and grievances I was used to—those heal, and often make a funny story later—but a real severing of connection, both physical and emotional. The other was a lawsuit, brought against my husband and me by a former friend who fell off a step in our house and broke her hip.

In both cases, anger itself was not the problem; anger is inevitable, as is conflict, between friends and loved ones. What was compelling to me about these sad events was the misery caused by the *form* of the anger expressed (in the family instance) and by the decision that anger was incompatible with friendship (in the friend's instance). In both cases, I learned, anger served an ulterior goal: It was merely the excuse, providing the energy to carry out a decision that had already been made.

In the family quarrel, the reasons for the anger did not cause the rift. The reasons were trivial in the great scheme of things, and, as is often the case with great angers, no one can remember them now anyway. The rift was widened, however, because the four participants all spoke different "anger languages," each with its own advantages and disadvantages. One of the four can be furiously, volcanically angry, which is intimidating to a calmer person, but he never says anything unfair or cruel; and then the tempest is over, done, forgotten. Another is more easygoing; he is rarely angry and has trouble expressing it when he is; his style is to accumulate his grievances, sometimes for years, and then spit them all in your face. The third is quick to express anger and moral outrage. When she is angry, she says anything that comes to mind, because she believes that anger is safe and empowering. For her, remarks said "in the heat of anger" don't count; you're supposed to forget them later.

My own style, as the fourth participant, is the one I liked least. I learned that I am slow to anger but, once angry, equally slow to forgive and forget. I take accusations and hard words literally, and brood over them. Tempests are over quickly; my storm clouds, once generated, hover for months.

"Writer, heal thyself," I hear you saying; I have used the opportunity of revising and updating this book to do just that. My experiences have not changed my views of anger, based on the research I did the first time around. On the contrary, they have enriched and verified them, because now I understand how applicable this information is in what psychologists charmingly call "real life."

I have also benefitted from talking with many people who labor in the anger trenches—therapists, teachers, parents, people living through the intense rage of divorce and disaster—who showed me how the research described in this book can be used. In lecturing and conducting workshops with all sorts of groups across the country, I was touched and impressed by the responses of these audiences. I heard from marriage and family counselors, who agreed that their problem is getting couples not to "express" anger, but to shut up long enough to listen to each other. I heard from people who run "ventilationist" therapies for violent adolescents, who told me that at last they understood why their programs weren't working and why their patients were getting angrier and more violent. I heard from countless parents who were raising little hellions they disliked, but who were afraid to "suppress" their children's "aggressive instincts." I heard from couples who had settled into patterns of exasperating, debilitating quarrels, sniping, and meanness, and mistook this for "honest communication of grievances." I heard from coaches and athletes, who told me encouraging stories of how temper control improves performance.

In the last few years, research on anger has blossomed. Most of it has confirmed and expanded the book's arguments in many spheres of life, and I have added this new material where relevant. On the other hand, new evidence persuades me that the physiology of emotion is not so similar across all emotional states, as I wrote in the first edition, and I have changed Chapter 3 accordingly. Chapter 3 also contains a new essay on the growing tendency in psychology and law to excuse angry outbursts and violence thought to be caused by biological "conditions" such as postpartum depression, high testosterone levels, or drinking.

I have also learned more about the importance of confession (as opposed to catharsis): The conditions under which the revelation of emotional secrets (not necessarily anger itself) is important to health. Thus Chapter 5 contains a whole new conclusion, in which I draw together five "conditions of catharsis" under which the expression of anger is likely to be effective. (Unfortunately, these conditions are rarely met in real life!) Thus an important addition to Chapter 5 is the clarification of the circumstances under which the expression of anger can be beneficial, and those under which it can be hazardous.

I have added more on the increasing problem of highway anger (Chapter 6) and expanded the discussion of anger and violence in sports; fortunately, many coaches and athletes are beginning to understand the value of anger control for better performance (Chapter 6). The studies *failing* to support the prevalent belief of sex differences in anger pile up like autumn leaves, and I have included more of this confirming evidence in Chapter 7. I have added what I believe to be an important new approach to anger in the family, the family-systems model, to Chapter 8; this view strikes me as a brilliant alternative to the usual "who started this, who's to blame" spiral of unanswerable, unresolvable family arguments.

I thought long and hard about what to do with Chapter 9, which uses the women's movement as a case study in the rise and fall of anger as a force for social change. Some of my readers wanted me to add more about men's anger at women, and not focus quite so much on the woman's perspective. However, my goal was not to delve into the fascinating and complex reasons that men and women are angry at each other, or to write up lists of what each gender objects to in the other. There are plenty of books that do that. I was trying to draw the reader's attention to the larger question: how changing economic and demographic conditions, and changing social roles—for men and women, for blacks and whites, for old and young, for gay and straight—tear up people's expectations of the "right" way to behave, and make them vulnerable to ideologies that direct their anger to the "right" sources to blame. The women's movement still makes an excellent illustration of these processes, so I decided to leave the original discussion virtually intact. I have, however, added a postscript on postfeminism, a look at what has happened to women's anger since the Reagan Revolution.

One friend of mine observed that the first edition was useful, as far as it went, in helping people think about "generic anger," but that in everyday life people have specific difficulties. Living with the anger at a spouse you are divorcing, she said, is different from working with an infuriating employer whom you dislike, feeling angry with a rebellious teenager whom you love, or transcending anger at an abusive parent who is dead. So I have added an entirely new concluding chapter on new approaches to living with, or getting through, some of these all-too-common difficult anger problems.

Revising this book helped me. I have learned to appreciate, if not entirely eradicate, the remarkable self-deception and self-righteousness that anger so often involves. I have certainly learned the truth of my own lesson in Chapter 4: Depression is not "anger turned inward"; if anything, anger is depression turned outward. Follow the trail of anger inward, and there you find the small, still voice of pain.

Acknowledgments

I am enormously grateful to my editor, Frederic Hills, and to Simon and Schuster for giving me the opportunity of revision. As ever, I am thankful for my agent, Robert Lescher, who, among other things, has taught me the virtue of the persuasive letter over the irritated one (while freely allowing me to rant at him). And every day I am thankful for my husband, Ronan O'Casey, who allows me to write cheerfully about anger because he bestows me with joy.

For this edition, I would like to add my special thanks and gratitude to Leonore Tiefer for her continuing editorial and moral support; my pen pal Harriet Goldhor Lerner of the Menninger Foundation for our years of correspondence on the subject of anger (and other matters); Charles Spielberger of the University of South Florida for our continuing discussions of "anger-in" versus "anger-out"; James Pennebaker of Southern Methodist University for our many helpful discussions on the difference between confession and ventilation; Robert Solomon of the University of Texas and Steve Gordon of California State University, for their non-psychological perspectives; and William Lee Wilbanks, Professor of Criminal Justice at Florida International University, for his staunch efforts to persuade people that they are not pawns of fate or biology.

I wish to thank also the following psychologists for sharing their clinical and research experiences so generously: Bernie Zilbergeld, Oakland, California; Robert Maurer of the Family Practice Residency Program at Santa Monica Hospital; Marion Jacobs, Co-director of the California Self-Help Center at UCLA; Christine Padesky of the Center for Cognitive Therapy in Newport Beach,

California; C. R. Snyder of the University of Kansas; and Richard Driscoll of Bearden Professional Associates in Knoxville, for allowing me to use his "anger spirals."

I wish to repeat my appreciation to the social scientists who, for the first edition, offered their time and ideas and who made available to me unpublished manuscripts: James Averill of the University of Massachusetts; Vladimir Konečni and George Mandler of the University of California at San Diego; Ernest Harburg of the University of Michigan; Ray Novaco of the University of California at Irvine; Don Fitz of St. Louis State Hospital; Suzanne Haynes of the University of North Carolina; Ralph Hupka of California State University at Long Beach; Faye Crosby of Smith; Karen Paige of the University of California at Davis; Norma Wikler of the University of California at Santa Cruz; Thomas A. Sebeok of the University of Indiana; Dorothy Otnow Lewis of Yale University and New York University Hospital. Naturally, responsibility for the interpretation of their work rests entirely with me.

I would like to convey my particular appreciation to Sally Koslow of *Woman's Day,* for her assignments on several facets of living with chronic anger—assignments that allowed me to investigate practical solutions for surviving rage, and report them here.

For this edition as for the first, I celebrate my mother, Dorothy, who is slow to anger; the memory of my father, Sam, who was quick to anger; and my uncle Reuben, who is quick to anger but slow to tell you—for showing me that all three reactions have their uses.

Finally, my thanks and gratitude to the men and women I interviewed, who so freely and cheerfully told me stories of bellowing, sulking, sarcasm, humor, ranting, and now and then reasoned argument; and to the readers of the first edition, for their letters and stories. They have reassured me that a book is not a message in a bottle sent aimlessly into the sea; they got it.

Introduction: A Point of View

Why is this woman angry?

> Arnold took the humidifier from the bedroom into the bathroom, filled it with water, and brought it back. An hour later, when I went to the bathroom, I saw the place was a mess—shower curtain askew, towels fallen into the tub, everything soaked, pools of water on the floor. I was furious. I asked him how he could be so thoughtless and insensitive—the equation between "thoughtfulness," that is, putting things back the way you find them, and "he loves me" is very clear in my mind. He apologized, sort of, but later that evening, over dinner, he asked me why this trivial episode made me so disproportionately angry.

How would you answer? Are any of the following facts about this couple relevant to your interpretation?

• Arnold and Jane have been having an affair for three years, but because he is married they have never lived together. The humidifier fight occurred on the first night of a two-week cohabitation made possible by the temporary absence of his wife.

• Arnold has been married for thirty years to a woman who has always looked after his needs and picked up after him.

• Jane is a feminist, an independent woman who has lived alone for ten years. She is used to doing things her own way.

• Arnold is a psychoanalyst. Jane is a historian.

• Jane has been told she will not get tenure at her university and she is worried about finding another job.

• Arnold takes long vacations with his wife. Jane is expected to have no other relationships with men.

Your judgment about why Jane was so angry with Arnold, and whether she *should* be angry, will depend on your age, sex, marital status, and politics. Perhaps you will agree with Arnold's psychoanalytic explanation that Jane was not "really" angry with him, but with her mother. Her mother, in his opinion, established an unrealistic, childish connection in Jane's head between "thoughtfulness," its behavioral expression, and Jane's curious idea that thoughtfulness is a sign of love.

Or you may prefer a feminist analysis: Jane should indeed regard the actions of her lover, including that psychoanalytic self-justification, as a sign of selfishness. The selfishness may have been inadvertent (he never learned to clean up because there was always a woman around to do it) or a political act of control (the male demand that women do all the housework serves to keep women in submission), but either way Jane is entitled to feel angry with him. By his action, Arnold was asserting her inferior status in their relationship.

Or perhaps you will find a physiological explanation congenial: Jane was already upset and agitated by other events in her day—stress and uncertainty at work—and this trivial irritation was the catalyst to discharge her accumulated energy.

Or you may agree with a newlywed's analysis: Jane and Arnold have nothing more serious than first-week-living-together crunch, a predictable collision between two sets of habits, preferences, and expectations. "They will either iron out their differences in time," says my friend Cathy, "or they'll settle into routine squabbling like the rest of us."

Or you may choose among an array of therapeutic analyses that look for unconscious motives. There are nearly as many of these as there are therapists, but they share what we may call the "really" question. Was Jane really angry with Arnold for not divorcing his wife? Or for his maintaining a double sexual standard? Was she really angry with herself for some mistakes she made at work that afternoon? Or for staying with Arnold in spite of having no future prospects with him? Was she really angry at her university for denying tenure to all of its female assistant professors? You could play the game all night, and this, mind you, is only a small incident. Imagine the explanations you could generate for a complicated, long-running marital battle.

The road to the understanding of rage runs two ways: in the direction of causes, and in the direction of results. Consider for a moment the *effect* of Jane's blowup and of Arnold's interpretation of it. Jane was saying, vehemently, that Arnold's behavior made her feel unhappy and unloved, that it displeased her, that she wished he'd cut it out. Arnold's response was to turn Jane's grievance aside, to make her feel that she had an "anger problem" and that the source of her complaint had to do with her mother, not with him.

Well, if she accepts his analysis, so what? The "so what" is that *the explanation Jane believes is the one that will guide her future action*. One of the founders of modern sociology, W. I. Thomas, observed that "if men define situations as real, they are real in their consequences"; so it is with psychological judgments. If Jane believes that she is not really angry with Arnold for leaving the bathroom in a mess, but "really" angry with her mother for teaching her to be angry with men who leave bathrooms in messes, her relationship with her mother is likely to be affected; her relationship with Arnold, unchanged. If she attributes her anger to the day's stresses, *she* may be the one who apologizes. If she thinks her anger with Arnold is legitimate, and if she convinces him that it is, she may get him to be more sensitive to her feelings. If she thinks her anger is really directed to sex-role inequities of national magnitude, she may join the women's movement and leave Arnold to do his own cleaning up.

The harder we try to pin down one explanation, the more certain we are to fail. The reason, I will argue, is that anger is not a disease, with a single cause; it is a process, a transaction, a way of communicating. With the possible exception of anger caused by organic abnormalities, most angry episodes are social events: They assume meaning only in terms of the social contract between participants. The beliefs we have about anger, and the interpretations we give to the experience, are as important to its understanding as anything intrinsic to the emotion itself.

This is why people don't always know whether they are angry;

sometimes it takes a friend or a therapist or a whole movement to persuade them. It is why people can feel very angry and not know why, or at what. There is no one-to-one correspondence between feeling angry and knowing why, because the "knowing why" is a social convention that follows cultural rules. We all seek meaning to our emotions and actions, and we accept the explanation most in harmony with our preconceptions, needs, and history.

I am not saying that all explanations are created equal; rather that we have to be careful which explanation we choose, because then we have to live with it. There are, certainly, ways to determine why we feel angry and how we might then behave, but they have to do with which actions will ease the feeling and which will escalate it. Many of us know people who have been in therapy for years and are just as scratchy as they ever were, still blaming their mothers for their unhappiness. Others blame their spouses, or life. The task for a quarreling couple, say, is not just to negotiate a mutually acceptable understanding of why they are angry with each other, but to decide what to do about it. And then to do it.

What we do about anger, though, depends first on how we think and speak about it.

> "Try another Subtraction sum," [said the Red Queen]. "Take a bone from a dog: what remains?"
>
> Alice considered. "The bone wouldn't remain, of course, if I took it—and the dog wouldn't remain: it would come to bite me—and I'm sure *I* shouldn't remain!"
>
> "Then you think nothing would remain?" said the Red Queen.
>
> "I think that's the answer."
>
> "Wrong, as usual," said the Red Queen: "the dog's temper would remain."
>
> "But I don't see how—"
>
> "Why, look here!" the Red Queen cried. "The dog would lose its temper, wouldn't it?"
>
> "Perhaps it would," Alice replied cautiously.
>
> "Then if the dog went away, its temper would remain!" the Queen exclaimed triumphantly.

The Red Queen's calculation is funny because it takes literally what our language intends metaphorically. A "temper" is not an object that can be misplaced, swallowed, sat on, or worn on one's head. Yet often in everyday speech this confusion occurs. Some people compare anger to a powerful force—a fever, a tornado—that "storms" or "rages" through the body. (Plato, Shakespeare, and Freud all compared anger to a high-spirited horse, ridden by reason.) When anger is not trampling roughshod through our nervous systems, it is sitting sullenly in some unspecified internal organ. "She's got a lot of anger in her," people will say (it nestles, presumably, somewhere in the gut), or, "He's a deeply angry man" (as opposed, presumably, to a superficially angry one). If anger isn't released, it "turns inward" and metamorphoses into another creature altogether.

Figures of speech like these, wonderfully vivid as they are, reflect something more than linguistic playfulness. When anger is reified—that is, transformed from a process or abstraction into a concrete material object—we think of it and act on it accordingly. The eminent British psychiatrist John Bowlby lamented the common tendency to "reify emotions, especially the more uncomfortable ones. Instead of describing the situation in which a person experiences a fear, the person is said to 'have' a fear. Instead of describing the situation in which a person becomes angry, he is said to 'have' a bad temper. Similarly, someone 'has' a phobia, or is 'filled with' anxiety or aggression. Once emotions are reified the speaker is spared the task of tracing what is making the person in question afraid or angry." But reification is not explanation.

The metaphors about anger infect research and therapy, too, for they encourage medical and psychological perspectives. If anger is sitting inside you *like* a gallstone, after all, you might as well treat it as if it *were* a gallstone. If anger can be redirected or remolded as if it were a river or a piece of clay, you do well to worry what "direction" it is taking or how it is "shaping up."

Most of us, of course, pay no attention to linguistic refinements and cheerfully use the word "anger" to mean whatever we want. We say we are angry about a broken shoelace, angry with our parents who have been dead for twenty years, angry at injustice, angry at life, angry at being fired, angry at burning the broccoli. Some popular writers and pop psychologists seem to believe that all of these experiences of anger are roughly equivalent and that one therapeutic stance (say, expressing the emotion) is appropriate to all. But as I will try to show, there are different angers, involving different processes and having different consequences to our mental and physical health. No single remedy fits all. Sometimes suppressed hostility can aggravate stress and illness, but sometimes suppressed hostility is the best thing for you. It used to be called common courtesy.

My husband, his then teenage son, and I were enjoying a lavish brunch with friends one August day, when a neighbor of the hosts dropped in to visit. She is a journalist, and a good one, and when she heard the subject of this book her curiosity was whetted. I was reluctant to talk about it, which aroused her interest all the more.

"Is it about women and anger?" she asked.

"Not specifically," I said.

"Is it about work and anger?"

"Not entirely."

"Then is it a sociobiology of anger?"

"No," I said abruptly, trying to discourage her . . .

"Is it political?"

"You could say so." . . . but I was failing.

"Is it a clinical analysis of anger in intimate relationships?"

"*No!*" shouted my stepson, slamming his hand on the table in mock fury. She visibly jumped, and then all of us laughed. The interrogation and my tension were over, and Matthew had demonstrated the point of this book: Anger has its uses.

The social perspective on anger, I believe, explains the persistence and variety of this emotion far better than reductionistic analyses of its biology or its inner psychological workings. This is a minority view in an era that celebrates medical and psychological models of the emotions: research on the brain and hormones, after all, promises exciting possibilities for "cures" of emotional abnormalities, and of course many people are accustomed to hunt for the origins of their emotional conflicts within themselves, rummaging around in their psyches. It is not that I think these approaches are entirely wrong; rather that they are insufficient. An emotion without social rules of containment and expression is like an egg without a shell: a gooey mess.

Our contemporary ideas about anger have been fed by the anger industry, psychotherapy, which too often is based on the belief that inside every tranquil soul a furious one is screaming to get out. Psychiatric theory refers to anger as if it were a fixed amount of energy that bounces through the system: If you pinch it in here, it is bound to pop out there—in bad dreams, neurosis, hysterical paralysis, hostile jokes, or stomachaches. Therapists are continually "uprooting" anger or "unearthing" it, as if it were a turnip. Canadian psychiatrist Hossain B. Danesh, for example, writes that his profession has "succeeded in unearthing" anger that is buried in psychosomatic disorders, depression, suicide, homicide, and family problems. Yale psychiatrist Albert Rothenberg is not so sure about this success:

> In depression we look for evidence of anger behind the saddened aspect; in hysteria we experience angry seductiveness; in homosexuality and sexual disorders we see angry dependency; in marital problems we unearth distorted patterns of communication, particularly involving anger. We interpret the presence of anger, we confront anger, we draw anger, we tranquilize anger, and we help the working through of anger. . . . We operate on the basis of a whole series of assumptions, none of which has been clearly spelled out.

That is precisely the problem. Clinicians devote a considerable portion of their energies to helping their clients "deal" with anger, yet few of them distinguish anger from rage, hatred, violence, or chronic resentment, and even fewer conduct the experiments to see how these phenomena might differ. Some clinicians deride research altogether, arguing that they are healers and artists, not scientists, and that they know all they need to know from their patients. Perhaps. But as a result of this attitude, too many clinicians illogically conclude that their observations of people in therapy apply equally to everyone else. Worse, they do not recognize how often they themselves *create* the problem they diagnose because of their particular school of therapy and their choice of methods. Sometimes anger, like beauty, is in the eye of the beholder.

And so let us spell out a few of the assumptions prevalent in the anger business:

• Emotional energy is a fixed quantity that can be dammed up or, conversely, that can "flood" the system.

• Anger and aggression are inextricably, biologically linked; anger is the feeling and aggression its overt expression, but both are aspects of the aggressive instinct.

• Anger is an instinctive response to threat and to the frustration of your goals or desires.

• If the outward expression of anger is blocked, anger "turns inward," where you feel it as depression, guilt, shame, anxiety, or lethargy.

To test the validity of these ideas, I have drawn together studies from the social and biological sciences (including psychology, sociology, anthropology, and physiology) and, to add descriptive nuance, I informally interviewed fifty men and women about their experiences with and beliefs about anger. I found that many of the assumptions of psychiatric theory are dated, flawed, incomplete, or wrong; that they justify our customs, they do not explain them. And so I began to question other beliefs about anger that affect our lives. Are men and women as different as the stereotypes say? Is ventilation of anger always good for you, and suppressed hostility dangerous? Does drinking liberate buried rage? Do sports displace anger? When does apathy over injustice turn to fury?

I believe that careful answers to these questions matter because the management of anger has such powerful and potentially dangerous implications for our private lives and our social policies. Our legal code distinguishes murder "in the heat of anger" from "cold" premeditated murder on the assumption that we have no control over the former. We make countless excuses for aggression in schools, sports, the streets, the family, on the grounds that anger is automatically caused by frustration, noise, crowds, and alcohol. People spend millions of dollars on treatments to prevent or cure the supposed consequences of suppressed rage, which has become an all-purpose diagnosis for such unlikely partners as depression, ulcers, and food binges. I have chosen to write about anger, instead of equally compelling emotions such as jealousy, joy, pity, or grief, because the filaments of anger affect the entire web of our social relations.

Most of all, I believe that a careful study of anger matters because anger, like love, has such a potent capacity for good and evil. And I do mean good and evil, not "adjustment and deviance," the gutless language that so often characterizes modern discussions of psychological topics. Anger, like love, is a moral emotion. I have watched people use anger, in the name of emotional liberation, to erode affection and trust, whittle away their spirits in bitterness and revenge, diminish their dignity in years of spiteful hatred. And I watch with admiration those who use anger to probe for truth, who challenge and change the complacent injustices of life, who take an unpopular position center stage while others say "shhhh" from the wings.

In the last several decades, biology and psychology have deprived anger, and our other emotions, of the human capacity for choice and control. My aim here, in evaluating and criticizing the prevailing wisdom, is to help restore confidence in those human gifts.

1

Rage and Reason—an Eternal Ambivalence

Be not hasty in thy spirit to be angry: for anger resteth in the bosom of fools.

—ECCLESIASTES 7:9

They have provoked me to anger with their vanities: and I will move them to jealousy with those which are not a people; I will provoke them to anger with a foolish nation.

—DEUTERONOMY 32:21

On the train to Brindavan a Swami sits beside a common man who asks him if indeed he has attained self-mastery, as the name "Swami" implies.

"I have," says the Swami.

"And have you mastered anger?"

"I have."

"Do you mean to say that you have mastered anger?"

"I have."

"You mean you can control your anger?"

"I can."

"And you do not feel anger."

"I do not."

"Is this the truth, Swami?"

"It is."

27

After a silence the man asks again, "Do you really feel that you have controlled your anger?"

"I have, as I told you," the Swami answers.

"Then do you mean to say, you never feel anger, even—"

"You are going on and on—what do you want?" the Swami shouts. "Are you a fool? When I have told you—"

"Oh, Swami, this is anger. You have not mas—"

"Ah, but I have," the Swami interrupts. "Have you not heard about the abused snake? Let me tell you a story.

"On a path that went by a village in Bengal, there lived a cobra who used to bite people on their way to worship at the temple there. As the incidents increased, everyone became fearful, and many refused to go to the temple. The Swami who was the master at the temple was aware of the problem and took it upon himself to put an end to it. Taking himself to where the snake dwelt, he used a mantram to call the snake to him and bring it into submission. The Swami then said to the snake that it was wrong to bite the people who walked along the path to worship and made him promise sincerely that he would never do it again. Soon it happened that the snake was seen by a passerby upon the path, and it made no move to bite him. Then it became known that the snake had somehow been made passive and people grew unafraid. It was not long before the village boys were dragging the poor snake along behind them as they ran laughing here and there. When the temple Swami passed that way again he called the snake to see if he had kept his promise. The snake humbly and miserably approached the Swami, who exclaimed, 'You are bleeding. Tell me how this has come to be.' The snake was near tears and blurted out that he had been abused ever since he was caused to make his promise to the Swami.

" 'I told you not to bite,' said the Swami, 'but I did not tell you not to hiss.' "

—*Rolling Thunder*

Many people, like the Swami's cobra, confuse the hiss with the bite. It is an understandable mistake, for ambivalence about anger permeates our society. Once thought to be a destructive emotion that should be suppressed at all costs, anger is now widely thought to be a healthy emotion that costs too much when it is suppressed.

In the abrupt transition from Puritan restraint to liberated self-expression, many people are uncertain about how to behave: Some overreact angrily at every thwarted wish, others suffer injustice in silence. We are told in one breath not to rock the boat, and in the next that the squeaky wheel gets the grease. Some people take a dose of anger like a purgative, to cleanse the system; others dread any ripple on their natural placidity and fear the loss of control that the demon anger, like the demon rum, might bring.

One friend of mine, a forty-year-old businesswoman, illustrates perfectly our culture's conflict about anger. She won't express feelings of ire, she said, unless she is really "boiling."

"What do you fear about expressing anger?" I asked.

"Retaliation—I don't want that. Or open warfare—very frightening. There's a fear that once you start screaming at people you'll end up like one of those hollerers on Forty-second Street. If you start, where's it going to stop?"

"But surely you've been angry at people before, and I don't see that you have lost all shreds of self-control."

"Actually, I think I'd be perfectly willing to get angry if I thought people would put up with it. But they don't. That's the kicker. They fight back. When you express anger, the person receiving it doesn't simply say, 'Point well taken!' "

"Well, then, what *do* you do when you are angry?"

"I retreat and sulk. Anger just sits there, like an uncooked doughnut."

It is instructive, if also comical, that two popular embodiments of anger in America are antithetical types—Superman and the Incredible Hulk. Clark Kent never really gets angry at injustice, merely impatient: "Oh, gosh, I'd better save the city again." Then he *chooses* to jump into his flying suit and charge off to right wrong. When David Banner gets angry, he becomes, *uncontrollably*, a giant green id, a bilious beast. He is not a man at all, super or otherwise. These incarnations of anger represent dual attitudes: *is* anger handsome or ugly, righteous or dangerous? Is it under our control, or do we have as much chance of telling it what to do as of regulating the carotid artery? Is it a human blessing, or a bestial sin? (The Bible does not answer, now

recommending the furious smiting of the unjust, then the ame-
liorative turning of cheeks.)

Although my friend occasionally berates herself for her ambivalence about anger—and spends a lot of time in therapy trying to
"resolve her feelings"—she is in fact part of a long and noble
debate in Western tradition. In the eighth century B.C., Homer's
Iliad offered an epic story of a man's anger—indeed, *The Anger of
Achilles* is the title of Robert Graves's beautiful translation of the
saga. When the Greek King Agamemnon appropriates Briseis, a
girl whom Achilles has won in battle, Achilles' masculine pride is
wounded. Stifling his angry impulses to kill Agamemnon at once,
Achilles retreats to sulk in his tent and pamper his rage. But
Achilles feels better about sulking than my friend does. "How
delightedly I nursed my grudge against the High King Agamemnon!" he recalls. "It smouldered in my heart, and was as sweet to
me as trickling honey." The tragic events of the *Iliad* unfold when
Achilles stops sulking and acts to avenge the killing of his friend
Patroclus.

In contrast, *The Trial of Sören Qvist*, written in the 1940s by
Janet Lewis, is an exquisite novella about a peaceful parson who is
roused to fury by his stupid, arrogant servant. When the servant is
found murdered, Qvist is arrested; and the trial that ensues for him
is both legal and spiritual. At last, although he knows he is
innocent of the deed, Qvist convicts himself of the desire. He
remembers an earlier time when anger had defeated him, an
experience that I expect is familiar to modern readers:

> No sooner did he feel himself alone than his anger disappeared. His
> bones seemed to turn to water, and a most awful sickness took
> possession of him. He sank to his knees, shaking, and covered his
> face with his hands. . . . This anger, which came upon him so
> suddenly and with such absolute power, had been the greatest trial
> of his life.
>
> Memories rushed upon him. The face of a young German
> student, blond, arrogant, and opinionated, rose before him. He felt
> again the sword in his hand, and in his heart the furious desire
> which had possessed him to kill that young man. The reason for the
> quarrel escaped him.

Two more unlike stories you could not find, for the anger that is sweet to one hero is anathema to the other; Achilles nurses his anger and Qvist curses his; one uses his anger and the other feels used by it. Over the centuries, the pendulum of opinion has slowly swung to the Qvistian position, a result of profound changes in our attitudes about the nature of humankind.

About as soon as man could think, he thought thinking was superior to feeling. (I use the word "man" advisedly, and not generically, either. I'm afraid man also thought thinking was not a female capacity.) The battle lines were drawn early for what Pascal would call the "internal war" between reason and emotion, and for most of our history a brave confidence in reason prevailed. Reason, or at least religious faith, gave man a fighting chance to control anger, pride, lust, covetousness, envy, gluttony, sloth, and any other deadly sin that happens to be his weakness; philosophers and theologians sought to distinguish man from beast, and from woman, by praising his intelligence, rationality, and upright posture (in both the moral and vertical meanings of "upright"). And so, for most of the twenty-five hundred years since Plato, the healthy individual was someone who did not fly off the handle, who was not, in Hamlet's felicitous phrase, passion's slave. Far from advising emotional self-expression, our predecessors came down firmly on behalf of self-control:

> *Hesitation is the best cure for anger. . . . The first blows of anger are heavy, but if it waits, it will think again.*
>
> —SENECA

> *In the march towards Truth, anger, selfishness, hatred, etc., naturally give way, for otherwise Truth would be impossible to attain. A man who is swayed by passions may have good enough intentions, may be truthful in word, but he will never find the Truth.*
>
> —GANDHI

> *To behave rightly, we ourselves should never lay a hand on our servants as long as our anger lasts. . . . Things*

*will truly seem different to us when we have quieted and
cooled down.*

—Montaigne

*The principal use of prudence, of self-control, is that it
teaches us to be masters of our passions, and to so
control and guide them that the evils which they cause
are quite bearable, and that we even derive joy from
them all.*

—Descartes

Short temper is a loss of face.

—fortune cookie

It is only in the last two centuries, just yesterday by historical
standards, that confidence in the power of reason yielded to doubt,
a transformation midwived by the work of Charles Darwin and
Sigmund Freud. Whereas Plato assured us that reason (ego) could
control our worst impulses, Freud and his followers bet gloomily
on the id, on the sway of instinct. Plato and his intellectual heirs
tried to show that man was better than beast; Darwin showed that
man was just another species of beast, and many of his successors
now argue that most beasts are wiser and kinder than man. Popular
ethologists (students of animal behavior such as Konrad Lorenz,
Robert Ardrey, and Desmond Morris) and lately the sociobiologists
(such as E. O. Wilson) make an impassioned case that man is not
a reasonable creature.

Because the legacy of Darwin and Freud has so profoundly
shaped contemporary attitudes about anger, I would like to offer a
few reminders of what they did, and did not, have to say about this
powerful emotion. I do not wish to imply a "great man" theory of
historical change here. It takes countless intellectual contributions
to chip away at an establishment view of the world, before it falls;
and although Darwin and Freud are the best examples of the
theories they promoted, they were by no means the only ones.
Further, scientific and theoretical ideas must fall on fertile ground

if they are to take root, and the social and economic conditions of the nineteenth and twentieth centuries have surely buffeted human self-confidence, making the world ready for evolution and psychoanalysis.

But Freud's and Darwin's theories represent a crucial pivot point in Western thought: for once the belief that we can control anger—indeed, must control it—bowed to the belief that we *cannot* control it, it was then only a short jump to the current conviction that we *should* not control it.

THE FALLACY OF THE SWAMI'S SNAKE

My neighbor describes a family crisis that she watched unfold on her patio. A baby bird, struggling from its nest, has made its way to a precarious perch on her clothesline. Terrified equally of flying and falling, it does not budge, but whimpers piteously. The mother, chirping her support and encouragement, shows her baby how to take off, flutter around, and land. No luck; baby doesn't move. The mother becomes chirpier. No reaction. She flies off, leaving baby in panic. Suddenly, from a nearby tree, comes an angry, unmistakable paternal note, a deep squawk: FLY! Baby stops whining at once and soars away.

The Bird Family scene seems so familiar to us that it is almost impossible to describe it without using anthropomorphic terms: The fledgling is "terrified," "panics," and "whines"; the mother "encourages," the father remonstrates sternly. Charles Darwin, for all his powers of observation, likewise had no difficulty in seeing human emotions in the animals he studied. In *Descent of Man*, he wrote that animals feel pride, self-complacency, shame, modesty, magnanimity, boredom, wonder, curiosity, jealousy, and anger—in short, all the blights and delights of the human species. "There can, I think, be no doubt that a dog feels shame, as distinct from fear, and something very like modesty when begging too often for food," Darwin wrote. (He was talking about dogs that live with people.) And one day, while walking in the zoological gardens, he observed a baboon "who always got into a furious rage when his keeper took out a letter or book and read it aloud to him; and his rage was so violent that, as I witnessed on one occasion, he bit his own leg till the blood flowed." One wonders what the keeper was reading . . . and why he persisted.

Darwin's purpose, however, was not to equate people with baboons, in spite of what we call each other in the heat of anger, but rather to demonstrate that the origins of virtually all the human emotions could be found in lower animals. Emotional expression, he said, serves the same adaptive purpose. The smile, the frown, the grimace, the glare: all were biologically based, common to many animal species through the course of evolution. Darwin sought to establish a theory that applied to human beings *and* to other species, and in so doing he significantly tipped the balance between reason and rage in favor of the latter.

When animals are threatened or perceive danger, they do respond in ways that we liken to anger: Hair (if the animal has hair) stands on end, pupils dilate, muscles tense, fins flap, warning growls or chirps or rattles sound, and the organism readies itself to fight or flee. When provoked by another stickleback, a male stickleback must attack, for it is programmed to be a feisty fish. If a foreign wolf enters marked territory, the defending wolf is not going to be laid-back about it. In *The Expression of the Emotions in Man and Animals*, written in 1872, Darwin argued that rage is a simple response to threat, which requires an animal to become aroused to defend itself. In fact, Darwin actually *defined* rage as the motivation to retaliate: "Unless an animal does thus act, or has the intention, or at least the desire to attack its enemy, it cannot properly be said to be enraged."

Because human beings so often seem to behave like sticklebacks, baby birds, and wolves, it seemed logical to conclude that the rage response is as programmed into us as into other species. Indeed, as Darwin's stringers in India, New Zealand, China, Australia, and Europe assured him, the symptoms of rage are identical in people throughout the world. The face of rage, for example, is not learned. It is as much a part of species equipment as a nose or a pair of eyebrows.

So far, so good, but then Darwin made a crucial error. Anger, he decided, was only watered-down rage. Anger and indignation "differ from rage only in degree," he said, "and there is no marked distinction in their characteristic signs." By lumping these three feelings together, however, Darwin severely restricted his analysis, for he was led to conclude that anger, like rage, is solely a response to threat and danger; and that anger, like rage, implies an instinctive aggressive response.

Darwin was a brilliant ethologist, but a poor psychologist. He had animal rage down cold, but human anger eluded him. His account of anger was oversimplified: Someone offends you, so you dislike him; your dislike turns to hatred; brooding over your hatred makes you angry. This progression of events is certainly possible, but by no means inevitable, or the only origin of anger. (Maybe it occurs the other way around for you: You hate someone's values, and therefore dislike the person; your dislike turns to anger; your anger causes him to offend you.) Further, it seems that Darwin did not have to deal with inept bank tellers and surly checkout clerks, for he assumed that "if the offending person be quite insignificant, we experience merely disdain or contempt." And he shared the delusion of his social class that a subordinate would never dare get angry with a superior: If the offending person is "all-powerful, then hatred passes into terror, as when a slave thinks about a cruel master." Clearly Darwin had never been a slave.

Because Darwin was interested in exploring the exciting similarities between humans and other animals, he understandably overlooked the differences. But in the case of anger, the differences are essential. The human symbolic ability and our enormously elastic capacity for learning give us a far greater range of choices than lower animals have. Human anger is not a biological reflex like the sneeze, nor simply a reactive display designed to ward off enemies. You may become roused to anger by memories and symbols as well as by real and present dangers, and you can maintain that anger for years. You may even decide retrospectively to get angry, which is the "more I thought about it, the madder I got" phenomenon. Beagles, in contrast, will know by your angry voice that you are displeased with them or about to punish them, but they will not bite you if you insult their intelligence or ancestors.

Further, human beings are able to lie. We can hide an emotional state if we choose to; and often, as on first dates and job interviews, we choose to. We can act *as if* we are caught in the throes of an emotion when we really feel quite cool; and often, when we feel obliged to show anger, sadness, or even sexual interest, we play a part. This ability is unique to us. A pouter pigeon's swagger reflects its biology, not its braggadocio. When a rabbit is afraid, it does not whistle a happy tune. But people know how to play angry for effect—as a lawyer does during a trial, to shake up a witness; as an assertive customer does to get action from a shopkeeper.

Modern psychologists have supported Darwin's idea that extreme emotions—great joy, rage, disgust, fear—are registered on the face, and that these facial expressions are universally recognized (and therefore biologically wired in). We should be happy for this bit of adaptive advantage, too, these researchers add, because it means we will always be able to tell whether a stranger is happy or about to attack us in a fury. However, the emotions they are talking about are, again, extremes. When most of us are angry we do not go around frowning, growling, and clenching our teeth, and when we are sad we do not necessarily continue weeping for days; we do not necessarily weep. A Japanese is expected to smile and be polite even if seething inside; a Kiowa Indian woman is supposed to scream and tear her face at a brother's death, even if she never liked him. Cultural masks overlay the face of emotion.

The idea that our emotions are instinctive has suggested, to some modern writers, that they cannot be controlled; no use trying to suppress your fury, this view runs, for the body will out. But Darwin himself would have disagreed, strongly. "The free expression by outward signs of an emotion intensifies it," he wrote. "On the other hand, the repression, as far as this is possible, of all outward signs softens our emotions. He who gives way to violent gestures will increase his rage; he who does not control the signs of fear will experience fear in a greater degree." But self-control, especially self-control in the pursuit of emotional restraint, is a human choice, beyond the limitations of instinct.

By equating anger with aggression, Darwin committed the fallacy of the Swami's snake. In human beings, this link is by no means inevitable. You may feel angry and express it in hundreds of ways, many of which will be neutral or even beneficial (cleaning the house in an energetic fury, playing the piano *forte*, organizing a political protest movement) instead of violent. Conversely, you can act aggressively without feeling angry at all, as a professional assassin or soldier does, as an employer who fires a competitive subordinate does. The very term "murder in cold blood" implies the absence of the "hot-blooded" emotion, anger. The fact that anger and aggression *do* coexist in many situations does not mean that, like Laurel and Hardy, the presence of one automatically includes the other.

Some ethologists and sociobiologists like to point out that "primitive" brain structures, such as the hypothalamus and limbic system, are responsible for most emotional behavior, by which they usually mean rage, fear, and sexual desire. The fact that human beings share these structures with lower animals, they argue, must account for the human similarity to sheep, dogs, and rodents. (But human beings and dogs have noses, too, which does not imply that the evolution of the human nose has proceeded the same way as that of the dog's nose; I have yet to see a man outsniff a bloodhound.) The so-called primitive brain structures have evolved just as much as more "recent" brain structures have, and they reach their greatest development in human beings. Moreover, they are as vital to thought processes as they are to emotion.

The Roman philosopher Seneca recognized the uniquely human aspect of anger nearly two thousand years ago. "Wild beasts and all animals, except man, are not subject to anger," he wrote, "for while it is the foe of reason, it is nevertheless born only where reason dwells." He meant that anger usually involves a conscious judgment that an injustice, insult, or idiocy has been committed, and a choice of reactions. James Averill, a psychologist who has extensively researched the social function of the emotions, agrees. Anger is a human emotion, he believes, because only people can judge actions for their intention, justifiability, and negligence. Each angry episode contains a series of split-second decisions: Is that fist raised in provocation or playfulness? Is that provocation dangerous or safe? Is that danger worthy of retaliation, a laugh, or getting the hell out of here?

Averill believes, and I concur, that animal aggression is reminiscent of human anger just as animal communication is reminiscent of human speech, but that the concept of "angry animals" is misleading and metaphorical. Human anger is far more intricate and serves many more purposes than the rage reflex of lower animals. We do not need to deny our mammalian, primate heritage, but we do not need to reduce ourselves to it, either. Judgment and choice distinguish human beings from other species; judgment and choice are the hallmarks of human anger.

Some people incorrectly assume that to emphasize the role of thought in anger is to strip the emotion of its passion and power. Just the opposite is true. As Robert Solomon, author of *The Passions*, observes, to say that emotions are generated by our thoughts and judgments does not "reduce the drama of emotion to cool, calm belief." On the contrary, our ideas, commitments, and values generate our grandest and most enduring passions: the social activist's sense of justice, the revolutionary's determination, the grudge-holder's sense of self-righteousness, the lover's lifelong devotion.

THE FREUDIAN LEGACY

Sitting in a café one afternoon, I overheard the following exchange between two women:

Woman A: "You'll feel better if you get your anger out."

Woman B: "Anger? Why am I angry?"

Woman A: "Because he left you, that's why."

Woman B: "Left me? What are you talking about? He *died*. He was an *old man*."

Woman A: "Yes, but to your unconscious it's no different from abandonment. Underneath, you are blaming him for not keeping his obligation to you to protect you forever."

Woman B: "That might have been true if I were ten years old, Margaret, but I'm forty-two, we both knew he was dying, and we had time to make our peace. I don't feel angry, I feel sad. I *miss* him. He was a darling father to me."

Woman A: "Why are you so defensive? Why are you denying your true feelings? Why are you afraid of therapy?"

Woman B: "Margaret, *you are driving me crazy. I don't feel angry, dammit!*"

Woman A (*smiling*): "So why are you shouting?"

It is not entirely easy to argue with a Freudian devotee, because disagreement is usually taken as denial or "blocking." If you do feel the emotion in question, you support the theory; and if you do not feel the emotion in question you also support the theory, because now you are demonstrating "reaction formation" or "repression." Such semantic contortions can themselves make one very cross.

We owe to Sigmund Freud, of course, the belief that our rational, conscious faculties do not know the half of what they are doing; that the unconscious, that seething cauldron of naughty instincts, guides so many of our feelings and actions. Freud regarded man as a creature at the mercy of his warring instincts—the innate conflict between love and hatred, life and death, sex and aggression—and he was pessimistic that the good side would win. Although Freud, like Darwin, regarded aggression as an ineradicable part of the human biological heritage, Freud emphasized the destructive, violent aspect of aggression, whereas Darwin saw aggression as self-defending and adaptive. Curiously, neither scientist paid much attention to anger. If they wrote about it at all, it was as a subcategory or weaker expression of the basic aggressive drive.

Yet, in the dark Freudian schema, so much unconscious rage and aggression! Everyone, at every age, is unwittingly furious with everyone else. Infants, for maternal abandonment. Toddlers, with the same-sexed parent who forbids incestuous lusts. Adolescents, for having to grow up and forgo childhood pleasures. Adults, for having to work and repress their instinctive passions. Freud penetrated the Victorian veneer of manners, to be sure; but, like prudes at a peep show, he was inclined to see more than was there.

Freud's theory and his language slowly filtered into the popular imagination through the writings and practice of psychoanalysts, but over the years Freud's disciples have diverged from the master's original arguments. In terms of the current thinking about anger, several of these discrepancies are significant:

The hydraulic model. Borrowing heavily from Hermann von Helmholtz's principle of the conservation of energy, Freud imagined that the libido was a finite amount of energy that powers our internal battles. If the energy is blocked here, it must find release there. As psychologist John Sabini put it: "Undischarged drives contribute their energy to the id, the reservoir of sexual and aggressive instincts. When the level has reached a critical point, overt aggression results." Freud chose all of his metaphors carefully, stating explicitly that although they were "incorrect," they were "useful aids to understanding" until the actual physiological mechanisms were discovered. Unhappily, many of Freud's followers confused metaphor with road map, and what was intended as a temporary concept assumed a life of its own.

Today the hydraulic model of energy has been scientifically discredited, but this has not stopped some therapeutic circles from *expanding* the "reservoir" idea to contain all the emotions—jealousy, grief, resentment, as well as rage. These therapists still argue that any feeling that is "dammed up" is dangerous, likely to "spill over" and possibly "flood" the system.

Catharsis. Freud and his collaborator Josef Breuer applied the catharsis idea specifically to aggression, using it to explain why, if we are all governed by violent instincts, relatively few of us were attacking each other on a daily basis. Catharsis, they suggested, empties the emotional reservoirs. Their definition was fairly casual: "The whole class of voluntary and involuntary reflexes—from tears to acts of revenge—in which, as experience shows us, the affects [emotions] are discharged." Actually, as experience was to show *them*, blubbering catharsis was not very effective therapy, and they later abandoned it for the talkier methods of psychoanalysis and conscious insight.

Today the catharsis question is with us again, but often with no better definition than Freud and Breuer had. Which elements of catharsis are essential to treatment and which are extraneous; for that matter, which are harmful? Some therapists imply that nearly all ways of "releasing" an emotion have equal therapeutic effect. Anger, for example, may be discharged by talking it out, shouting and hurling dishpans, exercising, playing football, watching a vigilante movie, throwing pillows, or plotting revenge. Freud and Breuer had used "catharsis" sparingly, but today it is nearly synonymous with emotional ventilation, "letting it all hang out."

Repression, sublimation, and guilt. Freud's use of these terms likewise was narrow and precise, but some popularizers broadened their meaning. "Repression," for example, came to refer not only to the process that keeps objectionable material from consciousness, but to a general (negative) state of keeping the lid on. "Sublimation" now covers not only the displacement of sexual energy into productive work, but also that of every other biological drive or impulse into unrelated activity.

Freud described repression as the pathogenic process that produces neurotic symptoms; psychoanalysis was designed to counteract these symptoms by bringing repressed material into consciousness. But he never argued that suppression of the instincts was undesirable. On the contrary: their suppression and redirection were necessary for the survival of the social system. Without repression, who would mind the store, build the bridges, create the Mona Lisa? Sublimation of sexual energy, while perhaps detrimental to the individual's wishes, served the greater good of society. And without guilt, the grease of civilization, hedonism would prevail. Society would disintegrate into anarchy.

Thus Freud was horrified by those who interpreted his descriptive statements as prescriptive, who wanted to expunge the controls of authority and guilt and "liberate" mind and body. "It is out of the question that part of the analytic treatment should consist of advice to 'live freely,' " he wrote, "if for no other reason because we ourselves tell you that a stubborn conflict is going on in the patient between libidinal desires and sexual repression, between sensual and ascetic tendencies. This conflict is not resolved by helping one side to win a victory over the other."

Yet that is exactly what many of Freud's successors attempted to do. Having decided that repression, sublimation, and guilt were merely Victorian cobwebs, they set out to sweep them away.

THE ANGER BUSINESS

There's a book by a female therapist who, in the name of feminism, admonishes her clients (and readers) to stop being nice. When you're angry, she says, just let it right out or you will channel your anger into overeating, overdrinking, skin disorders, colitis, or migraines. Late in her book, we learn where her data on psychosomatic symptoms come from:

> What affected me most adversely as a girl was my family's illusion that nice girls (indeed, all nice people) didn't have and certainly didn't reveal hostile feelings. Although I was in many respects a normally nasty little girl, I always felt extremely guilty about my bad temper and "selfish" behavior. Only recently have I been able to experience my average nasty self without feeling that I must produce, along with the awareness of my hostility, punishments such as headaches, rashes, and fatness.

Then there is the male therapist who, in the name of men's liberation, likewise advises his clients to abandon niceness, no matter how difficult this is to do: "It requires a constant self-awareness and sensitivity to himself in order to avoid the temptation to be the 'nice guy' rather than to do what is real and true for himself," he writes:

> As a general rule, put yourself first, except for those occasions when you genuinely want to make your wife's needs primary. Assume the risks of owning up to who you really are, completely and joyfully.

The author does not discuss what you should do if you are "really" a wife-abusing alcoholic, a supercilious prig, or an aggressive bully.

Freud would be appalled by these two characters: by their desire to behave like self-indulgent children with no responsibilities to others, no guilts about antisocial behavior, no restrictions on what they want to do. But they are a measure of how far our attitudes have come in a few decades, and they demonstrate the intimate connection between a culture's values and the popular advice that passes for scientific wisdom.

Therapies today differ in the solutions they recommend for people with "anger problems" (displacement, catharsis, fighting with foam-rubber bats, sports, rational problem-solving, years of analysis) and they have different theories about the causes of anger (accumulated energy, a crisis in infancy or childhood, years of resentment at one's mother). There are, of course, many sensible, practical therapists and therapies that can help people get through angry times in their lives, as I will be discussing.

But some of the descendants of Freud and Darwin have established schools of treatment based on the principle that anger, aggression's handmaiden, must not be blocked or silenced. Social psychologist Leonard Berkowitz calls advocates of this view "ventilationists," because they believe it is unhealthy to bottle up feelings. "Many go further," he writes, "and argue that if we could overcome our inhibitions and show our emotions, we would eliminate disturbing tensions, conquer nagging aches and pains, and promote 'deeper' and 'more meaningful' relationships with others." In the 1960s and 1970s, encounter groups adopted ventilationist therapies as vehicles for the let-it-out theory: William Schutz and Frederick (Fritz) Perls at Esalen, George Bach and Frederick Stoller in Los Angeles.

Lest you think that these are merely the weird fringes of psychology, dangling far from the mainstream, consider the arguments of psychoanalyst Theodore Isaac Rubin. In *The Angry Book*, Rubin warns us, without supporting data, of the familiar dangers that await those who bottle up their anger (or who "twist it" or "pervert it"). A "slush fund" of accumulated, unexpressed anger builds up in the body, just yearning for the chance to produce high blood pressure, disease, anxiety, depression, alcoholism, sexual problems, and the blahs. Rubin acknowledges that he has not measured the influence of this "slush fund" exactly (and concludes that it is "impossible" to do so), but this does not stop him from offering advice to his unknown readers. At the end of the book he provides a list of 103 rhetorical questions designed to give the reader therapeutic guidance:

Have you ever experienced the good, clean feel [sic] that comes after expressing anger, as well as the increased self-esteem and the feel of real peace with one's self and others?

(Actually, studies show that many people say that their self-esteem drops when they have let themselves express anger, that they feel depressed for several days, and that a gloomy pall envelops them. It depends on the situation and the object of their anger.)

Are you solidly aware that the purpose of warm, healthy anger is to deliver an affective (emotional) message in order to clear the air and to make corrections and reparations if necessary?

(Yes, and I'm also aware that corrections can be made without anger.)

When was the last time you got solidly angry? Did the world cave in?

(No, but sometimes it does. Some people get angry with positive results; others find that anger makes matters worse. It is misleading and naive to argue that *all* expressions of anger are beneficial.)

Are you aware that your anger will not kill anyone and that no one's anger will kill you?

(Yes, but only because I am a woman who has never been beaten by her husband or father. I imagine that thousands of battered wives in this country would have a far different response.)

Are you aware that people can feel loving and make love after a "fight" because an emotional traffic jam has been cleared?

(Those are other people, then, because most people report that they need time to cool down after a quarrel before they "feel loving" again. Besides, the trendy notion that fighting is sexy produces an association between sex and aggression that I, for one, find abhorrent.)

> If you cannot extricate yourself from the slush-fund morass, are you wise enough to seek expert professional help? This means going to a psychiatrist who is a graduate of a psychoanalytic institute recognized by either The American Academy of Psychoanalysis or The American Psychoanalytic Association.

(No other form of therapy will do? Actually, studies find that cognitive-behavioral and family-systems therapies are demonstrably more effective than psychoanalysis in helping people control and manage angry feelings, learn constructive new anger habits, and break out of repetitive family battles.)

The ventilationist view is widespread not only among clinical psychologists and psychiatrists, but also among the general populace as well. For her book *The Cycle of Violence*, sociologist Suzanne K. Steinmetz studied the attitudes and experiences of typical families, and she found that a majority of adults endorse the catharsis notion. "This myth is widespread in both popular thinking and among certain social scientists," she wrote. "[For example, Bruno] Bettelheim suggests that the excessive training in self-control, typical of American middle-class families, denies the child outlets for the instinct of human violence and thereby fails to teach children how to deal with violent feelings."

But Steinmetz hardly found "excessive training in self-control" in the families she observed. Instead, she found a common belief among parents that it is better to spank a child than to restrain one's anger; that siblings should "fight it out" (even though parents hate it when they do); that screaming matches between husband and wife, and between parent and child, are normal, healthy, and good for the relationship. One father thought that the regular use of physical punishment "lets out the parent's frustration." One wife who used to be "very quiet" when she was angry said, "Now we get into loud discussions where I just get things out. It doesn't solve anything, but I do feel much better."

"I do feel much better." Is this what it comes to, then, the ultimate rationale for emotional release? Never mind whether your emotional release makes those around you feel worse, or fails to solve the problem. If you can do what you want, it must be good for you. That's the American way, after all.

THE USE AND ABUSE OF ANGER

If anger is not only a biological reflex or an unconscious instinct, why has it persisted? One answer, I believe, is that anger survives because anger works. Preaching against it, like preaching against the other deadly sins, has not had much luck in the West. In America, the judicious application of a furious speech or a determined roar often gets the results that kindness, unfortunately, does not. Anger in America restores the sense of dignity and fair play ("I told that crook off good"), it feeds ambition and competitiveness ("I'll show the bastard how the job is done"), it asserts the individual in an anonymous world ("Listen to *me*").

But fair play, competitiveness, and individualism are by no means universal values. Try getting angry in front of an Utku-hikhalingmiut Eskimo, as anthropologist Jean Briggs did, and you will be ostracized for your childishness. Try demanding your rights in England, Japan, or Peru in the irate tone that would be effective at home, and you will be regarded as just another uncouth, noisy American. In highly cooperative small societies like the !Kung-san of Africa (the ! represents a click sound in their language), the provocations of anger that we take for granted—no, that we take for *instinctive*—are unknown. It is not that feelings of anger are unknown in such societies, rather that whether and how one acts on those feelings are managed by culture and by learning. The rules that govern anger do not spring arbitrarily from the brows of local shamans, witch doctors, and therapists; they serve their culture.

In some unspoken sense, most people understand this. In spite of certain gurus' admonitions to stop being nice, they know that niceness makes society possible. In spite of certain glowing promises that anger will make you feel good, they know that anger can be an uncomfortable emotion, for it means that something in your life is wrong. But this attitude is not bolstered by a society that praises aggressiveness, or rewards it tangibly when it condemns it verbally. We are ambivalent about anger not because of an "internal war" between reason and emotion; we are ambivalent about anger because sometimes it is effective and sometimes it is not, because sometimes it is necessary and sometimes it is destructive.

I dislike pop-psych approaches that persuade people that anger is buried "in them" because I think such notions are dangerous to the mental health of the participants and to the social health of the community. Such views get people ventilating and agitating, but they rarely recognize or fix the circumstances that make them angry in the first place. When Aesop's lion roared, no one thought the lion had a hostility complex or a problem with temper control; they knew a net had trapped him. No amount of chanting or shouting or pillow pounding will extricate us from the many nets of modern life.

Anger, therefore, is as much a political matter as a biological one. The decision to get angry has powerful consequences, whether anger is directed toward one's spouse or one's government. Spouses and governments know this. They know that anger is ultimately an emphatic message: *Pay attention to me. I don't like what you are doing. Restore my pride. You're in my way. Danger. Give me justice.*

As the Swami knew, anger is the human hiss.

2

Uncivil Rites—the Cultural Rules of Anger

The full potential of human fury cannot be reached until a friend of both parties tactfully intervenes.

—G. K. CHESTERTON

The young wife leaves her house one afternoon to draw water from the local well. She saunters down the main street, chatting amiably with her neighbors, as her husband watches from their porch. On her return from the well, a stranger stops her and asks for a cup of water. She obliges, and in fact invites the man home for dinner. He accepts. The husband, wife, and guest spend a pleasant evening together, and eventually the husband puts the lamp out and retires to bed. The wife also retires to bed—with the guest. In the morning, the husband leaves early to bring back some breakfast for the household. Upon his return, he find his wife again making love with the visitor.

At what point in this sequence of events will the husband become angry or jealous? Is his anger inevitable? The answer, observes psychologist Ralph Hupka, depends on the tribe and culture he belongs to:

• A Pawnee Indian husband, a century ago, would, in fury, bewitch any man who dared to request a cup of water from his wife.

• An Ammassalik Eskimo husband who wants to be a proper

48

host invites his guest to have sex with his wife; he signals his invitation by putting out the lamp. (The guest might feel angry if this invitation were not extended.) An Ammassalik husband would be angry, however, if he found his wife having sex with a man in circumstances other than the lamp game, such as that morning encore, or without a mutual agreement to exchange mates.

• A middle-class husband belonging to most modern American tribes would tend to get angry with any guest who, however courteously, tried to seduce his wife, and with the wife who, however hospitably, slept with their guest.

• A husband who belonged to the polyandrous Toda tribe of southern India at the turn of the century would find the whole sequence of events perfectly normal; nothing to raise a fuss about. The Todas practiced *mokhthoditi*, a custom that allowed both spouses to take lovers. If a man wanted to make love to a married woman, he first got her permission and then the permission of her husband or husbands; a yearly fee was negotiated; and then the wife was free to visit her new lover and the lover free to visit the wife at her home. But a Toda husband and wife would undoubtedly be angry with any man who tried to establish an affair by sneaking around the husband's back (and not paying the proper fee).

People everywhere get angry, but they get angry in the service of their culture's rules. Sometimes those rules are explicit ("Thou shalt not covet thy neighbor's wife"); more often they are implicit, disguised in the countless daily actions performed because "That's the way we do things around here." These unstated rules are often not apparent until someone breaks them, and anger is the sign that someone has broken them. It announces that someone is not behaving as (you think) she or he *ought*. This "assertion of an ought" is, according to psychologist Joseph de Rivera, the one common and essential feature of anger in all its incarnations. "Whenever we are angry," he writes, "we somehow believe that we can influence the object of our anger. We assume that the other is responsible for his actions and ought to behave differently."

This "ought" quality suggests that a major role of anger is its policing function. Anger, with its power of forcefulness and its threat of retaliation, helps to regulate our everyday social relations: in family disputes, neighborly quarrels, business disagreements, wherever the official law is too cumbersome, inappropriate, or unavailable (which is most of the time). Psychologist James Averill observes that for most of Western history, it has been up to individuals to see to it that their rights were respected and justice seen to; in the absence of a formal judiciary, anger operates as a personal one.

Perhaps the best way to understand the policing power of anger is to step outside of our own complex environment, and observe the way anger works in small societies. Small societies are highly revealing, whether they are families, tribes, high-school marching bands, or the U.S. Congress. Members of such groups understand very well the importance of the rules that govern anger, because everyone has to get along with each other in the morning. Anger is society's servant, and you can see this in the day-to-day life of small tribes. They may seem exotic, but they are, close up, a mirror on ourselves.

THE JUDICIAL EMOTION

N!uhka, age seventeen, was furious. Her father had reminded her that she was getting on in years and that it was high time for her to marry. N!uhka, who was rebellious and vain, was uninterested in the eligible young men her father suggested, and at last, in the heat of argument, she cursed him aloud. He was shocked. *She* was shocked. So were all the neighbors and relations who had overheard her.

Now N!uhka was angry and also ashamed of her disrespectful outburst. She grabbed her blanket and stormed out of the camp to a lone tree some seventy yards away. There she sat, all day, covered in the blanket. This was not a trivial penance, since the temperature that day was 105 degrees Fahrenheit in the shade (without a blanket), but by the time she returned to camp her anger and embarrassment had subsided.

The !Kung hunter-gatherers of the Kalahari Desert are called "the harmless people" because of their renowned lack of aggression. This does not mean that they are free from the petty plagues of human life, such as jealousies, resentments, suspicions, and sulks. Teenagers disagree with their parents' wishes, relatives squabble about who owes what to whom, and husbands and wives bicker about marital matters. The difference is that the !Kung know that they must manage these emotions and dampen them down to tolerable levels, and that if they don't their very survival is endangered.

The !Kung are nomadic, foraging constantly for food, and their only insurance against hard times is each other. No individual can lay in a supply of frozen pizzas and beer in the event of famine and drought, and no individual could long survive on his or her own. Sharing is therefore the dominant value and obsession of their society. As one of their principal ethnographers, Elizabeth Marshall Thomas, observed: "It has never happened that a Bushman [today they are called !Kung or !Kung-san] failed to share objects, food, or water with the other members of his band, for without very rigid co-operation Bushmen could not survive the famines and droughts that the Kalahari offers them." Under such conditions, any antisocial or angry outburst threatens the whole group; so it is to the !Kung interest to avoid direct physical confrontation or violence, and to be suspicious of individuals who cannot control their behavior or their tempers. "Their hold on life," says Thomas, "is too tenuous to permit quarreling among themselves."

The same structure of camp life that increases the chances of group solidarity and survival—lack of privacy, each hut close to the other huts, extended family nearby—also means that every flare-up and dispute is immediately available for public discussion and resolution. Such lack of privacy would be cause enough for anger in the West, where "It's none of your business" is an accepted refrain. Among the !Kung, everything is everyone's business. "Once a person attacks his victim he is like a fly that attacks an insect already caught in a spider's web," writes anthropologist Patricia Draper. "Immediately both are caught. If the combatants forget the sticky web in the heat of their anger, the onlookers do not. Real anger frightens and sickens the !Kung, for

it is so destructive of their web of relationships." Anyone who
becomes angry will have the assistance ("interference" to the West)
of the entire tribe, if need be. Perhaps this is why, in nearly a year
and a half of fieldwork, one anthropologist saw only four examples
of overt discord and heard of only a few others. Another recorded
only three serious disputes: one over possession of an animal that
had been killed, another about a marital disagreement, and a third
in which a mother raged at a curer who failed to attend her sick
child.

Although the !Kung are not aggressive, they are expert at
bickering and complaint. "The outsider wonders how the !Kung
can stand to live with each other," says Patricia Draper. "In the
early months of my own fieldwork I despaired of ever getting away
from continual harassment." Some psychoanalytically inclined
observers take this as evidence of the !Kung's "displaced" aggressive
instinct, which, if not released physically (they say), takes this
verbal outlet. But a closer look at the content of the bickering
reveals two things about it: It has a distinct social purpose, and
although it may seem to outsiders like a sign of anger it is really a
ritual game, devoid of anger's heat.

After several months, Draper discovered that the key to !Kung
bickering was its emphasis on dunning for food. What idle
conversation about the weather and the economy is to Europeans,
she noticed, reminders about food obligations were to the !Kung.
In time she learned the "properly melodramatic disclaimers" that
allowed her to join the game:

> You expect *me*, one lonely European, a stranger in this territory,
> living away from my own kin, without even one spear or arrow or
> even a digging stick, and with no knowledge of the bush . . . you
> expect *me* to give *you* something to eat? You are a person whose hut
> is crammed full of good things to eat. Berries, billtong, sweet roots,
> stand shoulder high in your hut and you come to me saying you are
> hungry!

The !Kung visitor would be delighted with such a spirited reply
(as would the inevitable onlookers), and once this exchange was

completed, Draper and the !Kung could go on to talk about other things. But food-dunning jokes and complaints are important because they remind everyone of the responsibility to recirculate food and property. The have-nots press for their share; the haves are reminded that their fortune is only temporary.

I have found Draper's observations useful in understanding my own particular tribe, Eastern European Jews whose forebears came from the shtetls of Russia and Poland, and for whom ritual dunning has been a long tradition. Indeed, the rich curse repertoire of Yiddish makes the four-letter-word grunts of English a pale and gutless thing. As Barbara Myerhoff recorded in *Number Our Days:*

Jake: In those days, everybody gave curses. You couldn't live without it. A woman there was on our street who could curse like Heifetz plays the violin. The things she would fix up for her enemies! 'May your teeth get mad and eat your head off.' 'May you inherit a hotel with one hundred rooms and be found dead in every one.' 'May you have ten sons and all your daughters-in-law hate you.' 'May all your teeth fall out but one, and that one has a cavity.' 'May your chickens lay eggs in your neighbor's house.' 'May the gypsies camp on your stomach and their bears do the *kazotskhi* in your liver.'
Basha: This last one you are getting from Sholom Aleichem.
Jake: And where do you think Sholom Aleichem learned it?

Today these curses are a fading talent (I think they require the original Yiddish), just as the ritual dunning is a mere shadow of its former self: "You don't call me any more"; "Write your Aunt Hannah a thank-you letter *today*"; "Do your fingers have leprosy that you can't pick up your socks?" But the curses and the dunning have their origin in survival needs as great as those for food in the African bush. The repeated bickering reminded shtetl Jews of their social obligations to the family and the culture, emphasizing the importance of staying in line and paying attention to the traditions that kept the precarious group together. A visitor to such cultures is likely, as Patricia Draper was among the !Kung, to feel under attack, at least until he or she learns the rules and can play the game.

Catherine Lutz, who lived among the Ifaluk in the Southwest Pacific, offers a good example of the deeply rooted community perspective of these close-knit tribes. She had asked a group of women: "Do you (all) want to come with me to get drinking water?" Their faces fell, until Lutz realized "that my pronouns were at fault"—*you* being separate from *me* in her sentence. The correct form of the question, she realized in time, is: "We'll go get water now, OK?"

Whenever a tribe must cooperate and struggle to survive—on the frozen tundra of the Northwest Territories, in the steamy jungles of South America, in the arid bush of Africa, as a persecuted minority in the heart of "civilization"—it must find a way to settle disputes without causing the offended party to leave the tribe in a huff. In the absence of formal laws to govern distribution of goods—in fact, in the absence of predictable supplies of goods—the problem of sharing is never permanently resolved. It is always vulnerable to dispute, and anger is the policeman of that dispute. Did I get my fair share? Did he get too much? Should I get more because I was sick or less because I couldn't hunt? The Siriono of Bolivia, for example, are forever accusing each other angrily of hoarding food, not sharing what they have, eating at night, or stealing off into the forest to eat. (Most of their remaining disputes have to do with sex, which also has its intrinsically uncertain aspects.) But anger over food distribution is not widespread in places such as Tahiti, where the food supply and other staples of survival are abundant and predictable.

The analogy of anger as policeman can be carried a step further, since policemen must themselves follow certain rules and are constrained from excessive violence. The anger that may be expressed in small tribes likewise must follow certain rules and constraints to ensure that anger does not become disruptive. The Siriono, for example, may throw a drinking feast in which serious complaints are aired. This is not an American-style drinking feast, where drinking is often assumed to lead to violence. The most that two Siriono men may do is wrestle, but if either man uses his fists he is promptly accused of "fighting like a white man" and stops, embarrassed, at once. More likely, Siriono men who feel angry with each other go hunting; if successful, they are too elated to be angry, and if not, they are too tired.

Perhaps the most vivid and charming example of anger being used to influence recalcitrant members of a tribe, while itself being controlled by ritual limits, is the "mad dance" of the Kapauku Papuans of West New Guinea. The Kapauku Papuans may not be familiar to you, but every culture, including our own, has its version of the mad dance.

A Kapauku wedding is, more than most, an obvious economic exchange, since the bride and groom have invariably been living together for some time before the ceremony. On the big day, the two families gather together for official payment of the bride price, and clan members gather from far and wide. Throughout the day, the groom's family displays the gifts they are offering, while the bride's family inspects them carefully, exchanging derogatory comments about their quality and quantity, muttering audibly about the stinginess of the groom's clan.

The groom's closest relatives, having set forth what they can afford to pay, now call upon their visiting kin to raise the ante. A few more shells and necklaces are added, but the bride's father still looks displeased. The local headmen, hoping to settle the matter quickly and avoid disputes, now try to drum up some financial support from the groom's kin with appeals to their pride and family loyalty. If this effort fails, the headmen will start *wainai*, the "mad dance," which is just what it sounds like: the dancers yell and scream their requests for the relatives to cough up some booty, all the while stamping their feet furiously in a fast rhythm, their arms mimicking the shooting of arrows.

If the mad dance doesn't produce the desired results, some of the bride's male relatives may get into the act, hurling insults and reproaches—not at the poor groom, who is broke, but at the groom's distant relatives. If all of this pressure fails, the bride's kin may be forced to join the mad dance themselves. Then all hell will break loose, for it means the end of negotiations. But usually the dance is effective, the bride's father gives his OK, the deal is settled, the groom gives his new in-laws a pig or two, and everyone goes home happy.

Now, apart from the pigs and the arrows, this is not so different from some American weddings, in substance if not form. I've watched a few mad dances in my time, and they usually get the same result: The errant relative shapes up. One woman I interviewed told me that her daughter's marriage was nearly called off by the groom's *mother* because the bride's family wasn't prepared to buy the newlyweds a house. After an exchange of enraged calls, foot stamping, and accusations of stinginess and bullying, a compromise was reached. The wedding went off as planned.

These economic exchanges are not simply outbursts of greed, however, in the Kapauku or any other tribe. They play an important cohesive role for the family and for the tribe; a lot more is going on than getting a few beaded necklaces or a silver teapot. Among the Kapauku, successful settlement for the bride price includes these benefits: The mother of the bride, who gets to keep most of the wealth, now has raised her status, for she has money to lend. The bride's brother receives a large enough portion to be able to get married too. The father of the bride, who has refereed the transaction, confirms his importance and position as head of the family. On the groom's side, the relatives who contributed to the bride price gain enormous public prestige for their generosity and, more important, the groom's undying gratitude. The groom will now call his creditors *naitai*, "my father," and be expected to assist them in their future troubles or debates. In sum, a satisfactory bride price unifies both sets of kin, forming alliances within each clan as well as between them. No wonder a mad dance might be called for.

Bickering, drinking feasts, and mad dances represent a spectrum of solutions that cultures have evolved to regulate disputes. Are the participants actually *feeling* angry? As observers, we cannot know for sure; but I don't think it matters. I suspect that among the Kapauku, as among Americans, some mad dancers are feeling enraged and others are behaving as if they were. Some jealous husbands actually do feel angry with wives who flirt, and others simply think they should. Some ritual bickerers, such as Pat Draper's !Kung friends, are playing a game quite consciously; others aren't kidding. The point is that the rules of the tribe regulate both the feelings of anger and angry behavior, establishing when anger may be expressed, and how, and to whom, and for what reasons.

To make sure, however, that anger does not become excessive and threaten the delicate internal mechanism of the group, small tribes rely on informal (but highly effective) ways to keep *inappropriate* anger in check: gossip, ridicule, witchcraft, public discussion, and in extreme cases ostracism. One of the most popular methods invokes the individual's bond to the community: shame.

"The only authority here," said the astute Semai informant, is *"slniil."* Among the Semai of West Malaysia, *slniil* (variously defined as "shame," "nervousness," or "reluctance") is the typical response to anger, whether one feels the anger personally or is the recipient of someone else's. A man who feels *slniil* will avert his eyes from the target of his wrath and refuse to talk or listen to him, thereby retreating from the conflict instead of confronting or escalating it. This is considerate behavior for a Semai, and no one will accuse him of repression, depression, or passive-aggressive manipulativeness.

Both parties to a Semai conflict feel shame; indeed, most close-knit tribes are as concerned about the person who provokes anger as about the individual who feels it. Arapesh adults (one of the tribes studied by Margaret Mead), who worry that strong bursts of rage will make their whole society vulnerable, will join in punishing the individual who *causes* another to engage in violence. Similarly, the Utku Eskimo worry about anyone with a volatile temper, even if that temper is, by Western standards, justified. Anthropologist Jean Briggs learned this the hard way. She lost her temper—"very mildly as we ourselves would view it"—with some Caucasian fishermen who, while visiting the area, broke one of the Eskimo canoes. Although she was angry on behalf of the Utku, although her annoyance was not remotely directed at them, the Eskimo saw only her anger, not its cause. She had revealed a sign of decidedly un-Eskimo volatility, and it was now uncertain whether she could be trusted. "As a result of my unseemly and frightening wrath at the fishermen," Briggs reported, "I was ostracized, very subtly, for about three months." (I think she felt a touch of *slniil*.)

Among the Temiar of Malaysia, according to Marina Roseman, anger in its late stages is expressed indirectly and formally in a "harangue." During the night, protected by darkness, the angry person speaks out from his or her sleeping compartment separate from the person being criticized. The target is referred to as "he" or "she" rather than "you" to further distance the confrontation. The target may respond in like fashion, or listen silently. In spite of these precautions of indirection, says Roseman, the Temiar still consider this expression of anger to be dangerous, capable of shocking the souls of participants or bystanders into taking flight. (The Temiar would be right at home among the haranguing inhabitants of a New York apartment building.)

Or consider the Toraja of South Sulawesi, Indonesia, who, like other groups in Malaysia and Indonesia, fear and dislike anger. The overt display of anger is "likened to that of amoral animals and is thought to be unworthy of human beings," says Douglas Hollan, an anthropologist who lived among them. In Hollan's year of fieldwork, he saw only three incidents of openly expressed anger, despite the occurrence of many events that "certainly tried people's patience." To "cool out," the Toraja call on their fatalistic philosophy, a belief that one's fate is determined at birth and can be changed only by the gods. They told Hollan they also avoid active rumination and brooding about their problems, and try to "talk themselves" out of it. In dealing with another person who is angry, the Toraja get out of the way and let the person calm down; challenging or confronting someone who is angry, the Toraja know, just enrages the person all the more.

I prefer the anger-calming approach of the Mbuti hunter-gatherers of northeast Zaire, who use humor to dissipate a quarrel. When rational discussion breaks down, Mbuti disputants (and their inevitable observers) begin to ridicule each other, acting out the argument, until everyone is rocking with laughter. Significantly, this stratagem is learned early in life. When a child teases another child into tears, guess whom the other children will rally around? The tearful victim. They will then begin a joyful game from which the teaser is excluded (a small but potent lesson in the hazards of antisocial behavior) until the teaser, the target, and the rest of the children are laughing and have forgotten the incident. Bullies don't succeed among the Mbuti.

Ridicule and humor are effective antidotes to anger in many small societies. Verbal dueling is high art where "fighting like a white man" is taboo or dangerous. In some Eskimo tribes, one man may challenge another to a drum match or song duel. He starts with a few brash insults and obscenities. His target replies in kind. The (inevitable) audience, which is enjoying the show, begins to take sides. Now the insults get juicier and the obscenities hilarious. The audience determines the winner by laughing louder and longer at his jokes, and the bloodless contest is over. "And that is precisely the point of the Eskimo song duel," writes Peter Farb. "Two disputants batter each other by the singing of insults rather than by blows, in that way preventing a quarrel from turning into a socially divisive feud." And a good time is had by all, besides.

A culture's values and needs determine not only our everyday angers but even when we may be allowed to "go crazy" with rage. "Anger," wrote Horace some two thousand years ago, "is a brief madness," succinctly noting the affinity between "mad" and "angry." The match is psychological as well as linguistic, because in many cultures (including our own) an enraged individual and an insane one are both regarded as being out of control, unable to take responsibility for their actions. Yet other cultures, such as the Eskimo, distinguish the two conditions: A person who is legitimately insane cannot be expected to control himself, but one who is merely angry can and must control himself. What distinguishes us from the Eskimo, aside from the weather? What role does the *belief* in the similarity between rage and madness play?

A BRIEF MADNESS

• One evening, apparently out of the blue, a young Malay man armed himself with traditional weapons, the parang and the kris, and embarked on a killing spree. By the time his rampage was over, several hours later, he had accosted customers in three local coffeehouses and murdered five innocent men. His friends were surprised that the young man had "run amok"; he seemed so polite and well mannered.

• In San Francisco in 1979, a civil servant named Dan White resigned his seat on the city's Board of Supervisors. Shortly thereafter he changed his mind, but he was too late: Mayor George Moscone had decided to give the job to someone else. White took his snub-nosed revolver, climbed in through the window of City Hall (so the metal detectors wouldn't reveal his gun), and pumped nine bullets into Moscone and supervisor Harvey Milk, who had been one of White's outspoken opponents (and who was a homosexual whom White disliked). In what the press played up as the "Twinkie defense," White's lawyers argued that his excessive consumption of junk food had caused his "diminished mental capacity," leaving him unable to premeditate anything, much less murder. The jury agreed. White was convicted of voluntary manslaughter and given a maximum sentence of seven years and eight months in jail. (Twenty months after his release, he committed suicide.)

• The Gururumba tribesman was behaving strangely. He had suddenly taken to looting his neighbors' huts, stealing food and objects, and one afternoon his kinsmen found him hiding behind a tree, shooting arrows at passersby. He was clearly suffering a mental aberration, the tribe agreed, which they diagnosed as "being a wild pig."

• In New York in 1980, Jean Harris shot and killed Herman Tarnower, her lover of fourteen years, in what the prosecution called a "jealous rage" and the defense a "tragic accident." Tarnower was found with four bullets in his body; Harris said she was trying to kill herself, not him. The jury did not believe her. She was convicted of intentional murder and given a minimum sentence of fifteen years in prison.

*　　*　　*

Running amok, being a wild pig, and temporary insanity are, within their respective tribes, legitimate signs of "a brief madness." These rages are, however, regarded as something other than psychosis, true mental illness, or other sorts of "long" madnesses, and they are often treated differently. Certainly some individuals who suffer organic abnormalities or psychoses that produce rage attacks can properly be diagnosed as insane; they do not, for one thing, revert to normalcy after a violent episode. And there are other individuals, such as the disturbed loners who have tried to assassinate or succeeded in assassinating our presidents and heroes, whose aggressive acts have little to do with anger and more to do with fantasies of power and fame. But most cases of "temporary insanity" caused apparently by rage, those heralded cases that capture the public eye, can be explained better in terms of their social causes than their organic ones, junk food to the contrary notwithstanding.

Start with "running amok," a phenomenon that originally referred to violent, often homicidal attacks among the indigenous peoples of the Malay Archipelago. Most people assume that the acts committed while a person is in such a state are unconscious, random, and without purpose. The *pengamok* (those who run amok) themselves think so, and so do their neighbors and relatives. But a closer look suggests otherwise. The frequency of this supposedly impulsive, uncontrollable act declined precipitately when the cultural response to it shifted from supportive tolerance to vicious punishment (at one point in Malay history, the *pengamok* were drawn and quartered).

Further, the objects of amok attacks are not random victims: Almost all of them are known to the amok and have been continuing sources of provocation. In one study that compared true *pengamok* to a control group of psychotics, the victims of the *pengamok* proved to be "rational" choices: a wife suspected of infidelity, a quarrelsome neighbor, an oppressive religion teacher. The Malay who killed the five customers of coffeehouses had carefully assured that his victims were Chinese: As his record showed, he had harbored anger at the Chinese who had killed some Malays several years before. The so-called psychotic symptoms of the *pengamok* vanish within a month or two of the episode, which is hardly the case for true psychotics.

Traditionally, the Malay are expected to be courteous and self-effacing, never to reprimand each other, and never to strive for success at the expense of another. Other cultures that have invaded the Malay Archipelago, such as the Chinese, have had rather more aggressive values, and therefore interpreted Malay behavior as signs of weakness and inferiority—which they promptly exploited. "Running amok," whether on an individual level or at a group level of rebellion, is a brilliant solution for Malay conflict: It allows the Malay to remain true to his cultural values while attacking the sources of his oppression and rage.

"Being a wild pig" is to the Gururumba what "running amok" is to the Malay. The Malay think that amok results from witchcraft or possession by evil spirits; the Gururumba think it comes from being bitten by a ghost. But wild pigs, like the *pengamok*, are not randomly distributed throughout the society. The only people who seem to get bitten, for example, are men between the ages of twenty-five and thirty-five, which is an especially stressful decade for the Gururumba male. He must abandon his youthful irresponsibility, take a wife, and assume a sudden burden of social obligations to the group. Success or failure at meeting these obligations will reflect not only on him, but on his clan.

Anthropologist P. L. Newman thinks that "being a wild pig" is a way of calling attention to the difficulties of shouldering these obligations. The victim of ghost bite, by his wild behavior, thereby announces to the tightly knit group that he wants to do something that his kinsmen might otherwise prohibit: change wives, move somewhere else, give up a particular responsibility. In the same way that a vociferous display of anger in our own culture finally convinces the recipient that the angry person *means* it, wild-pigdom convinces the Gururumba that the victim really is having a hard time and that something must be done. (Some Gururumba, consciously or not, put themselves in places where they are likely to be bitten by a ghost—a remote part of the forest or a gravesite.)

The Gururumba react with tolerance to a man who is being a wild pig. They are sympathetic to him, because they believe he is not responsible for his actions; they expect the seizure to run its course in a few days, like the flu. While the man is in this state they gently direct his "craziness": They leave food and little things for him to steal, and they don't let him hurt anyone seriously. The victim retreats to the forest for a few days on his own—not unlike our paid vacations—and if he returns still in a "wild" state, the tribesmen set up a ritual to cure him. They "capture" him and treat him as if he *were* a pig that had gone wild: They hold him over a smoking fire and rub him all over with pig fat. (This, the anthropologists assure us, is not as bad as it sounds.) A prominent person kills a real pig in the victim's name, and the victim is given a feast of pig meat and roots. Most important, however, are the reassessment and usually reduction of his obligations that occur after this ritual. That component of the procedure seems most likely to prevent remissions.

The Malay and Gururumba examples suggest that acceptable varieties of "temporary insanity" occur in cultures in which two equally powerful value systems conflict. In Western culture, a powerful taboo exists against intentional acts of violence, especially murder; yet the culture often counteracts that taboo with as great a passion for revenge, retribution, and defense of moral values. In America, when "an eye for an eye" meets "turn the other cheek"; when "thou shalt not kill" meets "thou shalt not commit adultery," temporary insanity is a temporary solution. This is a legal loophole in a Gordian knot: the law allows individuals to become angry enough to kill, but only if they kill in the service of society's dominant values, and only if they kill without premeditation or self-control—"in the heat of passion."

This is one reason, I think, that Dan White got off with such a light sentence for murdering two men and Jean Harris got a severe sentence for killing one. White and Harris both had had time, before their actions, to think about what they were doing. Both packed up their little guns at home and sought their victims. Both believed that they had been cruelly and unfairly treated by their victims. But Dan White's lawyers played on his "diminished mental capacity" to the hilt, bringing in plenty of psychiatrists to testify to his unstable mental condition. "The killing was done out of a passion," the foreman of the jury later said, "given the stress he was under." Jean Harris's defense emphasized the "tragic accident" explanation, and called on no psychiatrists to exonerate her behavior or describe the stress she was under. The only person to describe her mental state was Harris herself, and that was her undoing; for the anger she expressed, even there on the witness stand, was cold and deliberate. She gave no evidence of having been enraged at Tarnower; angry with the "other woman," yes, but with the lover who left her, no. Had she done so, had she used the enormous sympathy usually extended to scorned lovers, had she argued that she had committed a crime of passion, I believe the outcome would have been different. But she did not. She took responsibility for her emotions. And so the jury had to find her guilty of her actions.

Although people frequently deplore the association between anger and violence in the United States, our customs and our laws (to say nothing of the easy availability of handguns) encourage the link. Why do we resist the idea that we can control our emotions, that feeling angry need not inevitably cause us to behave violently? Seneca the Stoic had a good idea of the answer. We refuse to follow his philosophy of self-restraint, he suggested, "Because we are in love with our vices; we uphold them and prefer to make excuses for them rather than shake them off." And why do we make excuses for them? *Because they excuse us.*

In a timely update of Seneca's observation, James Averill notices that we do not abdicate responsibility for all of our emotions, just the negative ones. No one apologizes for being swept away by a tidal wave of kindness and donating five thousand dollars to a worthy cause. A bystander who intervenes to prevent an assault or mugging is unlikely to apologize for acting courageously. We want credit for our noble emotions and tolerance for our negative ones; and losing one's temper, "misplacing" it in a fleeting hour of insanity, is the apology that begs such tolerance. While anger serves our private uses, it also makes our social excuses.

MANNERS, EMOTIONS, AND THE AMERICAN WAY

The class was basic English for foreign students, and an Arab student, during a spoken exercise, was describing a tradition of his home country. Something he said embarrassed a Japanese student in the front row, who reacted the proper Japanese way: He smiled. The Arab saw the smile and demanded to know what was so funny about Arab customs. The Japanese, who was now publicly humiliated as well as embarrassed, could reply only with a smile and, to his misfortune, he giggled to mask his shame. The Arab, who now likewise felt shamed, furiously hit the Japanese student before the teacher could intervene. Shame and anger had erupted in a flash, as each student dutifully obeyed the rules of his culture. Neither could imagine, of course, that his rules might not be universal.

Because a major function of anger is to maintain the social order, through its moralizing implications of how people "should" behave, it is predictable that when two social orders collide they would generate angry sparks. It is easiest to see this when the colliding cultures are foreign to each other, but we have plenty of such collisions within our society as well. For some groups in America, anger is an effective way to get your way; for others it is the last resort. (Some groups have to learn assertiveness training to deal with others.) You may find your attitudes about anger, and the rules you learned to govern it, in conflict with those of different groups. Often it is this conflict about anger rules, not the rules per se, that can stir up trouble.

Each of us is tied to a group—a minitribe, if you will—by virtue of our sex, status, race, and ethnicity, and with countless unconscious reactions we reveal those ties as surely as Eliza Doolittle did when she opened her mouth. Anthropologist Edward T. Hall speaks of the "deep biases and built-in blinders" that every culture confers on its members. You can observe them at work every time you hear someone grumble, "I'll never understand women," or, "Why can't he just say what he feels?" or, "The (Japanese) (Mexicans) (Irish) (etc.) are utterly inscrutable."

Hall, who lives in New Mexico, has long observed the clash that occurs between groups when deeply felt rules about the "correct" management of anger are broken. The Spanish are sensitive to the slightest suggestion of criticism, Hall explains. "Confrontations are therefore to be avoided at all costs." The resulting misunderstandings between Spanish- and Anglo-Americans, he says, would be amusing if they weren't so often tragic.

When Anglo-Americans are angry, they tend to proceed in stages from small steps to larger ones: First, they hint around ("Mort, are you sure that fence is on *your* side of the property line?"). Then they talk to neighbors and friends of Mort. If they get no results, they may talk directly, and calmly, to Mort ("Mort, can we discuss our fence problem?"). Next they will express anger directly to Mort ("Dammit, that fence is on my property"). Eventually, if they are angry enough, they will take the matter to the courts. And as a last resort, they may resort to violence—and burn the fence down.

These steps, from smallest to largest, seem natural, logical, and inevitable. Actually, they are not only not natural, they are not even very common, worldwide. In many societies, such as in Latin cultures and in the Middle East, the first step is . . . to do nothing. Think about it. Brood. This brooding may go on for weeks, months, or even years (some cultures have long memories). The second step is . . . to burn the fence down. Now that matters are back to square one, participants are ready for direct discussions, negotiations, lawyers, and intermediaries. But notice, says Hall, that the act of force, which is the last step to Anglos, signaling the failure of negotiation, is the start of the conversation to Hispanics.

A culture's rules of anger are not arbitrary; they evolve along with its history and structure. The Japanese practice of emotional restraint, for example, dates back many centuries, when all aspects of demeanor were carefully regulated: facial expressions, breathing, manner of sitting and standing, style of walking. Not only were all emotions—anger, grief, pain, even great happiness—to be suppressed in the presence of one's superiors, but also regulations specified that a person submit to any order with a pleasant smile and a properly happy tone of voice. At the time of the Samurai knights, these rules had considerable survival value, because a Samurai could legally execute anyone who he thought was not respectful enough. (You may notice the similarity to American blacks and to women, who likewise had to be careful to control anger in the presence of the white man.)

Even today in Japan, an individual who feels very angry is likely to show it by excessive politeness and a neutral expression instead of by furious words and signs. A Japanese who shows anger the Western way is admitting that he has lost control, and therefore lost face; he is thus at the extreme end of a negotiation or debate. In other cultures, though, showing anger may simply mark the *beginning* of an exchange, perhaps to show that the negotiator is serious; a man may lose face if he does *not* show anger when it is appropriate and "manly" for him to do so.

Psychotherapy, of course, takes place within a culture and is deeply embedded in cultural rules. Arthur Kleinman, himself both an anthropologist and psychiatrist, tells of a psychiatrist in south-central China who was treating a patient who had become depressed and anxious ever since her demanding mother-in-law had moved in. "She is your family member. It is your responsibility to care for an old mother-in-law," the Chinese psychiatrist said. "You must contain your anger. You know the old adage: 'Be deaf and dumb! Swallow the seeds of the bitter melon! Don't speak out!' "

I am not recommending that Americans learn to "swallow the seeds of the bitter melon"; in our society, most of us would choke on them. Cultural practices cannot be imported from society to society like so many bits of cheese, because they are part of a larger pattern of rules and relationships. Indeed, that is the reason we cannot avoid the anger we feel when someone breaks the rules that we have learned are the only civilized rules to follow. But we might emulate the Arapesh, who criticize the provocateur; or the Eskimo, who settle in for a good round of verbal dueling; or the Mbuti, who have a good laugh, understanding as they do the healing power of humor. We might also retrieve the old-fashioned standard of manners, which is, as small tribes teach us, an organized system of anger management. The conventions of the U.S. Senate, for example—the ornate language, the rules of debate—regulate anger over disagreements into acceptable channels. A senator does not call his or her opposition a stupid blithering moron, for instance. He says, "My distinguished colleague from the great state of Blitzhorn, an otherwise fine and noble individual, is, in this rare moment, erring in judgment." The elaborate language that seems so comically deceptive to the rest of us is what keeps political conversation going without bloodshed and mayhem.

Good manners melt resentment because they maintain respect between the two disagreeing parties. Indeed, one of the basic principles of parliamentary law is courtesy, "respect for the rights of individuals and for the assembly itself." You don't have to join Congress to feel the effect of this principle at work. Someone steps on your toe, you feel angry, the person apologizes, your anger vanishes. Your toe may still hurt, but your dignity is intact. (A friend tells me he loudly shushed a talkative man sitting behind him at the movies, and immediately felt bad that he had expressed himself so angrily. After the show, the man touched him on the shoulder. "You were quite right to tell me to keep quiet," he said, "I was rude." "I could have kissed him," said my friend.)

Without rules for controlling anger, it can slip into emotional anarchy, lasting far longer than its original purposes require. Observe how friends and family react to someone undergoing a bitter divorce: They extend sympathy and a willing ear to the enraged spouse for a while, but eventually they expect the person to "shape up" and "get on with it." What these friends and relatives are doing is imposing unofficial rules of anger management. The victim may grouse and mutter about the loss of sympathy, but actually the friends and relatives are doing what any decent tribe would do: keeping anger in bounds after it has done its job and making sure the victim stays in the social circle. Well-meaning friends and therapists who encourage a vengeful spouse to ventilate rage for years are doing neither the spouse nor the tribe a service.

People in all cultures, even the pacifistic !Kung and the Utku, do occasionally feel irritable and angry. But they do not *value* anger. They strive for a state of mind that philosopher Robert Solomon calls "equanimity under trying circumstances," the worldview of small societies that live in dangerous environments. "The Utku," says Solomon, "much more than any of us, are used to extreme hardship and discomfort. Their philosophy, therefore, is that such things must be tolerated, not flailed against. Captain Ahab and Sisyphus would have no role in their literature."

In this country, the philosophy of emotional expression regards self-restraint as hypocrisy. The cultures of the Far East do not have this conflict; a person is expected to control and subdue the emotions because it is the relationship, not the individual, that comes first. Here, where the reverse is true, some people express their emotions even at the expense of the relationship, and manners seem to be as rare as egrets. This analogy is not arbitrary, for the same ideology that gave us emotional ventilation is responsible for the scarcity of egrets: the imperial "I."

Consider the gentle, forgiving environment of Tahiti, where people learn that they have limited control over nature and over other people. They learn that if they try to change nature, she will swiftly destroy them, but if they relax and accept the bounty of nature—and the nature of people—they will be taken care of. Anthropologist Robert Levy calls this resulting world view among the Tahitians "passive optimism."

Such a philosophy would not have lasted long among the ancient Hebrews, whose God gave them "dominion over the fish of the sea, and over the fowl of the air, and over the cattle, and over all the earth, and over every creeping thing that creepeth upon the earth" (Genesis 1:26). And a good thing He did, too, because in the harsh deserts of the Middle East, adherents of a laissez-faire Tahitian religion would have met a swift demise. The Judeo-Christian philosophy, however, produces "active pessimists": people who assume that nature and other people are to be conquered, indeed must be conquered, and that individual striving is essential to survival. But a universe defined as the Tahitians see it is intrinsically less infuriating than a universe in which almost everything is possible if the individual tries hard enough. The individualism of American life, to our glory and despair, creates anger and encourages its release; for when everything is possible, limitations are irksome. When the desires of the self come first, the needs of others are annoying. When we think we deserve it all, reaping only a portion can enrage.

3

The Anatomy of Anger

"O, preposterous and frantic outrage, end thy damned spleen!"

—*Richard III*, II, iv

When you get angry, what happens to your body? How do you feel? Try to recall a recent incident of anger and compare your reactions to the following list of symptoms:

- changes of muscle tension
- scowling
- grinding of teeth
- glaring
- clenching your fists
- changes of arms and position of body
- flushing (getting red in face or body)
- paling (losing color)
- goose bumps
- chills and shudders
- prickly sensations
- numbness
- choking
- twitching
- sweating

- losing self-control
- feeling hot
- feeling cold

These are a few of the items from the first modern, scientific effort to study anger. In 1894, psychologist G. Stanley Hall collected 2,184 questionnaires from people who answered his complicated queries in revealing detail, and Hall certainly wanted detail. He asked people to provide examples of their angriest episodes—what provoked them, what they did, how they felt later, any physical and mental changes. By today's standards, Hall's survey was too demanding, unsystematic, and imprecise. It was also lots of fun, and its findings entirely contemporary.

One of Hall's most curious results was the *physical* variation in people's experiences of anger. Some said that anger made them feel good, and others that it made them feel sick. "I have found it a not altogether unpleasant sensation to be in a great rage," wrote one informant; "It wakes me up and makes me feel very much alive." But another said, "I am often frightened that I can get so angry, and often have a nervous headache later." And some reported they had both reactions, depending on circumstances:

> When angry I feel all of a sudden burning hot, stifled and compelled to make a noise. Sometimes I grow icy cold and feel as if I was all blancmange inside. This feeling is worse than the heat, for I seem to be a stone.

Hall's respondents told him that anger produced "cardiac sensations, headaches, nosebleed, mottling of face, dizziness," tears, snarls, or "a complete inability to vocalize."

This array of physical reactions to anger was matched by the array of causes of anger. One category of provocation was what we might call the Stupid Inanimate Object, the idiot thing that produces immediate (usually brief) fury. "Our returns abound," wrote Hall calmly, "in cases of pens angrily broken because they would not write, brushes and pencils thrown that did not work well, buttonholes and clothes torn, mirrors smashed, slates broken, paper crushed, toys destroyed, knives, shoes, books thrown or injured, etc." When inanimate objects don't behave as they "ought," said Hall—there is that moralizing ought again—we lapse momentarily into the child's confusion between objects that are alive and those that are not, and act as if the offending brick, pen, or tool were capable of feeling our resentment. By so doing, naturally, we compound the injury—as when you kick the vending machine that has swallowed your money, thereby breaking your toe. You are not alone.

But another category of anger was more cerebral, and consisted of the idiosyncrasies, the "special aversions" that irritate us. One hundred and thirty women spontaneously told Hall that earrings on men were abhorrent to them. (I was surprised that enough men were wearing earrings in 1894 for this to be of such concern.) Men and women alike reported irritation at "thumb rings, bangs, frizzes, short hair in women, hat on one side, baldness, too much style or jewelry, single eye glass, flashy ties, heavy watch chains, many rings," and the like.

But it was the third category of angry incidents, anger caused by one person's treatment of another, that drew the greatest numbers and the greatest passion: Injustice. Stupidity (one's own or another's). Cheaters. Bootlickers (the modern equivalent still infuriates, although the term has advanced up the anatomy). Insults. Condescension: "To be treated as if I were of no account." One woman summarized the lot:

The chief causes are contradiction, especially if I am right; slights, especially to my parents or friends, even more than myself; to have my veracity questioned; the sight of my older brother smoking when we are poor; injustice, dislike or hate from those who fear to speak right out; being tired and out of sorts, etc. In the latter mood the least thing [will make me angry] like finding books out of place . . . stupidity in people who will not understand—these make me feel as a cat must when stroked the wrong way.

The angers that fell in this category combined physical reactions, in all their startling variety, and mental perceptions of insult, condescension, and the like, in all of *their* startling variety.

Research has progressed apace since Hall's time, and efforts to track down the physiology of rage have not abated. We are so much more sophisticated now, we think. Modern scientists have fancy equipment at their disposal and needn't rely on what people merely *say* happens to them; electrodes, chemical assays, EEGs, blood tests, computers, and other hardware will surely find some objective answers. In this pursuit, some researchers seek the genetic origins of temperament. Others try to pinpoint the neural circuits in the brain that stimulate anger and violence, or to locate the "master switch" to aggression. Some construct ingenious experiments to reproduce real-life emotions in the laboratory, where blood pressure, heart rate, sweat, skin temperature, attitudes, and lip chewing can be measured.

Biological explanations are appealing because they seem to be the purest, most fundamental. Many of my interviewees kept asking me about them: Why was my baby born as cranky as his uncle Mort? Is my husband genetically argumentative, did I think? What about the *feeling* of being angry, that out-of-control sensation? Scientists are discovering unanticipated (and controversial) answers from their studies of the brain, genetics, and bodily changes during emotional states.

An implicit assumption in many of the biological studies, as in the minds of many laymen, is that if we can nab those neurons that cause anger, we can prevent war, murder, and family quarrels. A fine and dreamy goal, no doubt, but some exciting research now suggests that it is misguided. Our emotions may emerge and differ primarily because of the *situations* in which they occur and because of the *interpretations* that we give to our bodily states—psychological and social matters, not solely biological ones. But perhaps the most revealing question is why it is that physiological explanations of our moods are so popular today. Researchers have made many advances in our understanding, but they have also shown that the anatomy of anger can be dissected many ways without reaching the heart of the beast.

EMOTIONS AND THE BRAIN

Tracy was a combative twelve-year-old boy who was highly excitable, given to aggressive outbursts, and had little self-control.

He also complained of constipation, muscle pain, and lethargy (which ruled out a diagnosis of hyperactivity). Nutritional bio-chemist Jeffrey Bland eventually traced the boy's problem to an "overconsumption-undernutrition" syndrome: Tracy was eating too many calories, in the form of sweets and junk food, and not getting enough nutrition, in the form of the vitamins and minerals that assure proper metabolism of calories in the body and brain. Tracy stopped eating candy, doughnuts, and ice cream, and began eating hard-boiled eggs, fruit, and whole-grain food, as well as taking B-vitamin supplements daily. In three weeks, Bland reports, Tracy's health had vastly improved and his "random aggressiveness virtually disappeared."

As I was gloomily debating the possible effects of chocolate on my personality, I opened the Pandora's box of brain research further. At once I wished I had stayed with chocolate. The list of brain diseases and abnormalities thought to cause rage, anger, and irritation is long: temporal-lobe epilepsy, viral encephalitis, brain abscess, stroke, presenile dementia, Huntington's chorea, tumors, hyperthyroidism, head injury . . .

In the early part of this century, for example, an epidemic of encephalitis lethargica swept the nation. "Lethargica," nothing. It could turn a placid child into a screaming devil. A physician who treated its victims described the stunning effects on one young woman who, he said, "used suddenly to become conscious of a rising surge within her, a seemingly physical wave which flooded her brain and caused her to clench her fists, set her jaws, and glare in frenzy at her mother." Had the mother said anything to displease her during one of these fits, the woman reported, "I would have killed her." She did not speak colloquially.

The phenomenon of explosive, sudden, apparently uncontrol-lable rage and violence, triggered by trivial provocation, is baffling. One psychiatrist, Sherwyn M. Woods, described the case of Steve, a fifteen-year-old boy who had murdered his middle-aged cousin when she nagged him about his dirty shirt. The boy described his feelings: "It's like a devil inside saying go ahead, grab her, stab her, choke her, kill her. You argue with yourself. It's like your hands aren't your own. Like a magnet pulling you. Once I start I can't stop until it's over."

Are these people all brain damaged, as some researchers think, or do they have psychological problems, such as lack of impulse control? Evidence of brain abnormalities in children and adolescents who had committed unusually violent acts turned up in 1951, when a peculiarity was discovered in their EEGs (called a 6- and 14-per-second positive spiking). More recent studies—such as one of thirty violent children, another with a sample of one thousand youngsters—found that a majority of those who had committed violent, antisocial crimes (such as Steve) had this odd EEG pattern. The trouble is that not everyone who has the abnormality is subject to rage attacks, nor is it clear whether the abnormality causes the violence or results from it.

However, among people who have suffered rage attacks *regularly* since infancy or early childhood, the cause can be traced frequently to genetic and other organic defects, to birth injuries, or to infantile convulsions. Other victims may have been injured in later childhood or adulthood, by illness or actual blows to the head. Some ominous studies suggest that many of the aggressive teenagers who make the newspapers these days are brain damaged. Angry, abusive parents may produce angry, abusive children not just by the example they set but by the injuries they inflict.

A compelling series of studies conducted by Dorothy Otnow Lewis and her associates demonstrates this point. First they compared delinquents and nondelinquents, finding that the former had significantly more hospital visits, accidents, and injuries than the latter. Then they compared imprisoned delinquents with delinquents who were not imprisoned (a measure of the seriousness of their crimes), and found that the two groups had similar medical histories in terms of *number* of accidents and injuries, but not in *kind*. Of the boys in prison, for example, 62.3 percent had had severe face or head injuries, many of them in the first two years of their lives, compared to 44.6 percent of the delinquents who were not incarcerated; indeed, a third of the imprisoned boys had been injured in the head severely enough to require skull X rays, compared to only 13.1 percent of the less violent boys.

It gets worse. Lewis's team next compared two groups of incarcerated delinquents: violent boys (who had committed very serious assaults, murder, or rape) and less violent boys (who had taken part in fistfights, threatened others with weapons, and the like). They discovered a much higher incidence of symptoms associated with temporal lobe seizures, neurological impairment (such as blackouts and stumbling), and paranoid thinking among the former than the latter. Nearly all of the violent boys (98.6 percent) had at least one neurological abnormality, and many had more than one, compared to 66.7 percent of the less violent boys; almost 30 percent of the violent delinquents had grossly abnormal EEGs or grand mal epilepsy or both, whereas none of the other delinquents had either sign. More than three-fourths of the violent boys, compared to "only" one-third of the others, had suffered head injuries as children, had had serious and extensive medical problems, and had been beaten savagely by their parents. Many endured abuse severe enough to have damaged their central nervous systems. One mother had broken her son's legs with a broom. A father smashed his son's fingers. Another father threw his son downstairs, after which the boy became epileptic.

Lewis does not conclude that there is a single factor that will make a child delinquent or violent. Violent delinquency is a combination of child abuse, social deprivation, trauma to the central nervous system, and other factors. But, she says, "our findings suggest a continuum of physical trauma corresponding to increasingly aggressive behaviors."

Now then, what do these grim studies tell us about brain mechanisms in anger? There is no doubt that some physiological conditions—food additives, disease, or injury—can cause a person to become irrationally enraged or violent or, less dramatically, to become cranky and irritable. This line of study helps researchers identify the areas of the brain that are implicated in rage and violence: particularly the hypothalamus (which controls autonomic processes such as respiration and heartbeat, hormones, and many emotional responses) and amygdala, both of which are part of the evolutionarily old limbic system. In the normal brain, inhibitory mechanisms regulate rage and aggression; in the malfunctioning brain, disease or injury may internally stimulate the "rage circuits" spontaneously and inappropriately.

Research on brain pathology sounds so basic and, well, au courant, but as a route toward understanding anger it has several problems.

True pathology is rare. Not all cases of explosive rage can be explained by brain damage, and not all cases of brain damage produce explosive rage. In one study of two thousand cases of head trauma, for example, only ten individuals became subject to spontaneous "rage attacks." And in most studies of people with temporal-lobe epilepsy, only 15 to 20 percent have such attacks, and some studies find that epileptics are no more likely than non-epileptics to have them. (Today, medication allows epileptics to lead normal lives.)

Or consider hypoglycemia, a trendy condition once thought to account for bad moods, fatigue, and a host of modern miseries. Strictly speaking, hypoglycemia is a chronic condition of low blood sugar that may occur because of a tumor of the pancreas or because the pancreas releases too much insulin after a high-carbohydrate meal. The symptoms do include irritability, fatigue, rapid heartbeat, and sweaty palms—symptoms that people may have for any number of reasons, such as studying for the bar exam or waiting to hear news of a promotion. But true hypoglycemia is rare: It occurs only once in every twenty thousand to one hundred thousand people (according to estimates at the National Institutes of Health), compared to diabetes, which affects one American in fifty, or high blood pressure, found in one in seven. The confusion about hypoglycemia seems to stem from the definition of "low" blood sugar. One common cutoff is 60 milligrams of glucose in a 100-milliliter blood sample; another is 44 milligrams. But in studies of *symptomless* men and women, about a third show fewer than 60 milligrams; if the same people take a blood test several times, even more of them will dip to that low point on at least one test. How can "low blood sugar" be an abnormal condition if it characterizes one-third of the population all the time, and up to two-thirds of the population on occasion?

Pathology, in any case, does not explain normality. The assumption in some brain research, implicit or explicit, is that by understanding abnormal rage we will understand normal anger. This belief is fallacious, even when the behavior in question seems superficially the same. Many people feel angry with their mothers or with cousins who nag them about dirty shirts, but we cannot thereby infer that they have abnormal brain-wave patterns. Most kinds and intensities of anger that we experience every day do not result from inflammation of a rage center or from a diseased neuron. They do not occur spontaneously while you are listening to a concerto. They occur in a social context, after an outside provocation—such as the phone ringing six times while you are trying to listen to a concerto.

The problem, therefore, is to distinguish people who suffer brain disease from those who suffer life. A juvenile delinquent may be neurologically impaired, or violence may be the only world he knows. A woman given to frequent rages may have not an allergy to onions, but an abusive husband. When I told a friend that one supposed sign of limbic brain disease is irrational, aggressive driving, he fidgeted and told me about "someone he knew" who once chased a car off the freeway because it cut in front of him. As far as I can tell, *everyone* has felt the Car Driving Furies. We can't all have lesions in the limbic system.

Further, to say that the limbic system contains mechanisms for anger, rage, and aggression does not imply that the limbic system is the *only* origin of such feelings and actions, or that all three are inevitably connected. The human capacity for cold, premeditated revenge, for violence for profit, for hatred at injustice, for anger at arrogance: these angers originate in the neocortex, the center for symbolic thought, logic, and reason.

Physiology needs an environment. Even if we wanted to reduce all kinds of anger to their corresponding brain centers, the task would be impossible. There is no such thing as a "rage circuit" that is unresponsive to, or independent of, environment and learning. When their amygdalas are electrically stimulated, for example, *previously violent* patients become violent. *Previously nonviolent* patients do not. In what sense, then, is the amygdala a "rage center"? As Leonore Tiefer, a physiological psychologist, summarizes the research, "Different amygdalas respond differently to the outside world, in different people in different societies. The brain does not operate in an all-or-none, on-or-off, yes-no fashion; that's not nature's way. Social experience can affect our basic physiology."

For these reasons, most researchers who are studying the role of the brain in emotion no longer look simply for "rage circuits" or "pleasure centers." New approaches emphasize the *interactions* between emotion and cognition in different parts of the brain, though researchers disagree about the nature and extent of those interactions. For example, certain regions of the left hemisphere appear to be specialized for the processing of positive emotions, such as joy, while regions of the right hemisphere are involved in the processing of negative emotions, such as depression. Patients who have lesions in one hemisphere often lose the ability to experience certain emotions. Damage to the left hemisphere tends to produce excessive hostility, tears, and pessimism. "Well," you might say, "wouldn't brain damage make anyone angry, sad, and pessimistic?" But damage to the right hemisphere is associated with excessive displays of happiness, joking, and laughing.

Other psychologists believe that there may be two parallel information systems in the brain, one for cognitive-interpretive explanations and another for "feeling." This would explain why someone can say "I am feeling anxious although I know there is no reason to be." According to psychologist Daniel Weinberger, the discrepancy between what we know and what we feel may have to do with different activities in the cerebral hemispheres. Weinberger distinguishes "suppressors," people who deliberately decide to postpone thinking about conflicts or negative emotions, from "repressors," who are unaware that they are feeling negative emotions in the first place. Suppressors say, "I prefer not to think about it"; repressors say, "There is nothing to think about." People with a repressive personality style convince themselves that they are *not* upset, when their bodies respond as if they are. Weinberger believes that repressors have deficits in transferring emotional information from the right hemisphere to the left. They may also have been raised by repressive parents who never allowed them to acknowledge, let alone display, a negative feeling.

The ongoing discussion about the relationship between cognition and "feeling"—are they parallel tracks or an inextricably woven web?—crops up again in the great Baby Facial Expression debate. It turns out that the specific muscles involved in the display of anger develop by four months of age; prior to that age, a baby communicates generalized distress. Some psychologists regard this fact as evidence that anger is wired in, and occurs long before the development of mental abilities. Others reply that an angry *display* does not necessarily imply an internal *feeling*. In their view, babies do not feel true anger until they are at least a year old, when they have developed the capacity to know, for one thing, that a feeling belongs to the self.

Certainly the first purpose of infant facial expressions of emotion is to communicate to others ("Mom, this psychologist is behaving weirdly; would you make him go away?"). But eventually these facial expressions also serve to regulate and activate our own feelings. When people are instructed to arrange their facial muscles in accord with an angry (or happy) expression, many of them report that they actually start to feel angry (or happy). Being angry may make you frown—but frowning will make you feel angry. "So there is some scientific support for the old advice to 'smile when you feel blue' and 'whistle a happy tune when you're afraid,' " says emotion researcher Carroll Izard.

These new directions in brain research show that emotion involves far more than a single spot in the brain that "turns on" anger, fear, grief, or joy. The energy of emotion, its intensity, its facial display, its origins and consequences, all depend on a complex network of brain, body, and environment.

TEMPER AND TEMPERAMENT: THE GENETIC INGREDIENT

"He was a very active, agitated kid, even from infancy," the woman said. "I used to think he would never hold still. I remember when he was an infant I could never just nestle him in my arms, because he was too busy, had too many places to go, always moving around." As all new parents know, a baby's personality seems apparent from Day One. Some babies gurgle, coo, and sleep contentedly; others seem especially sensitive, cranky, and unconsolable.

Like many couples in mixed marriages, Daniel G. Freedman, who is Caucasian, and his wife Nina, who is Chinese, were amused by the differences they observed between their respective families: The Chinese babies of her relatives cried less, were calmer and less excitable than the Anglo babies on his side. The Freedmans decided to put their anecdotal observations to the test. By studying newborns, untainted by experience, they hoped to see whether the differences in temperament were a result of inheritance.

With Harvard pediatrician T. Berry Brazelton, Freedman developed assessment tests of infant reactions that could be given to any newborn. Does the baby quiet easily? Does she settle down by herself or does she need to be picked up and consoled? Does the baby respond to the examiner's face and voice? Does he respond better to face *or* voice? Is the baby more interested in voices than in balls or rattles, or vice versa? Is the baby very active, or does he lie quietly where he is placed? Does the baby, like my friend's, resist being held or does she rest comfortably in an adult's arms?

The Freedmans applied this test to twenty-four Chinese and twenty-four Caucasian babies in a San Francisco hospital, when the infants were about thirty-three hours old. The Freedmans did everything they could to minimize differences between parents. The Chinese parents were all of Cantonese background; the Caucasians, all of North European stock. The mothers were about the same age, had had the same number of previous children, had had the same quality of prenatal care and the same kind and number of drugs during delivery. All the parents came from the same income and educational bracket.

Freedman apologizes for observing that he may have found one origin of what seems to Westerners like Asian inscrutability, but that is exactly what he got. "Caucasian babies cried more easily,"

Freedman reported, "and once started, they were harder to console. Chinese babies adapted to almost any position in which they were placed; for example, when placed face down in their cribs, they tended to keep their faces buried in the sheets rather than immediately turning to one side, as did the Caucasians. In a similar maneuver (called the 'defense reaction' by neurologists), we briefly pressed the baby's nose with a cloth. Most Caucasian and black babies fight this maneuver by immediately turning away or swiping at the cloth with their hands, and this is reported in most Western pediatric textbooks as the normal, expected response. The average Chinese baby in our study, however, simply lay on his back and breathed through his mouth, 'accepting' the cloth without a fight."

Freedman has studied babies in Nigeria, Kenya, Bali, Italy, Sweden, India, Australia, and (Navaho babies in) Arizona; each group, he says, has a typical pattern. Australian aborigines struggle with the nose cloth, like Caucasian babies do, but they are easy to calm and console, like Chinese babies. African and Australian infants have exceptionally strong necks; they can raise their heads and look around, which Caucasian babies cannot do until they are about a month old. Most Navaho babies calmly accept the tribal custom of being strapped to a cradle board until they are about six months old; those few who protest are taken off. But when Caucasian mothers in the Navaho community tried to use the cradle board with their own newborns, the babies cried and fussed so persistently that the mothers finally had to release them to preserve everyone's peace of mind.

Some researchers have taken the next step beyond description of differences. Andrew Sostek and Richard J. Wyatt of the National Institute of Mental Health, for instance, find that one enzyme that circulates in the blood and the brain, monoamine oxidase (MAO), is related to behavior even in newborns. Babies with low levels of MAO tend to be more excitable and crankier than babies with high levels. Levels of MAO, say the researchers, seem to be "biologically fixed": They run in families, and the variation in levels among infants is about the same as the variation in adults. However, the amount of MAO has nothing to do with the type of delivery, race, gender, birth weight, or prenatal medication given the mother.

Perhaps, as Freedman's work so provocatively suggests, there are temperamental differences among the human races, but there are also wide variations *within* racial groups. Psychologists Arnold H. Buss and Robert A. Plomin believe that there are at least four temperaments that have a strong hereditary component and therefore are stable aspects of personality: *emotionality*, or intensity of reaction, which may appear as "a strong temper, a tendency toward fearfulness, violent mood swings, or all these together"; *sociability*, a strong desire to be with others; *level of activity*, or total energy output; and *impulsivity*, the tendency to respond to events immediately without inhibiting one's feelings. As partial evidence of the genetic factor in these traits, identical twins (who share the same genetic makeup) have strongly correlated scores on tests that measure these qualities, whereas the scores are unrelated for fraternal twins (who have no more genes in common than any other pair of siblings).

Now this is all very interesting, but no one in the field of genetics is suggesting that individuals, or races, are born with an anger-at-injustice gene or a fury-at-frustration gene (or lack thereof). Racists, but not reputable scientists, subscribe to the single-gene notion—that there is a key gene that makes you smart or stupid, superior or inferior. Unlike spiders, who inherit a specific blueprint for web spinning, and unlike salmon, who for genetic reasons do go home again, human beings acquire most of their habits by learning. Any inherited predispositions we have are more diffuse and generalized than those of lower animals; genes merely provide us with a *reaction range*, and environmental events determine where in the range an individual will fall. Genes set the range of your adult height, for example—let's say five feet three inches at the shortest and five feet six inches at the tallest—but your actual height will depend on weather, vitamins, posture, diet, health, and so on.

One problem with this question of genetic components is that the "emotionality" of an infant, a four-year-old, and a forty-year-old takes (one hopes) different forms. Most forty-year-olds do not hurl themselves to the floor and pound their fists when they are angry, unless they have been in Primal Therapy. It is intuitively tempting to assume that cranky (or placid) infants will grow into cranky (or placid) adults, but the fact is that some do and some don't. Efforts to demonstrate emotional consistency from infancy through childhood to adulthood are contradictory and inconclusive. In one study, for example, researchers followed 136 New York children for six years, testing them for passivity, adaptability, responsiveness, intensity, and mood. The researchers could find *no connection* between their ratings of the children's temperament during their first year of life and the children's behavior at age five. Studies like these, and his own work, have persuaded psychologist Jerome Kagan that "the fears and joys of the first year seem to be part of nature's script for development, not harbingers of adolescent anxiety or prophetic signs of childhood happiness."

The confusion, I think, has to do with objective descriptions of baby behavior and subjective interpretations of that behavior. Parents do not say of their week-old infant, "Oh, look! Little Reginald has inherited his aunt Margaret's extreme volubility and arousability quotient!" They say: "Little Reginald is as mad as a newt this morning." Parents scrutinize each flounce of a fist, each hearty cry, for its "emotional" meaning, and in so doing they are rehearsing their own culture's customs about emotion and preparing to instruct their baby. Infants certainly behave in emotionlike ways from the first—their faces crinkle up and redden, they stretch and arch their backs—and attentive parents are quick to attribute an internal feeling to these actions.

Such attributions are made with degrees of seriousness. "My baby was angry from the start," one woman told me. "She hissed at passersby when I carried her home from the hospital." She was (I think) speaking figuratively, but some philosopher-psychologists speak literally about the "anger" the infant feels about being born, about the primal pain of separation from the mother. Because such speculations are entirely in the head of the observer and because no one can ask the baby, they are a matter of faith. I fail to see why it is not equally possible for the infant to feel Primal Joy at birth—relief at finally getting out of cramped quarters and cheer at finally having a colorful world to look at.

There may be, then, some genetic contribution to the fuel of emotion—those aspects variously called "emotionality," "arousability," "tempo," "metabolism," "excitability," and the like. What these terms have in common is the amount of energy the individual summons during an emotional response. We know that adults differ markedly in their normal (resting) levels of epinephrine (adrenaline), in their output of epinephrine in response to stimulation, and in the time it takes for their epinephrine levels to return to baseline after stress. The healthiest individual, like the best-made car, is well-tuned: neither sluggish nor overcharged, but able to pour out quantities of energy when called upon.

How that energy is channeled, however, and whether it creates a consistent personality style depend on what the child learns and whether that child grows up in China, Arizona, Australia, or New York. As psychologist L. Alan Sroufe once put it: "A child who has a rapid tempo may be seething with anger, hostile to other children, unable to control his or her impulses, and filled with feelings of worthlessness. But a child who has a rapid tempo also may be eager, spirited, effective, and a pleasure to others, and may like him- or herself." It is the world, not the genes, that determines which way it will go.

THE FUEL OF ANGER

When I am angry I can write, pray, and preach well, for then my whole temperament is quickened, my understanding sharpened, and all mundane vexations and temptations gone.

—MARTIN LUTHER

Betty. *They are gone, sir, in great anger.*
Petulant. *Enough, let 'em trundle. Anger helps complexion, saves paint.*

—CONGREVE, *The Way of the World*

You're beautiful when you're mad.

—infuriating male remark

What all three remarks have in common is their recognition of the effects of epinephrine, popularly thought to be the "anger hormone." A rush of epinephrine, scientists found years ago, prepares the body to respond to danger by fighting or fleeing. It must therefore be intimately associated with the experience of anger and fear.

This argument got a boost in the late 1940s, when it was discovered that the adrenal medulla produces a second hormone in addition to epinephrine, called norepinephrine (noradrenaline). It seemed logical to suggest that each hormone had its own emotional responsibilities; perhaps one accounted for anger and the other for fear. Albert F. Ax, working at the Boston Psychiatric Hospital in the early 1950s, did an experiment that seemed to demonstrate precisely this reasoning. This was the Grandfather Study of the physiology of anger, and its tentacles were to reach far into psychosomatic and clinical research.

Imagine that you are in Ax's lab, wired to an electroencephalograph that is measuring your heart rate, blood pressure, face and hand temperature, skin conductance, and muscle tension. (Other than that, nothing is unusual.) There you are, lying on a table and trying to relax, while a nurse takes your blood pressure every minute. (Relax, now.) You have no idea what the researchers are trying to find out, but you are in an accommodating mood.

Suddenly you feel an intermittent shock in your little finger, coming from a wire attached to it. It isn't painful, but it is noticeable, and you casually mention it to the experimenter. He checks the wiring, presses a key on the EEG machine that sends sparks flying, and panics. Suddenly he shouts: "This is a dangerous high-voltage short circuit!" He and the nurse dash around in agitation, but they eventually fix the wiring, assure you that everything is safe and sound, and try to get you relaxed enough to continue.

Would you be frightened? Worried about that wire still connected to your hand? Most of your fellows in this experiment were certainly scared. "Well, everybody has to go sometime," said one. "I thought this might be my time."

Fifteen minutes pass, and you are feeling better; damned

relieved, actually, when the polygraph operator enters the room to check your electrodes. You can tell at once that this guy is an arrogant goon. He pushes you around, criticizing you for moving, being uncooperative and useless to the study. (You, who have just survived a dangerous short circuit!) He insults the nurse. He is surly, rude, and offensive. But before you can insult or assault him, he is gone.

Would you be offended by this treatment? If so, you are in good company, since nearly everyone in the experiment did feel angry. Some of the men were about to deck the abuser if Ax himself had not intervened. "Say, what goes on here?" said one man. "I was just about to punch that character on the nose!" (I know it sounds like 1950s movie dialogue, but this *was* 1953.)

You don't know it, of course, but you have just been measured for your physiological reactions while you were afraid and while you were angry. Both scenarios were concocted by Ax to generate the emotions he wanted to study. As it happened, his play was a hit, and thirty-seven out of forty-three participants—men and women, ages twenty-one to fifty-five—got sufficiently frightened and furious to justify fourteen physical comparisons, of which seven seemed to discriminate anger from fear. The symptoms of fear resembled those produced by an injection of artificial epinephrine (at that time, the hormones could not be measured directly), and that the symptoms of anger seemed to be those produced by a combination of epinephrine and norepinephrine.

Ax's clever study was quickly ensconced in the field as fact: Fear = epinephrine; anger = epinephrine plus norepinephrine. His work is cited respectfully by his followers: "As Ax found . . ." they begin. But there are some significant problems with what Ax found. One is that the compelling scenarios confounded *type* of emotion with its *intensity*. The imminent danger of a life-threatening short circuit is not parallel to a brief annoyance caused by an incompetent bully, so you cannot say whether resulting differences are truly linked to each emotion or to how strongly each is felt.

But most important, the differences between fear and anger that Ax thought he found were minimal. All seven measures that supposedly distinguished the two emotions were actually correlated: that is, *the same bodily response occurred in fear as in anger*, differing only in degree. Moreover, if anger and fear each were identifiable by a pattern of physiological reactions, you would find those reactions clustering together reliably; for instance, the drop in heart rate and the rise in diastolic blood pressure for anger would be strongly correlated. In fact, Ax noted to his surprise, there was a general *lack* of correlation between the reactions of each emotion.

One reason for this result, we now know, is that some of Ax's measures are not exclusive indicators of emotion. Heart rate, which Ax thought decreases with anger, is a sensitive indicator of your attention to an event. Your heart rate *decreases*, other things being equal, when you are paying attention to things you want to accept: say, watching a play, taking instructions . . . or attending to a compelling experiment. (Even infants show this heart-rate drop when they are paying attention.) But when you need to concentrate on a problem and block out irrelevant distractions, your heart rate *increases*. Certainly Ax's participants were paying close attention to the irritating goon who insulted them.

What Ax learned, I think, is not that anger is different from fear, but that what happens to my body when I get angry (or afraid) is not necessarily what happens to yours. My body may even behave differently depending on what is making me angry. Ax discovered just what G. Stanley Hall had a half century before: the odd idiosyncrasies of anger.

Naturally some progress has been made. Ax was right about one thing: Anger does feel physiologically different from, say, fear or grief. In anger, skin temperature and pulse rate rise, which is why we feel "hot and bothered." With sadness and fear, skin conductance drops, which is why we feel "cold and clammy." Thus our metaphors of anger ("hot under the collar," "all steamed up," "he blew his stack," "flipped his lid," "hit the ceiling," "lost his cool") fit our physiological experience. (These metaphors of anger as explosions, steam, and heat are common in other languages and cultures.)

However, more accurate ways of estimating hormone levels

(from a urine test) now show that epinephrine is an all-purpose fuel. It is the energy behind most of our emotional states: fear and anger, yes, but also excitement, anxiety, jealousy, and joy. Epinephrine will rise if you are laughing at a funny film or playing an enjoyable game. In short, *any* event that is unfamiliar, intrusive, and compelling—and that potentially requires you to respond—will stimulate the production of epinephrine and, to a varying extent, norepinephrine as well.

The list of things now known to cause a rise in these two hormones reads like a catalog of modern life: heat, cold, pain, (true) hypoglycemia, low blood pressure (hypotension), hemorrhage, burns, physical exercise; drugs such as caffeine, nicotine, and alcohol; and "psychosocial stimuli," or what people do to you—an unexpected elbow in the ribs, an insult from a stranger or spouse, a dashing of your hopes for a promotion. Epinephrine rises not only in response to overstimulation, but also from understimulation. The body must cope with the exhilaration of a walk through a high-density, complex, strange new city, and it must cope with the boredom of repetitive, tedious chores. The production of epinephrine is lowest not when you are feeling bored or overworked, but when you are doing something that is mildly engaging, such as practicing the guitar.

Epinephrine and norepinephrine are what provide the *feeling* of a feeling: that tingle, arousal, excitement, energy. The adrenal hormones act on all organs of the body reached by the sympathetic nervous system, stimulating the heart, dilating coronary vessels, constricting blood vessels in the intestines, and shutting off digestion. That is why, when you are excited, scared, furious, or wildly in love, you don't want to eat.

These hormones also help the brain to learn. As levels of epinephrine and norepinephrine rise, memory, concentration, and performance are sharpened and improved, up to a point. If the body is flooded with epinephrine and you are *too* excited, concentration and performance worsen. A little nervousness when you take an exam or perform in an oboe duet is, in short, a good thing. A modicum of stage fright improves your act; too much, and you'll be frozen to the spot like an igloo. This is why you are likely to remember details of a mildly angry argument or a brief but irritating encounter, yet have trouble recalling the content of a really furious, all-out screaming match.

But the arousal effects of epinephrine are not enough to produce an emotion. For one thing, new research in psychology and neurology has found that "arousal" takes several forms, not just one, and these forms may involve different areas of the brain and different hormones. Further, arousal does not distinguish one emotion from another, and it does not distinguish emotions in general from other states of excitement. And it cannot explain why, of two people about to give a speech, one feels "psyched up" and the other feels overwhelmed by anxiety.

Moreover, epinephrine is not even directly related to the intensity of emotion. Injecting people with ephedrine, a powerful stimulant, has no effect on how afraid they feel about being threatened with electric shock. Conversely, drugs that lower the heart rate have no effect on people's *subjective* reports of feeling anxious. Indeed, people can experience intense emotions without the sensation of arousal. Several researchers interviewed spinal-cord-injured people, people with other handicaps, and nonhandicapped people to investigate the relation between arousal of the autonomic nervous system and emotion. The people with spinal cord injuries reported intense emotional experiences, and some said they felt more intense emotions than before their injuries. One man, with a high and nearly complete cervical lesion, reported being so angry at one of his instructors that he wanted to "run over him a few times" with his wheelchair. A woman who had a complete loss of sensation from her neck down following spinal-cord injury showed normal levels of joy, annoyance, and grief.

All of this suggests that the relationship between epinephrine and emotion is a murky one at best. Certainly, when the "fight or flight" response is all revved up, it does create the sensation of being out of control of one's emotions. In a basic sense, we *are* out of control, because, without portable biofeedback machines or advanced yoga training, we cannot consciously alter our heart rate, blood pressure, lung function, and digestive tract. Yet even this fact does not necessarily imply that we are "ruled" by emotion. Great physiological excitement does not instinctively feel unpleasant. Some people learn to associate it with the positive sensations of risk, fun, vibrancy, and power; for others, that rush of epinephrine signifies fear, danger, and powerlessness. The difference is a matter of attitude and experience, not of surging hormones. Without psychological perceptions, epinephrine has no content. It's that sinking feeling in your gut or the nervous palpitations of your heart or the fine sweat across your brow. Are you angry or apprehensive? Are you sick or just in love? Your body alone won't tell you.

THINKING ABOUT FEELING

One afternoon, as I was leaving the subway at rush hour, trudging tiredly up the stairs, I felt a hand brush my rear. It was an ambiguous gesture, considering the size of the crowd, so I did nothing; but my heart began to pound and my face flushed. I felt a mixture of excitement (My first New York pervert! Wait'll I tell the gang!) and fury (How dare this creep molest me?). The hand struck again, this time unmistakably a pinch. I spun around, umbrella poised to strike a blow for womanhood and self-respect . . . and stared face-to-face at my husband. He took one look at my apoplectic expression and burst out laughing, which was a good thing, as I might have whomped him anyhow.

This example shows the speed with which a single judgment—"This man is a friend with a rotten sense of humor, not a pervert"—transformed my apprehension and anger into delight. For heat to be transformed into hostility, uncertainty into fear, general distress into depression or rage, there must be a provocation, perception of injustice, or some interpretation of events.

Let's say you have succeeded at accomplishing something you have been trying to do for a decade: You got the lead in the play, you are promoted to executive VP. How do you feel? The answer, studies show, depends on why you think you succeeded. If you give yourself responsibility for your good fortune, you are most likely to feel proud, competent, and satisfied. But if you think your success was a matter of luck, good timing, nepotism, or some other reason out of your hands, your mood will be subdued; you will tend to feel grateful and modest. (Of course some people who have remarkably high self-esteem will assume control over any chance stroke of luck that befalls them, even winning the lottery.)

And what if you fail? What emotion do you feel? Again, if you take responsibility, your dominant feelings will be guilt, regret, and resignation. But if you have someone else to blame, another person or "the system," you are more likely to feel—you guessed it—angry.

Or take another example. You are working on a company report at your office, and a consultant is brought in to supervise your work. He is rude, arrogant, and insulting. Do you feel angry with him? Wait. Suppose a friend tells you that the man is suffering from a deteriorating illness, or that his wife left him and denied him visiting rights to their children. Suppose the friend tells you this man is habitually obnoxious and rude—to everyone, not just you. Or suppose the friend tells you the consultant is a high-achieving, ambitious expert in his field and that your work is essential to his success. Which description of the man will make you feel angriest with him? Most of us will answer: the ambitious expert. We forgive those whom we regard as sick or *habitually* unpleasant on the grounds that such people cannot help themselves. But we regard the "expert's" insults as intentional and controllable, and therefore worthy of legitimate rage. To most of us, anger (in others) that is motivated by personal gain deserves retaliation and punishment; anger that is expressed for unselfish motives or because of pain does not. Most of the events that happen to us are ambiguous, and our emotional responses to them depend on how we explain them: Did she mean to insult me? Is he unhappy or angry with me? Should I blame myself?

Psychoanalyst Silvano Arieti once criticized the efforts of Freudian theory to "minimize the role of the *idea* as an emotional force and to see it in a physical sense, as a quantity of energy." The ideas we have, he argued, cause us to interpret our past and present experience and, in so doing, we change our emotional associations. In short, we are not always at the mercy of unconscious emotional forces, because the ability to think, symbolize, and select among interpretations itself shapes our emotional experiences.

It is this cognitive capacity that may account for one of the most exasperating problems in the physiology of emotion: the sheer variety and complexity of emotional experience in people's lives. For example, psychologist Janet Polivy was going about her business, as good researchers do, trying to get her students to feel one emotion or another in the laboratory. The trouble was, her students refused to feel one emotion or another. They said they felt one emotion *and* another. When they got angry, they also reported feeling anxious and depressed. When they were afraid, they also said they felt depressed and hostile.

Polivy herself felt baffled by and curious about these results. What was going on here? Was this a result of an artificial lab situation, or something true to the nature of emotions? But when she asked her students to keep a daily record for several weeks, the same clumping together of moods occurred. Polivy is not sure whether she should blame her students for their "introspective laziness," or whether fear, anger, and sadness are emotional allies in some real physical sense. Perhaps, she suggested, anger, "an emotion not encouraged in our society, does in fact cause people to feel depressed and anxious." True, but this idea overlooks the fact that anger is not encouraged in *any* society in an indiscriminate way, and that anger *is* permitted in every society under specified conditions. Nor does it explain why fear should provoke anger and sadness; if people feel afraid when they are angry, they also feel angry that they are afraid! Our language discriminates between emotions, implying that each is a discrete entity; but in some African languages, in contrast, a single word represents both anger and sadness.

Not only do people experience clusters of emotion—anger and hurt, happiness and guilt—they differ in how intensely they experience their emotions. They differ too in emotional range: Some seem to have a limited number of emotions—they go from happy to sad, and that's about it. Others play on a keyboard of emotions—nostalgia, melancholy, gloom, euphoria, embarrass-

ment, jealousy, you name it. Cognitive differences may have more
of a role than physiological ones in accounting for these many
varieties of emotion.

Thus, in one study that nabbed college students before and after
an exam, students often reported mixed feelings, such as "hope"
and "fear" *before* the exam, or "anger" and "guilt" afterward.
These emotional blends resulted from the students' appraisals of
their performance, the importance of the exam, their own effort in
studying, their degree of certainty about how well they would do,
and so on. The students who felt angriest about their poor grades,
for example, believed the exam was unfair. This anger, though,
was often combined with guilt ("I should have studied harder"),
fear ("What if I don't pass?"), or apathy ("I don't care about this
course anyway").

Likewise, people who experience emotions intensely have typical ways of thinking: They *personalize* events ("I thought about
how I would feel if my friends, family, or I were in that situation");
they *pay selective attention* to the emotion-provoking aspects of
events ("I focused on the worst part of the situation"); and they
overgeneralize, taking a single event as a sign of a general state of
the world. They exaggerate, in positive as well as negative
directions.

Even one's emotional range seems to be more strongly related to
values and a basic "way of life" than to basic temperament. For
instance, psychologists Shula Sommers and Anthony Scioli found
that men and women who have a limited emotional range tend to
value a way of life based on pleasure and self-indulgence, and to
reject the values of responsibility and loyalty. In addition, women
who have limited range are more likely than other women to feel
powerless and entrust their lives to fate.

Thus the psychological factors involved in anger range from
your immediate perceptions of an event to your basic philosophy
of life. If you think a friend's criticism is intentionally mean, when
your friend intended to be well-meaning, you may respond with
anger rather than gratitude. Observe anyone who believes that
winning is everything and trying your best counts for nothing:
Such individuals feel miserable and depressed if they "only" come

in second. Our emotions cannot be separated from our mental lives.

Social scientists have been no less fascinated than philosophers by the mind-body distinction. They don't divide the body at the neck, as Plato did; instead they divide the brain by its hemispheres (the right side for passion and intuition, the left side for reason and intellect) or by its sections (the limbic system for primitive instincts and emotions, the neocortex for thought and rationality). Physiologists study what happens to the body during an emotional episode; psychologists try to find out how emotions feel subjectively and how people decide what emotion they feel. Researchers and therapists have gotten into heated debates about anger because often they are talking about different things: the anger that consists of cool thoughts, unaccompanied by pounding pulse, of hostility or resentment; the intense "reflexive" rage that follows danger or threat; the momentary annoyance that accompanies the behavior of Stupid Inanimate Objects.

But both sides are beginning to realize that no matter how you slice the problem, or the body, the distinctions are artificial. To understand anger, the dualist approach beloved for centuries will not do. Anger and its expression are a result of biology *and* culture, mind *and* body.

BIOLOGICAL POLITICS

In Los Angeles, a woman was acquitted by a judge for the murder of her infant son. She killed him, the defense claimed, while suffering from postpartum depression. In England, a woman was acquitted of the murder of her boyfriend—she rammed him into a utility pole with her car—because she had been suffering from "premenstrual syndrome." In San Antonio, Texas, a man confessed to raping a woman three times, but the jury agreed that *he* was the victim—of a high testosterone level. Across the country, clinicians are treating the "sexually compulsive man" who "just can't control his sexual desires," and angry couples who "can't control their tempers."

We are in the midst of an excuse epidemic, in which more and more physiological "conditions" are considered legitimate pardons for behavior that is immoral, illegal, or fattening. To William Lee Wilbanks, Professor of Criminal Justice at Florida International University, these excuses are all variations on the same theme: "I can't help myself." Wilbanks regards this phrase as an offense "to the core concept of humanity": that human beings have free will and are capable of self-discipline and responsibility.

"There is a growing tendency in the scientific community to view human beings as objects who are acted upon by internal and external forces over which they have no control," says Wilbanks. "We mistakenly infer that people *cannot* exercise self-control because they *do not* exercise self-control." We overlook the millions of men with high testosterone levels who do not rape, the depressed women who do not murder their children or lovers, and the angry couples who do not blurt out cruelties. "The idea that 'you can't help yourself' only convinces the person that their problem is hopeless, and they might as well give up," says Wilbanks. "It thereby produces the very kind of problem behavior it attempts to explain. The medical model of misbehavior completely ignores the idea of moral choice and resistance to temptation."

Psychologist C. R. Snyder, who has been studying the psychology of excuses for years, observes that "Excuses—such as 'it's not my fault,' 'the dog ate it,' 'I didn't *mean* to break her jaw'—soften the link between you and an unfortunate or negative action. The excuse lessens the degree of one's responsibility and minimizes the badness of the action. Excuses protect our self-esteem, but they also rationalize the destructive things people do."

As a psychotherapist as well as a researcher, Snyder is particularly concerned about people who move from *making* the excuse to *being* the excuse. "The excuse becomes incorporated into their identities," says Snyder. "They say: 'I couldn't help myself; I *am* a rapist/abuser; I *am* a depressed or angry person.' " Studies find, Snyder reports, that people lower their expectations for those they regard as "sick," "drunk," "depressed," or "out of control." So people with incorporated excuses don't even have to anticipate making one. "A man who blames his unacceptable behavior on his temper," he says, "finds that his future transgressions are automatically attributed to his problem. We call this a self-handicapping strategy. It excuses his behavior in the short run, but in the long run it undermines his self-esteem and sense of personal control."

Snyder observes that it is easier to treat people who make excuses ("I'm sorry I got angry and said that") than those who live by them ("I'm sorry but that's the way I *am*"). Once people define themselves as helpless slaves of a problem, they hand over control of the problem to others. Or they find an excuse that is out of their hands: "I can't help the way I am; my mother made me this way" (an ever-popular choice for blame). Successful therapy, says Snyder, depends on breaking down people's self-deceptive, self-protective excuses, and making them face the link between themselves and their actions.

Both Wilbanks and Snyder recognize that a humane legal system will permit some conditions to be legitimate excuses for a defendant's violent behavior, such as defending one's family or oneself or having an organic brain disorder. But they oppose the growing tendency in psychology and law to confuse moral judgments for scientific ones, and to confuse learned habits with organic deficiencies.

In today's world, in which people eagerly consume news of genetic, hormonal, and other organic explanations of behavior, it is easy to make this mistake. Once you begin to discover some organic causes of anger and rage, the temptation to see your explanation in every grumble and shout is nearly overwhelming. Neurologist Frank A. Elliott thinks that the "dyscontrol syndrome," a theoretical result of limbic brain disease, is "an important cause of wife and child battery, senseless assaults, motiveless homicides, self-injury, dangerously aggressive driving, domestic infelicity, divorce, and (in children) educational and social difficulties." Some food-allergy enthusiasts attribute the same list of woes to food deficiencies, additives, and allergies:

Many hyperactive children, cranky adults, warring couples, and outright psychotics, they say, are just eating the wrong thing. Richard Mackarness estimates that fully one-third of all cases of mental illness are produced by food allergies, and he cites examples of hospitalized patients who returned to normal lives after they stopped eating veal, or drinking instant coffee, or whatever. Physicians Paul H. Wender and Donald F. Klein, in their intelligent book *Mind, Mood, and Medicine,* get so excited by the remarkable cures that new drugs have effected on mood disorders that they see biochemical imbalances nearly everywhere they look, even as they recognize that the "realistic" problems of life can make us euphoric, depressed, or angry as well.

The appeal of biological reductionism, and its danger, lie in its influence on solutions. The diagnosis you make suggests the cure: food allergy, diet; brain disease, psychosurgery; chemical imbalances, drugs; social conflict, social negotiation. You might think it would be easy, not to say morally obligatory, to tailor a problem to its solution, but in practice there is much inflexibility. For example, what do you make of psychologist Kenneth E. Moyer's following observations?

I once had a neighbor who met all of the accepted criteria of freedom from pathology. She certainly should not and could not have been committed. However, her aggression circuits were easily fired. She felt hostile most of the time. She was irascible and uncomfortable, and though she reported that she tried very hard to inhibit her hostile behavior, she found herself frequently shouting at her children and her husband. Certainly, most men would agree that she should be freed of this unreasonable hostility if she is able to find a drug that will help her control it.

"Most men"? Perhaps, but I bet most women would prefer other solutions, or at least ask what this woman was angry *about*. If she was free of pathology, how do we know her hostility was so "unreasonable"? What if one man's "unreasonable" is a woman's "basic necessity"? Will drugs make her better able to enjoy her family and control her life, or will they make her more submissive and apathetic?

Not long ago, surgical intervention seemed a simple way to reduce rage. Once an electrode is implanted in the brain's diseased area, it takes only a zap of electricity to destroy the abnormality. "The wild cat Lynx rufus can be made tractable and friendly by an amygdalectomy," Moyer wrote. "There are wild men as there are wild cats, men who have so much spontaneous firing of the aggressive circuits that they are a constant danger to all around them and to themselves." People have returned to normal life after such easy operations, he said. Some were able to smile for the first time in their lives. Psychosurgeons tell horror stories, such as the one about the patient with a brain tumor that produced headaches, nausea, and vomiting. His psychiatrist, who opposed neurological surgery, decided the patient's symptoms were caused by "a hatred of his mother and a lack of regard for his father."

Persuasive, but it is only half the story. For all the magnificent revelations the brain has yielded in the last decades, our knowledge of its workings is still cloudy. In one group of twenty-five chronically hostile and violent patients, lesions of the amygdala had unpredictable effects: seizures were eliminated completely in only four patients, and "reduced appreciably" in another eight; the other thirteen did not change. Nor could the doctors predict which patient would improve as a result of the operation. Moyer himself, a devotee of psychosurgery, admitted that it is simply not known whether it is possible to reduce rage surgically without also reducing creativity, ambition, intelligence, or resistance to injustice. Yet he cited one patient who, after lesions of the temporal lobe, said that he couldn't get angry even if he wanted to.

This is why I call the diagnostic problem one of biological politics: Values and goals determine the diagnosis as much as "scientific" criteria. Some people refuse to believe that there are any genetic or organic causes of emotional disorders, preferring to spend useless years in therapy or to suffer privately (or to condemn others to those alternatives). But others embrace physiological explanations to be absolved of responsibility: "It's not *my* fault, darling, that I snap at you; it's low blood sugar." "So that's why I'm so impatient at work—I'm allergic to corn." "I just can't help these jealous rages; it's my low temper threshold." The remedies are as unthreatening as the cause: Taking a pill, rearranging a diet, and swallowing a vitamin are all far easier than taking a new job, rearranging one's life, or swallowing an unpalatable truth. So, of course, is doing nothing at all, an appealing route for those who look to genetics or instinct to excuse their lousy tempers.

Whatever diagnosis we choose to make about our emotions, the unmistakable lesson from biological research is that there is no such thing as "pure" biology untouched by perception and culture. Efforts to locate anger in the cardiovascular system, the gut, the muscles, the brain centers, the facial expressions, or bodily organs have all proved inadequate for this reason. Psychologist Joseph de Rivera despairs of these scientific assaults on the emotional Hydra, for as soon as one hypothesis is cut down, other bodily systems are quickly proposed. Because bodily sensations are clearly *involved* in emotion, he adds, people readily, but incorrectly, infer that bodily sensations *are* the emotion.

For society's sake, as well as for the thousands of people who are being taught to think of themselves as helpless victims of life or biology, it is time to restore confidence in our abilities of self-control and self-determination. I think that biological research helps us to do this, for it shows that while anger is a normal, physiological process, it is one that is generated, and can be reduced, by our interpretations of the world and the events that happen to us. It shows that the very act of defining an ambiguous emotional state as anger may create anger where none previously existed. It shows that while we may not be able to control the fight-or-flight response that protects and defends us, we *can* control what we do about it—express it, deny it, defy it, transform it, use it. Most of all, biology teaches that we need not be hostages to our emotions: We are restored a measure of responsibility for how we act on them. We can't plead that the devil (or Henry) made us do it.

4

Stress, Illness, and Your Heart—Myths of Suppressed Anger

Strategies for keeping anger in include denial and rage against the self . . . perhaps accompanied by hypertension and coronary disease. Inwardly screaming at oneself, on the other hand, may lead to depression, sometimes with high blood pressure, migraine, and impotence thrown in.

—Fortune

Most often the result of pent-up frustrations, repressed anger can turn inward in destructive, paralyzing ways. It can prevent us from dealing positively with problems or relating lovingly to others, and can also lead to serious health disorders.

—Harper's Bazaar

These quotations from two popular magazines certainly sound logical. Most of us know the uncomfortable feeling of holding back when we really want to let that so-and-so have a piece of our mind; if the so-and-so is persistently infuriating and the uncomfortable feeling gets worse, it makes sense to worry that an ulcer, or something worse, is on its way. And so it follows that if we express or act out our emotions as we feel them, we will avoid psychosomatic illness.

All sorts of psychosomatic illness, in fact. A Dutch psychiatrist in the Netherlands, J. J. Groen, listed some of the illnesses that doctors and clinicians believe are largely caused by emotional inhibition: "the cardiac arhythmias and tachycardias, Raynaud's disease, migraine and tension headaches, the hyperventilation syndrome, functional diarrhea, habitual constipation, dysmenorrhea [painful menstruation], ejaculatio praecox, vaginismus, and impotence . . . peptic ulcer, ulcerative colitis, essential hypertension, bronchial asthma, anorexia nervosa, and obesity (voracity)." Mercy! Much better to shout at your landlord or spouse! The assumption in such cases, Groen continues, is that these patients cannot act out their emotions in a simple, direct way, so the internal discharges of the autonomic nervous system are disturbed; this gives rise to clinical disease. Starting from this belief, many doctors advise (and therapies teach) clients to "get in touch with their feelings."

In my efforts to track down the role of suppressed *anger* in disease and psychosomatic illness, however, I was thwarted at every turn. The first obstacle was that our emotions are not especially distinctive. As I noted in Chapter 3, emotions tend to come in bunches, like grapes, and it is very rare to find a single emotion causing trouble on its own. Groen himself, for example, reviewed much of the research on psychosomatic illness and concluded that "only in relatively few of these conditions has it been possible to designate the pertinent emotional states in the simple terms of, e.g., anxiety, rage, or depression." Emotions *combine* in complicated ways, he said, to produce abnormal conditions.

A second obstacle I encountered was the confusion between *causes* of illness and *results*. It is easy to make this error. Doctors and therapists, after all, see people *after* they get sick or develop emotional problems. There the patients sit, angry or depressed that the marriage, job, or ulcer is not improving, and it is a simple if fallacious jump to the impression that the anger or depression caused the ulcer or emotional problem. The fact is, when people feel ill, that alone can make them irritable, afraid, and unhappy.

Third, a surprising number of studies investigating the role of emotions in health do not take health habits into account. Before you could conclude that "suppressed anger causes cancer," for example, you would have to rule out the possibility that people who suppress anger are more likely to smoke or drink. Yet many studies not only ignore relevant risk factors, they also overlook the possibility that something else entirely affects anger *and* disease. For example, perhaps an over-responsive nervous system leads to the development of frequent anger and, independently, to the development of heart disease.

Finally, the role of anger in illness is obscured by the confusion between psychological causes of mental and physical problems and organic, physical causes. As Susan Sontag rightly observed in *Illness as Metaphor,* whenever the medical origins of a disease are unknown, people make up psychological explanations. In the nineteenth century, before the bacillus that causes tuberculosis was discovered, "personality" explanations of TB were popular. The villain "suppressed anger" has been held indiscriminately liable for problems that now seem to be predominantly physiological or genetic in origin (such as overweight and ulcers); for vaguely defined problems that may have different causes for different people (such as depression and stress); and for complicated illnesses (such as hypertension and heart disease) in which anger must take its place, if at all, at the end of a long list of contributing factors.

A word, however, about terms. In popular parlance, "suppressed" and "repressed" anger are often used interchangeably to mean any of the following: anger that you feel but do not express openly and directly; anger that you "should" feel toward someone else, but which you instead direct toward yourself; and unconscious anger that is blocked from awareness because it is too threatening to the ego. For our purposes here, I will be talking primarily about the first two meanings, which I will call "suppressed" anger, to distinguish them from the psychoanalytic concept of unconscious repression.

EATING DISORDERS, OVERWEIGHT, AND ULCERS

*But I've been obsessed with food ever since I was a child.
I was rail thin, and quietly struggled to force down food,
but inside my resentment was seething.*

*Today, when I gorge myself, I'm using food as a
weapon, lashing out at my parents, my husband and
myself. Every cookie is an attack . . . I use food to avoid
responsibility, to satisfy the inner conflicts and emotional needs I can't handle alone.*

—JACKIE BARRILE,
"Confessions of a Closet Eater"

Sounds plausible, doesn't it? Unfortunately, this pop psychologiz-
ing is vague and superficial enough to be meaningless—there is
certainly no way to verify it—but clinicians feed such arguments to
their overweight clients, who swallow them with gusto. Anger is
often involved in the explanation of why people are overweight or
why they have a particular eating abnormality, such as anorexia
(eating virtually nothing) or bulimia (episodes of gorging and
vomiting). Like Jackie Barrile's seething resentment and food-
as-weapon theory, suppressed anger is frequently assumed to be
buried under the fat—or the fear of fat.

For many decades, research psychologists and psychotherapists
have tried to find consistent psychological causes of obesity or
simple overweight. As physician William Bennett and *American
Health* editor Joel Gurin report in their excellent book, *The
Dieter's Dilemma*, all efforts to confirm the psychodynamic
explanations for fatness have failed. This was not for lack of trying.
As early as 1957, psychiatrist Harold Kaplan and clinical psychologist Helen Singer Kaplan summarized the published notions of
the causes of overeating. These included:

• a means of diminishing anxiety, insecurity, tension, worry,
  indecision
• a means of achieving pleasure, gratification, success

- a means of expressing hostility (conscious, unconscious, denied, or repressed)
- a means of rewarding oneself
- a means of diminishing guilt, including guilt due to overeating

"And on and on," report Bennett and Gurin, "through some twenty-three more sets of mutually contradictory examples." In other words, for someone who thinks she eats when she feels angry, someone else eats when she feels terrific (it is often the same person, in fact). For everyone who thinks he's fat because his parents didn't love him enough, someone else thinks he overeats because his parents loved him too much: "My mother never fed me enough" coexists as an explanation of overweight right along with "My mother overfed me."

Today obesity is no longer recognized as a sign of emotional illness; the American Medical Association has been unable to find any distinct psychological or behavioral syndrome associated with it. Indeed, the only psychological differences between thin people and fat people, on the average, have to do with the social stigma of being overweight and the disdain this culture shows toward even the mildly plump. In short, most of the psychological problems that fat people have, with anger or anything else, are typically a result of overweight, not a cause. The stress they are under is almost always not a result of emotional conflict . . . but of dieting.

Binge eating, for example—Ms. Barrile's problem—is not particularly related to suppressed anger or seething resentment. It is primarily a response to *hunger*. It typically occurs among people who are dieting, whether as a four-week effort, a crash diet, or as a restrained, constant attempt to hold one's eating in check. Notice that dieting is the key here, not overweight: Many very thin people, especially women, keep themselves fashionably gaunt, but at a high emotional price.

Psychiatrist Hilde Bruch, author of *Eating Disorders*, described the dilemma of "thin fat people"—normal-weight individuals, usually women, who are obsessed with being thin. "Many women," Bruch wrote, "make a fetish of being thin and follow reducing diets without awareness of or regard for the fact that they can do so only at the price of continuous strain and tension and some degree of ill health . . . Never having permitted themselves to eat adequately, they are unaware of how much of their tension, bad disposition, irritability, and inability to pursue an educational or professional goal is the direct result of chronic undernutrition. . . . It has become customary to prescribe tranquilizers for them; three square meals a day would be a more logical treatment."

"Dieters, like starving people, are often irritable, tense and depressed," write Bennett and Gurin. Chronic dieting and restrained eating make people of all weights hungry; the body doesn't know whether you are starving voluntarily or not. Fat people (and "thin fat people") have been told to look for all kinds of unconscious motivations for their eating "troubles," but as Bennett and Gurin convincingly demonstrate, "In most cases fatness is just a biological fact, like baldness or green eyes; it is not the result of deep-seated psychological problems or abnormal 'obese eating habits.' "

People are ready to believe that allergies or junk food can make children cranky or given to aggressive outbursts, but they seem less ready to believe that dieting can do the same thing to adults. Imagine how the irritability quotient in this country would drop if people went off whatever currently idiotic, abnormally restricted diet they were on (and simply practiced good nutrition)! Instead of speculating about mysterious resentments they may have had as children, most dieters would do better to become angry not with their parents but at a society that has made an enemy of their bodies.

It may seem a long way from overweight to ulcers, but they share the same theoretical origins, if not results. A physician who wrote a book on ulcers in 1978 reported as fact that "the duodenal ulcer patient seems to have learned at a very early age to prefer to keep peace rather than to flail out with his hands or tongue." This statement seemed odd to me at the time, since the few people I know who have ulcers, or had them, also have had no problem flailing out with hands or tongue. They are straightforward anger-expressers, in fact.

Sure enough, the latest evidence has pretty much disproved the suppressed-anger theory of ulcers. Calm, relaxed people get ulcers as often as hard-pressed, competitive people do, and lower-status workers get ulcers as often as higher-status ones. Ulcers occur as often among bus drivers, farmers, and construction workers as among the occupations famous for producing them, such as movie moguls and managers. Ulcers aren't even more likely than usual to strike air traffic controllers, who certainly work under pressure. Ulcers turn up among people who express anger readily, and among those who don't. The popular picture of buried anger doing its nasty work, making painful sores, is imaginatively clever but medically unsound.

The strongest factor in the onset of ulcers is not an emotional state at all but the presence of high levels of serum pepsinogen I (a biochemical genetic marker) in the bloodstream. Studies of twins indicate that these levels are genetically determined, so apparently some people are put at risk of developing ulcers when they are under stress. Duodenal ulcers tend to occur among close relatives, especially identical twins, and are somewhat more prevalent among people with Group O blood type. (There are different kinds of ulcers, though, not all of which have the same cause. In one study, one-third of the patients hospitalized with duodenal ulcer had normal serum pepsinogen I levels.)

So relax. "Flailing out" with your hands or tongue won't protect you from ulcers (or keep you thin), and sitting on your hands or biting your tongue won't give them to you (or make you fat). Nor will either approach to anger make you lose the ulcer or lose unwanted pounds.

ANGER AND DEPRESSION

In the standard psychoanalytic formula, depression is anger turned inward. The idea was born in 1911, when Karl Abraham hypothesized that hostility about the loss of a loved one becomes self-directed, through incorporation of and identification with the beloved, and this process leads to depression. Freud, in *Mourning and Melancholia* (1916), added that guilt over a loss produces a need to suffer and a resulting drop in self-esteem, which triggers self-directed hostility. Most psychoanalytic writers subsequently put aggression or anger at the center of their theories of depression.

But if anger is a fixed quantity that can be maneuvered in this direction or that, why stop with "depression is anger turned inward"? Why not argue that anger is depression turned outward? Surely the one is as plausible as the other. A social worker I interviewed told me that she has trouble tolerating the rage of friends who are going through divorces or other emotional detachments. "I don't have the patience I used to," she says, "to listen to people rail about their ex-lovers. It keeps them stuck in the mire of their anger, for one thing, and I think it masks their real feelings of hurt and sadness."

"Real feelings of hurt and sadness"? The mistake, in this direction game, is to assume a one-to-one correspondence between anger and depression. This mistake does justice to neither emotion. Sometimes depression is "anger turned inward," but sometimes it is only depression, which is bad enough. Sometimes an angry person is "really" hurt, sad, or worried, and sometimes he or she is really angry. Just as there are different kinds and causes of anger, there are different depressions, and different relationships between the two emotions.

First, depression may be the sequel to anger. When anger is unsuccessful in averting danger or removing obstacles, when it does not restore your sense of control over the environment, you may eventually begin to feel apathetic. According to the *hopelessness theory of depression*, the key cognitions in depression are that nothing good will ever happen ("It's all hopeless"), and that the person is helpless in changing this bleak future. Depressed people tend to believe that negative events have internal, stable, and global causes ("It's my fault; it will always be my fault; and it will affect everything I do"). In such cases of depression, though, it is not quite right to say that anger has been "turned inward." More accurately, it has been extinguished.

Second, anger and depression may be wholly different, learned reactions to prolonged stress, depending on a person's social history and possibly also on genetic differences in hormone metabolism. Some individuals learn that by responding to a bad situation with judicious anger, they can change their predicament; others, feeling helpless and powerless, learn (or believe) that anger will only boomerang. Over time, anger *or* depression may become habitual strategies for accommodating to difficult circumstances.

Third, and most commonly, anger and depression may occur simultaneously. If depressives are "turning anger inward," we should find that they are not expressing anger or hostility "outward" verbally. But it turns out that most depressives *do* express anger and hostility to others. The idea that they cannot has not been scientifically confirmed; it came primarily from clinicians' hunches or personal observations. But perhaps, suggest physicians Paul Wender and Donald Klein, depressives do not express anger *to their therapists*, not wanting to antagonize someone who represents to them their only hope. They cite one long-term study of depressed women, in which hostility not only increased during episodes of acute depression, but also continued after the depression ended. Once again, simple equations between depression and the "direction" of anger were unsupported. Indeed, if depression were anger turned inward, we would expect that antidepressant medication would "release" or "redirect" the anger. This too does not seem to be the case. "Depressed patients who respond positively to antidepressants become *less* irritable and angry," report Wender and Klein, "contrary to the common psychodynamic explanation."

Because most of us have a stew of emotions when something troubling has occurred, to emphasize one emotion and exclude another may simplify the problem, but it restricts our choices. Therapists who see anger behind the mask of depression may be attending to only half the problem. Aaron Beck, a renegade psychoanalyst who has rejected the Freudian depression-and-anger formula, describes the typical vacillation between anger and sadness in the case of a man whose wife had criticized him severely:

> One moment he would think about how unjust she was to criticize him, and he would feel angry at her. Then, he would shift to the

idea that he had lost her affection, and would feel sad. All day the focus of his thinking alternated between blaming his wife and being deprived of love, with corresponding oscillations between anger and sadness.

Notice that what affects the man's mood is what he is thinking, not what he is feeling. This observation led Beck to break with tradition and devise a therapeutic approach to depression that emphasizes the distorted *ideas* that depressives have about themselves and the world. A wife whose husband has left her may be depressed because she blames herself, feels she has lost all appeal to men, and hasn't the energy for her work. A young student feels lonely and insecure and attributes this feeling to permanent failings instead of a temporary condition (being a freshman). A lawyer thinks his wife trapped him into marriage. In each case Beck, and others of the cognitive-therapy school, help the individual understand how his or her attitudes are responsible for the depression and try to correct the distorted ideas. Cognitive therapy, according to recent reports, is much more effective than drug therapy alone (antidepressants) or psychoanalysis for changing a person's misguided notions and low self-esteem.

Finally, anger and depression may be entirely unrelated. In doing research for their book *Social Origins of Depression*, sociologists George W. Brown and Tirril Harris interviewed a random sample of 458 women in an English working-class district, comparing them to more than 100 women in psychiatric treatment for depression. The researchers wanted to identify the life stresses that are implicated in the onset of depression, and they found several factors which, in combination with a particularly stressful catalyst, predicted which women in the random sample would become clinically depressed. These factors were a woman's lack of an intimate, confiding relationship with her husband; the loss of her mother before age eleven; three or more children under the age of fourteen in the home; and lack of outside employment.

Well, who *wouldn't* be depressed under such conditions? Add to the everyday problems these women face—isolation, loneliness, the demands of many young children, poverty—one last straw, such as illness or bereavement or violence, and imagine the strength they would need not to succumb to hopelessness. But in what way is this depression "anger turned inward"?

A good case could be made, of course, that these women *should* be angry. You could argue persuasively that if they did get angry at their husbands' lack of support (emotional as much as financial), or at the government's lack of jobs and child-care services, they would find the energy to change the entombing conditions of their lives. You may believe that a person should be angry rather than depressed, because focused anger has a better chance of producing practical solutions to one's misery than apathy and tears do. But the minute "should" creeps into the conversation we are into politics and away from biological or psychological givens. The goal of reform movements and of some therapies is to persuade the hopeless and disenfranchised that there are practical solutions to help them. To succeed in this persuasion, reformers must kindle anger from the coals of depression. But this is a social process, a matter of new motivation and new perceptions of the old situation, not of redirecting anger—suppressed or even unconsciously repressed—somewhere else.

One reason for the contradictory theories of anger and depression is that depression, like anger, comes in degrees of severity, including tearful tiredness, a chronic state of the "blues," and an inability to get out of bed. Moreover, depression, like anger, has many causes. One person may be suffering from the aftereffects of having been sexually abused in childhood; another may have a predisposition to respond to any stress with melancholy; a third may have a pessimistic personality style that fosters depressive interpretations of events. The relationship between anger and depression in any of these cases is likely to be very different.

The psychiatrist and essayist Leslie Farber once observed that depression is always about something that has gone wrong in one's life, but that people now regard it as a diagnostic category instead of an understandable response to troubled times. "No longer is a patient likely to arrive in my office declaring his distress to be marital tension, job insecurity, or generational conflict," he said. "What he announces is that he is depressed, as though that explained something. Of course he is depressed: Marital tension or job insecurity or generational conflict of some sort is making him miserable; depression is not a surprising component of his outlook."

The same may be said of anger, which also is always about something, and which is frequently a predictable response to troubled times. Whether anger and depression are related in a given instance, and which of them is appropriate, depends on the event that has caused them—and on our interpretations of that event.

THE STRESS CONNECTION

The clinical assumption that stifling anger can have psychosomatic consequences got a big boost in the late 1950s, with a book called *Mastery of Stress*. The three authors (Daniel H. Funkenstein, Stanley H. King, and Margaret E. Drolette) wanted to know whether the way we handle anger is connected to the ability to reduce stress. If you are enduring a year of particular frustration and worry, do you feel angry more often than usual? Or do you feel anxious, or another emotion altogether? What do you do when you feel angry: express it or keep it to yourself? Does any of this matter to your body's ability to acclimate to stress?

To answer these questions, the researchers got 125 healthy young Harvard men to volunteer for the project, which consisted of three stress tests (one a week for three weeks). The researchers repeated the series one year later, so they could see whether the men "mastered stress" in the short run and the long run. By "mastery" they meant the physiological acclimation of the body, rapid reduction of signs of tension (such as high blood pressure) to normal.

I liked the researchers' stress tests, because they were so similar to situations that most of us encounter all too often in daily life. In two different stressful settings, the men were frustrated in their efforts to solve the assigned tasks. As the researchers explained, their aim was both to interrupt the young man and assault his feelings of self-regard, without actually preventing him from doing the work. The experimenter would be just threatening enough and harassing enough to justify the young man's anger if he felt so inclined, but he wasn't mean enough to be the obvious source of the young man's problems. Just as in real life, the source of the difficulty was ambiguous, and each young man had the choice of blaming himself or the experimenter for failing the tests.

At the end of each stress session, the experimenter interviewed each young man about his feelings, giving him permission to rage, rant, weep, tell jokes, or do what he liked. The researchers were then able to categorize the *feeling reported* (anger, anxiety, amusement, and so forth) and *direction of the feeling* (expressed outwardly at the experimenter, directed inwardly, some of both). In shorthand, they could then speak of "anger-in" or "anger-out." Anger-in (feeling angry but directing it toward oneself), they assumed, would be the bad guy.

Certainly lots of people who read *Mastery of Stress* assumed it was. Hardly had the book landed on their desks when psychologists and physicians hustled off to construct anger-in, anger-out tests and relate them to one psychosomatic ailment or another. Anger-in, alias "suppressed hostility," fit nicely in the Freudian mold, and within a few years it was implicated in dozens of diseases. A bit of sleuthing, however, reveals that some of these researchers galloped off down an unpaved road. *Mastery of Stress* itself did not prove what its authors thought it would about the role of anger in stress:

• Anger—in, out, or ambidextrous—was characteristic of only 68 boys out of the 125. That is a majority, to be sure, but not much of one, which means that anger and stress are not necessarily related.

• Anger, no matter where it was directed first, *rarely stayed put.* Among the "anger-outs" who started out roaring at the experimenter, some changed their minds and felt angry with themselves for having let themselves get angry, or for failing the experimenter, or for other reasons of self-responsibility. Others felt anxious about having expressed their anger. Some, having expressed anger, then saw through the experimental manipulation and had a good laugh about it, while others got still angrier, feeling they had been duped. Similarly, some of the anger-ins shifted to anger-out, some kept on blaming themselves, and some eventually shrugged off the whole business.

• The direction of anger was *not related* to the ability to master stress. The kingpin of the whole anger-in-causes-stress argument was never supported! The researchers had believed that the ability to adjust to stress (according to various physiological measures) would be related to a person's emotional style, but this is not what they found. They reported, instead: *"In two years of testing, no relationship was found between the acute emergency reactions of the subjects [that is, anger-in, anger-out, or anxiety] and their ability to master or failure to master stress as time passed."* In other words, the young men who responded to stress with anger-in, anger-out, or anxiety had equally good chances of adapting to physiological stress.

• By thinking of anger-in and anger-out as rather fixed styles of coping, the researchers discounted the ways that situation and status influence anger. You may be an anger-out with a bank teller, but an anger-in with your mother-in-law. Many people are anger-outs at home and anger-ins at work. Funkenstein and his associates did not find out how their healthy young Harvard men expressed anger to other healthy Harvard men, or to their parents, or anyone else. So they could not say whether they had identified a personality trait (the man always keeps quiet about feeling angry) or a situational state (the man keeps quiet about anger toward experimenters).

To pursue the question of whether anger is a "state" or a "trait," Charles Spielberger, director of the Center for Research in Behavioral Medicine and Community Psychology at the University of South Florida, has developed a measure of people's characteristic anger patterns. Anger-outs make sarcastic remarks, slam doors, say nasty things, and strike out at whatever infuriates them. Anger-ins pout or sulk, harbor secret grudges, are "secretly" critical of others, "boil inside, but don't show it," and withdraw from conflicts. But over the years, Spielberger has observed that some people follow a third strategy, which he calls "anger control." When provoked, such individuals keep cool, control their behavior and angry feelings, try to be patient and understanding, and are able to stop themselves from sounding off. As a result, they actually experience anger less frequently, and are less likely to behave aggressively, than people who either sulk or explode.

Spielberger also found that although most people assume that anger-in is the opposite of anger-out, the two strategies are independent of one another. This result, coupled with his findings on anger control, suggest that the *context* of anger shapes our responses to it. Think for a moment about how you would feel and what you would do if:

- your boss blew up at you for no good reason
- a policeman shouted at you for something that was not your fault
- a homeowner refused to sell you the house of your dreams because of your race or religion

Would you reveal your anger? How would you feel about doing that? Would you try to talk reasonably to your unjust opponent, after he or she had calmed down? If you don't express your anger, would you brood about your grievance yet feel too guilty to do anything about it? Are any of these answers related to your chances of increasing, or reducing, your blood pressure? It would be nice to report yes, but no such luck. The connection between anger (expressed or suppressed) and high blood pressure depends on your age, race, sex, social class, and primarily on the reason you feel angry.

For example, in a random sample of men and women (black and white, middle-class and working-class) living in Detroit, the majority of the working-class men said that they would report an unjust boss to the union or to someone higher up, or they would protest to him directly. Yet this commendable, nonsuppressed anger strategy was related to the *highest* blood-pressure levels of all groups, especially for young black men living in stressful neighborhoods (where unemployment, crime, and divorce rates are high and job opportunities are low). Their blood pressure was higher than that of their peers who would just walk away from a belligerent boss and let the storm blow over or who would try to reason with him. The study investigators, headed by Ernest Harburg of the University of Michigan, are not recommending that we should let bosses treat us badly. Rather, the implication is that going over the boss's head, or confronting him directly, are anxiety-producing activities that carry certain risks of their own.

But expressing anger toward a prejudiced homeowner or an explosive policeman is another matter. People generally regard anger in these situations as legitimate; they have right on their side, since homeowners and policemen are forbidden by law to discriminate. (We feel pretty good about righteous anger, it seems.) So in these circumstances, the people who would keep quiet about their anger and who would feel guilty about expressing it were the ones who had the highest blood pressure. Even this relationship didn't hold for everyone—only for black working-class men and white middle-class men, whose culture and class, perhaps, have defined the proper "manly" role.

In all three situations, however, there was one anger strategy that seemed to produce the lowest blood pressures of all, and it was neither exclusively to suppress anger nor to ventilate it. Harburg calls this approach *reflection:* Like Spielberger's "anger control," it involves waiting until the angry person who insulted you has calmed down (and presumably waiting until you have calmed down as well), and then trying to reason with him or her. This strategy, most popular among women of both races and classes, can be learned, with healthy results.

Anger and its expression, therefore, do not exist in a vacuum. In all the varied areas of our lives we make choices about how to behave, when to speak, whether to reveal anger. Suppressed anger can be "bad" if, by not revealing our feelings, we allow the stressful situation to continue; expressed anger can likewise be "bad" if, in revealing our feelings, we make the stressful situation worse, say, by getting fired.

Nevertheless, efforts have continued for many years to find predictable links between stress, illness, and anger. A particularly intriguing riddle is essential hypertension, a condition of chronically high blood pressure; "essential" means that the cause is unknown. Clinicians have long been trying to identify the psychological traits of the "hypertensive personality," and hostility is frequently implicated as a prime culprit. By constantly suppressing their anger, some psychologists believe, hypertensives keep their blood pressure elevated. Release the anger and blood pressure should fall.

To read the research on hypertension and anger is an exercise on a mental seesaw. Some studies report that hypertensives bottle up their anger. Others report that hypertensives are *more* irritable and explosive than normals. Others find no differences. In one project that compared 332 essential hypertensives with 335 normals, the hypertensives said they felt more hostile than the normals did, and that they held grudges longer and calmed down more slowly than the average person. But in another survey of thousands of men between the ages of thirty and fifty-nine, the hypertensives showed neither a higher level of hostility than the normals nor a greater tendency to direct anger inward. One reason for these discrepant findings has to do, I think, with the appearance of a second emotion that turns up regularly in this research, tagging along after anger like a fretful sibling. It is anxiety.

Twenty-five people with moderate to high hypertension volunteer to take their own blood pressure four times daily for seven weeks, each time rating their feelings of anxiety and anger. What happens? It's *anxiety* that is more strongly related to blood pressure than anger. "Theories which propose that hypertension is related specifically to anger and hostility," the researchers concluded, "are not supported by these data." That's a mild way of putting it: The researchers also found the same persistent idiosyncratic differences between individuals that have plagued so many efforts to track down the physiology of anger. For some of the hypertensives, for example, anger and anxiety paired off like happy couples—one rarely showed up without the other. For others, though, anger and anxiety behaved like estranged spouses—where there was one emotion, the other was sure to be absent. And for still others, the two emotions were as independent as grapefruit and pickles.

These findings do not make sense if we are trying to identify the emotions that cause hypertension. But they do make sense if we regard them as the results of hypertension. Anger, anxiety, and hypertension share certain key symptoms of physiological arousal, that internal churning that is preparing the body to cope with emergencies. But anger is the only one of the three conditions that is specific. We are angry *about something*; anxiety and hypertension share the attributes of nonspecific arousal. Given a provocation, a hypertensive might readily become angry; without a reason for the arousal, anxiety might be the predominant sensation. (None of this need be conscious, by the way. Most people, hypertensive or normal, cannot tell when their blood pressures are elevated, although most of them believe they *can*. However, moods can be predictably tied to physiological symptoms even when individuals consciously think they are not.) Hypertensives are quick to respond physiologically to stress, and unlike normals they are slow to calm down. But this is not, I think, because they "hold grudges longer" or cannot "let go" of their anger; they hold grudges longer and cannot let go of their emotions because their arousal is above normal and slow to abate.

Ironically, hypertension may have a short-term advantage for its sufferers as an insulation against pain. In Barry Dworkin's experiments at Rockefeller University, rats that had high blood pressure (produced by an injected drug) were slower to avoid painful electric shock and were less sensitive to it than rats with normal blood pressure. Perhaps human beings, Dworkin suggests, develop hypertension in the same way, as a response to painful and prolonged difficulties that they cannot control. This might explain why blacks in this country have higher blood-pressure levels and a much higher death rate from hypertension and related disorders; they also are more likely than whites to live under conditions of economic stress (unemployment, blue-collar jobs, low income and education) and social stress (high rates of divorce, juvenile delinquency, and crime).

What then produces the elevated blood-pressure levels and the body's inability to regulate them? The full answer is not known, but part of it apparently has to do with a combination of relentless environmental stress and, just as in the case of ulcers, genetic susceptibility.

ANGER AND HEART DISEASE

The "Type A" personality, that achievement-driven, highly competitive soul who feels pressured for time, works too hard, swears impatiently at delays, and snaps irritably at the slightest interruption, has long been thought to be vulnerable to heart disease. Anger, we are told, is at the heart of their problem.

The Western Collaborative Group Study is an enormous research project that has followed 3,154 men, aged thirty-nine to fifty-nine, for years to see which of them develop coronary heart disease. The researchers identified Type A's in a direct structured interview: For example, the interviewer could note down whether a man revealed "many signs of hostility toward others, including the interviewer." Two aspects of Type A, competitive drive and impatience, were associated with the eventual occurrence of heart disease. The men at risk of illness were also more likely than healthier men to *direct their anger outward* and to *become angry more than once a week*. The researchers concluded that a high drive level, coupled with impatience and hostility, is typical of the Type A's ambitiousness and persistent efforts to control his world.

At the other end of the country, in Framingham, Massachusetts, another enormous long-term study got a somewhat different picture. *Suppressed* hostility, not the overt kind, was implicated in heart disease. These investigators found that the people who eventually developed coronary heart disease scored higher on a Type A questionnaire *and* they were more likely, when angry, to keep it to themselves than the adults who remained free of heart disease.

Well, you ask, what's an angry person to do? You're damned if you let it out and you're damned if you sit on it? Maybe it depends on which coast you live on?

All of this Type A business was gloomy news to me and to everyone I know who (a) works under deadlines, (b) gets irritated waiting for elevators, salesclerks, and bank tellers, (c) becomes enraged at idiotic drivers, (d) has too much to do and too little time to do it, or (e) lives in New York. Some of my Type A friends tried to change themselves into Type Bs with fierce and competitive determination, which rather missed the point. Others regarded

Type B-ness as a fate worse than death. Type As had to decide whether to give up their careers, cars, and cities—that is, everything they loved—to live longer, more boring lives.

As it happens, most of us can relax (if we have time to relax). Although "Type A" is, in the popular imagination, a killer personality trait, it turns out that it is not necessarily a killer and not necessarily a personality trait. Type A did prove to be a risk factor, but even so, most Type As never get coronary heart disease (CHD), and some Type Bs do. (This is why many scientists prefer to use the term "coronary-prone behavior" instead of "Type A personality.")

Researchers have made enormous progress in identifying the emotional and behavioral contributors to CHD. They have focused on two questions: What is it about Type A that is risky to health? And what protects the Type As who do not get heart disease? Consider first these anomalies about heart disease:

• After reaching a peak in the 1960s, deaths from heart disease have declined steadily for both sexes. The reason is not known. Better screening and testing? Possibly. A decline in risk factors? No; levels of serum cholesterol and blood pressure have not markedly changed, cigarette smoking has declined for men but not for women, dietary habits are not appreciably different.

• Although older women have higher blood pressure and serum cholesterol levels than men their age, they are still less likely to get heart disease. What protects them?

• Speed of activity, achievement ambitions, and involvement in one's job are *not* related to heart disease. Type A people do set themselves a fast work pace and a heavy workload, but they love it that way; most of them cope with hard work better than Type Bs who have a lighter workload. In fact, people who are highly involved in their jobs, even if they work hard, have a relatively low incidence of heart disease. What protects them?

• Among Japanese-Americans, those who retain traditionally Japanese customs and relationships have a very low incidence of heart disease, whereas those who adopt an "American" way of life sharply increase the likelihood of getting heart disease. This is true even though the two groups do not differ in diet, smoking, cholesterol, or blood pressure. What protects the traditionalists?

• Among immigrants to Israel, the highest rate of heart disease does not occur for the men who had uprooted their families and moved to the new country; the rate is highest for their *sons*, the first generation. Second-generation Israelis, the grandsons of the original immigrants, have the lowest incidence of heart disease. There is no difference in dietary habits or fat intake among the three generations, and no relationship between fat intake and heart disease. What makes the first generation so vulnerable?

• Heart disease is by and large a disease of industrialized urban societies. As rural people move to such nations or cities, or as nations industrialize around them, the rate of heart disease increases. What protects farmers, who are under as much stress as city workers?

Two researchers, epidemiologist Lisa Berkman and sociologist Margo MacLeod, think the answer has to do with the insurance that strong social bonds provide against stress, especially the stress of massive societal change. What all the protected groups have in common is close ties to a group: family, religion, community, business network, gender, or generation. The Israeli immigrants brought their old-world culture and customs to bolster them in the new country, but their children felt conflict between their parents' ways and the new ways; the next generation, "full" Israelis, had no such conflict. The Japanese are a nation noted for their strong group attachments, even in business. Indeed, so important is social interdependence to the Japanese, according to the psychiatrist T. Doi, that they have a special word to denote the need to be loved, to be dependent: *amaeru*, which has no English equivalent. Conversely, the Western notion of independence holds no charms for them. If you ask a Japanese about "independent action" or "independent judgment," observe Richard Pascale and Anthony Athos, authors of *The Art of Japanese Management*, you will get a puzzled response. "While the word for independent exists, it is uncommon and not relevant to the way a Japanese manager thinks," they add.

And what, after all, is the key quality of the hard-driving, competitive Type A man? Independence and individualism: getting ahead of others, striving to succeed. In the American corporate system, this often means leaving friends behind and sometimes families, too; in the Japanese business system, it does not. Japanese businessmen are no less ambitious and competitive than their American counterparts, but these traits are not related to heart disease in Japan, as they are here. Neither is suppressed anger. As one Japanese psychologist, Y. Matsumoto, explained:

> . . . it is not unusual for the individual in the West to spend the major portion of his working hours among persons in whom he cannot usually confide or from whom he can expect little guidance. The Japanese individual, however, is sheltered within his personal in-group community with built-in social techniques and maneuvers for diminishing tension.

The difference between the Japanese and the Americans is summed up in their opposite reactions to the proverb (popular in both nations), "A rolling stone gathers no moss." Epidemiologist S. Leonard Syme observes that to the Japanese, moss is exquisite and valued; a stone is enhanced by moss; hence a person who keeps moving and changing never acquires the beauty and benefits of stability. To Americans, the proverb is an admonition to keep rolling, to keep from being covered with clinging attachments.

And who are the women who are at risk of heart disease? Those who have lost their traditional social networks: housewives who are isolated in the suburbs, and for whom the danger signs of heart disease are not anger and irritability, but tension, depression, and anxiety. (This suggests that they are under as much pressure and stress as employed women, but haven't the identifiable targets, such as a boss, that can become the focus of anger.) Among employed women, those who are most at risk of heart disease are not successful, high-achieving career executives as the new stereotype suggests, but clerical workers; in particular, clerical workers who are or were married, have children, are stuck in low-paying jobs with little chance of promotion, and who work for bosses who they feel are unsupportive. Like the depressed housewives in that English working-class village, they must cope not only with a load of stressful problems, but also with social isolation—having no one to complain to who is supportive, who helps solve problems. Finally, there are some Type A women, employed and unemployed, who have adopted the individualism, impatience, and ambitiousness typical of Type A men.

The specific aspects of Type A that continue to be related to heart disease are hostility, explosive reactions, competitiveness, impatience, and irritability. "In a word: anger," says Spielberger. "Anger in all its forms is the connecting link between the Type A pattern and coronary-prone behavior." Spielberger calls those forms of anger the "AHA" syndrome: Anger, an emotional state ranging from irritability to fury; Hostility, negative attitudes such as hatred, resentment, and cynicism; and Aggression, overt antagonistic actions.

Indeed, at Duke University Medical Center, psychiatrist Redford B. Williams, Jr., has assembled several studies suggesting that hostility and individualism interact to affect health. Constant, chronic feelings of anger, hostility, and aggression increase the risk of atherosclerosis and coronary heart disease by as much as five times over normal. In one study, researchers followed up 255 physicians who had, as medical students twenty-five years earlier, taken personality tests—including a measure of hostility toward others. The chronically hostile physicians were far more likely than the non-hostile physicians to have coronary heart disease or to have died from it: 15 percent to 3 percent. And another study followed up on 1,877 middle-aged men, interviewed in 1957-8, all of whom were free of heart disease at the time. Twenty years later, the researchers found that hostility was a strong predictor of mortality rate—death from all causes combined.

Researchers are even refining the question of what kind of hostility is hazardous to health, and it's not just any old kind, either. According to psychologists Theodore Dembroski and Paul T. Costa, Jr., some facets of hostility are more "toxic" than others. "Neurotic" hostility, typical of grumpy, surly, "nothing-can-please-me" people, seems to be part of a larger personality trait of neuroticism. Although this trait isn't much fun to live with, there is no evidence that it can kill you. "Antagonistic" hostility, on the other hand, is aggressive, inflammatory, and quick to erupt. This kind of hostility may contribute to illness for two reasons. First, it pumps up the blood pressure and keeps it up there. Antagonistic people, who regard others as dishonest, immoral, mean, and untrustworthy, are disposed to explode at the slenderest excuse for provocation. But second, their antagonism keeps other people at a distance (naturally, the hostile person takes this as further evidence of human meanness); it creates a barrier between the individual and the close connections that, as Syme showed, are a kind of social vitamin that protects one from stress and illness.

We might summarize the findings this way: Hard work and deadlines are OK; being a bully or hothead because you have hard work or deadlines is not. Working hard in order to do as well as you can is OK; working hard in order to get back at your boss for being such a jerk and a bastard is not. Being irritated at slow elevators is OK; kicking the elevator and breaking your foot is not. Feeling angry when another car cuts in front of you is OK; chasing the car off the road and trying to kill its driver is not.

To the question—"Which Type As are not vulnerable to heart disease?"—the answer seems to be: Those who are ambitious and energetic, but who are motivated by challenge and intrinsic satisfactions instead of by external pressures and anger. They tend to feel in control of their work instead of controlled by it, but they also know when to accept the inevitable. They have close friends and good relationships. The coronary-prone elements of Type A, in contrast, are chronic, intense anger, social isolation, and a continuing feeling of frustration and fury about events that are out of one's control.

Still, it would be a mistake to regard Type A as if it were as unchangeable and genetically based as blood type. Anyone who has been the victim of a crime or lived though a grueling divorce knows the temporary madness that can seize the most mild-mannered Type B—the chronic anger, sense of powerlessness, and feelings of isolation. And many apparent Type As calm down and lose their irritability when they, say, change from a depressing, dead-end job to a more interesting one.

So it seems unlikely to me that suppressed anger itself is a contributor to heart disease; if anything, the men who are most at risk are overexpressing anger. Again, anger appears to be a symptom instead of a cause of the basic problem. What matters more is the reason that people feel angry, and whether they feel they can do anything about it. Might they be fired if they express anger? Do they feel they have control over the people who are making them angry? Do they have friends, a union, a supportive family network they trust and can talk to? The answers are yes, no, and no for the working men and women who are vulnerable to heart disease.

CONSIDERATIONS

The popular belief that suppressed anger can wreak havoc on the body and bloodstream has been inflated out of realistic proportions. It does not, in any predictable or consistent way, make us depressed, produce ulcers or hypertension, set us off on food binges, or give us heart attacks. I am not saying that constant, excessive feelings of rage are good for you; constant anxiety or depression aren't good for you, either. But that is different from maintaining that *suppressed anger* is responsible for our ills.

As *Mastery of Stress* showed, most of us develop habitual reactions to stress that allow us to cope successfully, restoring the sense of control over a challenging or difficult situation and reducing bodily arousal. For you, that reaction might be expressed anger; for your neighbor, suppressed anger might get desired results. Clinically pathological, psychosomatic, or self-defeating habits may be acquired, however, when *nothing you do* causes the stress and arousal to abate; when every action is met with inconsistent or controlling responses from the situation or person causing your predicament.

Negative emotions may be related to illness, but, as I noted at the beginning of this chapter, only in a general way; specific emotions are not the culprits in specific diseases. Howard S. Friedman and Stephanie Booth-Kewley selected several emotions that have been implicated in illness (anger, hostility, depression, introversion, and anxiety) and five diseases believed to have psychological components (asthma, arthritis, ulcers, headaches, and heart disease). The researchers used a sophisticated statistical method to combine the results of 101 studies.

Friedman and Booth-Kewley *failed* to find specific, disease-connected traits, such as the "arthritic personality," the "coronary-prone personality," or the angry "ulcer-prone personality." But the researchers did find evidence for a "generic, disease-prone" individual who is chronically depressed, angry and hostile, and anxious. Depression was most strongly implicated in four of the five diseases (excluding ulcers), and depression and anxiety were independently related to coronary heart disease, along with anger.

"Personality may function like diet," the researchers concluded. "Imbalances can predispose one to all sorts of diseases." Psychological disturbances affect the immune system in general, they observed. The occurrence of a specific illness depends on other factors, such as whether a person drinks excessively or smokes; the person's genetic vulnerabilities; and the biology of the disease itself.

I do not wish to imply that suppressed emotion carries no risks. There is fascinating evidence that the prolonged inhibition of thoughts and emotions requires physical effort, which is stressful to the body. Therefore, when people try to inhibit secret thoughts and feelings that make them angry, ashamed, or depressed, the effort places continuing stress on the system and can lead to long-term health problems. In study after study, such individuals prove to be at greater risk of eventual illness than people who are able to talk about their tragedies, even though disclosures of traumatic events are often painful and unpleasant at first. (In the next chapter, I will discuss this research further, along with the differences between disclosure and ventilation, confession and obsession.)

One reason, I think, for the contradictory findings about anger and illness is that researchers have rarely asked what the people in their studies were angry about, or even what "suppressed" anger meant to them. It is one thing to trace the irritability and anger that white, middle-class men show when they deal with roadblocks and puddles on the path to success. It is another to trace the effects of anger in black, working-class men who cope with poverty, discrimination, and community instability. And it is yet another to talk about the suppressed anger of female clerical workers who have two jobs, at work and at home, without the income or satisfaction to show for them.

Suppressed anger is unlikely to have medical consequences if we feel in control of the situation that is causing the anger, if we interpret the anger as a sign of a grievance to be corrected instead of as an emotion to be sullenly protected, and if we feel committed to the work and people in our lives. For those who are not in that enviable position, though, it won't be enough simply to "rethink" themselves out of bad working conditions. As Anne Hill, an organizer of office workers, put it: "Ultimately, the only way to get at the real sources of stress—things like work overloads, harassment, and arbitrary treatment by male supervisors—is to organize."

In many pop-psych discussions of the danger of suppressed anger, the content of the anger is regarded as less important than what we do with it. This mistaken emphasis ignores the lessons of history, anthropology, and Freud, all of which show that sometimes suppressed anger makes social life possible. The idea that it is always medically bad for you has, unfortunately, led to some odd conclusions that are less likely to produce emotional health than emotional tyranny. One man, for example, rationalized his twelve-year-old son's tantrums to me by saying that they would stave off ulcers and heart attacks later. (He assumes that the boy will make it unscathed to adulthood.) To doubt the validity of such medical justifications is not, let me repeat, to deny anger that is legitimate and useful. "What's called for today," writes Walter Kiechel, "is not the ungoverned gush of raw feelings, but a new civility that accommodates the expression of angry emotions."

5

"Getting It Out of Your System"—Myths of Expressed Anger

. . . the reason we have so much abuse in our families is that we do not allow anger in our families. If rage can come out, it can spend itself and be done with . . . It's not the hatred expressed that's the problem; it's the hatred swallowed.

—JOHN BRADSHAW,
in *Lear's*

When anger is properly elicited and responded to in psychotherapy, the benefits include riddance of psychosomatic symptoms, hostility and the depression that is caused by anger suppressed or turned against the self.

—NOLAN SALTZMAN, director
Bio Psychotherapy Institute, New York

I was angry with my friend:
I told my wrath, my wrath did end.
I was angry with my foe:
I hid my wrath, my wrath did grow.

—WILLIAM BLAKE

William Blake was no scientist. He may have intended the sensible suggestion not to nurse grudges, but in fact he confused the object of anger (friend or foe) with angry reaction (silence or revelation). He omitted two other logical possibilities: What if you hid your anger from a friend and expressed it to your enemy? Perhaps, in the first case, your wrath would dissipate and you would decide the matter wasn't so important anyway. And surely if you expressed anger to your foe, the fellow (being your foe, after all) would get angry right back at you, and maybe this time add injury to the original insult? If Blake thought that revealing your anger keeps your friends friendly, while suppressing it makes foes more furious, then he was a good judge neither of human history nor of friendships.

The contemporary ventilationist view, that it is always important to express anger so that it won't clog your arteries or your friendships, and so it will *reduce* rage, commits Blake's error. It tends to overlook the social context and the consequences of anger. If your expressed rage causes another person to shoot you, it won't matter that you die with very healthy arteries.

"There is a widespread belief that if a person can be convinced, allowed, or helped to express his feelings, he will in some way benefit from it," writes psychiatrist John R. Marshall, who was among the first to question the belief. "This conviction exists at all levels of psychological sophistication. Present in one or another form, it occupies a position of central importance in almost all psychotherapies. . . . The belief that to discharge one's feelings is beneficial is also prevalent among the general public. Friends are encouraged to 'get it off their chests,' helped to 'blow off steam,' or encouraged to 'let it all hang out.' Sports or strenuous physical activities are lauded as means of 'working off' feelings, particularly hostility, and it is accepted that there is some value in hitting, throwing, or breaking something when frustrated."

But is there? It seems to me that the major side-effect of the ventilationist approach has been to raise the general noise level of our lives, not to lessen our problems. I notice that the people who are most prone to give vent to their rages get angrier, not less angry. I observe a lot of hurt feelings among the recipients of rage. And I can plot the stages in a typical "ventilating" marital

argument: precipitating event, angry outburst, shouted recrimina-
tions, screaming or crying, the furious peak (sometimes accompanied by physical assault), exhaustion, sullen apology, or just
sullenness. The cycle is replayed the next day or next week. What
in this scenario is "cathartic"? Screaming? Throwing a pot? Does
either action cause the anger to vanish or the angry spouse to feel
better? Not that I can see.

Debate over the nature and value of catharsis, variously defined
but commonly meaning some kind of emotional release, has
continued for centuries. Plato would have censored tragic drama
in his ideal Republic because he believed it would arouse the
passions of pliant audiences and thereby undermine the State's
cerebral ideals. Aristotle, in contrast, thought that drama produces
catharsis in its viewers by purging them of pity and terror. He did
not mention purges of anger and revenge, though, as some
modern writers do when they speak of the supposedly cathartic
effects of violent movies and theater; and I doubt that Aristotle
would have had much truck with therapists who set their clients at
each other with foam-rubber bats. He did believe in the golden
mean. Excess was to be eschewed.

Most ventilationist theories today concentrate on what a person
should do to bring down angry arousal, to reduce tension. But it is
as true of the body as of arrows: What goes up must come down.
Any emotional arousal will eventually simmer down, if you just
wait long enough; although some people must wait longer than
others. This is why the classic advice for anger control—count to
ten—has survived for centuries, with variations:

> When angry, count ten before you speak; if very angry,
> an hundred.
>
> —THOMAS JEFFERSON

> When angry, count four; when very angry, swear.
>
> —MARK TWAIN

Some ventilationists, however, believe that counting and swearing
aren't enough. They maintain that certain actions, particularly

aggressive ones, will bring arousal back to normal *faster* than waiting, indeed, will "get rid" of the anger; further, that without aggressive release, angry energy will do internal damage.

But perhaps you already disapprove of aggression, even the kind that is "displaced" in sports, and instead hold the diluted view that when you feel angry you should "let off steam" by talking out your emotions. Even this apparently rational approach, I have found, has unanticipated consequences.

By looking at what happens, physically and psychologically, when people "let anger out," we can see that the ways that we express anger actually affect how we feel. The decision about whether or not to express anger rests on what you want to communicate and what you hope to accomplish, and these are not necessarily harmonious goals. You may want to use anger for retaliation and vengeance, for improving a bad situation, or for restoring your rights. Your goals determine what you "should" do about anger.

In particular, consider three popular notions about anger: that aggression is the instinctive catharsis for anger, that talking anger out reduces the feeling of anger, and that tantrums and other childhood rages are healthy and beneficial. "Letting off steam" is a wonderful metaphor and seems to capture exactly how angry outbursts work, but people are not teapots.

Myth #1: Aggression is the instinctive catharsis for anger.

> For he who gives no fuel to fire puts it out, and likewise he who does not in the beginning nurse his wrath and does not puff himself up with anger takes precautions against it and destroys it.
>
> —PLUTARCH

Plutarch's apt and accurate observation was drowned in the reservoir theory of catharsis. Many clinicians, following Freud, turned their attention to the matter of emptying that reservoir. What action quickly and effectively reduces the arousal of anger?

What will make your head stop pounding and your heart calm down? Is some kind of aggression necessary, physical or verbal?

Jack Hokanson, who is a veritable Sherlock Holmes of psychological sleuthing, has been tracking catharsis theories for years, using clues from one experiment to pose questions for the next. In the early 1960s, for example, Hokanson found that aggression *was* cathartic: The blood pressure of angry students would return to baseline more quickly when they could retaliate against the man who had angered them than when they could not. But then Hokanson noticed that this was true only when the man who angered them was a fellow student; when he was a teacher, retaliation had no cathartic effect. Naturally. In those days, teachers were still regarded as legitimate authorities, and one did not snap back at them in a cavalier manner. Expressing anger to a superior, then and even now, is itself an arousing, anxiety-producing action (as the medical studies in Chapter 4 also discovered), no matter how justified you think you are. Far from reducing anger, it complicates it.

So, after a flurry of studies on the *target* of your catharsis, the first modification of catharsis theory appeared: Aggression can be cathartic only against your peers and subordinates; it does not work when the target is your boss, another authority, or an innocent bystander. If the reservoir-of-energy model were correct, though, ventilating anger against anyone or anything should reduce tension. It does not.

Then Hokanson noticed something that most of his fellow psychologists were ignoring in the 1960s: women. They were not behaving like the men. When you insulted them, they didn't get belligerent; they generally said something friendly to try to calm you down. When Hokanson wired them up to a physiological monitor to see whether they were secretly seething in rage, he discovered that one man's meat was a woman's poison. For men, aggression was cathartic for anger; for women, *friendliness* was cathartic! For them, any aggression, even toward a classmate, was as arousing and upsetting as aggression toward authority was for the men.

This difference gave Hokanson the idea that aggressive catharsis is a learned reaction to anger, not an instinctive one. People find characteristic ways to try to handle obnoxious others, he concluded. Whatever works will feel good because it brings a removal of the threat and a sense of relaxation. In the case of sex differences, "what works" has a lot to do with the requirements of one's role. When women react to attack or threat by smiling, being friendly, and making gestures of accommodation, they traditionally have assuaged the other person's anger (often, however, at the cost of their own rights). When they act angrily and aggressively they typically provoke a critical reaction from others ("What a bitch"), which in turn increases their arousal and anxiety. The reverse is true for men: Aggression and anger typically bring respect and results, whereas friendly accommodation is a sign of "caving in" ("What a weakling").

But sex roles are not straitjackets, and Hokanson's next experiment was a prescient sign of the women's movement.

Imagine that you are seated at a console, facing an array of impressive gizmos and gadgets. Your partner, a fellow student who is of your gender and age, is sitting at an identical console nearby. You will communicate by pressing one of two buttons marked "shock" and "reward." You are probably in a friendly mood— Only an hour of this, you think to yourself, and I'll be done with my psychology requirement—when suddenly *zot!* Your partner has sent you an unpleasant shock.

If you are male, you are instantly irritated. "What the hell did the SOB do *that* for?" you mutter. "I'll show him he can't do that to me." So you press your shock button to give him a taste of his own medicine. Relief surges through your veins, according to that damned machine you're hooked up to.

If you are female, you are instantly puzzled. "I wonder why she did that?" you murmur. "Maybe she hit the wrong button. Maybe she got a bad grade on the intro exam. I'd better be kind." So you press your reward button, which awards her a point in whatever mysterious game the experimenters have up their sleeve. You feel so good about your forgiving response that relief surges through your veins, according to that interesting machine you're hooked up to.

This mechanical conversation between you and your partner goes on for thirty-two rounds, and half the time the partner responds to whatever you do with a shock and half the time with reward. If you are a man, you notice the shocks. Why, the bastard, you say to yourself, he persists in attacking me. If you are a woman, you notice the rewards. She must be feeling better, you think, she's not sending me as many shocks. In either case, your blood pressure is down and your spirits are up.

Little do you know that those thirty-two rounds are only to inform the experimenters about your typical reactions. Now you go sixty rounds with new rules. If you are a man, your partner will reward you every time you are friendly in response to his shock. If you are a woman, your partner will reward you every time you are aggressive in response to her shock. In short, a woman could stop being victimized or treated unfairly if she was aggressive, and a man could shake the bully by being friendly.

Hokanson and his associates observed that two things happened as a result of this new situation. First, the women rapidly learned the value of being aggressive and so became aggressive in response to shock more frequently, whereas the men learned the value of a generous reaction to insult. Second, the traditional form of catharsis for each sex was reversed. Women showed catharsislike reduction in blood pressure when they responded aggressively and had a slow vascular recovery when they were friendly. The opposite was the case for men: catharsis now followed friendliness, not belligerence.

Still Hokanson was not satisfied. To show how remarkably susceptible to learning catharsis is, he constructed an ingenious variation to the shock/reward experiment. This time, participants learned that by giving *themselves* a shock they could avert a stronger shock from the partner. When self-punishment was the lesser of two evils, it reduced arousal and felt cathartic. Hokanson had demonstrated that anyone may acquire self-defeating, even injurious, habits in an effort to avoid hostility or injury from others. In sum, he created masochism in his laboratory, and showed that even masochism can offer physiological relief.

The learned aspect of catharsis, it now seems, works like this:

You are upset. Someone irritates you or goads you and finally provokes you over the edge of self-control. Now you do something: You lash out, or hit, or practice Stravinsky on the piano. As a result, the unpleasant arousal and the sensation of anger diminishes, and you feel better. You no longer want to lash out or hit, and you switch to a peaceful Chopin prelude. All of these reactions to anger may be cathartic, that is, lessen your physiological arousal and its corresponding sensation that your blood is boiling. *At the same time, you are acquiring a cathartic habit.* This habit does not mean you will be less angry in the future. It means that when you *are* angry, you are likely to do whatever worked for you before: swearing noisily, writing a letter, having a few drinks, listening to music, punching the person who crossed you. As a young man in G. Stanley Hall's 1899 study recalled:

> Once when I was about 13, in an angry fit, I walked out of the house vowing I would never return. It was a beautiful summer day, and I walked far along lovely lanes, till gradually the stillness and beauty calmed and soothed me, and after some hours I returned repentant and almost melted. Since then when [I am] angry, I do this if I can, and find it the best cure.

Personality and personal experience, therefore, interfere between anger and aggressive catharsis. The people for whom aggression is not cathartic, as you might imagine, tend to feel guilty about expressing hostility; they have a strong need for approval from others; and they are likely to respond to stress by denying it rather than by meeting it head-on. These qualities do not fall on one side only of the gender line. Some men, by virtue of their temperament and history, are less aggressive than others, and their cathartic patterns reflect this. In one group of male prisoners, for example, some responded to threats of violence with characteristically aggressive retaliation, but others responded passively or submissively. Such men felt a catharsis, that is, had faster vascular reduction in blood pressure, only when they were allowed to respond to aggression with their customary pacifism. When they were required by the experimenter to behave aggressively, their vascular recovery was very slow.

Some schools of therapy, such as Alexander Lowen's bioener-getics, recommend any form of aggressive anger release that comes to mind, or foot: shouting, biting, howling, kicking, or slapping (anything short of physical assault and battery). Such aggression is supposed to get us "in touch" with our feelings. But aggression frequently has precisely the opposite effect of catharsis: Instead of exorcising the anger, it can inflame it.

One of the first studies to quarrel with the Freudian ventilation-ist position was conducted by Seymour Feshbach in 1956. Feshbach gathered a group of little boys who were not aggressive or destructive and encouraged them to play with violent toys, kick the furniture, and otherwise run amok during a series of free-play hours. This freedom did not "drain" any of the boys' "instinctive aggression" or "pent-up" anger. What it did was lower their restraint against aggression. On later occasions, the boys behaved in much more hostile and destructive ways than they had previously.

When you permit children to play aggressively they don't become less aggressive, as the catharsis theory would predict; they become more aggressive. Indeed, aggressive play has no cathartic value at all. In one study in which third-grade children were frustrated and irritated by another child (whom the experimenters had enlisted in their cause), the children were given one of three ways of "handling" their anger: Some were permitted to talk it out with the adult experimenters; some were allowed to play with guns for "cathartic release" or to "get even" with the frustrating child; and some were given a reasonable explanation from the adults for the child's annoying behavior. What reduced the children's anger? Not talking about it. Not playing with guns; that made them *more* hostile and aggressive as well. The most successful way of dispelling their anger was to understand why their classmate had behaved as she did (she was sleepy, upset, not feeling well).

The same principles of anger and aggression apply to adults. Murray Straus, a sociologist in the field of family violence, finds that couples who yell at each other do not thereafter feel less angry but more angry. Contrary to the popular view quoted at the beginning of this chapter—that "hatred expressed" will reduce family violence—verbal aggression and physical aggression are highly correlated, which means it is a small step from bitter accusations to slaps. Leonard Berkowitz, who has studied the social causes of aggression for many years, likewise finds that ventilation-by-yelling has no effect on the reduction of anger. "Telling someone we hate him supposedly will purge pent-up aggressive inclinations and will 'clear the air,' " he observed. "Frequently, however, when we tell someone off, we stimulate ourselves to continued or even stronger aggression." This is why a minor annoyance, when expressed in hostile language or behavior, can flare into a major argument. Letting off steam can make the atmosphere very hot and humid.

"There is an element of truth in the catharsis notion," says Straus, "but not in the usual idea of physiological relief. If a couple doesn't deal with what is causing their anger, it will remain, or worsen. Unfortunately, most people don't know how to express anger without attacking or belittling." Many psychologists therefore distinguish *verbal aggression* ("You bitch" or "I'll kill you!") from *reporting one's anger* ("I'm hopping mad"). Thomas Gordon, the originator of Parent Effectiveness Training, calls this the difference between I-messages and you-messages: the difference between "I feel hurt and anxious when I'm left on my own at parties, dear" and "You son of a bitch, how dare you treat me like dirt all evening!"

Verbal aggression usually fails because it riles up the other person and makes him or her inclined to strike back, whereas a description of your state of mind constitutes less of an attack, inspiring the other person to make amends. People who shout and yell when they feel angry thus tend not to get the results they hope for (that is, apologies and changed behavior from the yellee), so the next time they feel angry they yell louder. The object of their wrath either counterattacks or ignores them, as the children of some weary parents do. "Yelling does not do any good," said a woman in Suzanne K. Steinmetz's study of families. ". . . Makes the neighbors think you are crazy. The children turn a deaf ear when you yell. Eventually, they say, 'Oh, there she goes again!' "
My mother once asked a cousin how he could tolerate his mother's

angry reprimands. "Isn't it just easier to do what she wants?" my mother asked. "No," said the cousin, "I just tune her out. Don't hear a word she says." You can imagine what this does to the mother's level of anger.

It's hard on the nervous system to live with yellers. Some members of a family learn to tune them out, but others become more aggressive or depressed. Videotaped experiments with young children who are playing together peacefully show that the toddlers, merely on hearing a furious parental quarrel in the background, begin to hit each other and show other signs of agitation. Adults who suffer from depression (or schizophrenia) show higher relapse rates when they return, after treatment, to families that frequently and noisily express negative emotions, criticism, and hostility.

The point is that aggression, in whatever form, is an acquired strategy for dealing with anger, not a biological inevitability. It is no use telling placid, pacifistic, and rational people that they ought to "let go" and ventilate their rage with a violent display, throwing saucepans or biting pillows. They will only feel worse if they do. Unless, of course, you can guarantee them that aggression will produce the results they want.

Myth #2: Talking out anger gets rid of it—or at least makes you feel less angry.

It feels good to complain to a sympathetic person. It's exhilarating. There's something euphoric about getting a supportive reaction that you don't get if you just wait for the mood to be over.

—thirty-eight-year-old reporter

Who would disagree? Like most people I know, I have always been a firm believer in the talk-it-out strategy. Talking things over makes you feel better. That's what friends are for. That's what therapists are for. That's what bartenders are for. But that's not what the research shows. Talking out an emotion doesn't reduce it, *it rehearses it*.

Anger is often socially created. Talking to friends is one way to decide, for example, that you feel angry instead of hurt, or more sad than jealous. Sympathetic friends who agree with your self-diagnosis, or who provide a diagnosis when you have none, are aiding that process of emotional definition.

The belief that talking it out is cathartic assumes that there is a single emotion to be released, but, as noted in previous chapters, clinically you seldom find "pure" emotions. Most are combinations that reflect the complexity of the problem and of our lives: hurt and jealousy, rage and fear, sadness and desire, joy and guilt. Ventilating only one component of the mix, therefore, emphasizes it to the exclusion of the others. If you are upset with your spouse and you go off for a few drinks with a friend to mull the matter over, you may, in talking it out, decide you are really furious, after all. You aren't only ventilating the anger; you're practicing it.

Three psychologists conducted a field experiment that showed just how this process works. Ebbe Ebbesen, Birt Duncan, and Vladimir Konečni were working in San Diego when the local aerospace-defense industry had to lay off many of its engineers and technicians. It was the right time to study anger. The employees were irate, and legitimately so, for they had been promised a three-year contract and the layoffs came after only one year. If this happened to you, at what or with whom would you be angry? Fate? The economy? The company? Your supervisor? Yourself?

The researchers seized this opportunity to interview one hundred of the engineers who had been fired, comparing them with forty-eight others who were voluntarily leaving the company at the same time. Birt Duncan conducted an exit interview with each man, during which he directed his questions—and the men's expressions of hostility—in one of three ways: toward the company (In what ways has the company not been fair with you? Are there aspects of the company you don't like?); or toward the company supervisors (What action might your supervisor have taken to prevent you from being laid off? Are there things about your supervisor which you don't like?); *or* toward the man himself (Are there things about yourself that led your supervisor not to give you a higher performance review? What in your past performance might have been improved?). Some men were asked neutral questions only, such as their opinion of the technical library.

Notice that Duncan was not telling the men what they *should* be angry about, but asking them what they *did* feel angry about. When the interview itself was over, he asked the men to fill out a report, including some questions about what the men felt now about the company, the supervisors, or themselves. *"Ventilation" of the anger during the interview did not act as a catharsis in any way.* On the contrary, the men become *more* hostile toward the company or their supervisors if they had taken an angry public stance against them in conversation. And their anger increased only toward the target they had discussed, not the others. The men who were asked to criticize themselves, however, did not blame themselves more later; a result I was happy to see, since clearly the engineers' ability was not at issue in the layoffs, and the men knew it. But neither did the self-criticizers get as angry at the company or with their supervisors as the men who had outspokenly blamed these targets.

The simple act of pinpointing the cause of your anger makes you more likely to repeat the explanation, even at the risk of harmful consequences (in this case, not getting rehired). As you recite your grievances, your emotional arousal builds up again, making you feel as angry as you did when the infuriating event first happened, and, in addition, establishing an attitude about the source of your rage. Friends and therapists, of course, often do just what Birt Duncan did with the laid-off engineers: ask probing questions, innocent or intentional, that direct us to a particular explanation of our feelings ("In what ways was Sheila not fair to you?" "Could you have done something to keep Herb from leaving?"). I am not saying we always accept other people's interpretations; I'm interested in the ways we come to an interpretation, and what happens to feelings of anger as a result.

In study after study that I could find, those results are clear: Talking can freeze a hostile disposition. This is true for children, teenagers, and adults alike. For example, in that experiment with the third-graders mentioned earlier, the children who were encouraged to express their anger toward the child who had frustrated them later liked that child less than the children who were *not permitted* to express their anger! And the same was true in a study of college boys, who remained angrier with someone who had irritated them and who liked the fellow less when they were allowed a catharsis of their angry feelings than when they were not.

One psychologist who shared the assumption of her colleagues that people who suppress anger are in worse mental health than "expressers" was Mary K. Biaggio, who gave 150 of her college students a battery of tests to prove her point. Instead, she found that the students who were quick to express anger were less self-controlled, tolerant, and flexible than students who kept their anger in check. They seemed, she said with surprise, "to take things seriously and personally and at the same time exercise little restraint over their angry feelings and impulses." The students who were slow to get angry did not, as she had predicted, have resulting worries and complaints about holding it in. Although they were more conforming and concerned about creating favorable impressions than were the "expressers," they were also more dependable and socially mature.

Psychologist Edward J. Murray, who has conducted and reviewed many experimental studies of anger, reports that when people have been denigrated and criticized, giving them the opportunity to express their resentment generally makes them angrier. "Expressing hostile feelings is *not* a sufficient condition for the reduction of anger," Murray concluded; expression itself increases anger "surprisingly consistently." (Psychologists are almost uniformly surprised when they get these results, so powerful is the myth of catharsis in our culture.)

Now, none of this is to make a case for keeping quiet when you are angry, as some people seem to think whenever I talk about these research findings. The point is to understand what happens when you *do* decide to express anger, and to realize how our perceptions about the causes of anger can be affected just by talking about them and deciding on an interpretation. Each of us must find our own compromise between talking too much, expressing every little thing that irritates, and not talking at all, passively accepting the injustices we feel. Discussing your anger can lead to practical solutions, but it can also become obsessive, useless wheel-spinning. Constant complaining and bickering can be a sign of capitulation to misery, or, as it is for many patients with serious illnesses or disabilities, a sign of determination to live and fight for life.

The cumulative effect of these studies supports good old-fashioned motherly advice: If you can't say something nice about a person, don't say anything at all—at least if you want your anger to dissipate and your associations to remain congenial. But if you want to stay angry, if you want to *use* your anger, keep talking.

Myth #3: Tantrums and other childhood rages are healthy expressions of anger that forestall neurosis.

> [The child should] gain no request by anger; when he is quiet let him be offered what was refused when he wept.
>
> —SENECA

A flat-out tantrum is an awesome event. The child screams (or holds his breath), kicks wildly (or tenses his body), and throws himself on the floor, banging his fists (or his head). He or she seems to be entirely out of control, a kitten turned into a hellcat.

In some psychoanalytic circles, the guiding belief is that a child's tantrum may be a sign of a "childhood neurosis," caused by repressed infantile anger. One man I spoke to had, in desperation, taken his little boy to a psychoanalyst:

When my son was very young, about toilet-training time, he began to have violent tantrums, rages, almost like fits. He was driving us crazy. We wanted to throw him through the window. So we took him to this psychiatric center, where they explained that he had a neurosis. If they can get it between the ages of two and six, it's apparently easier to get out. The longer it's in there, the harder it is to release.

The analyst decided that the toddler's anger had something to do with the fact that the boy's mother was ill for the first few months after he was born and could not give him all the attention he needed. Eventually, his rage with her "surfaced" in the form of tantrums.

The analyst recommended therapy, four days a week, where the boy could ventilate his rage. Eventually, the analyst explained, the breakthrough occurred: The boy transferred his anger with his mother to the therapist. "He raged and screamed and cried," the father said, "and got it all out of his system." The little boy raged and screamed and cried in therapy for about a year, when his tantrums began to subside. In nursery school, during the same year, he was beautifully behaved.

Child development and anthropological studies cast doubt on the accuracy of the analyst's diagnosis and suggest, to the contrary, that the child would have "got it all out of his system" simply in the normal course of growing up. The research shows that:

• Tantrums first appear during a child's second year, peak between the ages of two and three, and are on the wane by age four. They typically run their course within a year.

• Some tantrums result from organic disorders, but most are the natural combustion of high energy and low self-control. They occur at a predictable stage in child development, when the child is forming a sense of self: The toddler is old enough to have a sense of "me" and "my wants," but is too young to know how to get them.

• It is difficult to know how a two-year-old can harbor an infant grudge at his or her mother, since the neurological pathways of long-term memory are not fully developed in children until they are two or three years old. Adults have ideas about how mothers should care for their newborns, and adults have memories of how their newborns behaved, but babies don't.

• Most children throw tantrums only in a particular place (school or home, say, but not both) and with a particular person (mother but not father, or vice versa). Thus tantrums are usually a public display, a response to the child's being told no to something he or she wants to do. They shut off immediately when

the child gets his or her wish and can be turned on as rapidly when
that wish is thwarted. One of G. Stanley Hall's observers wrote:

> A 3 year old girl of violent temper, once punished by being kept
> home from a ride, broke out in sobs that appeared uncontrollable.
> Suddenly she stopped short and calmly asked if papa was in. Being
> told no, and realizing that there was no possible restraint from that
> quarter, she resumed her sobs.

One man I spoke to watched his three children travel through the
tantrum phase and is now convinced that tantrums are produced
with deliberate calculation for the benefit of the target parent:

> You're trying to get out of the house to go to a movie, and they
> cling to you like chimpanzees—a double clutch, arms *and* legs
> wrapped around you. You have to peel the kid off. Then they moan
> and yell as if you were leaving them with Godzilla instead of the
> familiar baby-sitter. Of course, the second you leave (the baby-sitter
> later tells you), calm prevails and they shut off the tears.
>
> One evening, after I'd had a bad day with my daughter Andy, my
> wife said to her: "I hear you were really bad for Maria [the
> housekeeper] and Daddy today." "Oh, no," says Andy, "I was only
> bad for Daddy."

The immediate fate of the temper tantrum depends on the
child's level of energy and the parent's level of patience. Because
a tantrum is rarely an expression of real anger, but rather a desire
to stay up later, have a cookie, not put on shoes, and not endure
the many frustrations of being only two and a half, then every time
the parent yields, the child learns that tantrums work. As one of
Hall's candid adults recalled: "My temper was so dreadful that I did
not mind what it cost, it must have way. As a child I would
scream, kick, rush at things and throw objects in the fire or out of
doors, if my plans were frustrated. To put me to bed disturbed the
whole house, so that my nurse usually gave way to me. Every
point I scored made me worse."

Psychiatrist John Bowlby, author of the three-volume
Attachment and Loss, observes that a child's anger has a social
purpose from the start. Instead of postulating anger as part of an

aggressive instinct, Bowlby asks the more useful question: What good is anger? Why, for example, do young children so often seem angry when their parents return ˙from an evening out or a short vacation? Bowlby hypothesizes that insofar as human survival depends on our attachment to others, "a potential to feel distress on separation from them and anxiety at the prospect of separation" is also an integral part of our makeup. In babies, distress shows itself as a wail, but it differentiates into sadness, anxiety, or anger by the time children reach the age of two. (In this connection it is significant, Bowlby adds, that *anger*, *anxiety*, and *anguish* share the same root.) The first protoemotion to emerge in babies and other primates is fear—of loss, of the unfamiliar, of strangers—but anger develops along with the child's mental faculties and the realization that anger has an *effect*.

Bowlby regards most of the angry demonstrations of young children as "the anger of hope." Reproachful reactions, the child seems to think, will be a forceful reminder to the parents. One little girl who was separated from her father during a tornado, Bowlby recounts, hit him angrily when they were reunited and accused him bitterly of leaving her. Whenever separation is temporary, which it usually is, anger has two functions: First, Bowlby says, "it may assist in overcoming such obstacles as there may be to reunion; second, it may discourage the loved person from going away again."

Under extreme and pathological situations, Bowlby notes, children may develop an "anger of despair": When children are subject to repeated, prolonged separations, each of which is another significant loss, or when they are constantly *threatened* with abandonment, they feel enraged at the person who inflicts such intense pain of loss. Children may develop an anger of despair for other horrible reasons, such as having parents who abuse them. If the parent or loved one never returns, despair will eventually turn to detachment and listlessness. This sequence, from protest to despair to detachment, characterizes people's reactions to separation all through life—even when the separation involves people they no longer love. (It is the same sequence that characterizes most people, for example, following divorce.)

Bowlby's argument draws our attention to the difference between *form* and *content* of children's anger. All children, like adults, will on occasion feel angry, unhappy, resentful, or frustrated, but they must learn what form of emotional expression is appropriate and tolerated. "Expressing anger" is not the same as "acting aggressively," but many parents, eager not to block the former, encourage the latter. When you allow a child to scream, kick, hit, or smash objects, however, you are not reducing the child's anger. You are increasing his aggressiveness. You are teaching a cathartic habit.

One consequence of the ventilationist approach, therefore, is to prolong tantrums past their normal life. "Letting dear Hermione get it out of her system" often has the unhappy side-effect of teaching dear Hermione how to use the tantrum as a weapon. When therapists encourage young children to throw darts and cut up dolls and create messes all over their nicely carpeted floors, the children learn not how to control their emotions or solve the problem that produced them, but where to express them. (The therapy is most beneficial, I suspect, for frazzled parents, who get an hour's rest; but that doesn't solve *their* problem, either.) Similarly, when a father says to his five-year-old son, "Ah, you little monkey, you're angry with me for locking you in your room all night, aren't you? Go ahead, kick the sofa. Get it all out!" he is attending to the form of anger while ignoring its legitimate cause. This evasion makes for a child who is still angry, and now a confirmed sofa-kicker as well. Conversely, a parent who consistently punishes or rejects a child for expressing any kind of anger is likely to create a person who, when feeling angry, withdraws into sullen resentment.

Of course for some children, like some adults, a tantrum is the only way to get the point across. Decades ago, psychologist Florence Goodenough asked forty-five women to keep a diary of their children's outbursts of anger. She, too, observed that tantrums peak in the child's second year, to be replaced by more mature ways to communicate or more devious ones. But she was among the first to notice that children, like adults, get angry for a reason, and one reason is the "self-righteous type of mother who continually irritates the child by a syrupy type of nagging." One such mother's questionnaire about her six-year-old son was laced with self-serving comments designed to show how considerate she was and how ungrateful her son was: "I spoke to him gently," "I inquired casually why he was so late," "Reminded him courteously that lunch would soon be ready," and so on.

I shall love Goodenough's comment on this case forever. "The child's response commands our sympathy," she wrote. "He kicked, snarled, and screamed at his mother, 'Don't talk! Don't talk!' "

The emotions, in any case, are as subject to the laws of learning as is any other behavior. Parents should be advised that the kind of anger they attend to in their children is the kind of anger they will have to live with. Those who believe aggression is necessary and healthy would do well to consider the experience of Boys Town, a village of some four hundred adolescent boys. These boys either are orphans or have parents who cannot care for them, and when they arrive they tend to be angry, rebellious, and antisocial. In 1975 psychologists Dean Fixsen, Elery Phillips, and their colleagues took over Boys Town (which has no apostrophe), swept away many of the cumbersome layers of bureaucracy, established family units instead of institutional dormitories, and set up some new rules to govern the boys' behavior.

The teenagers had been getting away with a lot of mischief and disruption, and the new administrators would have none of it. The staff, they observed, was "not helping the boys by being overtolerant, nonjudgmental, and nonevaluative. If two boys got into a fight, perhaps they just needed to 'ventilate some pent-up emotions.' Unfortunately, such ventilation in the real world may land a man in jail. If a boy was late for work or class, perhaps 'he'd had a rough time lately and ought to be extended some understanding.' Unfortunately, such tardiness on a real job may cost a man his employment."

The well-meaning staff had previously exhorted the boys to "behave themselves," but by "understanding" their violent quarrels they were tacitly approving of them. Fixsen and the rest of the staff forbade the boys to fight, rage, sulk, pout, hit, curse, and bully each other. These acts are usually unacceptable between adults and unlikable besides. Why should adults tolerate in children what they dislike in other adults? The new Boys Town system rewards the boys for desirable behavior, such as the peaceful settlement of disputes and nonviolent resolutions of angry feelings, teaches them *how* to behave well, and punishes them with loss of privileges for any of the unacceptable actions. Both steps are essential, by the way. Being punished for what you are doing wrong does not instruct you in what to do right.

The result of the Boys Town experiment is a society of teenagers who are less angry, less violent, and happier than they were under the previous indulgent staff who, with the best of intentions, had inflamed the very problems they hoped to eliminate.

The kindest parents often do the same thing. Consider the example of Ellie Seif, whose two daughters, six-year-old Debbie and nine-year-old Karen, could have been textbook cases of the uses of anger. The children made everyone miserable with their constant rages. "Karen was becoming more and more difficult for me to handle," this young mother said. "She was angry, hostile, unhappy, unsure of herself, demanding. And I was too." Mornings in the Seif household had become intolerable. "When I awakened the girls Karen's reaction was to snarl, 'You woke me too late.' Then she'd demand, 'What's for breakfast? Where are my shoes?' Finally she'd order her six-year-old sister: 'Debbie, get out of my room!' By this time my stomach would be in knots. On many days I'd either scream at the girls or try to smother my anger; on other mornings I was full of tears."

So far, a household like many others, especially on school days. But the Seif family was fortunate to find a sensible therapist who treated all of them instead of the apparent "neuroses" of the children, and who observed that the family's problems derived from the parents' overinvolvement, not underinvolvement, in their children's lives. The girls had become completely dependent on their parents to solve their conflicts and organize their lives, and every instance of misbehavior—yelling, whining, and crying—was a plea for a parental solution. Step One, therefore, was to give each girl an alarm clock and the responsibility to get herself up and ready for school every day. "Amazingly," said their mother, "mornings in our household improved 100 per cent."

Next they tackled the problem of sibling rivalry. Debbie and Karen fought all the time; days went by when they did not speak a civil word to each other. The therapist observed that Mrs. Seif was continually involved in their battles, sometimes by trying to settle the issue, always by being psychologically "with them." She was instructed to stay out of it and let the girls solve their differences by themselves.

Now, if you were a child whose rage and complaints had always won your mother's attention, what would you do if her attention suddenly shut off? Why, at first, you would rage and complain even more. (Maybe she hadn't heard you.) The Seifs were warned that any change in their usual reactions to their daughters' fights would cause upheaval.

"Much of the girls' negative behavior escalated," said Mrs. Seif "—the anger, the demands for special attention, the sibling rivalry, the hostility, whining and dependency. Dr. Beck said it was as if I had an imaginary red button pinned to my chest that read 'push.' The children knew how to push that button—by fighting, whining, crying and so on. And to push it was to involve me in some aspect of their lives. As we began to extricate ourselves the button got pushed harder and more frequently. Louder screaming, fiercer fighting, more whining and crying—all were designed to re-establish the old patterns of overdependency."

After a couple of tumultuous weeks, the girls stopped testing and pushing, and began to take care of themselves. The result, however, was not that they "bottled up" their anger with each other, *but that the anger dissipated.* The realization that they could take responsibility for their problems and could find things of their own to do was an enormous boost to their self-esteem. That alone reduced their anger. Karen, Mrs. Seif reported, became less tearful and threatened, and more talkative and secure. "In Karen's everyday life, occurrences that once would have thrown her into a tantrum or a state of depression now were taken almost matter-of-factly," she added. "And as Debbie has come to understand that her misbehavior won't bring back the old attention she too has become even-tempered, happier and more easygoing."

*   *   *

Cultures and generations, of course, disagree on the normalcy and desirability of tantrums and other childish outbursts of rage. Some parents worry about spoiling their children, others worry about causing a childhood neurosis, and these concerns are translated into the way they treat their children and the standards of behavior they accept. By and large, American parents tend to tolerate a great deal of aggression and hostility from their children; even so, they do not go as far as the Siriono of Bolivia, who actively encourage their children's outbursts:

> A young child in a temper tantrum may ordinarily beat his father and mother as hard as he can, and they will just laugh. When children are neglected or teased by their parents, they [the children] often pick up a spindle or stick and strike them with considerable force without being punished. I have even heard fathers encouraging their young sons to strike their mothers. Eantándu [a Siriono chief] told me [anthropologist Allan R. Holmberg] that such expressions of anger in a child were a sign that he would grow up to be a valiant adult.

The Utku Eskimo are also tolerant of their young children's rages, but not because they think tantrums have much to do with adult character. Just the opposite. The Eskimo accept childhood outbursts because they know that babies and toddlers have no *ihuma* (reason, thought). Anyone who has reason, however, is expected to control his or her anger, and that includes children over the age of three or four. The only adults who are exempt from this expectation are idiots, the insane, the very sick . . . and *kaplunas*, white people.

THE CONDITIONS OF CATHARSIS

Usually our fights end in frustration all the way around and in a very empty feeling. For the next day or so I feel definitely terrible. I'm tempted to totally abase myself just to get rid of the feeling, the horrible emptiness. We don't make connection in our fights at all, and when they are over I feel so dead, so lonely. How could we have misunderstood each other so totally?

—MARGIE B.

I told him he was a colossal son of a bitch . . . and who the hell did he think he was, he'd taken off when we were kids and never knew what we were doing or what college we went to, or anything. I screamed at him. He didn't say much . . . But the next day, I'll never forget, I felt as if I weighed eight ounces. I felt so light, and so happy, because I had confronted him. It was maybe the single most liberating thing I ever did in my life.

—ALISON K.

What is the reason for the different experiences of Margie and Alison? The prevalent view of anger emphasizes the benefits of ventilation, which are said to include:

• improved communication with target of anger
• increased feelings of closeness with target
• physiological relief/catharsis
• raising self-esteem
• solving problems instead of brooding about them
• "getting rid" of anger
• becoming a happy person
• getting results from the target of one's anger

Yet, as I have been describing and as Margie could tell you, the weight of the evidence indicates precisely the opposite effects, including:

• worsened communication with target of anger
• feelings of distance from target
• physiological arousal; higher blood pressure
• feeling terrible; lowered self-esteem

- making the problem worse
- "rehearsing" the anger
- becoming a hostile person
- making target angry at you

The question is not, "Which list of consequences is correct?" because both are—under some conditions. The question is, "Under what conditions will expressing anger produce beneficial effects, and when will it produce hazardous ones?" The question is not, "Should I express anger or suppress it?" The question is: "What can I do to ensure the benefits of the first list, and avoid the problems of the second?"

After reviewing the evidence and interviewing clinicians and researchers, I believe that the expression of anger is most effective under the following five conditions:

First, anger must be directed at the target of your anger. If you are angry with Ludwig, all the discussion in the world with your best friend will not solve the problem. Unless that discussion results in your changing your perceptions of Ludwig ("Oh, I hadn't realized he didn't mean to insult me"), it is likely to reinforce your own interpretations, with the result that you rehearse your anger rather than ridding yourself of it. If you displace your anger by punching pillows, conjuring up vengeful scenarios, telling nasty jokes, or hitting your child, your anger will not be diminished nor will the displacement be cathartic. This is because the *cause* of your anger remains unchanged.

Second, the expression of anger must restore your sense of control over the situation and your sense of justice; it must inflict appropriate harm on the other person. Some experiences of emotional release feel awfully good. Telling off someone you believe has mistreated you is especially satisfying. Publishing the true story of how you were victimized by the bigwigs makes you feel vindicated, especially if the bigwigs are thereby brought to court or to public condemnation. Watching a villain get his comeuppance is a gratification of which we are too often deprived these days. These cathartic experiences do not feel good because they have emptied some physiological energy reservoir, but because they have accomplished a social goal: the redemption of justice, reinforcement of the social order.

For your sense of justice to be appeased, however, you must perceive some equity between the severity of the other person's alleged offense and your retaliation. If your child accidentally creates a minor mess and you overreact, screaming and shouting that your child is a thoughtless oaf, you are likely to feel embarrassed and foolish later; your self-esteem will plummet (so will your child's). In contrast, if your father has been vindictive and aloof all your life, and one day you whisper to him that his behavior has, um, well, "bothered" you, you are unlikely to feel that justice has been achieved. Your punishment hasn't equaled his crime.

Note that the goal here is restoring justice. Anything else that accomplishes this goal will also help reduce your anger. If you see your target get his comeuppance from someone else—for example, if the boss who fired you is likewise fired on short notice—your own anger will probably subside.

Third, the expression of anger must change the behavior of the target or give you new insights. One benefit of expressing feelings is that often we learn that we have been perceiving somebody's behavior incorrectly. Sometimes the act of writing down hostile feelings or talking about them produces new insights into one's own and the target's behavior. The changed awareness is what is critical. Some people stay in therapy for years, "expressing" anger about their parents, or life, or whatever. Such repeated expressions, without illuminations, are not cathartic.

Fourth, you and your target must speak the same anger language. As I have emphasized repeatedly, anger is a form of communication; whether it "works" depends on whether its message is received. For example, the calm, nonaggressive reporting of anger (those "I-messages" that so many psychologists correctly recommend) is the kindest way to express anger and usually the most effective. But even this method depends on its context. One woman told me that to her dismay, an abusive rage is the only way she can convince her husband that she is *really* angry. Calm discussions of her feelings, she said, may be the preferred middle-class way, but they get her nowhere.

The next day [after a furious argument], he ran around and mowed the lawn, and cleaned the gutters, and washed the kitchen floor. And he said he was sorry he was so lazy. Then he said, "You'll never get me to do anything unless you get flat-out mad, like you did," which puts me in an awkward position because I hate getting angry.

As this example shows, "letting off steam" is cathartic (and effective) only if the recipient of the steam sits up and flies right; the same goes for talking things over rationally. You and your partner must speak the same temperamental language. Thus there are no simple guidelines to determine when talking is better than yelling, because the choice depends as much on the receiver of the message as on the sender. Many of us know this intuitively, and tailor our communications to fit the purpose. A forty-two-year-old business-man, Jay S., described how his eyes were opened when he overheard his usually even-tempered boss on the phone one afternoon:

I've never heard him so angry. He was enraged. His face was red and the veins were bulging on his neck. I tried to get his attention to calm him down but he waved me away impatiently. As soon as the call was over, he turned to me and smiled. "There," he said, "that ought to do it." If I were the guy he'd been shouting at, let me tell you, it *would* have done it, too. But it was all put on.

When you "let out" anger it usually lands on somebody else, and how you feel—relieved, angrier, depressed—is going to depend on what the other person does.

Fifth, there must be no angry retaliation from your target. If you express your anger to your spouse, and your spouse says: "My goodness; I had no idea you were so angry with me! I'm shocked! I'm alarmed! Whatever can I do to make amends?" you are going to be delighted that you revealed your anger. You'll wonder what took you so long. Unfortunately, it is rare for a person to stand still and let you heap calumny on his head, no matter how justified you think you are. "Oh yeah?" the other person is bound to reply, "well, let me just say why I'm so angry at *you* . . ."

They say that expressing your anger is so good for you, so good for all concerned, but I don't think it has very good results at all. My therapist was always saying to me, "Well, can't you just say, in a calm but irate tone of voice, 'You know, it's driving me crazy that you're doing this'?" But I've never found that using that tone does any good, cuts any ice. Either people ignore you, or else you get a little *too* angry and they get angry right back and you get in a big fight that settles nothing.

The no-retaliation condition is, I believe, the reason for the apparent catharsis effect of writing angry letters to the editor or sending anonymous hate mail. Editors rarely respond in kind, and anonymous writers can't be sent retaliating insults. (Perhaps if they got some, they would think twice about sending the rude and vile letters they do.) But writing (unmailed) letters or diaries may also help people who need to reveal feelings toward targets who are not available, such as parents who are emotionally disturbed or deceased.

These conditions help explain, I think, the success of healing rituals, in which people express anger in a once-and-for-all way that allows them to leave it behind. The anger is expressed to the target; in a way that restores the sense of justice and balance; with resulting new insights about one's own or the target's behavior; with no angry response from the target.

Alison K.'s "catharsis," quoted earlier, fit all of these criteria. Alison's father had abandoned his family when Alison and her brother were young. Although he would turn up at infrequent, erratic intervals for brief visits with his children, he never showed continuing interest or support. One year, when Alison was about twenty, she and her brother were summoned to visit him at their grandmother's house. "It was one of the rare appearances he deigned to grant us," she remembers. "I wasn't feeling well and went into the bedroom to lie down. My grandmother asked, 'What's the matter with Alison?' and I heard my father say, 'I don't know. I've just given up on Alison. I don't know what to do with her.' I heard that—'I've just given up on Alison'—and I *flew* into that living room and told him off."

Alison's rage at her father was effective because she told him, at

last, exactly what she wanted to, instead of complaining *about* him
to her brother or friends; because she gave him exactly what she
felt he deserved; and because he stood there and took it, without
counterattacking. Had he said something like, "Well, if you had
not been such an unpleasant and mean little girl I would have
wanted to spend more time with you," I am sure Alison would
have relapsed to square one. Alison's expression of anger also led
her to a new insight: "My fear had always been that confrontations
would mean rejection. But the reality was that he had rejected me
years before."

A woman I'll call Marian S. is another case in point. To
exorcise the anger she felt after her divorce (her husband of many
years left her when she was fifty-two), she walked through every
room in her house with a rolled-up towel as a club. "For five or six
hours," she recalls, "I relived all of our old unresolved arguments.
I screamed and yelled and hit the walls, and when I was through
I lit candles, opened the windows, and let all the old demons out
of the house once and for all. I felt cleansed." Marian S. marked
the end of her anger, and of her ex-husband's ability to trigger it,
with this experience. She said what she had to; he wasn't there to
respond; she felt justice had been served; as a result, she stopped
blaming him. (I'll have more to say on anger and divorce in
Chapter 10.)

Perhaps most important, I believe that these five conditions of
catharsis explain the difference between the healthy benefits of
confession and the unhealthy consequences of *obsession*. In Chapter 4 I noted that the suppression of important, traumatic secrets
places continuing stress on the body. It takes considerable effort
not to think of something that is bothering you. James Pennebaker, a psychologist who has extensively studied the effects of
secrets and confession, finds repeatedly that people who have had
no traumas in their lives have the fewest illnesses. Those who have
suffered a trauma but were able to confide in others have the next
fewest number of ailments. But those who endured a trauma and
did not talk about it to anyone have the greatest number of
illnesses.

What kind of secret trauma? Pennebaker has interviewed

Holocaust survivors, most of whom, contrary to what you might think, had never talked about their experiences with anyone outside the camps—yet they thought about them all the time. Pennebaker has also worked with hundreds of other adults and college students, who, sadly, have all too many traumas to report: sexual abuse, abandonment, humiliations, beatings, secrets of all kinds.

"Many upheavals, such as the death of your parent or being laid off from work, are socially acceptable," says Pennebaker. "It's OK to talk about them with friends. Other experiences aren't easy or acceptable to talk about—having been raped, serving in Vietnam, being involved in an illicit relationship, having been humiliated. In these cases, the act of not discussing or confiding the event with another may be more damaging than having experienced the event per se. The reason seems to be that long-term inhibition of a secret increases physiological reactivity, which is associated with stress-related diseases."

So Pennebaker has been asking people to confess their "deepest thoughts and feelings" about their experiences, sometimes by writing them down, sometimes by talking to a tape recorder or an anonymous listener. (A control group of comparable individuals simply talks about trivial events.) His remarkable findings show an astonishing link between confession and improved health. When he followed up on the Holocaust survivors fourteen months later, for example, he found that the more they had originally disclosed, the fewer their subsequent visits to doctors and the fewer illnesses they reported. The more that bereaved individuals had talked about their spouses' deaths, the fewer health problems they had the following year. The more that college students had written about early traumas and even their normal (but secret) feelings of homesickness and school anxiety, the fewer visits to the campus infirmary they later paid, and the less likely they were to resort to drugs.

Why is talking or writing about a trauma different from thinking and obsessing about it? Obsessional thoughts, says Pennebaker, are poorly organized and incomplete. They occur as vague, fragmented images, nightmarish glimpses of the trauma. Being forced to write down one's thoughts or articulate them clearly gives shape, focus, and structure to the event. For example, the more that the bereaved spouses in Pennebaker's studies thought or ruminated about their spouses' deaths, the *more* health problems they had; but the more they talked openly with others, the less they ruminated.

Now of course not everyone is confessing feelings of anger here. But even when they do, Pennebaker and I agree that there is a world of difference between confession and repeated, prolonged ventilation. "Any cathartic effects of confession are due to insight, not physical 'release,' " says Pennebaker. "Confiding or consciously confronting the perceptions and feelings associated with a trauma allows for the integration or cognitive reorganization of the event."

In other words, the critical benefit of confession lies in reframing or reinterpreting the event, finding meaning in it, and putting it behind you. Pennebaker believes that "the failure to confront a trauma forces the person to live with it in an unresolved manner." Actively writing or talking about it aids people in assimilating the tragedy and coming to a sense of completion about it. It also helps them lose the secret feeling of shame.

For example, Pennebaker's students who wrote about the same experience each day for four days gradually gained insight and distance. One young woman, who had been molested at the age of nine by a boy a few years older, at first wrote about her feelings of embarrassment and guilt. By the third day, she was writing about how angry she felt at the boy. By the last day, she had begun to see the whole event differently; he was a child too, after all. After the experiment, she said: "Before, when I thought about it, I'd lie to myself. . . . Now, I don't feel like I even have to think about it because I got it off my chest. I finally admitted that it happened."

But revealing your "deepest thoughts and feelings" is not therapeutic if, once you start, you keep rehearsing and confessing them endlessly to all who will listen. It is not therapeutic if you get stuck at a middle stage, feeling angry and outraged, or depressed and humiliated, and never get beyond it. A colleague and friend of mine, Carole Wade, once invited a student to speak to her human sexuality class about her experience of sexual abuse. As the student talked, she began to cry, and everyone in the class was naturally deeply moved. "I've invited the student back each semester," Carole tells me, "and each time she gives the same performance. It's beginning to seem unsettling to me rather than touching. She has now defined herself as a wounded victim, and she gets a lot of sympathy for doing so. She's not moving beyond her victimhood."

Most of the time, we can conclude, expressing anger makes people angrier, solidifies an angry attitude, and establishes a hostile habit. If you keep quiet about momentary irritations and distract yourself with pleasant activity until your fury simmers down, chances are you will feel better, and feel better faster, than if you let yourself go in a shouting match. If you want to scream at your children, berate your spouse, or ventilate all over a powerless telephone operator, you can't call on the medical or psychological professions to justify your actions.

These conclusions are *not* a recommendation for moral passivity. Some expressions of anger are morally and socially necessary. Bureaucracies, hospitals, and other large institutions "cool out" the anger of mistreated clients by making them feel that they, the mistreated customers, are crazy, misguided, or stupid. People who sustain their anger under such trying circumstances often choose a lonely but heroic course.

And these conclusions are *not* a recommendation for brooding and resentment. Silent sulking is a lousy and deadly weapon. Few people are magnanimous enough never to bear a grudge, nurse an indignity, or express their anger in devious ways—such as to "forget" to do something they promised to do, hold back sexually, or sulk irritably around the house. I would argue, though, that these are not examples of not-talking; they are examples of talking to yourself. You know that you feel angry, but in the guise of magnanimity or self-righteousness, or because you are afraid to announce your feelings, you pretend everything is fine. Meanwhile, you are muttering imprecations to yourself and holding elaborate conversations in your head. This is not going to reduce your feelings of anger, either.

People who are anxious and tense about feeling angry can be

helped by therapies that know the difference between acknowledging anger and acting it out. You can learn to be more assertive
and say what you really feel, instead of resentfully bearing grudges;
you can learn to admit what makes you feel angry and how to
talk about that anger in ways that do not insult your target and
escalate the quarrel. (For more on therapeutic interventions, see
Chapter 10.) But as Leonard Berkowitz notes, "I do not think it is
necessary to *act out* one's hostility to achieve these benefits . . .
We can talk about our feelings and describe our emotional
reactions without attacking others verbally or physically, directly or
in fantasy."

Ultimately, the purpose of anger is to make a grievance known,
and if the grievance is not confronted, it will not matter if the
anger is kept in, let out, or wrapped in red ribbons and dropped in
the Erie Canal. But there is an unexpected benefit to knowing
about the hazards of ventilation: It might help you get along with
people who ventilate at you.

A friend of the screenwriter and humorist Larry Gelbart was
irate because his tyrannical employer had chewed him out for
some insignificant matter once too often. "I will not be treated like
a worm," he raged to Gelbart. "I'm going to punch him on the
nose the next time he shouts at me like that. How dare he—"

"Hold on, hold on," Gelbart said. "I think I see the problem.
You're not Jewish, are you?"

"What the hell has that got to do with anything?" his friend
replied irritably. "We're talking about common courtesy."

"Listen," Gelbart said, "relax. What any Jewish person would
know is that he's not *yelling at you*, he's yelling *for himself*. Next
time he shouts at you, this is what you do. Lean back in your
chair, fold your arms, and let his screams wash over you. Tell
yourself: 'Oy, such good it's doing him to get it out of his system!' "

The friend says this advice works wonders. The mogul won't feel
any better for yelling (in fact, as we now know, he's bound to feel
worse)—but Gelbart's friend will feel better for thinking he does.

6

"Seeing Red"

[When reason] is asleep, then the wild beast within us, gorged with meat or drink, starts up and having shaken off sleep, goes forth to satisfy his desires; and there is no conceivable folly or crime it won't commit.

—PLATO

• It is a perfect spring day in New York, a day to banish winter surliness. Buoyant and happy, my husband and I emerge from the Museum of Modern Art late in the afternoon, when we realize that our sojourn has delayed us in meeting friends for dinner. Every phone booth on the block is occupied. We walk down several streets, but apparently the rest of New York City is going to be late for dinner, too. We see a young couple standing at a pair of public telephones, and as the woman finishes her conversation and is about to start another I ask her politely whether I might make the briefest of calls. Suddenly, the young man, a natty fellow in a business suit and gold chains, whirls around and spits obscenities at us. He is so vicious, and his anger so unexpected, that we feel physically violated.

• A thirty-six-year-old dentist describes an embarrassing experience. After a vigorous workout playing racquetball, he went, as usual, to lift weights in the cooling-down room. Another man accidentally bumped into him. "Why don't you look where you're going, asshole?" the dentist shouted. "Those weights could have

161

fallen on me!" Naturally, the asshole felt it behooved him to reply. Harsher words followed and blossomed into lawsuits. The dentist is no longer angry and wishes he could back out. "I guess I overreacted," he says.

• A friend of mine is crossing a street in midtown Manhattan, with the green light. Suddenly a car makes a sharp turn and nearly runs him down. My friend, heart racing from the close call and furious at the driver's carelessness, slams his hand on the car's trunk as hard as he can. The car screeches to a halt. The driver leaps out, holding a handgun, and assumes a military shooting stance. "Don't you f—— with my car, you f——m——f——," he screams. (My friend did not pause to comment on the driver's limited and unimaginative vocabulary.)

Urban rages like these are all too familiar experiences for most of us in these trying and hostile times. No one seems to have learned, or can remember, the magic words that calm people when they are frightened or threatened: "I'm sorry; I didn't see you; are you all right?" The inability to speak these words, I observe, goes right along with a propensity for mindless insults.

Certainly there are plenty of outrageous events in modern life that make us feel angry—threats, assaults, grotesque murders, injustices—but in this chapter I want to consider another matter: the ways that provocations intersect with the background buzz of our busy lives. The stresses of urban life itself are highly stimulating. By overlooking the heat of the stresses and concentrating only on the provocations that inflame them, we miss a crucial component in understanding urban angers.

For example, suppose that a couple goes to see a pornographic movie and are turned on by it. Now suppose they get into an argument about finances on the way home. Their heightened emotional arousal from the movie is likely to inflame their quarrel, making them feel angrier with each other than if they hadn't seen the movie. But what if they have the quarrel on the way *to* the movie? Now the film is likely to act as a diversion, redirecting their angry arousal into feelings of sexual stimulation. (Three psychologists, Edward and Marcia Donnerstein and R. Evans, have actually conducted the experiment that demonstrated this.)

Clearly, the answer to such questions as "How does pornography affect its viewers?" is complicated. So is the answer to "What provocations make you angry?" because anger will often depend on whether your level of physiological arousal occurs before or after a specific provocation. Anger depends on some things you are aware of (such as the rude young man at the phone booth) and others that you are not aware of (such as your heart rate and epinephrine level). This is why events that you may find amusing on Tuesday seem infuriating on Friday, or why the mannerisms of your beloved that you usually find charming are today grating on your nerves.

If you put a few rats together in a small cage, it is easy to set up circumstances that will soon have them at each other's throats. You can blast them with loud, incessant noise. You can crowd them together like rush-hour commuters. You can give them the rat equivalent of a long hot summer. Rats are physiologically humanish, which is why they are used reliably to test our foods for cancer and our stresses for disease. But human beings differ from rats in (at least) one respect: The things that will agitate a rat will anger a person only under certain psychological conditions.

In today's conservative climate, where much effort is being made to demonstrate the genetic (and by inference ineradicable) components of human behavior, I think it is especially important to try to specify those psychological conditions. If frustration is dangerous, we had best be careful not to place obstructions in the way of our children, lovers, friends, or co-workers; indeed, we'd better be certain not to let our frustrations mount up. If noise and crowds generate aggression, there's not much point in trying to improve urban conditions; it's urban life itself that is making us miserable. If aggression in sports is at least one way to absorb our city rages, then let's encourage those hockey and tennis players who celebrate violence. If people are not responsible for their actions when they drink, then we and our laws might as well continue to forgive drunk drivers, abusive spouses, and assaultive individuals who "only had a couple too many." In the examples that follow, a pattern is apparent. Frustration, noise, crowds, alcohol, and sports do not instinctively generate or "release" anger;

they generate physical arousal, which, when coupled with a psychological provocation, can *become* the feeling of anger. The failure to understand the connections between arousal, attitude, and aggression has led to a host of misunderstandings in our laws, entertainments, love affairs, and daily lives.

FRUSTRATION

In 1988 the *Journal of the American Medical Association* reported a new medical problem, which we might call Vending Machine Madness. The author of the article reported fifteen serious injuries, three of them fatal, as a result of irate men kicking or rocking soda-vending machines that had taken their money without producing the drink. (In the fatal cases, the men rocked the machine so hard that it fell over and crushed them.) "Soda machine injuries can seem comical until the costs . . . are listed," wrote the author of the article. Indeed. Trying to argue with a vending machine reminds me of Sancho Panza's observation that whether the stone hits the pitcher or the pitcher hits the stone, it's going to be bad for the pitcher.

The vending-machine problem seems a classic case of the frustration-aggression hypothesis, first proposed by John Dollard and his colleagues in 1939. Frustration, they said, is always infuriating. The blocking of a goal (frustration) activates your aggressive drive (anger), which in turn causes you to behave aggressively (preferably toward whatever is blocking you). Frustration *always* causes aggression, these psychologists argued, and aggression is always preceded by frustration. This testable idea sent hundreds of researchers to their laboratories, where they promptly found that some frustrations make you angry, but lots of others do not. If you do not get the job you want or the lover you long for, you are as likely to be disappointed or depressed as angry, and maybe even relieved. Frustration causes many reactions, including a craving for ice cream or a desire to see a mindless movie.

Between frustration and anger, as between anger and aggression, lie the mind and the culture. The frustrations that would make many Americans angry produce indifference in societies that are not as goal-directed. Many years ago anthropologist Gregory Bateson observed that the Balinese do not mind being interrupted at work or play; they don't feel angry if you get in their way. The Balinese feel angry, all right, if you steal a cow or renege on a bet; but frustration itself does not especially faze them. Within our own culture, some groups impose frustration on themselves all the time: ascetics and academics, for instance, frustrate their immediate pleasures for long-term rewards—salvation or tenure.

Whether or not frustration makes you angry depends on several intermediate, learned conditions: How have you learned to cope when things don't go your way? Are there extenuating circumstances that make the frustration seem legitimate, or at least tolerable? Are you a perfectionist? What are your basic expectations about how the world works? One middle-aged lawyer says she won't allow herself the small frustrations at all:

> I just tune them out. I'm built for war. I mean I like a certain amount of anarchy—it confirms my whole dreadful view of the world that *of course* these things happen all the time, and I take them in tremendous stride. For example, I will never run for a train or bus or taxi. If I miss it, I miss it; there's always another one. This attitude protects me from disappointments and blowups. And I get a lot of pleasure out of seeing people blowing their cool over these little frustrations.

A Southern friend says that frustration never bothers him if the task at hand is unimportant or something he isn't good at anyway. He can be interrupted in the middle of any mundane matter, or stymied in his attempts to hang a painting, and all he feels is his natural cheerfulness. But what sends him into an absolute sit-spin of rage is the frustration of not being able to do something he thinks he should be able to do. "In the South," he says, "we call this 'feeling sent for and can't get there.' "

The once-neat line of the frustration-aggression hypothesis sags appreciably under the weight of its exceptions and modifications. In the list of things that make most people feel angry, frustration has to take its place after attacks to self-esteem; criticism of one's clothes, friends, and personality; direct insult; and the reverberating lament for centuries, unfair treatment. Further, it turns out that frustration usually does not make people behave aggressively unless they think the aggression will get rid of the frustration—another support for the argument that aggression is a strategy, not an instinct. And finally, not just any frustration, but the belief that the frustration is *unjustified*, is what makes us angry.

Most of us are intuitively aware of these qualifications. When you are struggling to glue a vase back together and the stupid glue tube won't cooperate, that is frustrating; but you probably won't feel angry until your beloved, watching you, comments wittily on your manual dexterity. When there's a war on and everyone, equitably, must accept gas and food rations, frustration is high but anger about rationing is not. When rationing seems arbitrary and uneven, however (for example during the gas shortages years ago), when some people have all the gas they want and you must wait hours for two dollars' worth, when you feel you are unfairly deprived of what you deserve, *then* frustration is likely to make you feel angry.

Because even the word "frustration" has a negative connotation, some psychologists, such as George Mandler, prefer to talk about "interruption"—a disruption of an ongoing act, thought, or expectation, which can be positive or negative. Let us say you have just sat down to dinner after a tiring day. The phone, that cursed blessing of civilization, rings. Grumpily, you answer it. If it is a salesman chirruping about encyclopedias, you probably will feel annoyed. If it is a long-lost friend returning home after five years in the Yukon, you probably will feel delighted. Same interruption of your dinner, but entirely different emotions. (Mandler's interpretation of my phone-booth experience, by the way, is that the abusive young man had been interrupted several times prior to my innocuous question, and that something in the nature of his call was itself upsetting him.)

Regardless of whether we speak of frustrations or interruptions, both are physiologically arousing; that is, they generate a momentary rise of adrenal hormones. The day is full of them, although most of these events are unimportant—a milk carton that refuses to open cleanly, forcing you to tear the stubborn spout—and the attending arousal rises and falls almost at once, like a sneeze. The frustration lasts a few seconds and is quickly forgotten. But consider what happens with repeated interruptions. Let's say a busy mother discovers a free forty-five minutes in her hectic morning, so she relaxes in her favorite chair with a new novel. Now suppose she is interrupted at five-minute intervals by her children:

"Mom! What's for lunch?"

"Hey, Mom, can I invite Jenny over to lunch?"

"Can we have peanut butter sandwiches?"

"Can we play softball in the patio?"

"Can we have hamburgers instead of peanut butter?"

"Mom! Jenny hit me with the bat!"

We could say that each interruption is frustrating her desire to read, but even so she will not feel angry if she expects her children's intrusions, welcomes them, or thinks they are funny. Again, it is her attitude that intervenes between the arousal of interruption and her emotional reaction.

But perhaps the best evidence for showing that frustration does not automatically produce anger comes unintentionally from the psychologists themselves. When they want to get their subjects angry, in order to study the effects of anger, they rarely frustrate them any more. They insult them.

NOISE

New York is a noisy place. It is filled with the sounds of drills and car honks and sirens, shouters and singers and musicians, blaring radios and shrill arguments. A New Yorker I know inhales the sounds of sirens as if they were magnolia blossoms. "I love that noise," he says. "It means someone is racing to the rescue. It means help. It means the city is working." "I hate sirens," his wife says, "that AW-oo, AW-oo at an intolerably loud and piercing level. A siren is a shriek that means another disaster."

The sound, therefore, is not always the fury. The anger provoked by noise has much to do with what the noise represents.

Many folks who hate loud street music and its intrusion on their private reveries often go home to apartments that have excellent stereo systems, where they play, at top volume, their preferences in rock, jazz, and classical. It's not noise alone that angers. It's what the noise means.

Loud sounds are arousing: They produce an increase in epinephrine that may feel uncomfortable. ("My father's loud Wagner operas made my mother feel she was going to cry," one woman told me. "He never believed her, though. He just thought she was out to deprive him of one of his few great pleasures.") The arousal of noise alone does not make people angry or aggressive, but noise *increases the likelihood* of anger when a catalyst is added.

To distinguish the effects of noise from the effects of human offensiveness, Vladimir Konečni asked 120 young men and women to participate in what they thought was an experiment on learning. Each student worked on an anagram test with Konečni's confederate, who either kept up a patter of insults and irritating mannerisms, or behaved himself and worked quietly on the anagrams. In the next phase of the study, each student read fifty words to the confederate, who had to give a one-word free-association answer. If the student thought the answer was "creative," he pushed a button marked *good;* otherwise, he pushed a button that supposedly administered shock.

All through this "learning" procedure, the students wore earphones and listened to a steady stream of music. Well, it wasn't exactly music. Because Konečni wanted to control the precise degree of complexity and loudness of the noise without contaminating these factors by the students' musical preferences, he programmed a computer to generate tones. The "music" ranged in complexity from nursery-song level to the highly avant-garde, and from soft (about 73 decibels) to loud (about 97 decibels). So some of the students heard computer compositions that were loud and simple (rather like disco); others got a soft and simple version (like Muzak); others, loud and complex (like jazz); and others, soft and complex (analogous, perhaps to a Bach fugue). A control group heard no sounds at all during the experiment.

Konečni found that people, unlike rats, need more than noise to provoke aggression. The students who had not been insulted by the stooge were completely unaffected by the noise. They dealt between eleven and thirteen shocks, on the average, whether they were listening to loud and complicated noise, soft and pleasant noise, or no noise at all. The students who had been insulted but who were not aroused by the music gave about fifteen shocks, not appreciably more than the noninsulted students. But when the music was loud *or* complex, and especially when it was loud *and* complex, the insulted students felt the angriest of all groups and readily seized the chance to get back at their offender. They blasted him with an average of five shocks more than anyone else gave.

Inadvertently, Konečni discovered the truth of one cliché, while adding a modern modification. The students who listened to the simple, quiet tones were the least likely to be provoked by the offensive partner. They didn't retaliate angrily against him when they had the chance. They didn't rise to his bait. Apparently it isn't just any music that soothes the savage breast, but Muzak!

The sheer decibel level of the noise around us is not enough to make us cranky, irritable, or aggressive. (It can, however, affect our mental and physical health, which is another matter.) Suppose a new highway is built near your house and now you have to put up with the rumble and buzz of traffic all day long. Does the noise annoy you? According to research, the answer is no if you believe that the road has brought economic benefits to your community—jobs and services—and therefore increased the value of your house. The answer is yes if you believe your property values have been diminished and if you bought the house in the first place to live in a remote spot. Even people who live near the deafening roar of airports are not irritated by the noise of airplanes if they believe in the importance and benefit of airports to their own economic health. Once again, actual anger depends on what the noise means to you.

Babies may seem a far cry, so to speak, from airports, but they too demonstrate the difference between the arousal that noise produces in us and the attitudes that can produce anger. A baby's cry causes (in anyone who is listening) skin conductance and diastolic blood pressure to shoot up. This is a disturbing sensation, even to a brand-new doting parent. A smiling, cooing baby may make an adult smile back and return to adult business, but no particular physiological arousal occurs. This system was very clever of nature. It is in the baby's best interests if adults are irritated by its cry, for then they will attempt to restore the baby's good mood, such as by feeding it. In turn, adults are deeply gratified and relieved when they are able to stop a baby's wails, and much of that relief is simply physiological: The arousal declines immediately, which is a relaxing and rewarding sensation. Incidentally, mothers and fathers do not differ in their physiological responses to crying infants. They may differ in knowing what to do about an unhappy baby, but that is a learned matter.

Nonetheless, the arousal caused by a baby's wail is rarely felt as rage or flat-out anger unless two things occur: The baby cries persistently and is difficult to console, even when picked up and fed, and the parent begins to think the child is crying intentionally. This distorted perception is common among child abusers, who typically complain, as one did: "When the baby was born I thought he would love me, but when he cried all the time, it meant he didn't love me so I hit him." Any parent will feel sustained agitation over a child who cries continually. Actual anger comes from misunderstanding why one is upset, and blaming the child.

CROWDS

Not long ago, a fashionable explanation of urban violence was population density. Comparing clustered people to trapped rats, some observers argued that crowded cities would turn into urban sinks. They produced statistics that correlated measures of density (such as number of people per residential acre or average number of individuals per room) with juvenile delinquency, infant mortality, VD, crime, and other forms of social pathology. The evidence looked good at first, but the theory subsequently fell into disrepute. The association between density and pathology disintegrates when income, education, and ethnicity are taken into account. In Tokyo, where population density exceeds that of any U.S. city, crowding is not associated with social pathology. In spacious Los Angeles, where you can drive for blocks and not see a pedestrian, the crime rate exceeds that of New York.

Further, some crowds are wonderful, even an essential part of the fun, such as at baseball games, carnivals, summer concerts in the park, jazz clubs, bars, and New Year's celebrations. One hundred scattered fans at a football game are depressing to viewers and players alike, and few would want to eat at a restaurant if only three of twenty tables were occupied. Crowded conditions in steerage, for immigrants fufilling a life's dream to come to America, did not produce the rage that crowded conditions in prisons do.

So it is not crowding itself that creates anger, but one's perceptions about the crowd. Does a crowd make you feel trapped, or do you know how to get around in spite of it? Did you choose to join the crowd, or did it join you? Is it temporary or permanent? What have your experience and culture taught you about crowds? Most of all, do you have control over your actions when you are in a crowd, or does the sheer force of numbers keep you from doing what you want?

The mere presence of many other people is indeed arousing—to a lesser extent, so is the presence of one other person—but whether that arousal is transformed into pleasure or anger depends less on whether you *are* crowded than on whether you *feel* crowded. Density itself does not make you angry until it curtails your sense of freedom and control. For example, when people are able to work effectively and without interruptions in a densely packed room, they feel less crowded than if they work with interruptions in the same room with fewer people. The same number of persons per square foot will feel pleasant in a cozy pub and frightening in a stalled subway. The dreadful failure of housing projects such as Pruitt-Igoe, which was nearly destroyed by its inhabitants before the city of St. Louis tore it down, was not a result of overcrowding but of bad design. Cold, impersonal, alienating structures can make people feel unhappy living or working in them, especially if they aren't designed to make human connections easy and regular. It is the mismanagement of density that creates the problem, not the density.

At the upper limits of density, of course, such as a traffic jam or a rock concert, crowding and loss of control are synonymous. But in everyday life, people learn how to work their own crowds; it's only unfamiliar crowds that unsettle them. Dense living conditions that are normal to a Japanese would be cramped to a Chicagoan, and Chicago's density would be intolerable to a Nebraskan.

The arousal of crowds may break into anger if the usual rules that govern crowd action are violated. Arabs and Latin Americans stand closer to each other in conversation than Americans do, taking detailed note of facial expressions and mannerisms. An American who does not know this is likely to feel "pushed" and annoyed when an Arab stands too close for comfort; he misinterprets the Arab's stance as a provocation. By and large, middle-class Americans have a greater need for distance and privacy than many other groups do. This is a learned, social need, not a biological one. Many Americans who visit China cannot understand how the Chinese can "crowd" several generations into small quarters. The Chinese are equally astonished to learn that American parents, who frequently give each of their children a separate room, would feel crowded if grandparents and other relatives lived with them. The Chinese and the Americans have entirely different family structures, values, and beliefs about crowding.

Feeling angry about being crowded also depends on what you have relative to what you used to have, as a famous old Jewish story teaches. It seems a poor man complained to his rabbi about the overcrowding in his house: a wife, six children, a mother-in-law, and a boarder were driving him crazy. The rabbi listened and offered one sentence of advice: "Bring your goat into the house." "My goat?" "Your goat."

A week later the poor man returned, complaining about the stench and dirt of the goat in addition to the crowd in his house. The rabbi said: "Bring your chickens into the house." "Oy, rabbi, my chickens?" "Your chickens."

A week later the poor man was a nervous wreck. "Rabbi," he moaned, "you have to help me." The rabbi listened. "Put out the goat." "Only the goat?" "Only the goat."

The poor man did as he was told, and returned to the rabbi in a few days. "It's better, Rabbi," he said, "but a house full of nine people and three chickens . . ." "Put out the chickens," said the rabbi.

A week later the man returned to the rabbi. "Rabbi, you're a genius!" he said. "Now my house is as roomy as a mansion!"

DRIVERS AND DAWDLERS

• In Los Angeles, the 25-year-old driver of a tractor-trailer deliberately rammed his truck into 24 separate cars. He told police he was weary of traffic jams: "If they [the cars] wouldn't get out of my way, I would hit them."

• In East Rutherford, New Jersey, a truck barely brushed the fender of a Mercedes-Benz. The two drivers got out. They exchanged harsh words, and the driver of the car punched the driver of the truck in the mouth, bloodying his lip. The truck driver then pulled out a semiautomatic handgun, and, with a single shot, killed the driver of the car.

• My mother, who was eighty-two at the time, turned right into a main street, causing an oncoming car to slow down by, oh, one-tenth of a mile an hour. At the next stoplight, the enraged driver got out of his car, went over to my mother's window, reached in, turned off her engine, and threw her keys across the street. (They were retrieved by two kind passersby.)

"Traffic anger" is a growing problem across the county, and the Car Driving Furies can strike anyone. Between November 1987 and August 1988 alone, there were 1,183 incidents of highway violence in California. (Although Easterners tended to believe, from the news, that hundreds of people were being killed in a wave of "drive-by" shootings, "only" four people were killed and a dozen wounded, which is bad enough.) In studies of 268 college students and 182 people found guilty of traffic violations, psychologist Ray Novaco found that 28 percent had chased another driver; 10 percent had thrown objects at another car; 16 percent yelled at least weekly at another car; and 6 percent had bumped other vehicles in anger. Apply those percentages to the millions of drivers on our highways, and you get thousands of people who, in anger, are doing dopey and dangerous things.

Even people who know better. Joe Kaplan, who was head of the
Greater L.A. Chapter of the National Safety Council, told a
reporter: "I will probably still get up and give my seat to a lady. But
when I get to an intersection, I'm ashamed to tell you, I'm going
to be there first." Why do Kaplan and others have to "be there
first"? Why do people who are kind to their families and pets
become rude, arrogant, and dangerous drivers? What happens to
people when they get behind the wheel that turns even Casper
Milquetoast into Torquemada?

There are several contributing factors to this problem. One is
the influx into a community of people whose driving rules differ
from those of the natives. Every city has its unspoken pace and
rhythms, and visitors violate them at their peril. Native Los
Angeles drivers used to be renowned for their courtesy and
law-abiding driving habits. Now there are millions of new arrivals
from what one reporter calls the "screech-and-batter schools of
driving," which has caused many natives to throw manners to the
winds. New Jersey drivers are famous irritants to New York drivers
because the former move at a slower pace.

Second, increasingly crowded driving conditions and clogged
traffic cause physiological arousal—increased blood pressure and
heart rate, signs of tension. Drivers feel confined, unable to control their pace and movement, and unable to get where they are
going, which adds to their impatience. If, in addition, they *used* to
be able to get where they were going more quickly—if they
remember the "good old days" before traffic jams—they have the
psychological burden of diminished expectations, which are annoying in their own right. "It isn't fair," drivers complain, "that I
used to get from A Street to Z Avenue in fifteen minutes, and now
it takes forty-five."

Third, drivers rehearse a "mental script" in which they
interpret the behavior of other drivers as intentionally rude or
insulting. "You can't ever say that someone else's driving *causes*
you to become angry or aggressive," says Arnold Goldstein,
director of the Center for Research on Aggression at Syracuse
University. "What's important is how you perceive the other
driver. If someone cuts in front of me near a hospital, for

example, I might think he's sick and not get angry. But if I see it as a deliberate act of aggression, I would be inclined to respond the same way."

A fourth contributing factor is the invisibility of other drivers and one's own anonymity. If you accidentally step on someone's foot in an elevator, you are likely to say "Excuse me." It is an unfortunate fact of human psychology, however, that the more distant we are from others, and the more anonymous they are to us or we to them, the less restrained, courteous, and empathic we become. The man who behaved so horrendously to my mother was not saying to himself: "There's a little eighty-two-year-old woman who reminds me of my grandmother; she probably didn't see me coming." He wasn't seeing a person at all, but a car that had gotten in his way—a thing, an obstruction. Moreover, had he recognized my mother when he approached her, he would immediately have become too embarrassed to behave as badly as he did. Why, she could have told someone.

Roger Brown, a Harvard social psychologist, described an experience common to us all when anonymity shifts to recognition. "I turned my car into one end of a narrow Cambridge street," he wrote, "just as someone turned his car into the same street at the other end. We came at one another like two combative mice, getting angrier as we approached, until at close quarters I recognized a colleague. We both switched to smiles and each offered to back out in favor of the other." It's both heartening and dismaying to know that experts can understand the rules of emotion, and still be subject to them.

Drivers are not the only category of people who are subject to the irritations of competing rhythms and rules, restraint in getting where they want to go, and perceived provocations. Dawdlers who get in the way of those in a hurry; thoughtless louts who block the fast lane (on highways or sidewalks); maniacs who zigzag carelessly through crowds, knocking down bystanders in their way: These folks are equally annoying to walkers and drivers. And to skaters, as Sara Davidson described in her account of the scene on the boardwalk in Santa Monica, California. When an eighty-six-year-old woman was run over and killed by a twenty-five-year-old bicyclist (who said, "She got in my way"), the Los Angeles City Council met to consider the situation.

On the boardwalk, it was war on wheels: Shouting and pushing erupted between skaters and bicyclists and joggers and senior citizens over who had the right-of-way. The skaters had the numbers and were gaining each day. People were skating to the bank, to the laundromat, to restaurants, to walk their dogs.

The City Council voted to ban skating on parts of the boardwalk, but people disobeyed.

"No skating on the boardwalk!"

"Up yours, ya jerk!"

A ninety-two-year-old woman struck a skater with her cane when he cut in front of her. "I'm living here twenty-five years," she shouted. "You should be ashamed."

"She got in my way"? "He cut in front of her"? What we are dealing with here is not a phenomenon unique to driving a car, but a special case of the crowding-and-anger question, a category of interference in getting where you are going. A Los Angeles freeway, a New York midtown street, and the Santa Monica boardwalk share certain prerequisites of rage: density high enough to curtail the feeling of having control over your movements; a clash of cultures (be they generations, ethnicities, or driving habits), each heeding its own rules of conduct; and high levels of epinephrine generated by the means of locomotion and the environment. Arousal is present, and so are the perceptions of provocation.

Driving a car is stimulating, especially in thick traffic, because it demands constant attention and split-second decisions; negotiating an urban street is stimulating, because of the arousal produced by crowds and noise; roller-skating and skateboarding are extremely stimulating exercises, over which even adept skaters lack complete control. This lack of control and the speed of movement inject an element of danger into one's travel: roller skaters *are* hazardous to ninety-two-year-old women, and to other living things as well; drivers who change lanes abruptly or who turn without signaling *are* threatening to your health. The same high arousal that skaters and fast drivers find exciting, however, can turn rapidly to anger (an intense anger, at that) when their movements are blocked by someone who can be blamed. Yelling "Up yours, ya jerk!" or honking the horn loudly is an effort to restore control, reduce the sense of danger, and retaliate against the offending person in your way.

Of course, these reactions, such as yelling offensive words and honking furiously, do not relieve your anger. They make it worse, both by pumping up your own blood pressure and by causing the target of your wrath to yell back at you, which in turn makes you feel angrier yet. That ninety-two-year-old woman on the boardwalk undoubtedly remembers more civil times, when pipsqueaks on roller skates would have been ashamed to knock an old woman down, and would have apologized to her if they had—a gesture that would have calmed both sides.

ALCOHOL

Alcohol, it is widely believed, loosens the social reins that keep people under control. Because so many crimes of violence are committed when the participants have been drinking, and because so many marital quarrels accompany drinking, alcohol is often assumed to be a releaser of anger and aggression. As one of my interviewees, a forty-five-year-old computer salesman, said:

> Alcohol used to make me furious. Sometimes, not all the time, it would evoke some horrible anger that was sitting there, which usually resulted in my getting furious at my wife. She used to say, "There's some terrible thing pent up in you that alcohol brings out, and I get it."

The examples of people who drink to *avoid* anger, however, rarely get into the newspapers or scientific studies. For them, booze soothes rather than strafes; they drink to drown their sorrows and forget their anger, not as an excuse to express it. Compare two former Yankee baseball managers, Billy Martin and Bob Lemon. "If Billy's in a bar," a Yankee coach told *The New York Times,* "he'll be in a fight before the night's out. Not Lem." When Lemon is angry he keeps it to himself; he drinks, but never becomes abusive or aggressive. In fact, drink seems to calm his anger: "A couple of C.C.'s and water'll do it to me," Lemon told the *Times*.

Large amounts of alcohol act as a depressant; drink enough, and you'll pass out. But alcohol is a stimulant at low levels. One or two drinks, and you perk up, your heart rate rises. As blood-alcohol concentration increases, your heart rate falls and drowsiness sets in. But even these changes are imprecise. They depend on your initial state of arousal—are you drinking to pick yourself up after a tiring day or to calm yourself down after a fight with your parents? —and also on your drinking history, tolerance for alcohol, and weight. The mood that accompanies drinking also depends on your mental *set*—your expectations about how alcohol will make you feel, the reasons you are drinking, whether there is something you want to do or say that alcohol will justify—and the environmental *setting* you are in: a small group of friends, an unfriendly bar, home alone. I can have a glass and a half of wine at dinner after a tiring day and conk out, but four glasses of wine at a dinner party and feel full of pep.

Researchers who are trying to identify the physiological reactions to alcohol and its relationship to anger often forget to account for set and setting. Then they get contradicting results, and wonder why. For instance, two experimenters let their volunteers drink as much bourbon as they wanted and then observed their reactions. Most of the drinkers became angry, depressed, fatigued, confused, and unfriendly. It apparently did not occur to the researchers until too late that people might become angry, depressed, fatigued, confused, and unfriendly because they were asked to drink bourbon at nine o'clock in the morning in a bleak hospital room. "This is an unnatural setting for drinking," the experimenters finally observed, "and our subjects did not appear to be having an exceptionally good time." Sometimes I worry about our scientists' common sense.

To complicate matters further, none of us has the same reaction to alcohol on all occasions, independent of the mood we are in when we start drinking. This is true even of alcoholics. David M. Rioch reported the case of one alcoholic

> who occasionally went to a party, was pleasant, friendly and entertaining, and could drink a dozen or more whiskey and sodas without showing any signs of inebriation. More frequently, however, he became antagonistic, critical, and sarcastic with one or two drinks, wandered off by himself with three or four, and was staggering and belligerent with five . . . The nature of his response to taking alcohol correlated with his dominant mood preceding drinking. This, in turn, was a function of his relationships with several people of importance to him.

The connection between alcohol and anger, therefore, is a social link, not a physiological one. People use alcohol as they use anger: as permission to do something they want. Psychologist G. Alan Marlatt has demonstrated this in the cleverest way: by comparing how people behave when they are *actually* drinking liquor (vodka and tonic) and when they *think* they are drinking liquor (tonic and lime juice). It turns out that thinking matters more than drinking. Men, for example, behave more belligerently when they *believe* they are drinking vodka than when they get the real thing but believe it's only tonic. Both men and women report feeling sexually aroused under the influence of *believing* they are high. And alcoholics who have a couple of tonics, thinking it's vodka, develop a "craving" for more liquor. Clearly, alcohol doesn't trigger some physiologically addictive mechanism or pull a "disinhibition" switch. Instead, it allows people to behave in stereotyped ways in accord with what they want to do and are used to doing.

Marlatt therefore concludes that alcohol itself "seems to produce little more than an indefinite or ambiguous physiological reaction, an amorphous change in mood, at least at the dose levels most social drinkers are accustomed to." What happens next to this "ambiguous reaction" depends on our beliefs about what alcohol does, the drinking environment, and, adds Marlatt, the "personal payoffs" we expect.

In numerous studies of family life, the pattern is depressingly the same: People drink and then abuse each other, sometimes physically, more often verbally. But as sociologist Richard Gelles observes in *Family Violence*, the bond between drink and aggression disappears once you consider whether people *believe they will be held responsible for their actions* if they are drunk.

> A counselor was interviewing a couple with a history of wife abuse. The counselor asked the husband, "Why do you beat up your wife?" The husband responded, "I can't control myself. I just lose control." The counselor, being a very wise person, asked, "Well, why don't you shoot her or stab her?" The husband had no response to that because the only answer he could have given would be "I can't shoot or stab my wife, I might hurt her." He knew very well what he was doing.

"The research shows," says Gelles, "that people *do* get drunk and beat their wives and children, but they are fully aware of what they are doing. So aware, in fact, that people will drink knowing that their inebriation will give them an excuse for violence."

The same may be said for anger. On further conversation with the salesman who thought alcohol "unleashed" his temper, for instance, it developed that the man had a good deal to be angry about. He had been fired unexpectedly, was out of work several months, and then took a job he disliked. His wife, who portrayed herself as the innocent victim of his inebriated rages, had been pressuring him to sell the musical instruments she thought he "didn't need," which he felt were his soul-saving pleasures; indeed, he was feeling altogether bullied by her yet incapable of telling her so. The "few belts of whiskey" gave him strength by absolving him of responsibility for his words or actions. But the reason for the anger was there before the first drink.

In most experiments, alcohol increases the chances of your feeling angry only if you are provoked or have a grudge: exactly the same pattern of results that the noise and crowding studies find. Alcohol can make you relaxed, giddy, and friendly, or abusive, tearful, and sullen, but if "liquor is quicker" it's because we want it to be.

In colonial America, in contrast, alcohol was believed to produce pleasant feelings and relaxation. (The Puritan minister Cotton Mather called liquor "the good creature of God.") If a person committed a crime or became hostile and aggressive while drunk, the colonials didn't blame the liquor; they blamed the person who consumed it. A person's own tendencies, they believed, led to drunkenness *and* crime.

Our culture today accepts drinking as an excuse for ventilating emotions that might be otherwise threatening or uncomfortable, such as sexual desire, love—and anger. And if people get too angry or too drunk, the law, accepting the assumption that they are blinded by passion, lets them get away with murder.

EXERCISE AND SPORTS

We were just getting on each other like everybody gets on everybody else. I don't know if Cliff [Johnson] was in an extra-bad mood or what. But he made the first move. I was in the bathroom and he took my head and shoved it. He wasn't kidding; he wasn't smiling . . . They say you should walk away from things like that, but what are you going to do? It's an instinctive thing.

—baseball player GOOSE GOSSAGE

Trust psychologists to take this instinctive thing into the laboratory, there to re-create locker rooms and exercise gyms. The high arousal produced by a strenuous sport or solo exercise makes emotion more likely—from exhilaration to anger, depending on what the people around you do, the rules of the game, or the provocation. A nudge in the ribs that would be thought amusing before a game feels deadly serious afterward.

Norepinephrine is part of the cardiovascular-response system that regulates reactions to muscular work, and it rises as you begin to exert yourself physically. If your physical endeavors become laborious and difficult, however, epinephrine increases as well. It seems that epinephrine is related to the emotional quality of physical activity, whereas norepinephrine is related to the degree of physical exertion. The next step, to show how these hormones become linked to an emotion, was taken by psychologist Dolf Zillmann and his associates, who have investigated the specific effects of exercise on anger. Regardless of whether insult preceded exercise or followed it, the people who got angry in these studies were those who were both aroused and provoked. But then Zillmann wondered whether people who know *why* they are aroused are as likely to rise to a provocation as people who are unsure about the source of their feelings. If I know that it is exercise, not anger, that is making my heart pound and stomach flutter, will I take your offenses, intentional or not, so seriously? The answer is no.

People who are physically fit recover quickly from exertion: Their pulse rates and heart rates return to baseline much faster than those of people who are less fit. It should follow, therefore, that people in top physical condition, for whom the arousal of exercise drops precipitously, would be less likely to mistake arousal-from-exercise for anger-from-provocation after a six-minute recovery period. And that is just what Zillmann found.

Experiments like this one indicate that the extent to which arousal increases the likelihood of anger depends on the ambiguity or certainty of the cause of the arousal. In real life, of course, ambiguity is the rule. The dentist mentioned at the start of this chapter was unaware of his high residual arousal in the cooling-down room—he was still exercising there, in fact—and as a result, it was easy to inflame his anger with a trivial catalyst. Postgame locker-room arousal also tends to stay high, as players relive their glamorous successes and (unwillingly) their embarrassing blunders.

Running is a good example of the relationship between arousal and emotion, because it is usually a "pure" and private activity rather than a team competition. Even in a marathon of 15,000 runners, 8 will be running for the world record and 14,992 will be running to beat their own previous records—or just to finish. I have listened to city joggers and country joggers alike complain about how irritated they get at dogs who jump on them as they run, slower runners who interrupt their pace, pedestrians, and other intrusions on their solitary pleasure; none of which would be so bad, or make them so cross, if they were not charged up by running. But, conversely, when the running goes well, when the runners surpass their own records, are cheered on by friendly onlookers, or have other cause for merriment, they will feel more intensely happy than if they were not charged up by running.

The specific emotion an athlete feels, then, depends on circumstances of the sport. I think that running has such a nice ambience to it, such good feelings for runners and observers alike, because it was (until recently) uncontaminated by big business, big competition, and big money. It represents an old-fashioned notion: sport for pleasure, not for winning. When millions of spectators turn out to cheer on the housewives, students, veterinarians, bus drivers, teachers, bankers, and other hardy souls who attempt a marathon, they are cheering for everyone; there's no one to boo. And the runners themselves have no one to blame, because everyone wins. No wonder the mood at most races is so cheerful.

This is not always the case, however, at some of our other sports, in which aggression is the goal and anger is the means. Psychoanalytic writers have done a good job of persuading people that aggression can be displaced by watching or playing competitive sports. "Competitive games provide an unusually satisfactory social outlet for the instinctive aggressive drive," wrote Karl Menninger. And Anthony Storr believed that "It is obvious that the encouragement of competition in all possible fields is likely to diminish the kind of hostility which leads to war rather than to increase it . . . Rivalry between nations in sports can do nothing but good."

Unfortunately for this sweet theory, wars are fought for political and economic reasons, not for the simple chance to ventilate violent impulses; God knows the 1936 Berlin games did not siphon off any of Hitler's aggressive drive. There is no evidence that competitive sports displace the "aggressive energy" of nations or of individuals. On the contrary. Anthropologist Richard Sipes selected a random sample of cultures around the world and rated them for the frequency of their wars and the presence or absence of combative sports (sports that involve body contact, the real or symbolic gaining of territory, and any "warlike" action). If the displacement theory were right, the societies that play hardest should be fighting least, since all that aggression is being sublimated on the playing field instead of the battlefield. Instead, societies that encourage violence in their sports are those that have the most wars. In the United States between 1920 and 1970, interest in football and hunting rose during World War II and the Korean War; affection for baseball dropped during war years and rose afterward, as it did after Vietnam. This pattern in no way supports the "aggression discharge" theory. (It doesn't mean that aggressive sports cause wars, or vice versa. It is more plausible that the level of violence in such societies is already high, and is expressed in games *and* warfare.)

In sports as in child-rearing, marital arguments, or tantrums, the same laws of learning apply: When an emotion is encouraged and the rules permit it, it is perpetuated, not "drained." Far from displacing the spectators' aggressive energies, sports violence sets an example for fans:

• Young men were randomly interviewed before and after an Army-Navy football game. (A comparison group of spectators was interviewed before and after an Army-Temple gymnastics meet.) The football fans felt more hostile after the game than they had previously, even when their team won. Watching gymnastics had no effect on spectators' hostility.

• Young men and women were randomly assigned to watch a hockey game, a wrestling match, or a competitive but nonaggressive swimming meet. The spectators' hostility levels rose after hockey and wrestling, but not after the swim meet.

• High-school and college athletes who participate in combative sports are more quick to anger, on and off the playing field, than nonathletes and athletes in noncombative sports. They also respond to frustration with a greater degree of aggression.

• When the Cowboys lose a football game, the crime rate in Dallas goes up.

• Professional athletes in combative sports become more, not less, aggressive and hostile as their season progresses, and during the off-season they are more hostile than noncombative athletes and nonathletes.

• Player violence and displays of temper do not "displace" such tendencies among fans; they teach fans how to behave. Nearly three-fourths of all incidents of fan violence are preceded by aggression by players.

Jeffrey Goldstein, a psychologist at Temple University, has been studying the effects of anger and violence in sports for many years. "The prevailing view of athletics is that they are constructive and healthy expressions of energy, including aggressive energy," he says. "They are said to build character, respect for authority, discipline, and perseverance. This is a view fostered by coaches, the sponsors of professional and amateur teams, and athletes themselves. It is, in all these instances, self-serving. And, for the most part, untrue."

Goldstein is not opposed to aggressiveness per se in sports, since some games require combativeness and competition, nor does he say that watching a terrific football game is enough to make everyone want to kick the cat or wreck the TV. Spectator hostility depends considerably on the eye of the beholder, and on whether the beholder enjoys violence or abhors it. For instance, hockey fans who agree that "fighting should be allowed to go unpenalized because it is an important part of the game" become more hostile and angry after watching a game than fans who dislike hockey violence. Fans who believe that boxers are unfairly trying to injure one another become more belligerent after watching a bout than spectators who think the boxers are just behaving professionally in order to win. In contrast, students of karate—who acquire a passive and peaceful philosophy along with their lethal skills—become *less* aggressive with increased training. "It's not aggression itself that makes people more aggressive," says Goldstein, "but the spirit in which the game is played."

"There is little doubt that many people find pleasure in watching others fight," adds Leonard Berkowitz. "What I do doubt is that this pleasure necessarily signifies a long-term reduction in some aggressive drive. Sometimes the pleasure stems from the ebb and flow of excitement; the game or match is simply an exciting event which is pleasant through the build-up and decline of internal tension." We should not underestimate the importance of anger and aggression as sources of *excitement* for sports spectators. In their essay "The Quest for Excitement in Unexciting Societies," Norbert Elias and Eric Dunning argue that in today's advanced industrial societies, "occasions for strong excitement openly expressed" are rare. But to say that people love excitement, or simply desire to be temporarily distracted from problems and worries, does not mean that sports "discharge aggressive energy."

Moreover, some kinds of anger in sports are part of the fun. You could argue that yelling at the umpire at a baseball game isn't *real* anger, it's *ritual* anger. "Kill da bum!" has a long history, and so does the tradition of having the team manager storm onto the field and wave his arms impressively at the stoic umpire. Some managers put on a full-dress performance, complete with kicking the dirt and flinging their caps to the ground and screaming. This ritual never causes the umpire to change his mind, of course, but it does have an important function. The manager is acting on behalf of his team and the fans, who feel their grievances have been heard, the rottenly unfair call has been protested, and the other side has been warned to look out. Now the game can continue.

In the last thirty years, however, ritual anger has been escaping its restraints. Temper tantrums, racket-smashing, insults, physical assaults, and a general philosophy of emotional release have come to dominate many of our sports. Some fans lament this change; some celebrate it as being more "honest," exciting, entertaining, and psychologically healthy. "It would hurt to repress my feelings," says a runner. "I don't see any violence in two players dropping their gloves and letting a little steam escape," a hockey player says; "if fighting is not allowed then another violent act will occur." (*Another* violent act?)

The prevailing belief that it would "hurt" to suppress anger and that it's "instinctive" and "healthy" to ventilate it confuses two things: the physical state of high energy and excitement generated by many competitive games, and what players do with that energy. John Ziegler, president of the National Hockey League, justified hockey violence this way: "We put men on the ice who are skating at full speed; the use of the body is an important part of the game; the players are surrounded with hard boards and they play at an intensity that, when they're out on the ice, is not demanded by any other sport. I do not find it unacceptable in a game where frustration is constant, for men to drop their sticks and gloves and take swings at each other. I think that kind of outlet is important for players in our games."

Ziegler is half right: The intensity of hockey is high. But that intensity can be controlled and directed in many ways, positive and negative. No instinct links energy with violence, and players have plenty of "outlets" that do not require taking swings at each other; they can play the game, for one thing. Hockey violence has more to do with what the rules (and fans) permit and encourage than with "natural" aggression, and even the law is beginning to notice this. Dino Ciccarelli, a hockey forward with the Minnesota North Stars, was jailed for a day for clubbing a Maple Leafs' player twice and punching him in the mouth. *Time* magazine said that "Ciccarelli was judged to have exceeded the National Hockey League's acceptable level of savagery, not an easy thing to do."

We are witnessing an increase in anger and aggression in contemporary sports not because of instinct, but because of rewards. In many cases, angry displays have become good business for management and successful strategies for players. For example, Kurt Neilson, an Australian tennis supervisor, once fined John Sadri, an American player, $250 for using obscene gestures and language and smashing an icebox with his racket. Some observers protested the low amount of the fine. Neilson agreed that Sadri's performance was "a shocking display of temperament," but then he added: "The professional code is not to punish or to penalize, but rather to move toward a better standard of behavior." Unfortunately, Neilson's action served the opposite of his intention, almost guaranteeing that Sadri would keep up his "shocking displays." Similarly, tennis stars such as Ilie Nastase and John McEnroe have had tantrums that entertain some spectators and horrify others, but these antics continue precisely because they draw so much attention or tolerance. Other tennis professionals, such as Bjorn Borg and Arthur Ashe, control their emotions beautifully and play the game without catharting all over each other or the fans.

Bjorn Borg's self-control was made, however, not born. "Once I was like John [McEnroe]," he recalled to a reporter. "Worse. Swearing and throwing rackets. Real bad temper. Ask anyone who knew me in Sweden then, 10 or 11 years ago. Then, when I was 13, my club suspended me for six months. My parents locked up my racket in a cupboard for six months. Half a year I could not play. It was terrible. But it was a very good lesson. I never opened my mouth on the court again. I still get really mad, but I keep my emotions inside."

For that matter, McEnroe's own famous temper is not the spontaneous, uncontrollable thing he tries to justify. McEnroe's tantrums persist because they work for him—they energize him against opponents, they draw tremendous attention and publicity (even critical attention, to a star, is valuable). But McEnroe can control himself, all right: "Against Borg I'll always behave," he said. "I have to. Yeah, it's not just the respect I have for Bjorn. I know I just can't afford to waste one bit of energy against him. That's in my mind. I know I won't get upset at anything."

McEnroe, in short, knows how to use his tantrums to his advantage and to control himself when *that's* to his advantage. A *New Yorker* writer, Herbert Warren Wind, observed an incident at a match between McEnroe and Vitas Gerulaitis. McEnroe, having noticed a small microphone on the court, hit it with his racket and broke a string. (He and his father had protested the mikes because they pick up everything the players say.)

> Since the umpire had previously given McEnroe a warning to proceed with play or risk the loss of a point, it was rather ironic that under the rules of tennis McEnroe could then take his own sweet time without fear of incurring a penalty as he meandered over to his paraphernalia along the sideline and got a new racquet. *This interruption, which affected Gerulaitis's play unfavorably, actually seemed to improve McEnroe's.* This is not the first time that this has happened, and it provoked, as it always does now, surmises that McEnroe deliberately baits umpires and linesmen when he needs an incident to fire him up.

But there are signs of change in the air. The Nick Bollettieri Tennis Academy, which has trained many stars, including Andre Agassi and Jimmy Arias, emphasizes anger control. Jim E. Loehr, who is the academy's director of sports psychology, says that in sports competition, players tend to respond to challenge in one of four ways. Some withdraw emotion and energy, giving up. Some struggle on with so much negative emotion that they become enraged and ineffective. (McEnroe, say Loehr, was one of the few players who could turn anger to his advantage.) Some become nervous, which at least may spur them to try harder. The ideal reaction, says Loehr, is the "challenge response," which is putting yourself 100 percent back into the game, using emotions in a focused way.

For instance, former baseball player Pete Rose was adept at the challenge response:

It is the fall of 1973, and the Cincinnati Reds are playing the New York Mets, who are only one game away from the pennant. The New York fans are understandably nervous, particularly of the Reds' hit-happy slugger, Pete Rose. Provocative banners have unfurled in the stands: "Rose is a weed," "This rose smells," and other pungent greetings. The team is unmoved by the fans' abuse. "The best thing you can do," Cincinnati catcher Johnny Bench remarks, "is get Pete Rose mad."

The score is tied in the bottom of the twelfth when Rose comes up to bat. After hitting a high fastball over the right-field fence, he runs the bases . . . with his fist held high.

Allen Fox, a psychologist and former tennis star at UCLA, now coach of the men's team at Pepperdine, emphasizes to his players the importance of breaking out of their negative emotional reactions to setbacks and defeats. "I need to call [players] repeatedly on *negative mental states* during practice, even during matches," he says. "We have a fining system during practice: If you curse or throw your racket, it costs you a dollar."

It works. And most interesting, the result of the ability to control anger is that people feel *less* angry, not more. They become better players, not so impulsive. (Recall the story of the irritable Seif children in Chapter 5.) William Wilbanks, a law professor who has written critically about the "I couldn't help myself" excuse, cured himself of his own anger excuses and his old tennis-racket-throwing habit. "That habit has disappeared," he says. "Because I believe I can control my temper I now do so. I used to hate myself for getting angry and that made me even more angry. I lost friends because of my temper and I really thought 'I couldn't help myself.' "

Habits always feel deeply ingrained, which is why they are habits, until a player has a reason for changing them. "I used to throw my bat after striking out, or I'd kick my helmet," former player and manager Joe Torre recalled. "Then, when I was catching, I'd see other guys do it. And it looked so silly. I realized it didn't make anyone a better hitter. The thing to do is to keep your cool."

Dave Righetti, a pitcher who earned a major-league record in 1986 for games saved, has one regret: angrily throwing a ball over the right-field wall after losing a game. "It really felt good at the time," Righetti said in an interview. "But you'll never see me do it again. I set the record, but everybody talks now about my throwing that ball. I think it tainted what I accomplished that year."

Actually, the best evidence to show that expressing anger makes you angrier, not less angry—riles you up rather than cooling you off—comes from the sports in which the expression of anger would be detrimental to players, where it would break concentration and cause poor performance instead of recharged efforts. You do not see many temper tantrums (during play, anyway) in golf, bowling, and chess. Golfers who allow themselves to become upset when they miss a shot don't do well on the next one; indeed, at the 1984 Andy Williams Open, Payne Stewart lost his temper—and lost the game. It's the players with the best self-discipline who succeed. Sandy Lyle once said that the secret of his success at golf was the refrain his father taught him to say: "Tempo, not temper . . ."

The purpose of sporting rules, like the purpose of manners, is to force us to put the game ahead of the individual. Yet by and large we are a nation that celebrates the individual over the team, the emotion over its control, rule-breaking over the rule, competition over cooperation. These values are apparent in the sports we most enjoy and the players we pay most highly. Why, we even call people who question such practices "spoilsports."

Our rules of emotion and sportsmanship are not etched in granite, but they fit the standards and practices of our culture. English rules favor understatement and restraint; American rules support overstatement and release. Compare the BBC coverage of Wimbledon tennis with American coverage, and you will have the cultural difference in a nutshell, along with the consequences of that difference. "The nine BBC commentators," observed *The New York Times*, "all decorous, knowledgeable and forthright, speak as little as possible during points, saving their observations for the changeovers." These qualities and this strategy do not fare well in the land of media hype.

> Geoff Mason, producer for NBC, which is televising more than 13 hours of Wimbledon, called the British telecasts "a little bit sterile for our audience.
>
> "We have to focus on emotion, be superaggressive and get closer to the action," he said. "Reserve and respect are not our way of doing it."

CONSIDERATIONS

The moral of this story is: When you feel provoked, count to ten; and when you are also hot, hungry, exercising, walking along a noisy street, booing the opposition in a crowded stadium, driving a car to (or from) work, or disturbed for the forty-fifth time when you have a deadline tomorrow, count to a hundred. The world being what it is, most of us do not realize how often we are agitated by the background stimulants of our lives. There is usually a lag between the source of arousal and a provocation, and the longer the lag, the greater the ambiguity of explanation. As research shows, when you have a choice between interpretations ("That anger must be my tension speaking" versus "Cynthia is truly obnoxious"), you are likely to choose the human provocation over the physical state. But when you know that your levels of epinephrine will jump sharply because of noise, heat, exercise, hunger, frustration, or crowds, you are better able to interpret your bodily sensations and are less susceptible to provocation than are people who do not know why they feel so jumpy. Knowledge is power—in this case, to decide whether you need a quiet evening alone or a discussion with Cynthia. And it suggests that, should you decide on the latter, you don't do it in the cooling-down room after a vigorous tennis game, or you may heat up the argument.

If we are not instinctively spurred to anger the way rats can be spurred to aggression, then we are offered greater chances of control over our emotions. With control comes responsibility. Questions about the level of anger and violence in sports cannot be shrugged off with "Oh, well, it's a good catharsis for players and audience," and belligerent drunks cannot get away with "Gee, it's not me, it's the booze that did it." We may continue to use anger, or the excuses for anger, as a way to get what we want; but how nice to be able to say, at least once in a while, that reserve and respect were our way of doing it.

7

Shouters, Sulkers, Grouches, and Scolds—Which Sex Has the Anger Problem?

"Come, come, you wasp; i' faith, you are too angry."

—Petruchio to Kate, *Taming of the Shrew*, II, i

"Out, you mad-headed ape!
A weasel hath not such a deal of spleen
As you are toss'd with."

—Lady Percy to Hotspur,
King Henry IV: Part I, II, iii

At a psychology conference in New York City, I spent a morning at a session called "Women and Anger." The topic was popular and the room was full, with nearly as many men as women. The two women who were conducting the program, both therapists, got things started by inviting the women in the audience to complete the sentence: "I get angry when others . . ." As the audience gaily offered examples aloud, the leaders wrote them on a large blackboard:

- don't listen
- put me down

- don't appreciate me
- tell me I'm as good as a man
- put me on a pedestal
- tell me what to do
- intrude on my privacy
- manipulate me
- tell me how I feel
- don't take me seriously
- give me lower pay for the same work a man does

Next the leaders asked the women in the audience to complete a second sentence: "When I imagine being angry directly I fear . . ." And they got this:

- losing control
- losing my job
- not being liked
- scaring or hurting someone
- getting physically hurt
- losing my credibility
- being called weak
- being labeled defensive
- being laughed at
- feeling guilty
- being called overemotional or unprofessional

Just as a laughing camaraderie was building up among the women in the room, a middle-aged man stood up. "With very few exceptions," he said, "the men in this room could generate the same list. I fear losing control when I get angry, and I certainly fear losing my job." "I work in the public school system and I'm angry all the the time," said another man, "but I still can't handle it." Now a third man spoke. "I hate to get angry," he said, "because I look so foolish when I do. I'm clumsy at it." The counterrevolution was building. "You women think you have the patent on not being *appreciated*?" asked a man in the back of the room. "I work goddamned hard every day of my life and my wife thinks she's the only one entitled to sympathy and anger because she's a housewife. She's furious at me for not appreciating her work, but do you think she gives a fig about appreciating mine?"

A buzz of consternation and debate filled the room until the leaders could reassert themselves. "The men have made some important observations," said one, "which should be incorporated into future conference planning. However, as the topic today is *women* and anger, we do think we should stick to the subject as scheduled."

The subject as scheduled included an analysis of sex differences, which by now has been repeated so frequently that it seems to be a set of truisms. Men feel angry; women feel depressed. Men express anger openly; women sneak around and shoot sarcastic verbal bullets. Men are allowed, even encouraged, to feel angry, because it is part of the masculine role; women are supposed to suppress their anger because it is unladylike to display temper. Women fear revealing anger more than men do. (The group leaders' second sentence-completion, "When I imagine being angry directly I fear . . . ," took this for granted. They did not offer the women the chance to finish the sentence "When I imagine being angry directly I enjoy . . .")

The ideas behind the women-and-anger symposium were typical of arguments that many psychologists have advanced in the last decade. "Women have special difficulty expressing their anger effectively and directly," writes clinical psychologist Harriet Lerner:

> Expressions of anger are not only encouraged in boys and men, but may be glorified to pathological extremes. . . . In contrast, women have been denied the forthright expression of even healthy and realistic anger. . . . To express anger—especially if one does so openly, directly, or loudly—makes a woman *unladylike, unfeminine, unmaternal* and sexually unattractive.

And therapist Celia Halas says:

> [Anger] is an emotion that women express far less frequently than do men. In fact, men generally feel quite comfortable with anger,

express it freely, and are reasonably careless about the problems it causes in other people. . . . Women are generally afraid to express their anger. They have been taught that to do so is unladylike. They fear the reaction they will get if their rage breaks forth.

And therapist Elizabeth Friar Williams says of a patient:

Like many women, Peggy had learned to be "ladylike." She had been forbidden as a child to express anger openly toward her parents or to criticize them.

I also subscribed to these arguments without closely questioning them: Which women are we talking about? All women? Middle-class women? Women in therapy? Nor did I stop to reconcile my assumption of sex differences with the evidence of my experience, in which "civilized" anger at dinner parties, "street" anger on apartment stoops or bus stops, outbursts of rage at children, and marital spats failed to occur appreciably more often among one sex than another.

I began to get an inkling that each sex thinks the other has cornered the anger market after I happened on Herb Goldberg's book, *The Hazards of Being Male.* Goldberg, a clinical psychologist, argues that if women had any trouble with suppressed anger, that problem is as rare as a dodo today. "Women across the nation have begun to experience and spit out their repressed anger regarding their old role," he writes. "While women have been quite free in expressing anger toward men, men are largely unable to express their anger toward women, particularly their resentment over loss of control in their relationships with women."

Goldberg's evidence for his assertions comes from his observations of people in therapy—his brand of therapy. Goldberg believes in "aggression training," and his method, which in spirit is not unlike the marines' way of provoking anger in their recruits, is called the "gender club." By this he does not mean a kindly social gathering, but a blunt instrument. Men and women in his group therapy are instructed to "spew out in turn their innermost hostile feelings toward the opposite sex." It seems that men have more trouble than women with this exercise. "Invariably, I've found that the supposedly aggression-phobic and passive female is able to do this quite readily, while the male is very blocked in his expression of anger toward women," says Goldberg. "It is 'unmanly' to acknowledge openly his vulnerability or his anger. Frequently it ties in with the fear of being a bully, and consequently his anger over the situation emerges only indirectly."

What's this? *Men* who suffer from indirect anger? Yes, because "Males learn very early in life that psychologically they will lose any confrontation with a female, because win or lose they will be labeled 'bullies,' " Goldberg explains. "Finally, the aggression and anger toward her that he has denied and defended himself against will emerge in countless indirect and hidden ways in the form of detachment and withdrawal, psychosomatic complaints, and sundry other passive forms of aggression."

What's this? Now it's men who suffer the psychosomatic symptoms? Men who lapse into passive aggression? Isn't this women's turf? Not any more, says Goldberg, who even encroaches on the feminist belief that women have trouble with anger because their childhood conditioning teaches them to be nice, be sweet, and never be angry. Nonsense, says Goldberg. Growing up is a piece of cake for a girl, but painful and difficult for a boy. "The emphasis [in school] is on politeness, neatness, docility, and cleanliness, with not much approved room being given for the boy to flex his muscles," says Goldberg. "From early boyhood on, his emotions are suppressed by others and therefore repressed by himself. In countless ways he is constantly being conditioned not to express his feelings and needs openly."

What's this? Men whose emotions are repressed and who suffer blighted childhoods? Yes, according to men's liberationists such as Jack Nichols, who maintain that women are able to ventilate any emotion they want to, whereas uptight men often suffer "a paralyzing inability to express what they feel," including anger. Nichols explains:

> A psychologist once told me that in his practice he had noticed that many men seemed to lack feelings altogether. On one occasion, he

said, he asked a patient how he felt about certain aspects of his wife's infidelities.

"How does it make you feel?" he asked the man.

There was no response. A bland silence prevailed . . . until the man dazedly admitted that he did not feel much of anything at all.

If you are a man, especially one who is having a bad time with a woman, you are likely to side with men's analysis. If you are a woman, especially one who is feeling dominated by her employer or husband, you are likely to side with the women's view. But personal experience is not the way to settle the debate. Everyone seems perfectly able to ventilate when it comes to personal experience, even if that ventilation complains of suppressed emotion. For example, which of these remarks were made by women?

It took me a long time to realize that sometimes you gotta get angry. Years and years to learn that sometimes you just gotta yell, and let everyone know it's over and *that's it*. Before that, I would sulk. I'd try not to sulk, but I'd sulk. Or maybe I'd try to be conciliatory: "Look, I've really got to talk to you about this."

My fear about anger is that if I let it go, I could destroy you. It scares me.

I'm afraid to get angry because no one will like me if I do.

All of my [siblings] and I developed some inability to express anger when we were growing up, on the theory that everybody will be better off if you can control it. We never shouted back to our parents; it never occurred to us. I find getting mad very disturbing. I'd rather avoid it. When I'm in a rage I don't express myself very well—I get incoherent.

Most of the time I'm not a particularly volatile, angry person. And when I do get angry I don't express it very well. I tend to oververbalize. I get snide.

These are all statements from men whom I interviewed, but they certainly match the female stereotype. The men and women I spoke with differed in what they had learned about anger as children, in what currently provokes them to anger, in their degree of comfort with feeling angry; but those differences were not predictably tied to their gender.

Indeed, of the many studies that have surveyed the kinds and causes of anger, very, very few have uncovered any sex differences; usually a surprised author will add a footnote to this effect and combine the findings for men and women. Given this consistent pattern, it is odd that only a few studies have been conducted expressly on the question of sex differences in anger. Apparently only a few psychologists have thought to doubt the basic belief that men are much more prone to anger than women. But the research that exists indicates that the impressions of clinicians, male or female, simply do not hold up.

That is, neither sex has a "special difficulty" in expressing anger. Many girls are indeed forbidden to express anger openly, especially to their parents, but so are many boys. It may be "unladylike" for a woman to lose her temper, but it is "unmanly" as well. A woman does have trouble expressing her anger directly to her boss, but so does a man, and if you doubt this, listen in to some bar conversations after work one day. People who feel they become angry too readily wish they could control it; people who don't feel angry very often think that they should; and both kinds of people are to be found among both sexes.

In the following discussion, I will be talking only about anger. The sexes do differ in their likelihood of expressing other emotions, notably fear and sadness, apparently because women don't have masculine standards of stoicism to live up to; and they do differ considerably in their willingness to *talk* about their feelings. (Remember how women's social networks and tension-reducing conversations seem to be a strong factor in protecting women's health.) However, as I am about to argue, neither sex has the advantage in being able to "identify" anger when they feel it or in releasing it once it is felt. Both sexes have trouble with anger, and this makes sense, for it is a troubling emotion.

THE STEREOTYPE UP CLOSE

For each of these eleven statements, please indicate how true or false it is of you:

1. I lose my temper easily but get over it quickly.
2. I am always patient with others.
3. I am irritated a great deal more than people are aware of.
4. It makes my blood boil to have somebody make fun of me.
5. If someone doesn't treat me right, I don't let it annoy me.
6. Sometimes people bother me just by being around.
7. I often feel like a powder keg ready to explode.
8. I sometimes carry a chip on my shoulder.
9. I can't help being a little rude to people I don't like.
10. I don't let a lot of unimportant things irritate me.
11. Lately, I have been kind of grouchy.

You have just taken the "irritability" scale of the Buss-Durkee Inventory. Surely, you would agree, men would be more likely than women to say they are blood-boiling, grouchy powder kegs with chips on their shoulders (psychologists never seem to worry about mixing metaphors), and women to reveal themselves as patient Griseldas . . . who are maybe irritated more than "people are aware of." In fact, according to Arnold H. Buss, coauthor of this scale, no sex differences have yet surfaced, on samples of college students and psychiatric patients.

Nor have sex differences turned up in large surveys of adults. In Charles Spielberger's studies of "anger-in" and "anger-out"—based on his State/Trait Anger Expression Inventory, which has been given to thousands of people of all ages—*males have higher scores than females on anger-in* (pouting and sulking, harboring grudges, feeling secretly critical of others, keeping things in, feeling "angrier than I'm willing to admit"). Spielberger has found *no sex differences on anger-out* (that is, the readiness to express anger, strike out, make sarcastic remarks, and so on).

Even among people for whom anger is a trait (a characteristic aspect of personality) rather than an occasional, temporary state, women are as likely to be found as men. Jerry Deffenbacher, a clinical psychologist and researcher at Colorado State University, has developed a successful therapy for people with problems with chronic anger—and that includes as many women as men. Deffenbacher treats men and women who "describe themselves as having a significant personal problem with anger and desire help for it." Males and females are angered by the same types of situations, Deffenbacher reports, and to the same degree, and they respond to treatment the same way.

Other researchers have set foot into the world to interview adults in their natural habitat. For example, two researchers recruited eighty men and women between the ages of twenty-one and sixty, and asked them straightforward questions about a real experience with anger that they had had in the last week. No self-delusions here about being patient or grouchy; each person had to tell exactly what happened, and to whom, and what they did and how they felt. The researchers then compared the men's and women's answers on a total of 128 items. The differences that turned up, they reported, were "surprisingly few, especially in view of the widespread assumption that women have particular difficulties in experiencing and expressing anger." For example:

Targets. Although women are supposed to have the greater difficulty expressing anger to their husbands or lovers or parents, women, like men, were most likely to get angry with someone they loved. Second choice: someone they knew and disliked.

Justification. Although women are supposed to have trouble with anger even when they feel it is justified, men and women alike reported that their anger was legitimate. Both sexes felt entitled to express anger, they said, because the culprit knew what he or she was doing but "had no right to do it," or because the infuriating event could have been avoided if the culprit had been more careful or thoughtful.

Causes. Men and women even feel angry at the same general things, such as violation of their expectations, plans, or wishes; attacks to their self-esteem; someone not behaving "properly."

Reactions. When they feel angry, these men and women behave the same way. Most of them (57.5 percent) said they let it out verbally, and not necessarily in dulcet tones, either. A smaller percentage (12.5 percent) become aggressive: hitting, slapping, throwing something. Men and women were equally likely to take anger out on a third person, to try to calm themselves down privately, or to talk over the incident with the offender.

Functions. Women, who supposedly fear the positive consequences of anger and see only its negative aspects, were as aware as men that anger has social uses. Both sexes cited the same reasons for expressing anger: to assert authority; to strengthen the relationship with the culprit—or to break it off; to change the culprit's behavior in some way; to "let off steam" over miscellaneous frustrations; to express dislike for the object of their anger; to get even for "past wrongs."

Aftermath. Even when women do allow themselves to reveal anger, it is said, they are subject to guilt and embarrassment for having behaved out of feminine character. Well, most women do feel awful after an angry outburst. So do most men. As we might expect from the evidence on catharsis, the aftermath of an angry episode leaves a sour taste for many people of both sexes. About two thirds of the men and women in this study, for example, said they felt irritable, hostile, or aggravated. About half added unhappy, depressed, gloomy, anxious, jittery, or nervous. (So much for overt anger "getting rid" of depression or irritability.) About a third of the group said that they felt relieved and satisfied about their bout of anger. Only 10 percent said they felt "triumphant, confident, and dominant."

There were, however, a couple of differences. More women than men said they were likely to cry when they felt angry, and to deny the object of their anger some "customary benefit." (The study did not include examples of these "customary benefits," but I imagine they include culinary and sexual activities. This is the "I'm mad at you so I won't make your favorite apple cake" approach to expressing anger, and women have a slight edge here.) But on the whole, the researchers concluded, "the women in this sample experienced and expressed their anger in much the same manner as did the men."

Now, consider for a moment the last time that you felt very angry but kept your mouth shut. The person who made you angry was your employer, maybe? A neighbor? Your best friend's impertinent kid?

Next, try to recall the last time you felt angry and spoke directly to the person who was making you so cross. Got it?

Third, how about the time you were so angry you thought you were going to burst with rage, and let it out by screaming or yelling at your target? At your spouse, perhaps? A child? Your parent?

Finally, when was the last time that you were so angry that you took it out physically on your target, say, by hitting, shoving, throwing an object?

These questions were part of psychologist Don Fitz's method of studying anger, a method that generates much more detail than asking people to recall only one recent experience. Fitz, too, was interested in the anger of men and women in real-life situations, and in one of his surveys he gathered 337 adults, ages seventeen to sixty-two, married and single, employed and unemployed, and asked them the details of four recent types of anger or annoyance, from silent to violent.

You might think that most people would have difficulty coming up with an example of all four. You might think that women would outnumber men at the "silent" end, and that men would outnumber women at the "violent" end. You would be wrong. Virtually everyone had a story to tell of each kind of anger (six women and eight men could recall no episode of screaming anger, though). Fitz found very few sex differences in his large and complicated survey. Overall, he said, men and women are equally likely to keep quiet when they feel angry, or talk it out, or scream it out, or even get violent; which course they follow depends on what is making them angry and where they are when they get angry. It does not depend on gender and it does not depend on personality.

Fitz had hit upon the clever idea of asking people to tell him *the location* of each example of anger—the street? the office? home? a friend's house?—and he struck pay dirt. With this simple question he uncovered one of the basic constraints on how people behave when they feel angry, and one of the reasons, I think, for the persistence of the belief in sex differences.

That is, work requires people to "stifle" or "bottle up" their anger, and it does not recognize gender. Men and women who are employed full-time cited work twice as often as all other locations combined for occasions of feeling angry but remaining silent. Neither sex yet feels free to tell its boss to go to hell, however nicely. Conversely, the most popular location for screaming arguments and physical violence is—as you might expect—the home. Especially, Fitz found, for housewives, who reported feeling angry more frequently at home than working wives or men did.

In public places, however, men are more likely than women to express anger, although not to feel angry. Both sexes may feel annoyed or angry with an insolent drunk in a bar, an arrogant maître d', a nervy fellow who cuts ahead of them in a movie line, a cabdriver who overcharges; but men are more willing to say or do something about it. (Not all of them, though. Several of the men I interviewed said they used to speak up to rude strangers, but now that the world is so crazy they fear that the rude stranger will shoot them.)

This sex difference contributes to the popularity of assertiveness training for women, which teaches them how to stand up for their rights in dealing with shoe salesmen, tradespeople, nosy neighbors, and waiters. Assertiveness in the home is apparently another matter. One woman I interviewed illustrated this point perfectly. At work, she is reluctant to reveal displeasure or anger:

> The secretary in my office was the kind of secretary who would give you a phone number with only five numbers in it. She would say, "Mr. HmmJmmm called," and I'd say, "Who?" and she'd say, "I didn't quite catch his name, but here's the number—" and it would be 83462. I'd say, "Where's he calling from, China?" "Oh, I didn't quite get the rest." Now that would make me angry, but I would never dream of saying anything about it to her.

But when she feels angry in the privacy of her family circle, this woman cries, yells, throws objects, and hits. "I never get angry at anyone," she explained, "except my husband, my baby, my sister, or my mother. I *never* get angry at friends or strangers. They might not like me!" Public disapproval worries her. Private disapproval does not.

The public-private difference between sexes accounts for a misleading fact that often turns up in laboratory studies of aggression. In a typical experiment, men and women rarely differ in their *readiness to feel angry*; they differ in their *willingness to express anger aggressively* (for example, sending an electric shock to their partner in the experiment, hitting him or her with a foam-rubber bat). But Fitz observed that lab studies usually involve students who are meeting each other for the first time. Such studies do not simply measure sex differences in aggression, but sex differences in aggression *toward strangers*. To prove his point, Fitz set up one of the standard aggression experiments, this time using husbands and wives. Guess what? The so-called sex difference vanished. Wives were just as willing as husbands to treat their spouses miserably.

Finally, Fitz turned his attention to the matter of personality. Do certain types of people respond to anger in characteristic ways? Of the four ways of handling anger—suppress it, talk about it, shout and yell, become physically violent—can four personality types be made to correspond, say "brooders," "constructive problem solvers," "screamers," and "fighters"? If so, Fitz reasoned, one would expect those who frequently fall into one category to fit into the others rarely. Further, according to popular assumption, women should tend to be brooders, men to be fighters.

But people are not easily confined to personality pigeonholes. They think of themselves as being consistent, but in reality they are not. The four ways of handling anger represent a range of solutions, and the one you choose depends on why you are angry, with whom you are angry, and the circumstances in which you find yourself. Sometimes you will keep quiet for your own good. Sometimes you will try to talk about it, and fix the problem that has caused your anger. Sometimes, when rational discussion breaks down, as with a two-year-old child or a forty-two-year-old child, you will amplify the volume. And in times of extreme rage, you are capable of physical assault. In case after case, my mild-mannered interviewees told me about reaching that threshold:

I'm not a fiery personality. I am not a person who loses her temper. Until I married. I have never been as angry at anybody as I have been at Mike and the kids. I can lose my temper with them *flat-out* four, six times a day, whereas in my previous life I would go for years without losing my temper.

If Kevin were my only child I wouldn't understand child abuse at all. But David has me up against a wall. He's a pusher. Once, when he was about two, he *insisted* that he wanted Cream of Wheat, and insisted over and over and over again, until I made it for him. And then he sat in his high chair and I put it in front of him, and he turned his face away—which meant he wasn't going to eat it. I picked up that Cream of Wheat and threw it at him. I didn't even think whether it was hot or not.

In my first marriage I was very rarely angry, maybe because my word was law. We had disagreements from time to time, but the fighting was never sustained. But my rage at my second wife is of a magnitude and dimension I've never known in my life. She can get to me faster than anyone else.

Now I ask you to bear with me for one last piece of evidence, a highly comprehensive and revealing report that summarized seventy-two studies of adult aggression. The authors, Ann Frodi, Jacqueline Macaulay, and Pauline Thome, concluded: "Commonly held hypotheses that men are almost always more physically aggressive than women and that women display more indirect or displaced aggression were not supported." Of the seventy-two studies, all of which included a test of actual aggressive behavior, fully 61 percent did not find the expected sex differences.

These studies, of course, concerned aggressiveness—a person's willingness to hurt someone else, sometimes physically, sometimes verbally. Anger itself was not the focus, but anger was a central part of most of the research. To see what differences, if any, exist between men and women, Frodi and her associates divided the studies into several categories, as follows:

• Think of a time when you physically injured or tried to injure the object of your wrath. Have you ever thrown Cream of Wheat at anyone? Or slapped a spouse? If so, this comes under the category of "direct physical aggression when participants are angry," and only a few experiments found any differences between the sexes. Husbands and wives are particularly "equal" in this way. In a national-sample study of 2,143 American families, 12 percent of the husbands and wives had attacked each other physically in the past year. In half of these violent families, both spouses attacked each other with equal frequency; in one-fourth, only the husband was abusive, and in another fourth, only the wife was. But wife abuse commands the medical and political attention for important reasons: Male violence inflicts more injury than female violence does, largely because men tend to use fists, guns, and knives, whereas women slap, punch, or throw something. The point here, though, is that women are not "naturally" less aggressive when they feel angry than men are, especially on home ground.

• Try to remember when you physically assaulted someone, although you were *not* angry at the time. Did you feel called upon to defend your own or a loved one's honor, perhaps, even though you thought the whole business was silly? Have you ever hit a bully on the nose, just for the satisfaction? This is called "direct physical aggression when participants are not angry," and here men take the lead, far and away. Just as Fitz found that men are more inclined to show anger to strangers, Frodi et al. found that men are more likely to behave aggressively with them. Many writers have commented on the stereotyped nature of male aggressiveness. When men talk with one another about episodes of aggression, for example, they tend to mention a precipitating event ("he gave me the finger"; "he called me a name") that clearly *required* an aggressive response and virtually bypassed personal feeling. This difference between the sexes has more to do with aspects of the male role than with "natural" differences in anger.

• How about the last time you hurled verbal abuse on the object of your wrath? Insults? Snide remarks? Hitting your target with verbal dumdums? This is "direct verbal aggression," and women hold their own, even on face-to-face insult. The females in these experiments did not suffer a failure of nerve or assertiveness.

"Angered adult women," the researchers concluded mildly, "have not been shown to be reliably more or less verbally aggressive than men."

• Well then, what about displacing your anger on some innocent bystander? That nice co-worker who stopped in your office to say hello after your boss vetoed the best idea you'd had in years? Shouting at the kids when you're really angry with your mate? Berating yourself instead of your friend, when your friend was the one who goofed? Women are supposed to be the artists of indirection and self-blame. But in this category of "indirect verbal aggression," eight studies showed that *men* were more indirectly aggressive than women, and another nine studies showed no differences at all. The researchers concluded that these experiments "offer little support for any hypothesis that women are as likely [as] or more likely than men to engage in indirect, or displaced, aggression."

• How about personality differences between the sexes? Is it possible to say that one sex feels angrier than the other, as a predisposition toward the world? If you believe what people say about themselves, you would conclude that men are the surlier lot. On projective tests, in dreams, in self-reports of their intentions and customary behavior, men come across as fast to flare up and quick on the punch. But if you believe what people *do*, you won't find that men and women differ very much. And when the sexes acknowledge their aggressive or hostile feelings, their general level of hostility, their awareness of suppressed hostility or "hostility turned inward," no differences appear. "The consistency of this pattern of results," concluded the authors with typical understatement, "is remarkable."

One reason for the difference between impression and reality may have to do with the changing rules for women's expression of anger. Francesca Cancian and Steven Gordon have analyzed nearly a century of expert advice on love and anger in women's magazines (from 1900 to 1979). The experts have consistently been lecturing women on how to define feelings of love and anger; when, how, and where to express these feelings; and what the consequences of that expression might be. But the specific lessons changed as women's roles did.

For example, "traditional" advice, prevalent at the turn of the century and during the 1930s, 1950s, and 1960s, regarded love as an emotion that required self-sacrifice and compromise. Sex, the experts said, was unimportant in true love, and a desire for romance and passion was a sign of immaturity. So was expressing anger. Wives were advised to suppress their anger and sacrifice their own interests for the harmony of the marriage, keeping up a cheerful, harmonious front at all costs. "Never criticize your husband," admonished a typical Depression-era essay. "He gets plenty of hard knocks in the outside world without your joining in the anvil chorus." ("The 'hard knocks' that women endured in the Depression were not mentioned," add Cancian and Gordon.)

The "modern" view, which emerged during the 1920s and the 1970s, regards love as a form of self-expression and individuality; it values passion and impulse, fun and novelty; and it considers good sex an essential part of true love. Women were advised to express anger and disagreements, and to confront problems directly. These changes did not occur arbitrarily; they parallel the changing roles of women toward a more egalitarian ideal. "Emotion norms are connected to waves of political and cultural liberation versus oppression," say Cancian and Gordon. "During the 1920s and the late 1960s, when people challenged the authority of the government and other major institutions, emotion norms began to challenge the authority of husbands over wives." The shift from self-sacrifice to self-expression, along with new advice to openly express disagreements and angry feelings, could occur only with the growing economic and domestic power of wives.

Perhaps the persistent belief that women don't express anger well, in spite of the findings that they express it all too equally with men, occurs because many women are caught in a time lag between traditional *ideas* ("be nice; suppress your feelings for the sake of your man") and modern *behavior* ("speak up; express your feelings for the sake of your relationship"). Whereas more and more women are behaving like men in the expression of anger, many experts continue to assume that they are not.

THE PERSISTENCE OF MYTH

I have been arguing that women find it just as easy or difficult as men do to identify and express anger when they feel it. But the zinger is "when they feel it," because men and women do not always feel angry about the same things. They become angry about the same *categories* of offense—condescending treatment, injustice, and attacks to self-esteem being the principal ones—but they often disagree about what they consider to *be* condescending treatment, injustice, or insult. Anyone who has lived through the past twenty years probably has the scars to prove this point. Men and women have grown baffled and angry as definitions of what constitutes a just division of labor in the home and in the work force have changed, along with definitions of the proper role of the sexes. Conflagrations have erupted over symptomatic issues (Is commenting on a woman's looks at the office a sign of courtesy or condescension?) and profound ones (How dare he deny my right to equal opportunity and economic security? How dare she abandon her responsibility to me and the kids?). The clear conclusion, though, is that men and women alike have trouble handling anger toward a major prop of their self-esteem: each other.

This is not the place to list the specific grievances that each sex has against the other, for the results would stretch from Pondicherry to Philadelphia. But it is important, I believe, to distinguish ideological judgments from psychological processes if either science or social justice is to be served. The confusion between them has created the illusion of sex differences where none exist, and obscured the importance of differences that do.

For example, psychiatrist Teresa Bernardez-Bonesatti writes:

Anger toward men, one of the most frequently encountered experiences among women, is thus redirected against the self or their own sex, displaced onto less powerful persons (children) or vented in inimical or impotent fashion. These alternatives are chosen rather than risk the loss of the support and approval of males as well as the concomitant loss of one's given self-esteem and appraised value.

I believe this statement is absolutely true—and that it would also be true if you replaced "women" at each mention of "men," and vice versa. Certainly anger toward women is a frequent experience among men, and many men fear to reveal anger toward their partners to avoid the risk of the partner's displeasure. Psychotherapist Bernie Zilbergeld tells me that, in the couples he sees for marital counseling, it is the men who have trouble admitting anger at their wives.

However, although men and women both react with anger to the usual provocations, they do seem to respond differently, on the average, to "ego insult," i.e., criticism. According to psychologist Mary Kay Biaggio, men tend to get angry, women tend to feel hurt. Women are also more likely than men to blame themselves instead of the other person, and to feel ambivalent about expressing anger (even when they do). Men are more likely to focus on their feelings of hostility (rather than hurt) and to blame the other guy for behaving badly (rather than blaming themselves).

Some clinicians regard these differences as a problem for women. They want women to adopt the male model of anger expression: Shuck that ambivalence, quit feeling "hurt," stop blaming yourself, and give the object of your wrath a piece of your mind. I agree that there are times when that is the best strategy to follow, but why is everyone so quick to admire the male ideal? What's so good about it? Why aren't we trying to get men to follow the female pattern, and become less aggressive, hostile, and challenging? It seems to me that people would be better off if they felt more ambivalent about expressing anger, not less; if they weren't so quick to blame the other guy and thought a while about their own role in conflicts and disputes. Moreover, consider the consequences of telling someone you feel "angry" versus telling the person you feel "hurt." Announcing that you're angry is likely to bring defensiveness and possibly counterattack. Announcing that you're hurt is more likely to bring sympathy and a willingness to solve the problem between you.

Such biases about the "ideal" or "best" way to manage anger influence other perceptions of people's behavior. A therapist who thinks that a client should be angry with her husband instead of herself, or who decides that the client is unconsciously angry with her husband, may overlook the client's actual testimony of what makes her angry and direct her to the therapist's own interpretation. Thus is born the idea that women have more trouble identifying and experiencing anger than men do. You can see the blur of objective and subjective interpretation in the following short excerpt, written by an eminent psychoanalyst, Jean Baker Miller:

> To compound the problem, like many other women, [Beatrice] had great difficulty in allowing herself to recognize her own wrath, much less express it. Even so, she was likely to become furious if the other person did anything that seemed to threaten to alter the bond [between them].

These two sentences utterly contradict each other. The first states the assumption: Beatrice, like many women, has trouble recognizing and expressing anger. The second states the real condition: Beatrice has no trouble becoming furious, and for an understandable, self-protective reason at that. The author continues:

> It seems clear that being in such a position is very conducive to rage. How could she not get angry at that other person to whom she had given so much control over her life?

Indeed, how not; but Beatrice *does* feel angry, and does express it, although not in a constructive way. The psychoanalyst, Beatrice, and I may agree that Beatrice should not be a doormat and surrender control over her life; and I bet we would all like Beatrice to *use* her anger to change or extricate herself from her predicament. But that is not the same thing as suggesting that Beatrice cannot recognize or express anger.

The author candidly offers a bit of dialogue between herself and another client, but this client knew the difference between what she felt and what the therapist thought she felt:

[MILLER]: "How did you feel when you did that?"
[CLIENT]: "Scared. Very scared."

[MILLER]: "Of what?"
[CLIENT]: "Of his anger."
[MILLER]: "That's all?"
[CLIENT]: "I know what you want me to say—of my own anger. But I don't think you're right. I know pretty well when I'm angry; so I can tell you I was just plain scared of his anger."

Some therapists further confuse matters by setting a standard of the ideal way to express anger, implying that any other way is incorrect, indirect, or unhealthy. If they do not like the *way* women (they think) express anger, they may infer that women are displacing or denying their "real" anger. Two feminist therapists once listed what they saw as the typical forms of women's "indirect" anger: "Pouting, whining, temper tantrums, manipulative attempts, 'backbiting,' gossip, sarcasm and anger at other *women* are classical ways women express anger with men."

I fully agree that these are not very nice ways to behave and that many women resort to them. But what, pray, are the classical ways that men express anger with women? Pouting and whining are among them, I promise you, and certainly so are temper tantrums, backbiting, and manipulative attempts. If anyone believes that men are above using gossip and sarcasm to express anger with women, let him listen to men's reactions to women who intrude on traditionally male bastions, such as men's clubs, corporations, and Congress. Herb Goldberg tells us that men are angry with women for being abandoned, frustrated, and trapped, "all of which [they] can't express directly." So they take it out on themselves, other men, their children, the dog.

Therapists may wish that everyone expressed anger in a direct, considerate, mature manner. But they should not err in thinking that only one sex has the edge on immaturity or manipulation.

Actually, as the research amply documents, men and women express their angers in many ways, some direct and some indirect, depending on the target of their anger and the circumstance. Thus if a woman cannot get up the courage to tell her boss that his patronizing remarks offend and enrage her, she is likely to think that she has a "woman's problem" with meekness. She tends to forget her ability to express anger forthrightly to other men who do the same thing, or to tell her children that she feels angry with them. She overlooks the fact that many men are silently outraged by their bosses, too.

Therapists and social reformers who are themselves angry at the injustices they see in their constituents' lives tend to regard actions they deplore as symptoms of anger. Claudeen Cline-Naffziger observes that "Some of the best places to discover angry women are in the usual stereotyped positions":

> Housewives who manipulate husbands and children in order to achieve some vicarious life, secretaries whose system of cross-filing is so complex that only they can trace the documents, teachers who hit pupils with rulers or inflict verbal abuse, and last but not least, lovers in bed who are passive and nonparticipatory. Most depressed, bored, self-destructive, and dependent women are angry.

No; more accurate to say that she would like depressed, bored, self-destructive, and dependent women to feel angry, because, as she herself writes, "anger indicates that action is needed." What her housewives, secretaries, teachers, and lovers may have in common is a lack of power, not necessarily a presence of anger. The two are by no means invariably linked, either; anger as a response to powerlessness is an acquired taste.

The negative stereotypes that promote the belief in sex differences, however, are ubiquitous. An angry man is considered assertive and strong; an angry woman is considered bitchy and overbearing. Both sexes, when asked, will say that women ought not to be the recipients or the instigators of anger or aggression, poor fragile creatures that they are. If the poor fragile creature steps out of character, she may be assailed with a battery of nasty words. The very fact that there are so many ugly words to describe angry women (such as bitch, virago, termagant, scold, fishwife, shrew) and only a couple of mild words that might specifically be applied to chronically angry men (hothead, grouch) is itself irritating evidence of the stereotype, which seems to allot women no choices other than Bianca the Meek and Katharina the Shrew.

These stereotypes draw our attention to the spheres of life in which the *consequences* of anger are so different for men and women: wife-battering; sexual harassment and abuse; discrimination. In such circumstances, women are in a double bind. If they express anger, they risk physical or economic harm, and they are blamed for being "shrews." If they swallow their complaints, they risk continuing abuse and hardship, and they are blamed for being too passive, self-destructive, or weak.

What insulting words and the stereotype of sex differences reflect, however, is not a real difference between men and women in the likelihood of feeling or expressing anger, but a *status* difference. Because women on the average occupy the lower rungs of the social and economic hierarchy, they find themselves more often than men in situtations in which either sex might have an "anger problem." Most people have difficulty expressing anger to others of higher status, especially when those others have the power to administer raises, pink slips, tickets, or contempt-of-court citations. If you compare female law secretaries with male lawyers, you might come away with the idea that women have more trouble expressing anger than men do. If you compare female lawyers with male lawyers, your sex difference is likely to be buried under a ton of torts.

One way to separate the effects of gender from the effect of status is to see what happens to an individual who moves from being an employee to an employer. One man I interviewed, Paul S., described two experiences of anger at work: the first, toward his boss; the second, toward a subordinate.

My boss [at my old job] was a very mean, slimy, political character. I really hated this guy. One afternoon, after a long boozy lunch, I was joking with my secretary about him. He came into my office just in time to hear me call him a horse's ass. That started an argument that must have lasted three hours. The result was that he said if I ever talked like that again to him he'd can me.

You understand I hate hollering. I get very nervous when I have to yell and scream. But when I was editor of [a national magazine] I had to battle nearly everyone at one point or another—each of them was a prima donna I had to shout down once. I remember one woman who had criticized the copy editor by sending around an open memo. I went into her office and just reamed her out. I really let her have it. I remember how proud of myself I felt that I hadn't got my words mixed up.

When Don Fitz found that "place" has such a large impact on the expression of anger, he may not have realized his double meaning. Men and women do know their place in the literal sense—home, street, or office—and they tend to be equally vociferous at home and equally subdued at work (unless they are in positions of power). It's when people leave their "place" in the social hierarchy that the trouble starts. It's when they start getting uppity and rebellious that they invoke the wrath of the complacent and of the powerful.

TWO CULTURES

I am twenty-one, a newly minted college graduate, and my roommate and I take a celebration trip to Mexico. She is blond, demure, very feminine. We meet two men: a CPA who believes in the emancipation of women (he chooses me), and an unemployed bullfighter who does not (he chooses my friend). The four of us have dinner, dance, tell stories, laugh; later, the bullfighter drives us on a tour around the city. Everyone is happy until the bullfighter tells my friend that he loves her and desires her desperately. She politely refuses. His demeanor changes at once: The gentle, whimsical fellow becomes a demented madman. Careening the car wildly along the road, shouting all the while at the object of his lusts, he drives us into the countryside. None of us, not even his compadre, can stop him.

Suddenly he stops the car and drags my friend out by her arm. As she stands, shaking, he drops his pants to reveal his private accoutrements. "Look at me!" he demands. "Can you still refuse my manhood?" Somehow, she can. After a few more tense minutes, the bullfighter shoves her back into the car and takes us home.

The next day the CPA calls to apologize to me. "This is the problem with Mexican men," he says sadly. "We must teach our boys to be hombres, real men, not these brutal machos. Will you have dinner with me?" He is so woebegone that I agree.

The bullfighter calls to apologize to my friend. If she spurned his sexual overtures, she must be a real virgin. He asks her to marry him, or at least to have a drink. She does not agree.

Postscript: I have dinner with the CPA. He attacks me in the street on the way back to my hotel, and I have to claw his face to escape. I get away with one last image of his eyes, suffused with loathing and rage.

Women don't have to go to Mexico to have an experience like this one. The communications gap between men and women is enough of an abyss right here, and God knows the number of misunderstandings and quarrels it causes. Even within the same ethnic groups, men and women differ in a universe of unconscious and nonverbal ways which mark their respective "cultures" as surely as the Balinese differ from the Eskimo.

For example, she says she doesn't want to go to bed with him, but she goes to his apartment for a drink. By this she means: I'd like to spend more time with you; I'd like that drink; who knows what will happen once I trust you and know you better? He figures: She's in my apartment, after all; she knows the game, she's not a kid; she's wearing a sexy dress; she must want me to make a pass. So he does. She turns him down, nicely. He persists. She turns him down, firmly. He is furious: What's this sudden coy act, this reluctant virgin? And she is furious: She *told* him she wasn't ready for sex; how dare he break his promise? Now each feels angry and betrayed by the other, but in fact they have both faithfully followed the unspoken rules of their gender.

Consider next a possible consequence of anger in such a delicate situation. There's the man, aroused for sex and aroused to righteous anger. If the woman believes that he is really angry, if she blames herself for having led him on (as he keeps insisting), if she wants to keep the relationship . . . well, he may get what he wants. (In many cases, she may be afraid of his becoming violent, as well.) The woman, eager not to hurt the man's ego, which she

has learned is a poor and flimsy thing, and afraid of hurting his
sexual equipment, which she has learned cannot tolerate the
slightest frustration without exquisite pain, may end up saying yes
when she originally meant no. Her acquiescence has two results.
It reinforces his anger, making anger an effective reaction to sexual
frustration and therefore a reaction he is likely to have again. And
it convinces him that her original no really meant yes, that women
are sexually indecisive creatures whose refusals are to be ignored.
(Just to complicate matters, some women *are* sexually indecisive,
having learned that saying no when they mean yes is a way to
preserve their reputations while doing what they want.) In this way
an association between sex and anger is established.

Problems of communication are built into the very language
habits that men and women have. Imagine this situation: A man
and a woman meet at a cocktail party and are attracted to each
other. They chat for twenty minutes or so, and as they do their
mutual attraction fades. Although they have been talking about
shared concerns—the cost of housing, good Italian restaurants,
bad movies—he walks off thinking she is a chattering, intrusive
nitwit and she walks off thinking he is an arrogant chauvinist
brute.

What went wrong? They may search for reasons for their
reciprocal irritation without hitting on a more subtle one: a clash
of conversation rules. When females talk to females, they ask more
questions, fill more silences, and insert more frequent "um-
hmms" and murmurs than men do. When males talk to males,
both parties tend to regard any interruption as a challenge to the
speaker, who may then yield his turn or speak louder to maintain
it. When females talk to males, their respective language rules can
create misunderstandings. He takes her supportive murmurs as a
sign of agreement rather than attention, and feels irritated by her
interruptions. She wonders why he isn't paying attention to her
and never seems to support what she is saying.

Although English does not have status markers embedded in its
verbs, as so many other languages do (there are at least six forms of
"you" in Japanese, depending on your sex, your status, and those
of the person you are addressing), status makes itself felt. When

women talk to women in natural settings, for example, they interrupt each other with equal frequency. When men and women talk, men overwhelmingly interrupt women. Women generally respond to male intrusions on their speech by yielding the floor, or by taking longer to reply (as if they were waiting to see if the conversational ball were truly in their court), or by leaving sentences and thoughts unfinished. A woman who does not behave this way is often regarded, by the man she interrupts, as being "intrusive" or "aggressive" or "a chatterbox." In fact, she may simply be following the same unconscious speaking rules that he is.

So of course there are differences between the sexes; it is just that the differences have less to do with innate or even learned ways of expressing anger and more to do with the intricate differences between their cultures and their circumstances. You can see this, I think, in the one setting where both men and women can be said to have an "anger problem"—whether as a minor skirmish in the sex battle or as open civil war—and that is the family.

8

The Marital Onion

"High-stomach'd are they both, and full of ire,
In rage deaf as the sea, hasty as fire."

—*King Richard II*, I, i

My father once reluctantly agreed to be the best man at a friend's wedding. He was reluctant because he feared that the marriage would end in three months or in murder, whichever came first. Still, friendship prevailed. As he drove the bridal couple to the judge's chambers, they bickered incessantly in the back seat about her choice of judge. As he drove them to the train station after the ceremony, they quarreled violently about the groom's choice of honeymoon hotel. My father predicted that the marriage would never last beyond the first night. In fact, the couple stayed together happily, fighting and cooing all the while, until the husband's death, of natural causes, thirty-five years later.

Like love, anger has many guises. The bond between lovers is an odd and magic thing, and if persistent anger is the sign of its dissolution for some, it is the sign of its strength for others. For some couples, noisy bickering and battling are as a gentle rain of kisses, signifying attention, affection, and life; the symbolic meaning of their rage is greater than its content. As my friend Janet said of her parents, who have been married forty-five years:

My father read in the paper one day about an unhappy hippo in a zoo. Somebody got the brilliant idea of putting a goat in with the hippo to keep it company. The goat, in the manner of goats, would butt the hippo all day long. And of course the hippo, in the manner of hippos, didn't feel a thing. It was the perfect marriage. The hippo went from lethargy and torpor into bliss. Finally he was getting some attention.

My father was very fond of that story. To him my mother was the goat, and he was the hippo who protested.

I'm fond of that story too, because it is such an apt and comical description of some marriages I know. In my experience, though, few of these miscegenetic unions are as jolly as Janet's father describes. Usually the hippo complains to you of being nagged and attacked all day long ("Never a moment's peace! Never a tranquil meal!"), and the goat gets you in a corner to grumble of the hippo's thick-skinned intransigence ("I might as well be a stone for all the attention I get! No one in this house ever does what I want!").

"Marriage and family living," says marriage counselor David Mace, "generate in normal people more anger than those people experience in any other social situation in which they habitually find themselves." *Normal people*, notice. Not sick, nasty neurotic types, as she will call him during a quarrel, and not self-destructive, bitchy, pathological types, as he will call her in return. James Averill observes that there are at least four perfectly normal reasons that people feel angrier with loved ones and friends than with strangers or people they dislike. Close contact provides more opportunities for anger; the irritating things that loved ones do tend to be cumulative and distressing; people are more strongly motivated to get loved ones to change their ways, and anger is one attempt to get them to change; and people feel more confident and secure in expressing anger to loved ones.

Efforts to dig up the "root" of anger in marriage aren't using the right metaphor; marital anger is more like the concentric layers of an onion. (The tearful aspect of both onions and anger is pertinent.) Most attempts to diagnose the causes of marital anger concentrate on one layer only: background differences, or the clash of personalities, or immediate issues of disagreement. But for most of us the layers overlap intricately, as you can see in the

example of a couple I will call Malcolm and Moira White. I offer
the candid revelations of the Whites not to play "Can this marriage
be saved?"—in this case, it can't, and it wasn't—but because in
kind if not quantity their conflicts are typical of those that crop up
in most marriages. The difference between the Whites and most
other couples is one not of substance, but of degree: Happy couples
think of each other as nice people who occasionally feel angry.
The Whites think of each other as angry people who occasionally
are nice. "You know how some people have mean streaks?" says
Malcolm. "Well, Moira has a sweet streak."

THE ONION UNPEELED

He says:

She has a fantastic armamentarium of devastating things to say.
Sometimes I will listen for perhaps half an hour before she gets to
me—she never stops until she gets to me—and then it's, "Aha.
See, you miserable, neurotic son of a bitch, why are you so angry?"
And if I try not to respond to her, she'll say, "Why are you giving
up so easily? Don't you want to solve this thing?" After I've been
frustrated and taunted and goaded and I walk away, she follows me,
yakking. She'll follow me through closed doors. She'll follow me
out of the house. "Look, I don't want to fight any more," I'll say.
"Well, *I* do," she says. I think she feels that when I blow up, she
wins.

The point is that I don't think people ought to behave this way.
I think people ought to be civilized and restrained, and if they have
differences they should try to iron them out rationally. If you want
to stay married, bite your tongue.

She says:

I've always had this honesty thing. I don't know if it's just trying to
bait everybody or what, but I have to say exactly what I think. I
remember once before we were married I blew off steam at him
about something that had happened at work, and he said, "I
understand that you're doing that because you're really mad about

the job, and that's OK." I thought, Oh! How grown-up! He doesn't take this personally! He's just like my parents, who know I'm not really mad at them but at something else. How forgiving! How grand! That's not the way he is now, but I remember how impressed I was. I thought, Wow, I can get away with murder, just like at home.

He thinks that I just bait him and want to have terrible conflicts, and that I'm a destructive person by nature. But I think those are two different things. I don't mind a fight per se, I don't fear them as he does, but I don't think I'm either self-destructive or destructive of others. [*Do* you bait him?] Well . . . it's usually not to provoke him, it's to express something indirectly that I'm not expressing directly. I don't just want to make him mad, because he's really ugly when he's mad.

On the face of it, Malcolm and Moira have little to argue about. They live in a cheerful house on a tree-lined block in an affluent suburb of New York. Malcolm, who is forty-three, is from a wealthy family and earns a large income from his work as an investment banker. Moira, who is twenty-nine, comes from a poorer family and worked, until the birth of their child, as an office manager of a thriving law firm. Now that their son is in nursery school, Moira has returned to graduate school for a music degree. Malcolm and Moira travel to sunny islands in the winter and to crisp New England harbors in the summer. But they do not notice that they are living the good life, because they are angry with each other nearly all the time.

The oddest thing about the Whites' anger, they will tell you, is that so often it seems to have no cause. They might be able to remember a precipitating event—such as the time she came home at 11:00 P.M. from a music class and he had left all the dishes for her to wash—but what they cannot explain is why the precipitating event seems to have so little connection to the ensuing argument. Moira says:

Ordinarily, finding the dishes in the sink like that, I would attack him in the morning with something like "You *never* clean up in the kitchen"—which isn't true—and "You are *not* supportive of my being in school or you would be trying to make this school-and-baby juggling easier for me." I would twist the issue. I mean, I don't know why he didn't clean up the kitchen, since he usually does. But then *he* would go to town on my saying he never cleans the kitchen, and then we would get into a "who-does-the-most-around-the-house" battle, which I find a breathtaking, mind-boggling thing, because it happens I do forty-seven times more than he does around the house—hanging pictures, unclogging the toilet, mowing the lawn—and the house is supposed to be his area, man, Mr. Suburban! He needs to have a nice big house but he can't fix a thing in it.

"I can never reconstruct our fights," says Malcolm. "Whether that is because I am so angry that I don't hear anything, or whether it's because I'm so busy fending off all the shot and shell that's coming at me, or countering the flaws in her logic that make no sense to me, I don't know. But very often I don't know what the fight is about, except in its broadest outline. And I always know there's another fight coming, no matter what I do or say." After one of these blowups, Malcolm withdraws and nurses his griev-ances. "I'll be bitter and sour and hostile," he says. "Moira will sometimes come to me, like a repentant kitten, and I know I'm supposed to behave like those husbands on the TV ads, you know, bring her flowers and scratch her behind the ears and flatter her, but I find that almost impossible to do. I find forgiveness very hard."

Naturally, Malcolm's retreat causes Moira's attack. "He doesn't start the fights as such," she says, "but he comes home so angry and he wakes up so angry that he provokes me. Often his attitude sets me off into thinking about some specific thing I can start a fight about. Like a lot of mornings he rolls over when the alarm goes off and says, 'Shit.' Now that's pretty depressing if you're right at his side. He says he doesn't start fights in the morning, but I feel that anyone who wakes up that belligerent has already started something." You can anticipate his version: "I feel that anyone who wakes up knowing that his day will be filled with bitter quarrels can be expected to say, 'Oh shit.' "

What's the matter with Malcolm and Moira? We might start

with their different backgrounds: Malcolm's Boston Brahmin, wealthy, Protestant family and Moira's lower-middle-class Irish Catholic family. Malcolm, for example, describes his father this way:

> Our family situation was generally *Life with Father*. I had a totally male-dominant, Victorian, rule-the-roost kind of father; kindly, well-meaning, by no means tyrannical, but he felt free to fulminate in grand fashion about the maids, or about us, or whatever, and my mother was totally submissive to him. None of us resisted him. When he was at the peak of his form he used to give my older brothers black marks and demerits, and they had to work them off by doing manual labor. There was nothing pathological about him, just occasional explosions. All within civilized bounds. I can't remember anything cataclysmic in my father's anger.

Moira describes *her* father somewhat differently:

> My father had a definite temper, especially if my sister and I did anything wrong or were nasty and disrespectful toward him or our mother. He'd spank us, and yell. When we were little he'd knock our heads together, so the thing was to wear a barrette all the time because it hurt the other person more if your barrette got bashed into her skull. But when I turned twelve I stopped being a good girl. I would bait him, on purpose, to see what would happen, and then I would run to my room and barricade the door. I was terrified that he would . . . [What?] spank me, I guess.

So we have diagnosis #1: a man who hates rising to the bait and a woman who baits; a man who believes in keeping the lid on, and a woman who is always trying to get the lid off. Certainly some of the Whites' difficulties stem from these early lessons in the management of anger. Malcolm had little experience with anger, his own or his parents', and prefers to stay in control. To Moira, control means coldness. She learned quickly that Malcolm's cool shell could be broken by persistent attack, and that once that happened she would get the passion (and attention) that she had gotten from her father.

Of course, the greater the discrepancy between two people's backgrounds, the more occasions for disagreement are likely to turn up. The background-difference approach can be the first step toward identifying the sources of such disagreement; or, what I think is more often the case, an excuse to avoid taking responsibility for one's behavior. After all, short of living alone or marrying one's clone, who doesn't live with someone of different temperament, habits, and pleasures? Short of marrying one's sibling, who doesn't live with someone from a different background? (Even there, I bet those Egyptian pharaohs and their sister-wives had marital squabbles.)

Contrast the Whites' attitudes, for instance, with those of the Ravens, another couple I interviewed who also came from widely divergent backgrounds and who have been happily married for thirty-five years. He is Jewish, she is Protestant. She came from a family of shouters and he from a family that expressed anger indirectly, through jokes and sarcasm. Jack Raven says:

My father never yelled, he never got angry. But he could cut you to pieces. He had a marvelous sense of humor, except when it was extremely snide. He'd make a joke, say, "You'd better save your money because I've seen the way you work"—I had to work as a kid—"and as a businessman, you're a great . . . basketball player." He was saying, of course, you don't know what the hell you're doing with money and you're a jerk. He thought by not saying it that way he wasn't insulting you, but he was insulting you anyhow.

When I was courting Dorothy I saw her yell a lot at her own family. She and her mother, especially, would have screaming arguments. I resolved that Dorothy and I would *talk* out stuff but that we'd never scream at each other. It took me a long time to learn that sometimes she was right—that sometimes you have to yell and let everybody know the matter is over, you've got something to say and *that's it*.

One of the things that got her angriest at me began with a small disagreement. She had said something about a party we'd been to and I said, "That's not the way it happened." We had a big argument about it. And finally she said, "Well, my God, we've lived two different lives." And I said to her, "*Everybody* lives two different lives. I don't know why you thought anything different. Two people living in a house, there's two different lives going on, two different worlds right there. Each one of our kids is going to grow up with a different set of parents. You and I can stand here, looking at the same room, and you'll see it your way and I'll see it my way, and it's always been like that." She was so surprised.

I asked Jack Raven how he and Dorothy got past the matter of their contrasting backgrounds. "We have a tremendous capacity for seeing somebody else's point of view, which is called"—he paused, and smiled—"immobility. When you see someone else's side as well as your own, you don't know what the hell to do! But if you can keep an outlook about the basic ridiculousness of petty disagreements, and keep your humor, you don't get angry."

Another popular explanation of marital anger concentrates on the expectations that people have when they get married. When these expectations, often overinflated at the start, are not met (this approach suggests), anger may follow. The Whites had big expectations of each other, for he left a fifteen-year marriage for a "new life" with her. With the wisdom of hindsight and the practice of battle, Malcolm and Moira can tell you just where the other let them down. She says:

> Malcolm seemed very mature, poised, and good at social events, which I was not. He's fourteen years older than I, and I was only twenty-two when we met. I thought he would be very together, real self-confident, and perhaps could give me advice on what I should be when I grew up. Not that he would *tell* me what to do exactly, but that I could bounce ideas off his great wisdom and expertise. He didn't do anything to help me, as it turned out.

And he says:

> Moira was the first person to generate a deep emotionalism and passion in me. You see what I had hoped—and I realize this is unfair of me—was that somehow the fresh presence would help me shuck off the stodgy, boring, WASPy fellow I am on the outside. I laid that responsibility at her door, which is one of the reasons I

now feel so betrayed by her, having given up home and hearth—
not to say a good deal of money—to find myself in this comic-book,
Jiggs-and-Maggie, dishpan-throwing marriage.

Diagnosis #2: the clash of impossible expectations and unful-
filled dreams: She wanted him for professional liberation and he
wanted her for emotional liberation. Marriage counselors now
confer this diagnosis wearily, since they see the symptoms so
frequently. It is chapter 1 in their book *Marriage as Impossible
Romantic Fantasy*.

Following this "he/she will change me" delusion, of course,
comes the "he/she will be different after we get married" fantasy.
Malcolm and Moira argued as bitterly before their marriage as any
time afterward, but each regarded these quarrels as aberrations.
She thought that if only he could make up his mind about
divorcing his wife once and for all, she would have nothing to be
angry with him about. He thought she was just young and naive
and would outgrow what he regarded as her "college-style bitchi-
ness."

"My shrink," Moira reports with satisfaction, "says I'm very
bitter and resentful about his not fulfilling those expectations."
And what do you say? I asked. "I don't know. I'll take what
anybody says."

The trouble with the Squelched-Expectation Hypothesis is that
any couple, looking backward, can find examples of what they
thought marriage would bring them that it did not. Some of these
expectations may be global and vague ("I expected a continually
romantic and happy life") and others more specific, even if
unarticulated ("I expect that now I'll have regular sex, at least four
times a week"). And anyone, looking forward, can describe what to
expect from his or her future spouse. In a survey of readers of
Mademoiselle magazine, a twenty-one-year-old from Austin,
Texas, wrote down what she will expect of her (still unidentified)
husband: "A life that is strong, exciting, stable, varied, rich,
meaningful, and always honest, both in our relationships with
each other and our relationship with the world at large." My first
reaction was to laugh out loud at this charming assemblage of

contradictory demands (I especially like "stable" and "varied"), and then to muse on the inflation of marriage standards. From a twenty-one-year-old, these earnest pomposities are naive. What will happen when she tries to translate them into an actual marriage with a human male instead of her dream mate? Will she feel angry that he has given her a life that is merely strong, exciting, stable, varied, rich, and honest, but not meaningful?

Everyone has expectations. They are the soul of the human condition, for they reflect the human ability to anticipate the future, to dream, and to hope. The complementary human ability is to bring those expectations into resolution with reality, what folks used to call maturity. Why should anger be the "natural" response to the thwarting of expectations, instead of laughter? It's not the missed expectations that can produce anger, but how you interpret them: as a personal affront, a betrayal, as the Whites do; or as an inevitable, mischievous side of life, as the Ravens do:

> Christ, I was only a kid when Dorothy and I got married. What did I expect? Everything! The Moon! Heaven! Forty-five bucks a week so I would feel like a grown-up! What did I get? Nothing—nothing I expected, anyway. We've had the moon and heaven after all, but not any of my goofy twenty-year-old visions. Thank God.

A third common diagnosis of anger in marriage ignores most matters of background and childhood and gets right to the specific, current complaints that each spouse has about the other—those things that make your hackles rise. The Whites, of course, have no trouble generating a list, from small things (he hates experimental art, and she loves it) to significant ones (she doesn't like the way he treats the children of his first marriage, and he thinks she is unnecessarily mean to them).

In many marriages, one spouse will have an irritating mannerism that the other cannot stand. In Suzanne Steinmetz's study of fifty-seven families, the husbands and wives grumbled about things like these:

> Well, if I told you what we really argue over . . . It's a gallon jug of cold water in the refrigerator in the wintertime. I want it in.

We just argue because he is too neat and I am too sloppy. He is a neatness nut about drawers and closets.

[My husband] has this terrible habit of rolling up the bathrobe and throwing it in the closet. [I like] things where they belong.

In *Behind Closed Doors*, sociologist Murray Straus and his associates asked their interviewees how often they agreed with each other on several marital matters: money, children, housekeeping, social activities, and sex. It turned out that gallon jugs of water in the refrigerator and neatness-versus-sloppiness conflicts are not so trivial after all. What people argue about most often is housekeeping: One out of three American couples (the Straus study was based on a national random sample of families) say they *always* disagree about cooking and cleaning. Thirty percent always disagree about sex, 25 percent about social activities and money (related issues, to be sure), and 20 percent about children. And these numbers do not include the large percentages who *occasionally* argue about such issues.

In my interviews the same pattern appeared. One woman told me that her parents were frequently roused to anger on the question of the dinner hour. "My father was a man of routine," she said. "He liked to have dinner precisely at six. My mother liked to relax, have a drink, let things slide . . . maybe eat around seven or seven-thirty. I never understood why she couldn't make that slight accommodation for him. Now that I'm wife and mother, I understand. But he never did." And I heard vivid stories of anger about the husband's eating habits ("with his mouth open—disgusting") or the wife's ("she holds the knife in her fist, like a baby"); or about his children, or hers; or, very often, about money, as this woman I interviewed described:

Our biggest anger in our marriage, our most intense fights, are about money. We have very different philosophies. He feels that debt is terrific, that money is to be spent, and who cares, it will all be all right; and I feel that a nest egg is equal to security and that we ought to save a *little* money. He claims that he agrees with me, but the fact is that he has lots of debts and it doesn't bother him and it bothers me tremendously. We had a terrible fight recently because I was so proud of having managed to save a couple of hundred dollars—so he decided to give me less money to run the house with since I hadn't spent all he'd given me! He was punishing me for saving money!

Conflict, over serious differences and silly ones, is in the nature of marriage. Some couples regard conflict as an internal problem that "self-destructive" neurotics insist on provoking (although it's usually the other person who is the self-destructive neurotic), and some therapists likewise regard conflict as a symptom of an "underlying" problem instead of as the problem itself. One such therapist counseled the woman who likes to save money that she wasn't "really" angry at her husband's prodigal spending; she was "really" using the money issue as a barrier to intimacy. This is a fashionable but facile argument I hear a lot of, these days, "intimacy" being the "in" word to denote closeness, affection, and trust. (And, I think, sexiness, what with its evocation of intimate apparel.) But few people try to specify what this goal of intimacy translates into—a life without quarrels? If so, you'd better reach for something nearer your grasp, such as climbing Mount Everest. Perfect agreement on everything, like perfect intimacy, is to be found only in romantic novels and heaven.

The modern family consists of several people of different ages, sizes, sexes, and interests. It has no overriding purpose, the way a company, church, or school does, to unite these disparate individuals. (Unless, like many minority families and immigrants, the family must be united to survive in the new culture.) The family has to make decisions on an impossibly broad range of activities from where to live to what to eat. Members of a family have that much more to disagree about than members of an office do, and often with a good deal more emotion.

Membership in a family confers concern over everyone's behavior, not just out of love but identification. People regard their children and spouses as extensions of themselves, and so do not take their actions lightly. "If, for example, a colleague spells or eats incorrectly, that can be mildly annoying, or more likely, a subject of derision and jokes," says Straus. "But if the bad spelling or table manners are those of one's child or spouse, the pain can be excruciating. And if, in addition, one attempts to correct those table manners, dishes may fly." Many American families, moreover, permit dishes to fly as a "normal" expression of anger; and because what happens in the confines of a family is considered sacrosanct and private, families are insulated from the social controls and social assistance that might help them resolve their conflicts. Malcolm and Moira's neighbors do not gather around, like the !Kung do, to make sure a dispute is settled amicably.

And so we have diagnosis #3 for the embattled Whites: an extreme condition of marital conflict that has been inflated out of containable proportions. The Whites, in this view, don't have particularly unusual conflicts, just more of them. Because the conflicts remain unsettled, a quarrel over one issue catches fire, until Malcolm and Moira find themselves unable to keep track of what exactly they feel so angry about.

After they get through listing their grievances, however, the Whites agree that their real problems with anger began when their child, now aged four, was born. He says:

I suppose you could make a case that she has a tough life, trying to get through university and take care of a baby. But nobody will ever convince me that she does. I don't think that a woman who has access to a hundred-thousand-dollar income, who lives in a nice house thirty minutes from New York, who could have a housekeeper all day and all night if she wanted, and who has one nice baby, should be bitching all the time. That might be sexist of me, but I've got my own worries, you know? I come in and worry about running this business every day, and times have been hard economically, and I have an office full of people making demands on me, to say nothing of tough decisions to make, and then I come home to a steady stream of how miserable her life is! She accumulates grievances all day long. The minute I walk in the door I get the pie in my face. Half the time I think, Oh, Jesus, can't I even take off my coat before you start in on me?

Most husbands, I suspect, will sympathize with Malcolm, whereas housewives who have young children may sympathize with Moira:

> There I was, in this pretty but boring suburb, with a sweet baby and nothing to do. I went to a doctor for a checkup, and there was nothing wrong. He said, "Is anything bothering you?" and I said, "No"—and burst into tears.
>
> Malcolm was very angry with me for being unhappy with all he had given me. We had a lovely house, a lovely boy baby, a quiet town, and he took it personally that I felt, "Yeah, this is a nice house, yeah, this is a nice kid, but I feel miserable." I was angry—I'm *still* angry—as many women are, that having a child changed my life so drastically and didn't change his at all. I'm bitter about that and resentful. I know it's a fact of life, and my mother thinks my generation is a bunch of prima donnas to expect anything else. "Oh, you girls today!" she says. "Sure it's a drag having kids, but who did you think would raise them? You think the men will? What do you have to complain about? You have a baby-sitter every Wednesday night and your husbands cooks dinner twice a week! What more do you want?"
>
> I can usually tell Malcolm—when he comes in the door at night—that I'm angry about the baby, not at him—that he wouldn't shut up for twelve hours straight and I couldn't get any work done. But even when I say, "Warning—coming into the kitchen is hazardous to your health tonight, it's not *you*," he will still take it personally. He will still get angry because he feels, Why do I have to come in the front door and be assaulted? I sympathize with him, sort of.
>
> I guess I realize that basically it comes down to your own attitude about these things. If you feel a child gets you down, it's going to get you down. I've used the baby as an excuse to be paralyzed and to bitch, and it's really not that awful.

Diagnosis #4: Well, Betty Friedan analyzed this one in *The Feminine Mystique*: the isolated suburban housewife who feels lonely, bored, and inadequate, and the husband who can't imagine what she has to grouse about.

There are working conditions to a housewife's job as there are to any other occupation, and they can make for contented employees or bitter ones. It is usually easier to see this at a company where you can identify the person or predicament that is making you feel angry: the woman down the hall who stole the credit for the work you did, the man who usurped your promotion, the gossip who won't give you a moment's peace, or a general state of stress and tension that are creating an environment of simmering hostility. Many housewives cannot identify the circumstances that create stress on them; they know only that they feel lousy. Some respond to "housewife's syndrome" with depression, psychosomatic symptoms, crying jags, drugs and alcohol, or lethargy. Moira, being rebellious, responds with anger.

This approach to marital anger regards any chronic emotional problem—anger or depression, primarily—as a sign of stress: a problem of working conditions, not of personality. Moira's unhappiness is typical of many housewives who are socially isolated (Moira has virtually no friends or relatives she sees daily), faced with repetitive tasks that go unrecognized and unrewarded (financially or emotionally), and who lack an independent source of self-esteem (being in school, as Moira is, often perpetuates insecurities and dependence). These conditions can affect people of any personality type, background, ethnicity, class—or gender. Househusbands will know what Moira feels like, and corporate women will understand Malcolm's view. Conversely, women who are happy, healthy, and satisfied in the job of housewife have excellent "working conditions"—they have busy social lives, they have lots of things to do, they get praise and attention from their husbands and friends.

When Straus and his colleagues investigated the factors that are related to continuing rage and eventual violence in the family, they found very few that had to do with "sick" psychological problems or childhood training. The main causes have to do with immediate sources of tension: There is more than one child at home; one or both of the spouses is under particular stress such as illness, having lost a job, moving to a new city; numerous continuing disagreements; and decision-making concentrated in the hands of one spouse. (The researchers asked the couples who has the final say about buying a car, having children, what house or apartment to choose, what job the wife or husband should take, whether the wife should go to work or quit work, and how much money should be spent on food. They could then determine whether a family was husband-dominant, wife-dominant, or democratic.)

The Whites fit these anger predictors closely. In recent years, they moved three times; Malcolm lost two jobs (and quickly got better ones); Moira quit hers to raise the baby. Their conflicts, of course, are plentiful, stemming from religious and generational differences. But most of all, the important decisions are in Malcolm's power, as is the case in most households in which the wife does not bring home income. Although Malcolm said he hoped Moira would "liberate him" from his "fuddy-duddy" businessman's ways, in fact his second marriage duplicated *in structure* his first one. He was again the dominant one. He decided where they should live, he decided that they would move for the sake of his career, he decided when they were ready to have a child, he allocated money. He did so benevolently, to be sure, taking Moira's opinions into consideration; it was just that her opinions had little effect on what they eventually did. Malcolm's magnanimity and Moira's inexperience combined to make her feel helpless to control her life, miserably low in self-esteem, and trapped. The fact that she was trapped in a golden cage didn't ease her ache. He saw only the gold; she saw only the bars.

Finally, consider the possibility that the content of a couple's anger matters less than the meaning and form of their anger. In a survey I did some years ago for *Redbook* magazine, I asked readers how they and their husbands argue—by calm discussion, shouting, withdrawal, tears, and so on. (I found no differences between men and women, by the way, except that women were somewhat more likely to cry during an argument.) The couples who were more happily married did not necessarily have fewer conflicts, nor did they feel angry less often, than unhappy couples; but they spoke the same emotional language when it came to settling their differences. And so we have a fifth layer: as the saying goes, a failure to communicate.

Certainly the Whites might as well be arguing in Swedish and Greek for all they understand each other. "I guess there are all those Italian families that have screaming matches all the time but love each other deeply so it's all considered normal and fine," sighs Malcolm. "Well, I'm truly lost at that." "When we get in a fight

I'm often in a rage, outraged by his inability to see what I'm saying," says Moira. "Sometimes I'd swear he understands perfectly well what I'm trying to say but he's determined to drive me crazy by denying it."

Anger means profoundly different things to the Whites, and they use it for different purposes. Moira likes the feeling of anger; she says it makes her feel hot and alive. It doesn't worry her to shriek, to say anything that comes to mind, even to throw an occasional pan. After an argument, Moira goes to sleep like a baby and awakes refreshed. Malcolm hates the feeling of anger; he says it makes him feel cold and empty. He believes in rational discussion. After an argument, he lies awake fuming and tossing, or maybe takes a couple of Valiums to get to sleep, and awakes still feeling surly.

To Moira, anger means power. It means she is back in control, or at least trying to assert some control. It is the weapon she wields to get her way; anger means strength to her, and she interprets Malcolm's pacifism as weakness. Moira trusts her family to understand her uses of anger; she believes that you should express anger only to your loved ones ("My parents understood I wasn't really angry at *them*"). To Malcolm, anger means powerlessness; it means he has lost control. He wouldn't want to get his way through anger, for anger to Malcolm is a last resort, a sign of failure; he thus interprets Moira's outbursts as a weakness. Malcolm believes that the people you love should be spared your rage.

Diagnosis #5, then: different symbolic meanings and uses of anger. This is not a superficial difference, because even if the Whites settled their specific conflicts they would still become angry with each other about symbolic issues. If Malcolm is feeling angry because his wife won't serve supper at six o'clock, whereas Moira is feeling angry as an effort to assert her dominance, they will be arguing to cross-purposes. They might solve the dinner problem and fight the dominance dilemma for years.

Have you taken sides in the Whites' battle? Of the five diagnoses mentioned—and I'm sure many others could be generated—does one seem to be the major cause of their anger? Are they victims of background differences, parental training, normal marital conflicts, Housewife's Syndrome, or different communication styles? The answer is: all of the above, and none of the above. Onions are not so easily peeled.

In the next section, I would like to consider an approach to anger in marriage that I find particularly constructive—even for (perhaps especially for) couples as embattled as the Whites. It represents an alternative to the "who's to blame," "who started this" debate that traps couples in repeated spirals of rage—a debate that has no answer, and therefore no end.

THE SYSTEMS SOLUTION

> *Mary got preoccupied by problems at work and stopped talking to Dennis.*
>
> *As a result, Dennis felt neglected. And he did what he usually does when he feels neglected: he felt like having sex.*
>
> *But Mary didn't feel like having sex, which made Dennis feel even more neglected. He became resentful and stopped talking to her.*
>
> *As a result, Mary felt cut off from Dennis. And she did what she usually does when she feels cut off from Dennis: she became preoccupied with resentment about his not helping more around the house.*
>
> —from DANIEL WILE, *After the Honeymoon*

Every couple can tell you about some recurring marital pattern that they have developed over the years. They usually don't describe it as a pattern, though. They describe it as "Dennis's laziness" or "Mary's coldness"—the other person's problem which provokes their own (good-natured) efforts at reform. Just to be perverse, Dennis and Mary refuse to reform, so the reform efforts escalate. Before long, the partners conclude that they have only two unappealing choices. As Wile says, they "may either express anger, which leads to fighting, or suppress it, which leads to boredom, loss of love, *and* fighting." What's a couple to do?

The family-systems approach emphasizes the patterns that occur in all relationships, rather than the personality problems of the participants. Were you irritable and reserved with your first spouse, yet remarkably relaxed and open with your second? The difference is not only in you, and not even only in your spouse—the difference is in how you are together. Family-systems theory regards the family as a whole that is greater than the sum of its parts.

Richard Driscoll, a psychotherapist in Knoxville, Tennessee, describes three anger patterns that are all too common in families. One is the "anger justifies itself" pattern:

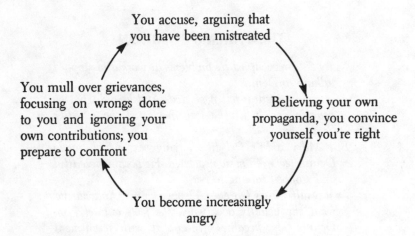

You accuse, arguing that you have been mistreated

You mull over grievances, focusing on wrongs done to you and ignoring your own contributions; you prepare to confront

Believing your own propaganda, you convince yourself you're right

You become increasingly angry

A second pattern, common among people who fear the expression of any form of anger or conflict, is the cycle of passivity and outburst:

Acquiescence, passivity, failure to confront problems

Remorse over outburst; fear of further confrontation

Grievances continue, resentment builds

Angry and apparently uncontrolled outbursts

A third pattern, common among individuals who are all too willing to express angry feelings (such as the Whites), is this:

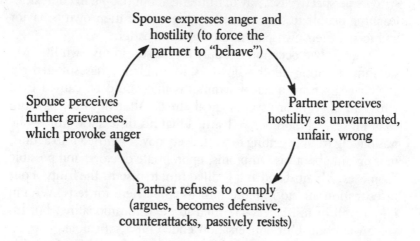

Spouse expresses anger and
hostility (to force the
partner to "behave")

Spouse perceives
further grievances,
which provoke anger

Partner perceives
hostility as unwarranted,
unfair, wrong

Partner refuses to comply
(argues, becomes defensive,
counterattacks, passively resists)

Notice that when a problem is framed this way—as part of a circle with no beginning or end, rather than a straight line with a start and finish—the question becomes "How do we break out of the pattern?" rather than "What should I do about my anger?"

Harriet Goldhor Lerner, a family-systems psychotherapist and author of *The Dance of Anger*, contrasts the systems approach with linear thinking—thinking in terms of cause and effect. "Whenever we have a problem, we tend to look for a person to blame," Lerner says. "Consider the too familiar situation of the nagging wife and the withdrawing husband. The more she nags, the more he withdraws, and the more he withdraws, the more she nags. Now some people might look at that situation and say, 'Aha, she's to blame, because first she nags, gets on the poor man's back, and he has no option but to withdraw.' Someone else would look at the same sequence, saying, 'No, no, you have it all wrong; he started it. First, he became unavailable and remote, and this poor woman had no option but to try to go after him.' "

From the systems perspective, it doesn't matter who started it. What matters is that each person is provoking a response from the other: the more he withdraws, the more she will nag. The problem is not in the specific trait of the individual—she's a "nag," he's an "avoider"—but in their *interconnected* responses. The family-systems perspective is a way of thinking about people in context, of teaching people to become better observers of their own behavior and to see their own part in an unhappy pattern.

I recently had occasion to apply this lesson to my own life. My stepson, a young adult who lives in England, has suffered for several years from a set of symptoms that could be caused by a virus, an allergy, or psychological stress. After not hearing from Matt for several months, we learned that his illness was worse—he was having trouble getting to work every day. I whirled into action, finding out about his symptoms, appropriate doctors, and possible diagnoses. My husband and I called him to discuss the fruits of our investigation and to implore him to come here for tests. We ran into a wall of resistance. He tried to be accommodating, but his voice was cool. Our conversation ended on a sour note.

My first reaction was to feel angry, and to blame Matt for being stubborn and ungrateful. After all my efforts! I was only trying to help! But by looking at the encounter through a systems lens, I could see how my behavior provoked his. There I was, dashing to the rescue. Everything I said implied that he was an incompetent child, that English medicine was inept, and that only by his coming here would we solve the puzzle of his illness.

So I called him back. "Matt," I said, "I'm sorry about that conversation and apologize for it. It must have sounded as if we didn't trust your judgment. Naturally, we were and are worried about you. So let's leave it at this: If you ever want to come here, if you ever want us to find out what doctors here have to say about your symptoms, we'll be happy to help." The relief in Matt's voice was palpable. "Thank you so much for saying that," he said. "I didn't want to disappoint you by saying I couldn't come over right now, but the fact is that establishment doctors haven't helped me and now I'm seeing a homeopath. It might work or it might not, but I'd like to follow this program though to its end."

The first step in breaking family patterns is to drop the fantasy of rescuing or changing one another. In family-systems language, what usually happens in the course of an ongoing difficulty is that one partner becomes *overfocused* on the other, and the other is *underfocused* on himself. Suppose the husband has a problem— he's out of work and won't look for a job. The wife, who is naturally sympathetic, becomes more and more focused on him and his problem, trying to help: Here's a counselor he can see, here's a book to read, and so forth. Yet the more he resists, and the longer he sits moping around the house, the angrier she becomes with his "laziness" and "lack of responsibility." Her sympathetic efforts to help, after a while, alternate with outbursts of anger, but neither approach gets him to budge.

The irony is that the more the wife focuses on his problem, the less motivation and competence he will feel in finding a solution. She may not see her own part in it. "Overfocused people tend to feel very self-righteous in their efforts to help the other," says Lerner. But in the course of helping they stop focusing on their own problems or asking the spouse for help. They excuse the "suffering spouse" from other responsibilities. Eventually, the relationship becomes polarized between the competent helper and the incompetent helpee. The more one spouse tries to change the other, the more deeply involved he or she becomes in supporting the status quo.

The second step in breaking the pattern, therefore, is admitting that what one is doing to change the other person *isn't working.* The wife has talked to her husband incessantly, she has clipped eight thousand job offerings from the paper, and he still doesn't have a job. Now the wife can put her energy into identifying her own options, given that he is the way he is. If she decides to stay with him, she must specify to them both what she needs to do so that she will not feel bitter about his behavior. "I can tolerate your not working," she might tell him, "but I can't continue to support you in the old way. So, in order to feel good about our relationship, I'm keeping a separate bank account and taking my own vacations." Or she might say, "I can see I'm not being as helpful as I'd hoped. I'm out of solutions. What ideas do you have for activities that will make you feel better?" "The virtue in seeing your own part in a system," says Lerner, "is that you have new options, more control."

The antidote to overinvolvement, however, is not *un*involvement. The middle ground is to be able to express love and concern, while acknowledging that the spouse must solve the problem him- or herself and that there are limits to what one is prepared to do. "I had a client once whose wife became terribly depressed and eventually wouldn't get out of bed," says Lerner. "By not setting limits of what he would tolerate, and by overfocusing on her unhappiness, he allowed her to get worse and worse. In contrast, another client of mine was in the same situation, with a depressed wife who got into bed. He looked after her for three weeks, and then said, kindly: 'You know, I can't live like this. It's making *me* depressed, unable to continue, and pretty soon I'll be in that bed with you. Then what will we do?' By telling his wife that he would not accept her depression, and by turning the situation away from blaming her to setting up a problem for them both to solve, he helped them both."

When a couple like the Whites is immersed in a cycle of repeated arguments that lead nowhere, the problem is not "expressing" anger or even "suppressing" it. Their problem is how to solve the problem that causes the repeated arguments, and to do this, both must learn to specify clearly what their real needs, responsibilities, and desires are. By blaming each other, the Whites avoided this difficult task. Lerner offers an excellent case study that I think highlights this point very well.

Dianna, age thirty, comes to therapy complaining of "depression." She feels her life is "going nowhere," and she is bored by her substitute-teaching job. At the same time, she feels bitter and resentful toward her husband, Jonathan, who adamantly refuses to "allow" Dianna to get professional training to improve her career options until their daughter is old enough for school. They repeatedly quarrel about Dianna's wish to go to graduate school, and about other issues too, but the fights are unproductive. Dianna feels dominated and controlled by Jonathan, and helpless to change.

A typical battle scene, Lerner describes, would unfold as follows: Dianna complains of her unhappiness at work and her wish to get an advanced degree. Jonathan replies that she should wait until their child is in school, "for Cara's sake." Dianna then cites chapter and verse of evidence from child psychologists, in an attempt to prove that happy mothers raise happier children. Jonathan clings even more tenaciously to his opinion that Cara would suffer. The argument becomes more and more intense and angry, until both withdraw in sullen resentment. After a few weeks of cooling off, they repeat the entire discussion.

"Venting anger is not much different from staying silent if our expressions of anger serve to block change rather than facilitate it," Lerner observes. "Like many women, Dianna was fighting in a manner that actually protected her husband and the status quo of their relationship. In a nutshell, Dianna was putting her emotional energy into trying to change a husband who did not want to change. In trying to do the impossible, she relinquished the power that she did have—the power to change her own self and to take a new and different action on her own behalf."

Efforts to change oneself mean that others will have to change too, and this is often scary and troubling to others—even when the change will lead to better relations all the way around. This is why so many people prefer the pain they have to the possibility of pleasure. Spouses don't say, "I'm so happy, dear, that you're changing all the rules of our marriage and making your own decisions." Any change within a system produces countermoves from the other participants, in which they'll try to get you to return to the familiar old ways. They may raise the ante: If you were fighting once a week, they'll try to provoke a fight three times a week.

By identifying the role and *purpose* of anger, the systems approach helps couples understand why they put up with horrible, unproductive quarrels: The anger might be protecting them from even scarier realizations about themselves and their marriage. For example, to return to Lerner's case, Jonathan's anger allows him to avoid his real concerns: "I am scared and worried about your going back to school. What if you like it too much? What if you meet someone else? What if you stop looking after me?" And Dianna's willingness to participate in the same old fights protects her from facing anxiety-arousing issues: "How will it affect my marriage if I become a stronger, more assertive person? Who has the power here? What are my own fears about returning to school? If my choice is to save my marriage or save myself, which do I choose?"

Dianna had to learn first to stop trying to get her husband to agree with her. "It is Dianna's job to clarify her own thoughts and feelings, and to behave in a manner that is congruent with her convictions and beliefs," Lerner says. "It is *not* her job to change Jonathan or make him see things her way. The more she tries, the more she will ensure that nothing will change."

Second, Dianna learned how to circumvent the angry arguments altogether. "Suppose that Dianna were to approach Jonathan when things were relatively calm between them," says Lerner, "and tell him the following, without apology or blame: 'Jonathan, I know you don't approve of my going back to graduate school at this time and I understand that you are concerned that Cara will suffer. Nonetheless, I've decided that I need to do this for myself and I plan to go ahead.' " Naturally, Jonathan will protest and offer up all the old arguments about Cara's well-being. *Dianna must refuse to take the bait*, Lerner emphasizes. "She might say: 'Perhaps you're right about Cara or perhaps you're wrong. I can't know for sure. What I do know is that I want to go to graduate school at this time, and if I put it off, I will end up feeling bitter and resentful. I am hoping for your support, but I certainly understand that you may see things differently."

Dianna must stand behind her decision with firmness and dignity, without anger or belligerence toward her husband (and perhaps with some empathy for his unexpressed worries). She must not try to change his feelings, for the simple reason that she can't: He is worried about future possibilities, and neither of them is a fortune-teller. The best they can do is strike a bargain, in which each partner acknowledges the other's concerns while, when necessary, agreeing to disagree. In Dianna's case, Jonathan may disagree with her decision about school, but perhaps they can agree on an intervening bargain on how to balance her schoolwork and Cara's care.

"Bargaining may be the most difficult step in breaking angry patterns," observes Richard Driscoll. "It requires both that we are clear about what we want, and that we listen to what someone else wants. And on those occasions when things do not instantly fall into place, which means just about always, it requires that we remain firm in our requests but friendly in our attitudes."

Before a person can change the rules of a relationship, Lerner believes, she or he must have a "bottom line," a standard of the other person's behavior that is ultimately unacceptable. And the person must have the self-confidence to maintain that standard in the face of pressures to relent. Setting a true bottom line is particularly difficult for women. "Instead, many women keep reacting to what the other person does or says, or they make idle threats they have no intention of keeping—'if you are late one more time, we're through,' " Lerner observes. "The ability to say *this far, and no farther* requires that a woman have a secure sense of herself."

Some people object to the systems approach precisely because it does not seek to apportion blame, and because it describes each participant's role in an interconnected network. This idea implies, critics say, that a woman who is beaten by her husband is as much to "blame" for his behavior as he is. It reinforces the view of woman as masochist: If she stays in a bad relationship, she must enjoy its pain. And it obscures the critical moral line between victimizer and victim.

I know of no systems therapist who would endorse any of these inferences. On the contrary, systems therapists want victims to become empowered enough to break away from the psychological and physical bullying that victimizers apply so freely. They want victims to understand the essential fact about any relationship pattern: that they have choices, and that they have the power to break out of the pattern. Far from blaming victims, I think, the systems approach helps them correctly identify solutions. It is not masochism that keeps women (or men) trapped in destructive patterns, but the fear of greater pain or loss if they change the pattern or leave. (Recall the Hokanson study on page 132, which showed that people can acquire self-defeating practices if these reduce their own anxiety or help them avoid hostility or injury from others.) Once "victims" understand why they are so overfocused on the relationship, even at the expense of their own happiness and self-esteem, they can begin to take the steps to free themselves.

On the other hand, it in no way excuses the behavior of the spouse who is abusive to observe that the abused spouse plays a role in the pattern. In many couples, an episode of verbal or physical violence is followed by tearful and remorseful apologies, and loving concern. The abused spouse forgives, and the cycle starts over again. And it surely will start over, because the violent episode has been rewarded with the affection that the couple should have been giving one another to start with.

Treatment programs for abusive couples who cannot manage their feelings of anger are generally based on three principles:

- Abusiveness is a mutual problem, part of the family system. One spouse may be abusive but the other may be rewarding it.
- Abusiveness is learned. It is not a personality defect or an illness, it is not as "automatic" as it may feel at the time, and it can be unlearned.
- Abusiveness is an effort to solve a problem, and other, more successful ways of solving problems can be learned.

For example, clinical psychologist Gayla Margolin teaches couples how to identify the specific things they do that set each other's teeth on edge. Specificity is the key. In one couple she treated, the husband would provoke his wife's anger by saying "Leave me alone" impatiently, hanging his head, or walking out in the middle of a discussion. She would provoke his by an unpleasant grimace, bringing up past matters, analyzing his behavior superciliously in the language she had learned in years of therapy, and raising her voice.

Next, the couple establishes certain ground rules (Lerner's "bottom line") for arguing, such as: "If you hit me, I leave this marriage for good." The rules must then be obeyed.

Third, the couple develops a plan to break up the established habit of conflict: *Nip anger in the bud. Disengage immediately from the argument.* In other words, *Shut your mouth.* You might say, "I'm starting to feel angry," or "This is becoming a fight," or some mutually recognized funny word or endearment, and *stop.* Then the couple agrees to return to the argument when both are feeling calm, a couple of hours later or the next day, and continue to discuss the issues.

Fourth, the couple learns to fix their habitual ways of thinking about the relationship and their anger. "You won't love me if I disagree with you" has got to go, says Margolin, and so does "It is best for me to hide my feelings and go along as though nothing is wrong." A common error, one that turned up in my interviews too, is persisting in an angry argument when it should be left for later. "The future of our relationship rests on being able to resolve this argument right now," runs this fallacy. No, the future of the relationship rests on the confidence that there will *be* a future, and giving both partners a cooling-down time.

Finally, people need to know not only *how* to argue, but *when* to argue. "You can't imagine the number of people who decide to 'express their feelings' on the way to a party, or when one partner has to leave in ten minutes for the dentist, or when the kids are underfoot," says psychotherapist Bernie Zilbergeld. "Then they're surprised when the partner blows up, or the evening is ruined, or the partner leaves or the kids interrupt in the middle of an important revelation. If you want to discuss a problem, choose a good time—when you're not angry, and have the time to talk about it."

Once old angry habits are changed, a couple can turn their attention to the problems they are having and try other ways of solving them than by shouting. Margolin teaches couples "how to express their dissatisfactions in a constructive, nonblaming manner rather than acting upon their anger with accusations, threats, and violence." She teaches them ways to solve some differences and live with others. She teaches them how to be polite.

IN PRAISE OF CIVILITY

I cannot count the number of times that married couples tell me: "I've got all this anger bottled up and I need to get it out." Sure you do, and I'll be happy to cater the divorce.

—BERNIE ZILBERGELD,
psychotherapist in Oakland, California

Anger is a sign of attachment, of connection. The attachment may be ambivalent, unhappy, or begrudging, as the Whites' is, or strong and thriving, as the Ravens' is. But people rarely feel angry with others who are of no consequence to them. The opposite of love, after all, is not anger, but indifference.

The actress Lynn Fontanne once said that the secret of her successful marriage and acting partnership with Alfred Lunt was that they were never impolite to one another. I can't imagine a more eloquent summation of the benefits of civility. Civility is not, mind you, the same as silence. It makes no sense to behave like writer Judith Thurman's father, who "ate a Danish for dessert most nights of his married life without mentioning to my mother he didn't like Danish." This is not being polite, this is being silly. But you can have a rip-roaring argument about Danishes, dinner, or any of the 412 conflicts that bother the Whites *without being rude*.

Managing anger in marriage depends only in part on making an accurate diagnosis of the reasons for feeling angry. Naturally it behooves you to figure out whether you are really angry about how she squeezes the toothpaste or about his making you move your entire household twice in one year, with no say in the matter. But for most of us, most of the time, there isn't a single diagnosis; there are many, intersecting, with one or another being more important this week and not so important next week. For most of us, most of the time, differences aren't "settled," once and for all; they just lurk there, waiting for the chance to wreak mischief and misunderstanding.

Couples who are not defeated by rage and the conflicts that cause it know two things: when to keep quiet about trivial angers, for the sake of civility, and how to argue about important ones, for the sake of personal autonomy and change. Malcolm tends to commit the former error, brooding and sulking for days in the name of manners; Moira commits the latter, shouting and inflicting wounds in the name of honesty. A wife may have every sympathy with a husband who stifles his grievances for the sake of marital harmony, but she may be forgiven for anger when he complains that she can't read his mind. A husband may have every sympathy with an anguished wife, sharing her resentment that society does not give equal breaks and equal power to women; but he may be forgiven for tiring of abusive rages.

As the catharsis studies convincingly show, sometimes the best thing you can do about anger is nothing at all. Let it go, and half the time it will turn out to be an unimportant, momentary shudder, quickly forgotten. The other half of the time, keeping quiet gives you time to cool down and decide whether the matter is worth discussing or not. As Moira and Malcolm could tell you, expressing anger *while you feel angry* nearly always makes you angrier. Recall Moira's description of a typical argument, which quickly advances into blind fury and unintended, unfair accusations ("You *never* do anything around the house"), with grievances tumbling over each other for priority. Actually, the Whites learned this by themselves during a two-week truce when they agreed they would not fight. They loved the resulting tranquillity and found, to their amazement, that they actually felt less angry with each other when they forced themselves to suppress their anger. Unhappily, they did not know how to take the next step and learn to negotiate differences, and so the truce did not last.

Because most couples are not experienced labor negotiators or diplomats, some of them, like the Whites, use angry abusiveness to get their way; it may be the only way they know. Couples like the Whites will not be helped much by therapists who encourage them to recall childhood memories or to practice "aggression-release" exercises. But therapists who understand the benefits of civility and the social uses of anger can be of practical and immediate assistance.

In the sixteenth century the essayist Montaigne wrote that "there is no passion that so shakes the clarity of our judgment as anger." Yet Montaigne's own judgments were perfectly clear, and he was a skilled practitioner of rage. People should "husband their anger and not expend it at random," he advised, "for that impedes its effect and its weight. Heedless and continual scolding becomes a habit and makes everyone discount it." Nor should we express anger alone, "in the air"; anger should reach its intended target. Montaigne especially disliked shouters, those who "go after their own shadow, and carry this tempest into a place where no one is punished or affected by it, except someone who has to put up with the racket of their voice." Montaigne would surely have been baffled by modern couples who, in the sweet name of honesty, confide every irritating act the other commits, "expending" anger every chance they get. One man I interviewed, a thirty-one-year-old singer, described how he had been "cured" of his anger problem:

> In Gestalt therapy they taught me to express my anger at once and not let it fester. I used to be a person who never expressed anger until I felt it was legitimate to do so—I'd only present my grievances if I felt I had a case for complaint. Now I don't worry about legitimacy; if I'm pissed off, I say so. It's usually a matter of hurt feelings—"Why did you look at me that funny way? Why did you ignore me?"

The singer also reported that he and his lover fight and snipe at each other frequently, but he doesn't see a connection between his newfound readiness to sound off and the emotional reverberations the sound produces. In contrast, here's Jack Raven:

> What I hate about the Me generation, or the Me psychosis, or whatever the hell it is, is the fact that you're supposed to exorcise whatever it is that's bothering you, but no one tells you to worry about getting angry at the people you *like*—who can be destroyed so easily by your so-called revelations. The relationship can be ruined. I get angry at the simplistic notion that you should get angry without taking other people's feelings into account.

Which attitude would you rather live with?

In the final analysis, managing anger depends on taking responsibility for one's emotions and one's actions: on refusing the temptation to remain stuck in blame and fury or silent resentment. Once anger becomes a force to berate the nearest scapegoat instead of to change a bad situation, it loses its credibility and its power. It feeds only on itself. And it sure as sunrise makes for a grumpy life.

9

A Rage for Justice

*Justice is my being allowed to do whatever I like.
Injustice is whatever prevents my doing so.*

—SAMUEL JOHNSON

*People are, if anything, more touchy about being
thought silly than they are about being thought unjust.*

—E. B. WHITE

Saint Thomas Aquinas imagined that people feel angry only when
they are offended by their inferiors: "Thus a nobleman is angry if
he be insulted by a peasant; a wise man, if by a fool; a master, if
by a servant." If the nobleman insults the peasant, on the other
hand, "anger does not ensue, but only sorrow." The irritating
habit of modern peasants to react to insult with anger instead of
sorrow, is, of course, the story of revolution.

Yet Aquinas was making an important point about the power of
authority to establish legitimacy, and legitimacy is death to anger.
For, in fact, most peasants, fools, and servants have not protested
the injustices done them, nor even regarded them as injustices.
The sense of injustice is made, not born, and although we think of
anger as the handmaiden of justice, it is not its inevitable
companion. Anger depends on our perceptions of a situation,
perceptions of injustice included.

Many people believe that if they feel angry now about something, they must always have felt that way, although the anger may previously have been repressed, distorted, or displaced. A woman who feels angry with herself for having dropped out of medical school for marriage twenty years earlier wonders what she did with the anger she assumes she felt at the time. A man who, as an adult, feels angry with his parents for making him eat all the food on his plate when he was young thinks he felt as angry when he *was* young. The ex-medical student and the little boy may truly have felt angry in the past, but it's more likely that they were just going along with the times, following the rules, with perhaps a squawk or two of protest. Not only do people attribute their emotions backward to what they felt years ago, they attribute them sideways, to what they think others should be feeling. Some attribute anger to women or minorities of previous generations and even centuries. When they wonder why a battered woman stays with a vicious husband, blaming herself instead of him for her abuse, or why a slave does not rebel, or why the untouchables accept their caste of degradation, they are assuming that these sufferers interpret the situation as they do—and see a way out of it, as well.

The forces that keep people in their places, if not entirely contented then at least not angry, are not always as irrational as they seem. The decision that a particular situation is unjust must overcome a few psychological and practical hurdles, and so must the next decision: that the injustice merits anger instead of apathy. The question, therefore, is not simply "Why do people become angry?" but why they do not.

THE RATIONALIZING SPECIES

Golfer Tom Watson seemed to be cruising to an easy victory in the $300,000 Byron Nelson Classic years ago, when the weather and his luck turned suddenly against him. From a comfortable score of eight under par he dropped to four over par. "It doesn't upset me," Watson told a reporter. "Golf is not a fair game."

Life is not a fair game, either, but people have a curious capacity to behave as if it were. We tend to equate what is with what ought to be, and react with outrage to attacks on our way of doing things. We accept injustices more readily when they are built into the system, because the roles we play seem so normal and inevitable. For example, we take it for granted that it is within a boss's right to set working hours; but Eskimo workmen in factories in Alaska found it hilarious that the white men responded so obediently to whistles summoning them to stop work or start it. To the Eskimo, the only authority that determines when men shall work is the tide. Yet American workers would find it just as hilarious, to say nothing of an infringement on their liberty, if they had to sing the company song in unison every morning, as many Japanese workers do, without question or anger.

What happens when people's faith in the legitimacy of the system is put to the test? Usually, it is the test that fails. The very organization of our mental faculties seems designed to screen out information we don't want to hear, information that is at odds with our basic beliefs. Psychologist Anthony G. Greenwald calls the self "the totalitarian ego," arguing that the ego organizes its knowledge, perceptions, and memory in predictably biased ways that are designed (like totalitarian governments) primarily to protect its organization.

The ego, says Greenwald, is a "self-justifying historian" which seeks only that information that agrees with it, rewrites history when it needs to, and does not even see the evidence that threatens it. The organization of knowledge in the mind is like a library system. Our built-in biases allow us to retrieve any specific information that we need rapidly; once we make a commitment to a particular cataloging system (say, a conservative ideology or a religious framework of belief), we spend more time maintaining the system than revising it. The biases of the mind persist because they work: They preserve self-confidence, they keep our mental organization in order, and they keep us persevering toward our goals, whatever those may be. The mind's cautiousness about accepting new ideas may seem foolhardy in a world bursting with innovation and discovery, but (at least until recently) it has been an adaptive success for our species. The flash of anger that people may feel when they are threatened with conflicting information is the mind's way of protecting its organization. "My mind's made up—don't confuse me with the facts" seems to have been an oddly successful strategy in the evolution of the brain. After all, if we kept "changing our minds" with each new bit of experience and observation, we would never know how to behave, what to think, or why we were working so hard for a future reward. Excessive "mind-changing" produces indecisiveness and anxiety.

The structure of the "totalitarian ego," which can mobilize considerable anger to protect itself and its beliefs, may actually be necessary to our mental health. After reviewing years of research, health psychologists Shelley Taylor and Jonathon Brown concluded that well-being virtually depends on the illusions of "overly positive self-evaluations, exaggerated perceptions of control or mastery, and unrealistic optimism." These illusions are both normal and necessary for the usual criteria of mental health: the ability to care about others, the ability to be contented, and the ability to work productively. In fact, the people who score *highest* on tests of self-deception (for example, who deny threatening but universal feelings, such as ever having felt guilty) score the *lowest* on measures of psychopathology and depression!

When a traumatic event occurs that cannot be ignored, the result is, literally, disillusion. Some victims see the world as less benevolent and less meaningful than it had been, and themselves as less worthy. Unable to create positive illusions, they become angry, depressed, and anxious. Others, finding meaning in the tragedy, eventually reestablish a positive view of the world and themselves.

Many psychologists have posed theories of cognitive consistency to predict how people handle information that conflicts with their beliefs: They shift the belief slightly, or more likely the new information, to make the two coexist harmoniously. One friend of mine, for example, who is a Freudian analyst, always orders the latest books that put Freudian theory to critical, experimental test. This allows her to feel that she is keeping up with the research. But she never reads the books, deciding in advance that they are full of holes. This allows her to keep up her analytic practice.

Consistency theories all assume that human beings have a fundamental need to find meaning and order in life's experiences. Psychologist Melvin J. Lerner adds that we need to believe in a just world, one in which people get what they deserve, good is rewarded, the sinful punished. The Belief in a Just World, he argues, is "a fundamental delusion" that is central to the way we organize experience, making sense out of confusion, justice out of cruelty and unfairness, and orderliness out of random events. And it protects the legitimacy of the established order. Researchers have by now conducted dozens of experiments that show what happens when the belief in a just world clashes with an obvious fact of injustice. If you cannot do anything about the injustice, you will tend to denigrate the victim, deny the evidence, or reinterpret the event entirely. You will go to great lengths to protect the basic faith.

Denigrate the victim. In a just world, innocent women are not raped. Women who are raped, therefore, must have "invited it"—by being seductive, or perhaps by merely being. Examples appear in the news much too often: a Wisconsin judge (since recalled) exonerated a teenage boy for raping a fourteen-year-old girl because she was "provocatively dressed," and another judge (still in business) excused a man for raping his *five-year-old* daughter because the child was "particularly seductive."

Similarly, some vehement antiabortionists cannot accept the statistics of rape, incest, contraceptive ignorance, and woman-battering, preferring to believe that it is only immoral women who have abortions. Women are blamed for "getting themselves pregnant," as one congressman put it, in that bizarre, anachronistic phrasing that exonerates the role of the male in conception. (The same congressmen who advise that "the best contraceptive is the word no" would not take it kindly, I bet, if their wives applied that word to them.)

Women are not the only objects of rationalizing denigration. The poor bring their suffering on themselves (say many of the well-to-do) because they are lazy, conniving, drunk, or violent; the millions of homeless people, said Ronald Reagan in the waning days of his presidency, prefer living on grates and park benches, even if they freeze to death. A man who is fired for trying to improve working conditions must have deserved it; he should have kept his mouth shut. Fighter pilots, on hearing that a buddy has been killed in a plane crash, will blame the buddy for having made a stupid error; if it was the plane that failed or the Air Force's error, the survivors are in danger too. All of these rationalizations help people avoid the panicky thought that poverty, job loss, or death could strike *them*.

Denial. Here's a familiar term for the psychoanalytic archives, this time referring not to an unconscious process but often a perfectly conscious one: screening out unpleasant information that might threaten one's convictions. Fundamentalist parents, fighting to have their children taught absolute values of right and wrong, worry that schools are subjecting their children to information that might jeopardize their religious certainty. When writer Frances FitzGerald asked one such mother whether she would consider sending her children to a nonfundamentalist school, the mother said, "No, because our eternal destiny is all-important, so you can't take a chance. College so often throws kids into confusion." To avoid confusion, many people prefer ignorance.

Freud and his followers regarded denial as a primitive, dangerous defense mechanism that meant a person was out of touch with reality—a hallmark of mental illness. Emotionally healthy people supposedly are good at "reality testing" and can face the truth about themselves and their dearest beliefs. Of course, denial can have disastrous consequences, as when a woman ignores a lump in her breast or when a man having a heart attack says, "It's only indigestion." Yet, as a general strategy of information-processing, denial and self-delusion protect us against anger, depression, and anxiety, which is why they are such characteristic responses to information that threatens our basic view of the world. People do not say, "Oh, thank you, Harry, for showing me why my philosophy of child-rearing is entirely wrong!" They say, "Oh, buzz off, Harry, and take your cockamamie ideas with you."

Certainly, denial lies at the heart of virtually all political philosophies. As a particularly depressing case, there are people who will tell you that the Holocaust never happened. But you can see garden-variety denial in the way individuals respond to the news that innocent people have been imprisoned or murdered by the Soviet Union, the United States, Israel, Vietnam, Argentina, Chile, France, Japan, South Africa, Haiti, Cuba . . . (fill in your choice for infamy). Depending on your politics, you will tend to deny the crimes committed by your favorite nations (for such crimes jeopardize your desire to believe in your allies' basic integrity and justice, and possibly jeopardize your economic interests as well), and emphasize those committed by your enemies (it is perfectly consistent to believe in the sins of your opponents). If, however, you believe in the basic corruptibility of the powerful—if you believe, with the historian Barbara Tuchman, that "every successful revolution puts on in time the robes of the tyrant it has deposed"—then you won't find it inconsistent evidence to be denied when your favorite country does something criminal, stupid, or cruel, or when your favorite oppressed group, in time, behaves oppressively.

Reinterpretation of the injustice and its outcome. This mechanism to preserve faith in a just world requires some flights of imagination. People "rewrite" the injustice they hear about so that is simply disappears, taking with it the need to be emotionally disturbed. For example, you might reinterpret the result of injustice, deciding that the victim wasn't such a victim after all; suffering is a good thing that builds moral character and makes the sufferer a better person. Or you might decide that the cause of the injustice was, let's say, not a company's decision to release toxic wastes into the local water supply, but a result of something the victims failed to do; perhaps those citizens who now complain they were poisoned just forgot to take adequate precautions. Or you might extend the time frame of the whole event to maintain your belief in ultimate justice: Eventually, heroes and bastards will get their just desserts, but it may take a few years. Maybe a lifetime. Maybe in the afterlife . . .

So great is the need to believe in justice and order, says Lerner, that many people will even assume a large burden of anguish, blaming themselves, rather than yield the belief. Parents of terminally ill children, the most poignantly undeserving of victims, frequently berate themselves for their children's fate: "If I had only done this . . ." "If we'd never done that . . ." This self-blame, paradoxically, allays the anxiety of the intolerable conclusion that no one is responsible. Or consider the puzzling fact that victims of rape often take responsibility for having provoked the rapist. When it is nearly impossible for them to blame themselves, for example when they have been seized and raped in their own homes by a man who broke through a window, they feel worse about themselves and take longer to recover than women who are raped outside the home. Why don't they become furious with the rapist? Self-blame restores the sense of control, predictability, and safety in a way that blaming the rapist does not. "If I have provoked the bastard," the reasoning goes, "I'll just take precautions to avoid such misery in the future; *I* will make sure it never happens again." But if rape can happen to you no matter what you do, even in the safety of your own house, then you are not safe anywhere; then there is no order, logic, or justice.

In the laboratory, psychologists have watched as before their very eyes the belief in a just world "cools out" anger. Young adults observed a videotape of what they thought was a real experiment in learning (in fact, it was staged), in which another young woman suffered a series of severe shocks whenever she made "errors." At first the observers would flinch empathically with each televised shock, and many expressed fury and indignation at the treatment they were watching: "I was really mad." "I felt like getting up and walking out." "I thought it was disgusting." In spite of these strong affirmations of anger, *not one* of the thousand people who have by now participated in this experiment have actually complained. Instead, most of them decided that the victim was a fool or a weakling for sitting still and allowing herself to be shocked. "I would never let anyone do that to me!" they asserted. Unable as they were to do anything about the injustice they observed, they condemned the victim and evaluated her critically. The more strongly the experimenters portrayed the innocent victim as a martyr, the more vehemently the observers condemned her.

Religion, of course, offers the ultimate just world, if not in this life then in the next. Religion and political ideology organize our angers as they legitimize our social systems. Indeed all of the great religions have made the management of anger a central concern, with prescriptions designed to protect the social order and to generate anger, if at all, only on its behalf.

For instance, although the Old Testament itself is a veritable catalog of family squabbles, internecine wars, and the smiting of heathens, it continually reminds its readers that "He that is slow to anger is better than the mighty"—surely a sermon that would reassure the mighty—"and he that ruleth his spirit than he that taketh a city" (Proverbs 16:32). Jehovah himself may be jealous and angry, but mortals must not be. God's anger in the Old Testament has a clear purpose: to keep the faithful in the fold.

> *Ye shall not go after other gods, of the gods of the people which are round about you; (For the Lord thy God is a jealous god among you) lest the anger of the Lord thy God be kindled against thee, and destroy thee from off the face of the earth.*
>
> Deuteronomy 6:14–15

Jehovah of the Old Testament and Allah of Islam are angry gods, who require anger to be used freely in their service against enemies, infidels, and the wicked; but anger *within* the community is to be suppressed. This was a smart and successful philosophy for small nations surrounded by competing groups, the situation then and now in the Middle East.

In contrast, the religions of Taoism, Vishnuism, and Buddhism advocate the complete eradication of anger and any other emotion that serves a this-worldly desire, such as lust and greed. Because everything that happens in this world is predestined, according to these theologies, there is no point in getting riled up about evil, war, and sin. There is certainly no point in protesting one's caste; obedient behavior in this life will be rewarded with caste advancement in the next incarnation. War and anger may be an occasional necessity, but they are not to be sought after or celebrated.

Christianity stands between the martial religions and the pacifistic ones. Anger may be used to combat evil and injustice; anger is good or bad depending on its use, not its nature. Although in the New Testament divine vengeance has subsided in favor of divine forgiveness, human beings are still supposed to wait for forgiveness in heaven and not raise their voices too loudly for justice on earth.

> *Let all bitterness, and wrath, and anger, and clamour, and evil speaking, be put away from you, with all malice: And be ye kind one*

to another, tenderhearted, forgiving one another, even as God for
Christ's sake hath forgiven you.

Ephesians 4:31–32

An eloquent, noble instruction. Unfortunately the Church had no qualms about whipping up a little bitterness, wrath, anger, and evil-speaking whenever it needed a Crusade or an Inquisition. Christianity, like other religions, knew that anger has the power to work on its behalf or to destroy it. If anger was one of the seven deadly sins, it had better be carefully contained. If we consider the secular results of Christianity instead of its religious intentions, we see that those who turned the other cheek usually got a slap in return; and that the meek did indeed inherit the earth—to plow, to plant, and to harvest for their masters.

The belief in a just world—a religious universe in general or a political arena of the world in particular—is only one of the forces that contain the disruptive potential of anger and keep people angry on behalf of the system instead of angry against it. As far as human society is concerned, if not all of its individuals, these forces are highly adaptive. They allow people to act with confidence that their environment is secure and orderly, to assume a cause-and-effect between what they do and any good results they get, to commit themselves to the long-range goals that societies need. In short, these beliefs allow people to be optimistic.

Ideas about justice are not all in the mind. Realistic, practical motives hold people in roles as victims of manipulation or injustice without their perceiving either. Sociologist Barrington Moore, Jr., calls their condition one of "exploitative reciprocity," and if revolutionaries emphasize the "exploitative," the people involved tend to emphasize the "reciprocity." Every social system, from the family to a nation, is based on a social contract of the rights and duties of its participants. The contract may be written or implicit, but the rules are usually clear to all, or become clear once they are broken.

Some feminists, for example, who feel angry about the genital mutilation (such as circumcision or even excision of the clitoris) that women in many Third World cultures endure, cannot understand why the women tolerate these practices and continue them. Yet these horrendous, painful customs are as essential to the woman's security and survival—because they guarantee that the woman will continue to be protected by men—as a job contract is to a union worker here. (Many Third World feminists themselves put food, education, and work at the top of their list of reforms for this reason.) In any relationship between authority and subordinate, the subordinate gives up something to get something: the benefits of the authority's protection, expertise, talent, access to the rain god, earnings. As Frances FitzGerald observes, the wives in Jerry Falwell's fundamentalist church get a great deal by paying the price of submission to their husbands, so heavily do the prohibitions fall on traditional male vices such as drinking, smoking, running around, and ignoring the children. People will accept their roles as long as they regard them as contributing to the social good and their own individual benefit, and as long as the authorities hold up their end of the bargain. They are usually prepared, though, to give the authorities an extended line of credit.

The anger that fuels revolt does not arise, therefore, from objective conditions of deprivation or misery. As long as people regard those conditions as natural and inevitable, as God's Law or man's way, they do not feel angry about them. So sociologists speak instead of "relative deprivation," the subjective comparisons that people make when they compare their actual lives to *what might be possible*. Alexis de Tocqueville observed that "evils which are patiently endured when they seem inevitable become intolerable when once the idea of escape from them is suggested," and the freed slave Frederick Douglass put the same idea more passionately. "Beat and cuff your slave," he wrote, "keep him hungry and spiritless, and he will follow the chain of his master like a dog, but feed and clothe him well, work him moderately, surround him with physical comfort, and dreams of freedom intrude."

In this country, the civil-rights, women's rights, and human-rights movements have been organized and sustained primarily by those who already had more education, opportunities, and success in the system than the less-fortunate members of their race, sex, or class. Paradoxically, some of the angriest revolutionaries came from worlds of privilege, not misery, such as Kathy Boudin, the daughter of a famous civil-rights lawyer, who became a member of the Weather Underground. In her work on the components of relative deprivation, social psychologist Faye Crosby finds that two conditions must be met before people will feel angry or aggrieved about an injustice: wanting what they don't have and feeling that they *deserve* what they don't have.

The inequalities between haves and have-nots lie at the heart of every society's organization. But the American notion that all men are created equal and deserve equal opportunities virtually guaranteed political turmoil, although many would say it is a noble turmoil indeed. The doctrine declared that the gap between rich and poor, ideal and practice, success and failure can be overcome in this world, in this land, in this lifetime; and that differences of class, inheritance, genes, and, lately, gender will fall before hard work and perseverance. In one stroke, this philosophy created a nation of relatively deprived people—some more relatively, others more deprived.

Margaret Mead once said of liberals that they are "the yeast within the body politic upon which American society relies to keep its dream worth following. Without them, we should be lost. Yet with them, we are uncomfortable. For they draw their strength from the discrepancies in the very heart of American life." Rebels and dissidents challenge the complacent belief in a just world and, as the theory would predict, they are usually denigrated for their efforts. While they are alive, they may be called "cantankerous," "crazy," "hysterical," "uppity," or "duped." Dead, some of them become saints and heroes, the sterling characters of history. It's a matter of proportion. One angry rebel is crazy, three is a conspiracy, fifty is a movement.

THE BIRTH AND DEATH OF ANGER

*I couldn't believe—still can't—how angry I could be-
come, from deep down and way back, something like a
five-thousand-year-buried anger.*

—ROBIN MORGAN

*They called me "the angriest Negro in America." I
wouldn't deny that charge: I spoke exactly as I felt. I
believe in anger. The Bible says there is a time for
anger.*

—MALCOLM X

Social movements are learned rebellions. We are now far enough
removed from the angry and exhilarating years of the rights
movements of the 1960s and 1970s to see how anger on a social
scale, like that on a personal one, ebbs and flows; to observe the
processes by which anger is aroused, sustained, and cooled out. I
use the women's movement as an illustration because I know it
best, but it is a paradigm of most of the social-reform protests that
have marked our history.

Like many suburban housewives Jan Schakowsky felt isolated in
1968 and 1969. She had few female friends and saw little chance
to find help and support from other women. "I felt real different;
my kids were both in diapers; I felt totally trapped." Then she began
to hear and read about the women's movement, "about the
injustices, and I started reading, you know, even women's magazines, and watching the talk shows." Her days became consumed
not only with diapers but also with news of feminism. "By the time
my husband walked in the door all hell would break loose. He was
responsible for all the evils of the world and especially responsible
for keeping me trapped. What kind of person was he? Didn't he
understand?"

—SARA EVANS, *Personal Politics*

My hunch is that this description of the flush of anger that
feminism wrought has a faintly dated ring to it. You may be

amused at Jan Schakowsky's reactions by now, or saddened, or irritated, but you recognize that you haven't heard much about her in years. The rage with all men and all marriages seems to have abated in favor of more selective targets. Jan Schakowsky's anger then, and your response to it now, tell a great deal about the mechanisms of this emotion.

In the beginning, there is no word: there is only private, unarticulated experience. A housewife, feeling depressed and lonely in the suburbs, given to crying jags and drinking binges, thinks she is the only one not carrying out her job as wife and mother. A token woman in a man's business thinks she is to blame when her colleagues refuse to accept her. The women in the accounting department of a large firm discover that they earn four thousand dollars a year less than their male peers, even though the women have more education and seniority; but they are complacent. The men, they say, need the money more than they do.

Consider the case of a woman I will call Louise Friedrichs, a superb student in her graduate class at an Ivy League university. When she received her Ph.D in 1969, her faculty mentor (himself a famous scientist) recommended her for a position at Johns Hopkins University. Back came a curt letter: "I am afraid I must admit that it is extremely unlikely that a woman would be appointed to the junior position we have open," the professor from the hiring committee wrote. "I'm afraid that although we have no prejudice against educating women, we are less willing to let them put their education to use." In spite of the writer's sheepish "afraids," he did not fear to reveal the fashionable bigotry against women. Louise was denied even the chance of an interview to change their minds. (As of 1989, Johns Hopkins had 1,692 full-time faculty members, of which 238 males have tenure—and 19 females. In 1980, 230 men had tenure, and only 11 females.)

When Louise read this letter, she said to her mentor, "My God, what should we do?" "Do?" he said. "Nothing. Nothing—do you want to destroy your career?" And she said no, she didn't, and that was the end of the discussion. Today, when she recalls the experience, she is surprised at how calmly she took the news. "I thought, 'Gee, isn't that too bad,' " she says. "But I was not angry. I was puzzled."

At this prepolitical stage, people's attitudes and experiences may have little to do with each other. In interviews with a representative random sample of American adults in Riverside, California, it turned out that people's attitudes about inequality of income and opportunity, welfare and welfare recipients, and their own position in society were inconsistent, contradictory, and uncertain. Norma Wikler found this too, in her in-depth interviews with Vietnam veterans in the early 1970s. Talking with army, navy, and marine veterans who had served in Vietnam between 1968 and 1971, Wikler observed that "the outstanding feature of the veterans' discourse was the confused and contradictory jumble of sentiments, attitudes, and political perceptions" about the Vietnamese, the military, antiwar demonstrators, and American politicians. A vet might shift from a leftist view ("It's the people making munitions that are keeping this war going while the poor people get screwed") to a rightist view ("It's the politicians I hate because they made the military fight a war with handcuffs on") with barely a pause for breath. In 1974, Wikler concluded, the veterans had to cope in isolation with the war's aftereffects. "One day," she predicted, "their 'private troubles' may be translated into public issues and yet make their impact on American society." This transformation finally occurred in the 1980s.

The situation was (and still is) the same for most working women in America, who distinguish discrimination against women in general from their own experience. Most women know full well the extent of job discrimination—that at all job levels women earn less than men and receive fewer fringe benefits—but they simply don't apply this knowledge to their own lives. "It is as if each woman considers herself to be the exception to the rule of discrimination," says Faye Crosby. "The step from knowledge of the group situation to an understanding of one's own situation, which is a small step logically, can become a chasm psychologically." The story of the women's movement in the 1970s is the story of efforts to bridge that chasm.

When the women's movement first emerged on the national scene, opponents argued that women were as usual whining and bitching for no good reason, that a few hotheaded neurotics and lesbians were "corrupting" good women who until then had been perfectly happy. Supporters countered that women had always had good reasons to be angry, that in fact most women already were secretly angry and had been for years. I think both views are wrong. The ideas of women's liberation, like those of virtually every successful ideology, follow and articulate the social and economic upheavals that cause disruption and distress. Most of the women who left the jobs they had during World War II and retired to the suburbs, where they produced a boom of babies, did not feel angry about doing so (although many were disappointed and wanted to stay in the work force). Most of them believed in the legitimacy of the division of sexual labor, even when that meant that he got the sex and she got the labor.

But over the next two decades that legitimacy was challenged as women entered the labor force in unprecedented numbers. This did not happen because a few uppity women decided to leave the nest. It happened because, while everyone was talking about woman's place at home, new technology and industry were making millions of white-collar service jobs available, and women were available to fill them. (Between 1947 and 1979, twenty-five million new jobs were taken by women.) The job market opened to women in the mid-fifties because the country needed not just more workers but specifically *female* workers. Women rarely *displaced* men; they *replaced* men as men got opportunities to advance.

In the 1950s and early 1960s, the middle-class married women who took jobs were doing so primarily to achieve consumer dreams—a first mortgage, a second car, a third child—but by the late 1960s most were working because they needed to. Inflation was starting to make the two-paycheck family a necessity instead of a luxury. Women went back to work not because they felt grouchy and frustrated at home, but primarily because the jobs were there. Nevertheless, many of the women who were not employed, like Jan Schakowsky (and Moira White), were finding that suburban life was not the twentieth-century paradise that they had been promised. It was lonely, remote, alien to community and continuity.

Another powerful but invisible demographic influence was affecting the emergence of the women's movement: a shifting sex ratio. Whenever there is a "surplus" of marriageable women in an age bracket, you get more women not marrying at the age they expected to; becoming economically independent; entering professional occupations; and pressing for equal rights. This imbalance, along with its social effects, has occurred throughout history and in many societies, for a variety of reasons. It occurred most recently in the United States, for example, with the postwar baby boom. The reason for the surplus of women was that as the baby-boom cohort of women came of marriageable age, there weren't enough men *slightly older than they* to go around. (Of course, the notion of a surplus rests on the tradition of women marrying men who are slightly older, better educated, and earning more money than they. It's a custom that has remained remarkably stable.) When men are a "scarce resource," they acquire emotional leverage, since they can always find another partner, whereas women must compromise or lose. Wherever there is a surplus of men, in contrast, as on the American frontier, men tend to value romance, marriage, and commitment.

Women's liberation was an articulation of changes that had already occurred for women, not a cause of those changes. But it had an excellent model to follow: the structure and philosophy of the civil-rights movement. Many of the women who went on to launch the women's movement in the late 1960s got their training, experience, and theory from New Left projects in the urban North and rural South. With the reform notions of the Great Society and the affluence that could afford to underwrite them, the dream of equality for all seemed tantalizingly near.

Louise Friedrichs has kept a detailed diary of events and her reactions to them since her high-school days, so she can reconstruct exactly how her perceptions and emotions changed when the women's movement appeared. She had taken a job in a small, academically unremarkable college after her rejection by Johns Hopkins in 1969:

I had been the only woman in my department for two years and never thought a thing about it. I never thought of myself as a joiner or a member of any group, women included. Once a man asked me to join his research team because he wanted "a woman's point of view," and I remember thinking, What does *that* mean? What *is* a woman's point of view? It was the first instance of my being treated as a representative of my class, and I didn't know how to react. It was ridiculous! My point of view was 183rd Street in the Bronx!

For anger to arise from change, confusion, and dissatisfaction, a person must have a coherent explanation: a new way to interpret old grievances, a theory that the individual can apply to his or her own life, and alternatives to that life that the individual thinks are feasible. What Betty Friedan's *The Feminine Mystique* was to housewives in the early 1960s, the statistics on salaries and employment were to working women (and by now there were very many of them) in the early 1970s: a bolt of shock and recognition. "That's me!" was the first cry. "That's not fair!" was the second.

These early buffets to women's confidence in the system as it was might have stopped there had it not been for public and private discussions of injustice. It takes only one voice to say aloud that the emperor is naked before many more will join in; a very small degree of social support is enough to generate critical dissent. A common element in studies and personal accounts of "raised consciousness" and ideological transformation, whether of religious or revolutionary converts, is social support. It is not alone a new theory that offers consolation and understanding, but a friend or helpful group of friends to introduce the theory. In his autobiography, Malcolm X described how this works. Alone, defeated, and isolated in prison, Malcolm X was visited by his brother, who had become a Muslim, and who offered him an explanation of his sorrows, the thesis that all whites are devils. Malcolm X tested the thesis against his own experience. "The white people I had known marched before my mind's eye," he recalled: the whites who killed his father, who committed his mother to an asylum, who split up Malcolm's brothers and sisters to be raised in different homes, who told him that his ambition to be a lawyer was foolish for a Negro and that he should take up carpentry instead.

For her part, Louise Friedrichs became aware of discrimination against women from a good friend, another woman on the faculty:

Then, in the fall of 1971, another woman joined the faculty, and she was very active in women's rights. She began agitating for a university commission on the status of women right away. By February 1972 I had read stacks of facts and figures about working women—salaries, all that "protective legislation," the gloomy prospects for promotions and tenure, and so on. I discovered, as if in a thundercloud, from reading this stuff, that I in fact *was* a member of a class, that in fact I had a male-identified ideology that was counter to my own best interests.

Suddenly everything made sense. No wonder my department was crazy about me. No wonder they gave me a good salary. *Because I deserved a whole lot better than I was getting, and they knew it*. I had twice the training and talent of those men, and was doing half as well. I deserved to be at Johns Hopkins.

Now, how are you likely to feel when this new information and a new worldview crash headlong into your self-concepts and private experience? When your just and orderly world is shattered by facts you cannot deny? Frequently, the first emotion that can be distilled from the stew of sensations is not anger, but embarrassment: loss of face. "Oh, God, how could I have been so *stupid*? How could I have wasted so much precious time? How could I have let them brainwash me?" Louise recalled:

I remember the feeling of being embarrassed, so embarrassed at everything I had done over the years. I had played the sex-object role so well and so successfully, and now it made me revolted and literally sick to my stomach to think about it. I wanted to jump out of my skin.

Sonia Johnson, the woman excommunicated from the Mormon Church for her support of the Equal Rights Amendment, had the same experience. Already in a support group of nine pro-ERA Mormons, she went to hear a church official explain the church's opposition. When he could not do this intelligently, when instead he made condescending jokes about the ERA and told the audience how much the church loved its women, Johnson became an immediate convert to the women's movement. She describes the "mass of emotions" she felt when she left that meeting: "I felt betrayed. I felt ashamed and humiliated that I, who should have known better, had been so easily duped for so long."

It can be intolerable, this embarrassment; so a common resolution at this stage is to conclude that the new information is wrong and your old ways are right, more right than you ever knew. In their autobiographies, many women of the conservative right— Marabel Morgan, Anita Bryant, Ruth Stapleton—describe the same frustrations and dissatisfactions in their traditional roles as deferent wives and mothers that Betty Friedan did; but their solution was to embrace religion, their husbands, and the traditional roles more tightly. And, not coincidentally, they gained thereby a large amount of money, approval, fame, and power in their self-appointed careers of telling women not to take careers.

But a second way to resolve the feeling of embarrassment and humiliation is to shift from self-blame to blaming others: "Well, I didn't know what I was doing, did I? They did it to me. *He* did it to me." (This attribution leaves unanswered the question: If you were only doing what was expected of you, why shouldn't he have been doing what was expected of him?) The potential convert tries out the new theory everywhere. Just as Malcolm X began to see evidence of bigotry in every white person, the new feminist may see sexism in every man. This shift of emphasis, from my fault to their fault, produces the phase of anger. As feminist Susi Kaplow wrote in the early days of the movement:

> Realizations are, at first, halting, and then begin to hit you like a relentless sledge hammer, driving the anger deeper and deeper into your consciousness with every blow. . . .This is an uncomfortable period to live through. You are raw with an anger that seems to have a mind and will of its own. . . .You yourself get tired of this anger—it's exhausting to be furious all the time—which won't even let you watch a movie or have a conversation in peace.

And Robin Morgan added:

> It makes you very sensitive—raw, even—this consciousness. Everything, from the verbal assault on the street, to a "well-meant"

sexist joke your husband tells, to the lower pay you get at work (for doing the same job a man would be paid more for), to television commercials, to rock-song lyrics . . . everything seems to barrage your aching brain, which has fewer and fewer protective defenses to screen such things out.

And Jane O'Reilly, in retrospection, says:

> There was a time, from about the middle of 1972 to the end of 1975, when I stopped speaking to old friends, provoked scenes in editorial offices, became irrationally attached to inexplicable love affairs. I could barely write, and finally I could barely speak. . . .[I] thrashed bitterly against the discovery that the only way out was forward. There was no going back.

"Consciousness-raising" groups validate the new experience of anger and encourage its expression. They also articulate those two conditions of relative deprivation that Crosby discovered—wanting something you don't have and feeling that you deserve it. To question legitimate institutions and authorities, most people need to know that they are not alone, crazy, or misguided. But more than that, group support generates anger by giving individuals a feeling of power. It creates the hope of change. The private listlessness of "Sure, he's unfair to me but what can I do?" vanishes in a group, becoming, "*They* are unfair to *us*, and just wait until we get them!" Anger, on a personal level or a social one, is the emotion of influence, and its use reflects confidence in its ultimate success.

The start of any protest, like that of any new organization, is emotionally stimulating. Novelty, freedom from old restraints and the challenge of new changes, the identification of a cause within reach, the heady rapport of unexpected allies: all produce high physiological arousal, an intense energy, whose content swings readily from exhilaration to rage. In their support groups, people ventilate (and reinforce) these new emotions. With anger rehearsed and practiced, it is more easily rekindled in daily life—at work, at home, on the street. I was interested to read Sonia Johnson's account of her first experience with expressing profound rage, because it met all the criteria for a successful cathartic session. Rage and fury emerged on the heels of her humiliation and sense of betrayal, and when she returned home from that disastrous Church meeting she locked herself in a room above her garage and "let God have it."

> For two solid hours I raged at God at the top of my lungs, screaming and sobbing. I think you must understand that this was quite unlike my usual parlance with God. I have a naturally quiet voice and am not given to raising it in anger, to say nothing of screaming. . . .When my vocal cords and lungs finally gave out . . . I discovered to my amazement that I felt wonderful— absolutely euphoric.

For aggressive anger to feel that euphoric, you may recall, the person must feel it is directed to the cause of his or her fury; it must seem to be appropriate redress ("I told him what I thought of a Supreme Being" who had created women to be treated so shabbily); and it must produce no retaliation from the target (Johnson was not "zapped" as she expected she might be). For most newly angry converts to a movement, however, these conditions are not met. They do not feel angry about just one thing, for example, but about entire institutions and thousands of individuals who are now defined as the enemy. Ventilating anger is not sufficient redress for grievances; only ending the grievances is. And the targets of rage, particularly lovers and employers, are notably prone to retaliate. So the anger escalates.

Rage, I believe, is essential to the first phase of a social movement. It unifies disparate members of the group against a common enemy; the group becomes defined by its anger. Like the judicious use of private anger, public rage calls attention to an issue and the importance the protesters attach to it. Calm discussion—"Er, fellows, we'd like to talk about these few points of salary inequities with you"—is unlikely to get the fellows to sit down with you. "Say, guys, we're getting tired of racial insults; how about giving us a fair shake?" would never have integrated the schools. There is, as Malcolm X knew, a time for anger, and only anger will do.

*   *   *

"All social movements," said Bertrand Russell, "go too far." And yet the brain and the body, it seems, are natural reactionaries. They enjoy a brief flush of adrenaline and challenge, but they conspire toward the conventional. The "thermostat of sanity," as John Leonard called it, sees to the calming of rage in both the individual body and the social one. At first anger is indiscriminate, the prism through which all experiences are refracted; slowly, anger becomes selective. At first whole categories of people are the enemy: men, whites, bosses, heterosexuals, anyone over thirty, the government, parents, women. "After a while," says psychologist Ernest Harburg, "you can tell the difference between intentional malice and stupidity. The awareness of stupidity among the opposition is a watershed discovery. It is harder to stay mad at someone who isn't evil, just incompetent. Or ignorant." Louise Friedrichs described the course of her anger from its initial stage:

On my thirtieth birthday, in 1974, I wrote in my dairy: "I seem to be out of my 'hate men' phase." This was interesting, because I didn't know I was in it! So much of the early theoretical writings of feminism consisted of "they are doing this to us" that I realized I had made an exception of my own husband. I wrote that I had never thought of John as a man, i.e., one of "them," but as a friend—a member of some neutral category.

By 1974, I began to realize that this was not going to be a short fight. I wrote in my diary, "furious over job discrimination in department"—I realized that nobody gave a damn about hiring women. At the beginning, in the days of such exhilaration and optimism, *anything* we got seemed good, and we wanted so many things that every little success seemed terrific. Showers in the women's locker rooms, for example. We got showers right away. Not *tenure*, mind you, nobody got *tenure*.

During that academic year, I realized that I had changed in ways that my colleagues had not. But I wasn't angry at them any more. They were misguided, maybe, but not malicious. I saw with great clarity that I had been taken in by the system, but they had been taken in too; they just didn't have the motivation or the opportunity or the energy to get out of it the way I had. So I was able to separate my personal feelings from my political commitments. I didn't feel the men were "doing it to me" any more; I felt that the system was set up for their benefit and they were getting a free ride. Change would have to come from political action, not friendly persuasion. I mean, didn't they know what was *right*? You mean they weren't going to hire women just because it was *fair*? *Now* what?

It is on the "now what?" stage that the fate of anger depends. You've got showers in the gym but not tenure; you've got the right to be called "chairperson" of the department but the department still has no women; you've won the support of the majority of the nation for the Equal Rights Amendment but it is defeated by a minority of powerful adversaries. Your support group, its consciousness raised to the rafters, fragments, each member going off to struggle with daily dilemmas and the mundane business of life. You realize, after the first flush of success, that you are not in a short fight. It was easier to maintain anger against specific individuals you hoped to change. It is harder to keep the anger flowing against something so huge and amorphous as "the system."

One solution you might adopt at this point is to turn from agitating for social change to concentrating on your own personal development. Ironically, you might even return to the reaction that characterizes so many victims of discrimination and injustice: You might blame yourself.

When powerless people are blocked from effective action, a typical response, especially in this highly individualized culture, is to redefine the problem as a private matter instead of an organizational one. This shift allows people to retain their awareness of the injustices that once infuriated them *and* to preserve their self-esteem in the belief that they are doing something about them. Because self-blame does not produce changes in the external causes of stress and anger, it works to the very detriment of the individual, while paradoxically creating the illusion that the individual can control his or her destiny.

For example, some women who once felt angry about their second-class status in America have now concluded that any problems women have are primarily their own fault. Colette Dowling's book, *The Cinderella Complex: Women's Hidden Fear of Independence,* was one of the first harbingers of this reversal. Dowling reduced women's issues—the lower pay that women earn, the huge proportion of women in low-status, low-income jobs, the double burden of work and family that employed wives carry, the absence of women in the top echelons of American business—to *women's* fear of independence. I find arguments such as these psychologically bankrupt and politically self-defeating, but I see their allure. Not only do they bring the support and praise of those around a former feminist, who are grateful that she has stopped holding them responsible for her grievances and bludgeoning them with statistics; it gives her an optimistic boost that change is possible. And not the long-term, difficult, unromantic kind of change that requires sustained collaboration, but the immediate, heady kind of change that lies in vague promises about one's inner potential. For if the problem is in you, in a "hidden" fear of inadequacy instead of some nebulous external situation, why, it's nothing that a few years and a few thousand dollars' worth of therapy can't cure. *You* can do it, this reasoning states, just shape up and fly right. And let go of those belligerent ideas about injustice while you're at it.

It is safer, certainly, to feel guilty rather than angry. Today women read self-help books with titles like *How to Raise Your Stupidly Low Self-Esteem, by Working Hard Enough and Being Thin and Pretty Enough, in Order to Get That Shlub to Stay with You and Treat You Right.* Guilt-inducing though they are, these books are less threatening than those that ask women to consider where their low self-esteem comes from, what causes their obsession with being thin and pretty, and why they should stay with a shlub in the first place.

The problem for many at this stage of social protest is finding the line between blame and responsibility. If some feminists obscured the line by blaming everyone else and everything in their lives for all their woes, many modern self-help books commit the opposite error. A harder but more honest route is to discriminate between the sources of anger that you can do something about and those you cannot, between taking responsibility for your own actions and failures and attributing blame elsewhere for events beyond your control. "Nowadays," wrote Jane O'Reilly as the 1980s dawned, "I divide the blame more equitably: half for me and half for societal arrangements."

That, I think, is a fair split in an unfair world.

In the 1970s the dirty word was *women's libber*, as in "I'm no women's libber, but I want to be a miner (fire fighter, senator, priest, lawyer, carpenter) anyway." Now that women *are* miners, fire fighters, senators, priests, lawyers, and carpenters, they are supposedly doing one of two things: returning to traditionalism, giving up hard-won careers to raise tomatoes and children; or advancing forward as superwomen, individualists in the best American tradition, maintaining they don't need "a whole movement" to help them. In either case, we are supposed to be in a "postfeminist" phase, whatever that means.

Actually, apart from the media anecdotes, women are not "returning to traditionalism." Most of those who could, don't want to, and most of those who want to, can't afford to. What *has* happened is that most young women today take the achievements of feminism for granted. If you ask college women to imagine their futures, they will tell you that the world is their oyster, that husbands are going to share the housework, that any career is possible, that women can raise two children with one hand and run a law practice with the other hand, and that inequities of pay or promotion are, like chastity belts, among the barbarities of the past.

This is not a sign of antifeminism; this is a sign of naiveté. Once women get jobs, get married, and get babies (in any order, nowadays), many are discovering that perhaps feminism isn't merely a dusty topic in ancient history, like, say, the Vietnam War. Two of my students illustrate particularly well how young women today regard the women's movement, and how anger relates to those attitudes. Louise Friedrichs would recognize herself in them.

One young woman, whom I'll call Eve Ramirez, now works at a television station, learning the business "from the ground up." Ramirez's parents were not especially affected by the women's movement. Her mother went to work outside the home only after Eve was in college, and her father never dried a dish, until recently. Still, Ramirez feels she was indirectly influenced:

> My parents never sat me down and told me this is what the women's movement was, but they brought me up thinking that by now things were going to be fair when I went out into the working world. My college courses woke me up a little bit, and then when I finally went out to go to work it *really* woke me up because there is such a big difference between how men and women are treated. It's not enough to keep me from doing what I want to do, though. And I'm sure things are much better than before the women's movement occurred.

Like many of her generation, Ramirez doesn't like the word *feminist* because it has bad connotations:

> I've always heard it in derogatory terms, like "Oh, those feminists." A lot of times men and even women use the word to say that someone is stepping out of line, shouldn't be doing what she's doing, not being feminine; that a feminist doesn't just want to do what a man does, she wants to *be* a man. But I think you can be feminine and be a feminist. It's not something you'd want to label yourself as, but if I had to, I would, because I'm sure I am one. Actually, I don't think the term is as derogatory now—maybe it's just because I'm older and I can take it.

Wendy J., a law student at an Eastern university (where more than 40 percent of the entering class is female), grew up with feminism and admits that for many years she could not separate feminist politics from her mother's anger at her father. Wendy's mother, an English professor who has long been active in women's issues, was divorced when Wendy was in the second grade. "At some level I blamed her for losing my father, and I was angry at her for being so angry and bitter," Wendy says.

By the time Wendy was an adolescent, she rebelled against everything her mother stood for:

I thought that the women's movement was much ado about nothing; there was no reason for it. I wore the sexiest clothes I could find—low-cut blouses, jeans that looked painted on—and tons of makeup, horrendous blue eye shadow. The only important thing was did the boy like me; it didn't even matter if I liked him. I was a typical "gotta be cute" teenager. My mother must have been horrified, but she never said a word.

After high school I began to grow out of the age when being sexy and dumb for the boys is important. The more experience I had, especially at work, the more I woke up. It doesn't take long. I lost a job because of sexual harassment. It's interesting—all the stories I'd heard from my mother and her friends, about losing jobs or not getting tenure, didn't mean much to me. But when it happens to you personally, the message hits home. I realized one day, for instance, that I have only one friend who has never been raped or had an experience with unwanted sex.

Wendy worries that many of the women in her law school have adopted the trappings of equality without its spirit. "They want to be feminine, by which they mean beautiful and anorexically thin, *and* professionally successful, *and* better than everyone else," she says. "If they aren't, the feelings of inadequacy are overwhelming."

Many of them are very scared of the word *feminist*. It creates an image of a person who hates men, who isn't feminine. Some of my classmates say, "I'm a feminist, but I want to be feminine, too," which tells me they don't know what feminism is. It's really humanism, the view that neither sex is superior to the other.

Wendy says that her feelings of anger depend on "whether you look forward to what remains or backward to what's been accomplished. My mom and I were talking about this recently. 'I never thought our efforts would make a difference so soon,' she told me. 'When we started out, law schools took only a very few women, and now look at yours.' " But she is not as optimistic as her mother:

I asked an older student here where the women's-issues groups were, and she said, "Oh, I'm not at all into feminism." "Do you object to the word," I asked, "or are you not 'into' equal pay and an end to discrimination?" This is not *Candide*, I said, and this is *not* the best of all possible worlds.

Eve Ramirez, for her part, plans to look forward:

My internship gave me a discouraging glimpse into the real world of television. But I think this is priceless information for two reasons. First, it made me become more realistic; I can now enter the work force with a truer sense of what I will be faced with. Second, it gives me hope. A lot has been changed already, but a lot more needs to be done. It is an exciting challenge that I am prepared to face and eventually conquer.

Social scientists Leonie Huddy and David Sears have reviewed fifty years of studies of American attitudes toward gender issues and toward feminism, as well as conducting a representative survey of 2,257 American adults. Contrary to the public impression that the next generation is "returning to traditionalism," Huddy and Sears found that the youngest women in America, those between eighteen and thirty-four, are the *most* in favor of women's equality. It is the oldest who are most opposed. These differences among women reflect a divided view on where their best interests lie—in the economic protection of husbands, or in economic self-sufficiency. I asked Huddy why, if that were true, there was such a prevalent impression that young women are in a postfeminist phase. "Many of them *are* feminist in their basic beliefs and ambitions," she said, "but they don't identify with feminism, and they hate the word. It connotes anger, militance, and lesbianism."

Sociologist Beth Schneider has been trying to find out why *feminism* connotes "anger, militance, and lesbianism," and why so many women support feminist goals but are reluctant to call themselves feminists. Schneider collected impressions of feminism from a diverse group of women, ages nineteen to sixty-six. The women's hostility was almost entirely directed at what they regarded as feminists' deviance in the private sphere of relationships, in the basic definitions and activities of "normal" womanhood—sexuality, maternity, and personality traits (nurturance, warmth, nonaggressive-

ness). Thus, although most of Schneider's group agreed that
feminists are doing good things to improve the status of women,
many also regarded feminists as being tough, aggressive, unattrac-
tive, and hostile—i.e., "afraid of being a woman." Feminists are
often assumed to be sexually deviant too: If they aren't lesbians, they
are "frigid" or "oversexed" heterosexuals.

The disclaimer "I'm not a feminist, but . . ." allows women to
endorse safe general policies, without being condemned by others
for violating traditional standards of femininity. It is safe to endorse
the practical, and now mainstream, goals of the women's movement, such as equal pay, fair promotions, and rape centers. It is
less safe to question the "personal," traditional requirements of the
female role. The goal is equality, without being thought unladylike while pursuing it.

The story of the women's movement in America is the story of the
rise and fall, and rise and fall, and rise and fall, of anger. Of all the
social roles that anchor our lives and give them meaning, none are
more deeply felt than the roles of woman and man. People do not
take kindly to challenges to this most central aspect of their
identities. When changes occur, they want to know whom to
blame—"Who started this?" Antifeminists blame uppity, frustrated
women. In her entertaining and provocative reply, *The Hearts of
Men*, writer Barbara Ehrenreich blamed uppity, frustrated men.
The women's movement began, Ehrenreich argued, as a response
to a "male revolt" against maturity and responsibility in general
and against women in particular. A generation of immature men
refused to honor their commitments to women and family, forcing
women into one of two choices: economic self-sufficiency (the
direction of feminism) or efforts to bind men more tightly to them
(the direction of antifeminism).

Other writers blame women for placing impossible demands on
men. Many men are certainly angry at what they perceive as all
the attention given to women's issues, and none to theirs. Warren
Farrell, in *Why Men Are the Way They Are*, cites dozens of
examples of what he calls "the new sexism"—female put-downs of

men that would never be tolerated if they were male put-downs of women. Anti-male greeting cards sell like hotcakes. Anti-male books imply that women are wonderful, though they occasionally make bad choices in the name of loving too much, whereas men are childish jerks. And, says Farrell, while women complain about all the pressures on them to be beautiful and feminine, men aren't supposed to complain about the impossible pressures on them to be handsome, masculine, *and* financially successful.

The who-started-this discussion has the virtue of reminding us that sex roles do not apply only to one sex. Women have not been the only gender to chafe under the restrictions of their "proper" place. For every wife who accuses her husband of being dominant and emotionally aloof, there is a husband who accuses his wife of being parasitic and emotionally pushy. To listen to the grievances of one sex and not the other is to hear the sound of one hand slapping.

But what, then, is the future of this debate, and the anger it generates between the sexes? In one scenario, things are getting better and better. Now that there are so many women in the workforce, sheer numbers will eventually crash through the "glass ceiling" of power. The Marlboro Man, who wouldn't diaper a baby with a barge pole, is rapidly becoming a laughable anachronism. Men are doing far more housework, cooking, and child care than their fathers ever thought respectable, which will allow women to succeed at careers and men to succeed at domestic relations. (In some books and movies, men are portrayed as better mothers than women are.) As women and men share more activities and qualities, their misunderstandings and animosities will decline.

A second scenario foresees that women will continue to work, but without corresponding changes from men. As a result, women will be expected to be traditional *and* liberated, in charge of the family *and* of their careers. Like Wendy J.'s classmates, they will try to be "feminine" *and* "feminist." Advocates of this prognosis observe that the Marlboro Man still sells plenty, and so does Rambo; the macho ideal continues to be glorified in film and politics. Men may be doing more in the home, but studies consistently find that the more they do, the less happy they are with their wives and their marriages. In this scenario, anger between the sexes will continue. Women will blame men for "not doing their share" or making them choose between work and family, and men will blame women for demanding too much and abandoning their domestic responsibilities.

Of course, both visions can, and do, coexist in our complex society, and as long as there is conflict about men's and women's roles and obligations, there will be tension and animosity between the sexes. But to make sense of this conflict, I think it is time to abandon the who-started-this debate, which commits the error of linear thinking so common to family quarrels. Beliefs about masculinity and femininity are, like hemlines, tied to larger economic and demographic conditions, such as the availability of jobs, the need for women's labor, and the ratio of men to women. This is why, as psychologist Lillian Troll observes, each "women's movement" is only a generation deep.

Perhaps one way to break out of the who-started-this trap is to look outward, to our social worlds, rather than inward to our own failings—or sideways, to our partners' failings. To understand why women feel such pressure to be feminine and feminist, to be beautiful and successful, we might begin with the conflicting demands on them from their jobs and their families. While we're at it, we might also look closely at the conflicting pressures on men to be both financial piranhas and soft-hearted dads.

Looking outward can help people better diagnose the origins of these conflicts, as well as find ways to resolve them. Otherwise, blame will bounce from court to court in an interminable game of sexual volleyball—and worse, people will find it difficult to separate what they want from what society wants of them.

TEMPER OF THE TIMES

I hope [journalists] will retain their curiosity—their interest; yes, and at their heart a touch of anger. When the adrenaline runs low, when the little flare of anger flickers out, I think it is time for the reporter to think about going into some more remunerative form of work.

—T.R.B.[RICHARD STROUT]

The belief in a just world is in trouble. Every day there are all too many flagrant examples of bad guys getting away with murder. Old women are mugged by young punks for a handful of dollars. Terrorists deal death to the innocent. The richest and most flagrant of criminals get the shortest sentences. The expectations that soared in the affluent postwar years—for safe retirement, a healthy environment, improved standards of living, compassionate care for the poor, the ill, and the old—now fall with national reverberations.

The anger that might protest such events is beset by pitfalls: howling, nihilistic rage on one side; apathy and sullen resentment on the other. Nowadays our public discourse has become increasingly polarized into these two detestable extremes. At one end is the Morton Downey, Jr., style of enraged hectoring that *Spy* magazine calls "populist fascism," in which "conversation" is transformed into the reciprocal hurling of names. Hatemongers, angry at everyone and everything that they oppose, do not argue; they attack. It is the shriek of the inarticulate.

The other extreme, just as troubling, is excessive denial. This attitude is, "Don't say mean things about that person; it might hurt his feelings." Many people seem to think it is rude to point out, for example, a politician's lies, evasions, and manipulations. On one of Bill Moyers's PBS shows on the 1988 presidential campaign, several commentators observed that the television media have rarely contradicted the packaged images and speeches of the administration in recent years. To do so, they said, would seem somehow "unfair," as if the media were out to "get" those in power. True investigative reporting, such as uncovering governmental corruption, is one of the essential aspects of the media's job. But by attacking the media for their alleged bias, the government has successfully cowed the very institutions that ought to be monitoring it—with the acquiescence of the public, who want to be polite, and who do not want to be angry with their leaders.

What's called for is a little flare of anger, enough to guarantee our use of anger and not its use of us. This is difficult. It is much easier to extinguish anger completely, and with it all sense of caring about community or hope of change; or to let go in aggressive displays at every perceived affront, fanning the fury past containment or direction.

Psychoanalyst Walter Bonime, noting that there are plenty of healthy reasons to feel angry in this society ("the denigration of women, blacks, the young, the old, all of whom are scorned in various ways"), distinguishes such realistic anger from the hostility that some people require to feel authentic. One woman told him that she "always wanted to feel like an oppressed person. That makes me feel alive. I have to keep facing the fact that [when] nothing is going wrong, then I become dead." This woman's lament is the signature of the alienated, who fear that their voices will not be heard in a nation of shouters unless they scream.

My friend Judy describes such individuals less clinically. "They think the world is there to do them in at every turn," she says. "Just as people who live in rain forests might conclude that life is a dark, damp, soggy business, they are walking around believing that the climate of the world is to do them in." New Yorkers, she adds, have a particular rain forest of their own:

Outside of New York people don't seem to realize how *infuriating* life is. I think New Yorkers are much more fragile than anyone knows—they're not hardened and tough, they're softies. They have a notion that life is supposed to be an idyll, and so they are always angry when it isn't. You see how farmers in the Midwest handle floods and droughts? It's a part of life—"Back to work, Maude." New Yorkers? A *faucet* drips and they go crazy. Enraged calls to the landlord! New Yorkers are the ultimate innocents. They don't see anything as a part of life; everything is a personal assault that happened to *me*: MY rent has gone up, MY faucet is leaking, MY job is lousy.

She has certainly captured the attitude, although I don't think it is limited to New Yorkers.

Private, reflexive ventilated rage is often justified today as a proper attack on "oppression"—sometimes actual oppression, and sometimes the normal constraints of maturity. The problem with it is that, once it has drawn attention to a grievance, it does not do much to change anything. Change, over the long haul, requires organization, patience, good humor, and the ability to negotiate and compromise; all of which may be energized by anger or killed by it.

Of course, as I have been arguing, there are times when only anger will make the necessary point, when gentle hints and persistent kindnesses go unheard and unheeded by the irritating spouse or government in question. A sociologist friend of mine thinks it is significant that there is a word for people who are not persecuted but believe they are ("paranoid"), whereas there is no word for people who *are* being persecuted but believe they are *not*. "Chumps?" he suggested. People who never feel angry even when it is in their own best interests to do so, who never take a stand against an injustice they can influence, win no prizes for courage, nor sympathy for their stoicism.

The moral use of anger, I believe, requires an awareness of choice and an embrace of reason. It is knowing when to become angry—"this is wrong, this I will protest"—and when to make peace; when to take action, and when to keep silent; knowing the likely cause of one's anger and not berating the blameless.

A story is told of the great Irish statesman and orator Tom Kettle, and his speech to the House of Commons in the early years of this century. A member of the opposition party rose to comment: "An excellent speech indeed, but I do have one quibble. The young MP says that one decision would be a *calamity* while another would be a *catastrophe*. Why, surely, these are the same."

Kettle rose immediately to reply. "Not so," he said. "Were the honorable opposition MP to be walking along the Thames and were he to fall in, that would be a calamity. Were he to be rescued—*that* would be a catastrophe."

It is, I'm sure, too much to hope for that we will ever have politicians as literate and deft in their insults. But it is not too much to hope for an electorate that can tell the difference between hatemongering attacks and legitimate accusations, a public that does not confuse brutality with "openness" or passivity with "politeness." Were the public to avoid all anger on the grounds of manners, that would be a calamity. Were the public to favor an unrestrained howl of rage on the grounds of honesty, that would be a catastrophe.

10

Rethinking Anger: Strategies for Living with Anger and Getting Beyond It

He always had a chip on his shoulder that he was ready to use to kindle an argument.

—FRED ALLEN

The person who pursues revenge should dig two graves.

—proverb

Over the years, I have been collecting messages from Chinese fortune cookies. Either the Chinese are very concerned about anger or somebody is trying to tell me something, but here is part of my collection:

Watch your temper. Short temper is a loss of face.
He that is slow to wrath is of great understanding.
Anger is as useless as the waves of the ocean without wind.
The greatest remedy for anger is delay.
Anger, like fog, often distorts the way.
Better not to see an insult than to avenge it.

And the latest addition to my collection:

Strong and bitter words indicate a weak cause.

Not once have I ever found a fortune that advised: "Express your fury, or you will get an ulcer," or "Self-control is a loss of face," or "Ventilate thy wrath, and fortune will follow." There is, of course, a chasm between fortune-cookie advice, which is concerned with the health of the community, and modern psychological advice, which is concerned with the health of the individual. There are, however, many psychologists whose work has been devoted to bridging that gap.

The diagnostic bible for psychologists and psychiatrists, *The Diagnostic and Statistical Manual of Mental Disorders* (called the *DSM* for short), contains many categories of "mood disorders": depression; fears and phobias; and many varieties of anxiety, including panic attacks, agoraphobia, post-traumatic stress syndrome, chronic anxiety, obsessions, and compulsions. But problems with anger are nowhere to be found. "People can have a 'generalized anxiety disorder,' " says clinical psychologist Jerry Deffenbacher, "but not a 'generalized anger disorder.' " Individuals can have a situation-specific phobia, such as a fear of driving, but not a situation-specific anger problem, such as intense anger *while* driving. The *DSM* recognizes that people may feel excessive anxiety or depression when they are going through a crisis, says Deffenbacher, but it completely ignores the extreme anger many people feel while going through a crisis, such as divorce. He adds:

> I think that we have too long ignored or avoided treating clinical problems of anger, particularly those in the mild to moderate range. These are often the anger reactions that influence health, relationships, vocations, and sense of self, but do not necessarily force people into therapy. . . . It is my impression that, as clinicians, many of us will dig right into a case of depression or anxiety, but shy away from anger. Our student clients, at least, seem aware of this. At the end of our treatment studies many have essentially said, "Thanks. I knew I needed help, but did not know where to turn." When asked why they didn't go to the counseling center, they would look at us in amazement and say that they were neither depressed nor crazy. They were not, just individuals struggling with a difficult and often socially unacceptable emotion.

Anger is indeed a difficult emotion, even in its "mild to moderate" forms, and in recent years clinical psychologists have made great strides in helping people manage, understand, and direct it. It's all very well to say that anger can be dangerous to one's relationships, but what if the relationship is over and your ex-partner continues to bait and provoke you? It's all very well to say that anger at your children or employer may not be accomplishing anything, or even making matters worse, but what if you *feel* it, and can't seem to shake it? Modern anger-intervention therapies recognize that the simple ventilation of anger is not enough to solve problems or change habitual family conflicts. They recognize that anger can be destructive, but it can also be a useful symptom that can lead to constructive changes.

CHRONIC ANGER

Anger involves the mind, the body, and the behavioral habits that people have acquired over the years in coping with emotions. Because the resolution of anger, like its creation, is a matter of mind and body, people who want to "let go" of anger have to rearrange their thinking as well as lower their pulse rates. This is why therapies that rely primarily on emotional release (Primal Scream, bioenergetics, and the like), or for that matter on relaxation techniques, are attending to only half the problem. Yelling "You jerk!" is rarely cathartic because it pumps up your blood pressure while doing nothing about the jerk who is bothering you. Floating for twenty minutes in an isolation water tank may be enormously calming while you're in it, but you still have to face the jerk the next day.

Successful anger therapies, therefore, attack the mind (teaching the person to identify the perceptions and interpretations that generate anger), the body (teaching relaxation and cooling-off techniques to help the person calm down), and behavior (teaching new habits and skills). These perceptions and habits might be summarized as follows:

Anger-Arousing Perceptions:

Injustice: "It's not fair"
Shattered expectations
Blaming: "Your fault"
"Not treating me right"
Shattered belief in a just world
"She's condescending to me"
"I deserve better than this"
"Those people are breaking the rules"

Anger-Reducing Perceptions:

"Bad things happen"
Empathy for the other person
"I can't fight every battle"
"She couldn't help it"
Humor and silliness

Anger-Intensifying Habits:

Yelling
Sulking and pouting
Plotting revenge
Hitting, other violence
Competitive games
Accusations ("You never . . .")
Arguing while angry

Cooling-Off Habits:

Count to 10 (or to . . .)
Sleep on it
Exercise (noncompetitive)
Nip argument in bud
Meditation, relaxation
Distraction (baking bread, reading, movies)

Ray Novaco, a psychologist who has developed a "stress inoculation program" for treating chronically angry individuals, believes that the first important step in anger management is for the individual to become an expert on his or her anger. "People say 'I'm angry all the time,' " he observes, "but what does that mean, exactly?" To find out, Novaco's clients begin by keeping an anger record, a diary that keeps track of what *triggers* the anger; the *frequency* of anger; the *intensity* of the anger; the *duration* of the anger (five minutes? three days?); and the *mode of expression* (What did you do?).

What happens, Novaco observes, is that people begin to see a pattern to their anger—that it occurs in particular situations, or with particular people, or under particular provocations. The person begins to see that anger is not entirely in the "self" but in the situation, and the focus of the solution changes. Keeping an anger diary also demystifies the emotion, showing the individual that anger isn't an "uncontrollable force." You were enraged at the traffic cop for giving you an unfair ticket, but you didn't hit her; you were furious at your boss, but you didn't quit; you wanted to kill that stupid driver, but you didn't.

Next, because anger is fomented, maintained, and inflamed by the statements we make to ourselves and others when we are provoked ("What a thoughtless lout!" "Who does she think she is!"), Novaco teaches people how to control anger the same way, by reinterpreting the supposed provocation: "Maybe he's having a rough day"; "She must be very unhappy if she would do such a thing." This is what people who are slow to anger do naturally: They empathize with the other person's behavior and try to find justifications for it. A telephone operator I interviewed, for example, told me that she no longer gets angry when customers rudely vent their anger at the world (or at the phone company) on her. "I bypass their anger entirely," she said, "and sympathize with them. I say nicely, 'Boy, you must be having a rough day.' They immediately calm down, realize how they must have sounded, and apologize."

The reappraisal method is being used with people who are exposed to constant provocations as part of their jobs, such as the police and bus drivers. New York City bus drivers, for example, learn that passengers who have irritating mannerisms may actually have hidden handicaps. Repeated questions ("Are we at Eighty-third street yet?") may indicate severe anxiety; apparent drunkenness may be a symptom of cerebral palsy; petit mal epileptic seizures can make a passenger seem to be deliberately ignoring a driver's orders. "Before, if a passenger rang the bell five times, I'd take him five blocks to get even," said a bus driver from Queens. "Now I'll say, 'Maybe this person is sick.' " These new attitudes reduce the arousal of anger by removing the perception of being under attack, which puts the individual—forgive me—back in the driver's seat.

Jerry Deffenbacher offers several examples of how people might talk to themselves when they begin to feel angry:

Cool thoughts. "Just stay cool. Getting all pissed off won't help." "This battle isn't worth it. Take a few deep breaths and chill out."

Problem-solving thoughts. "It's OK to feel annoyed, but it's just a hassle to be dealt with." "OK, develop a plan. What's the first thing that I want to do?"

Ultimate control and escape routes. "Bottom line, I'm in control. I can always walk away rather than lose it." "It's OK to take time out. Move away, get your act together, then come back and deal with it."

Self-rewarding thoughts. "Good, I'm hanging in there." "I feel great because I am coping with a hassle rather than screaming."

Deffenbacher also teaches clients to use silly images to reduce their anger and rethink provocation. "People often use inflammatory labels or phrases when they are angry," he observes, "which adds to their own anger. A helpful technique is to make those images *concrete*. You're driving along, calling the driver in front of you an ass. Well, 'ass' has two meanings—can you visualize either one of them actually driving a car?"

Certainly humor is the ultimate form of reappraisal, and the one that feels the best. I'm talking about funny, good-natured humor, by the way. Sarcastic, insulting humor does not reduce anger; it tends to increase hostility, and make other people angry and defensive. I'm not even talking about the ability to tell jokes or one-liners, although that's fun. I'm talking about the ability to see the lunatic or absurd aspects of life, including the tendency to take life too seriously.

Humor transforms injustice into absurdity, which is why it is the finely honed weapon of minorities and individuals who dare not or who cannot fight back directly. People who mistakenly believe that humor is never as serious or valuable as tragedy miss the point entirely. Not taking something seriously is a supreme act of defiance. The Czechoslovakian writer Milan Kundera says he learned the value of humor during the Stalinist era: The ability to laugh was a sign that a person could be trusted, because it signified an irreverent attitude toward history and its policemen. Kundera is, he says, "terrified of a world that is losing its humor."

On a mundane level, humor is therapeutic because it has a physiological component (it reduces tension) and a psychological one (it helps people rethink a problem and get some distance on it). When used on the target of your anger, it often defuses hostility and makes friendly discussion possible (or at least defangs the opposition). It allows people to travel the middle route between passive submission on one side and a futile battle with reality on the other. A friend of mine told me about a visit with her aunt, who, though due to have a mastectomy in a few days, was remarkably cheerful. "Listen," she said to my friend with a smile, "I told your uncle not to complain; he's had forty good years on that side."

Good-humored laughter at oneself may really be the best antidote to anger. "The affectionate admission of one's own foibles in a way that leads to spontaneous laughter," says sociologist Thomas Scheff, is a sign of "reconciliation—not only with others, but with one's true self, the suffering, foolish, awkward, impossible animal that is a human being." Harvey Mindess, a psychotherapist who has long been a believer in the healing power of laughter, tells of a patient who came to this "reconciliation." The woman concluded her sad saga of endless miseries by saying, "My problem's simple. I'm a total mess." In context, it was very funny, and they both broke up laughing. By exaggerating her plight, the woman had paradoxically reduced its significance. She was only a *partial* mess, which didn't seem so bad.

Because people who are angry, depressed, or anxious are usually self-absorbed and solemn about their feelings, some psychologists actually use "humor therapy" as a tactic. The theory is that you can't laugh and frown at the same time. My father, not knowing that he was anticipating a therapeutic method, often applied this approach on me when I was a child. Once, when I was enjoying a sullen and irritable mood, he insisted I accompany him to an afternoon of Charlie Chaplin movies. (He had the good sense not to try to reason me out of my anger.) There I learned that you cannot maintain a sullen mood when you are laughing out loud.

All of the techniques for chronically angry individuals focus on prevention (learning how to avoid getting angry in the first place); regulation of the intensity of anger (learning how to relax and calm down); and learning new skills to break the habitual response to anger. All three of these elements are important, though individuals differ in which skill they most need.

For example, some angry people are stubbornly resistant to changing their perceptions and ideas ("Look, the guy is a jerk and an idiot, period") until they have learned relaxation methods to help them cool off. Others find that changing their perceptions is fine as far as it goes, but it doesn't go far enough. It is not enough to learn to say of your three-year-old, "Young Barnaby is not *intentionally* trying to drive me crazy by screaming and painting the walls purple; isn't that cute?" You must also learn how to discipline young Barnaby and let the child know when you are displeased.

Further, some events cannot be reappraised. A friend of mine who has multiple sclerosis was asked to leave her elegant health club because, the manager said, "beautiful people" don't want to exercise with the disabled. (The extent of her disability at the time was a cane and a brace, and in fact, she told me, other women in the club were extremely nice to her.) When she told me this appalling experience, I found I had no desire to worry about the manager's personal woes in order to reduce my feeling of outrage. My friend went home and cried, and then thought about what course of action to take. She decided to demand her money back, plus interest—which they gave her—and put the whole business behind her. "There are other battles to fight," she said. "This one wasn't worth it to me."

Chronically angry people can learn to decide, finally, which battles are worth fighting, and which ones are best left alone. "Sometimes," Ray Novaco says, "it's just fine to accept cold soup." For some of the large indignities of life, the best remedy is direct action. For the small indignities, the best remedy is a Charlie Chaplin movie. The hard part is knowing the difference.

THE DIFFICULT PERSON

Everyone must confront a thorn or two in the rosebush of relationships: the difficult person. I am not speaking here of the nuisances who cross our paths and vanish, such as mean-tempered drivers, surly salesfolk, or rude moviegoers who talk all through the movie. I refer to the people who drive us crazy, but whom we can't ignore or leave—co-workers, neighbors, relatives, friends. These are the relationships that fill "Dear Abby" columns and therapists' offices: "My neighbor refuses to do anything about his dog, which runs wild and tramples my begonias." "My friend is always late, and when I try to talk to her about it she bursts into tears and says I don't like her." "I have to work with Manny on this project, but every time I offer a suggestion or criticize his ideas he gets belligerent and hostile."

Most people, faced with the unhappy task of dealing with such individuals, do what they assume any normal person would do: They set about trying to change the other person into a pussycat. They begin rationally: "Erwin," they say, "you are behaving in a rude and irritating manner, I wish you wouldn't do it, so please stop." When rational discourse fails—and it always does, because, after all, this is a *difficult* person or they wouldn't be having the problem in the first place—they do not conclude that the method failed. They conclude that Erwin was not paying attention, and they increase the volume: "*I said, you are behaving like a lout.*" And when that doesn't work, they often end up in repetitive efforts to get the friend or relative to change. The difficult person, of course, calls these efforts "nagging," and refuses to listen.

What's a person to do? The answer, many psychologists agree, contains a lovely irony: To change a difficult person, you must first change yourself—your way of thinking about the person and your way of responding to the familiar provocations.

The first question to resolve is what "difficult" means. Christine Padesky, director of the Center for Cognitive Therapy in Newport Beach, California, observes that many people create trouble for themselves by being too judgmental. "We decide that others *shouldn't* be 'difficult,' and that we *should* be able to influence and control them," she says. "Instead of focusing on their strengths and what they do right, we focus on their flaws and what they do wrong. I think that people need to examine their expectations of others. If you think that half the people in the world are difficult, because they refuse to do what you want or to agree with you, then most of the difficulty lies in you—in your expectations, which need to be reevaluated."

But what if, as is usually the case, it's only one or two people who get on your nerves, who seem impossible to deal with? Harriet Lerner, whose work on family systems I described in Chapter 8, takes a systems approach to the problem. This means that people must learn to see their own part in making the "difficult person" difficult. Once they recognize that their efforts to change the difficult person aren't working, says Lerner, they need to break the old pattern.

Suppose you have been covering up your co-worker's constant tardiness. You have spoken to him about it dozens of times, to no avail. You've tried everything and nothing has worked. In this case, you must state the new conditions of the relationship as clearly as possible. "I can't continue to cover up for you or delay meetings because of you," you might tell him. "So I've decided that I will simply go to meetings on time, and hope you can get there for them. If you don't, you'll have to find out what you missed from someone else." The virtue in seeing your own part in a system, Lerner adds, is that you are no longer at the mercy of the difficult person.

Managing a difficult person means, therefore, first managing oneself. But it is not easy to break away from the familiar actions and emotional blackmail of a difficult person. Along with Lerner, Padesky advises people to adopt a shared, problem-solving approach instead of the usual win/lose attitude. "The idea is to *collaborate* with the difficult person on trying to fix the problem between you," Padesky explains. "If you're working *with* someone, you'll make better headway than if you're locking horns with them. You focus on solving the problem, not on getting revenge or making the other person feel bad."

For example, Padesky had a client (I'll call her Julie) who had a "difficult" secretary. Julie needed the secretary and liked her, but the woman could not tolerate the slightest criticism. Whenever Julie tried to discuss her work with her, she would burst into tears and then not come to the office for three days.

Padesky first asked Julie to try to understand the reasons for the secretary's behavior. "Very often people who are difficult to deal with are themselves frightened or insecure or troubled in some way," says Padesky. "Maybe they're in chronic pain, or simply not imaginative enough to cope with the demands on them. So when they have a problem, they respond by being belligerent or stubborn or tearful. In such cases, empathy goes a long way, and it may provide the key to changing the difficult person's behavior." In this case, it turned out that the secretary was afraid of being fired or thought incompetent. In fact, neither of her fears was justified, and Julie conveyed this reassurance to her.

Next Padesky taught Julie to give the secretary constructive feedback on what she was doing right, and how to create a collaborative mood. "I know you have a lot of work and conflicting demands here, which you manage brilliantly. But I'm unhappy about the number of errors in these weekly reports," Julie might say. "What do *you* suggest we do to solve this problem?" Now the problem is framed in terms of time and task management, not in terms of the secretary's "difficult personality."

"Insecure people usually need specific feedback that tells them how they're doing and what they need to do to improve," Padesky observes. "Don't let tears deflect you from your goals, though. You don't have to be cold, but neither should you be too supportive of the emotional display. Instead, keep the person talking; ask specific questions, such as 'What are we going to do next?' "

With a difficult person who becomes belligerent, Padesky again recommends sidestepping emotional displays and concentrating on solving a problem together. Padesky told me about an exasperating situation she herself was in with such a person. She was head of a committee at work, and one of its members was a man who would fly off the handle at even the most reasonable requests. Every time she asked him about his willingness to take on some task, he would become angry, accuse *her* of being difficult, and attack her, in essence, for doing her job.

"My first response," says Padesky, "was to get angry back. 'You don't have the right to talk to me like that! What I'm asking is very reasonable!' We'd have an argument; I'd storm out of the room, furious, and only much later realize that he had successfully avoided agreeing to do any work. He was using belligerence as a way of intimidating people out of requiring work from him. We were playing his game on his turf."

So Padesky changed the rules of the game. She stopped interpreting his belligerence as a personal attack on her, and concentrated instead on what she wanted from him. Their ensuing conversations, she recalls, sounded pretty strange at first, because what she said did not follow from what he said. "You must not say what the other person expects," Padesky advises. "Just keep your eye on the goal." Instead, she would simply repeat her question to him: "You know, you said you would do some work for this committee. What did you have in mind?" When he would make outrageous accusations against her ("You're out to get me! You have some hidden grudge against me!"), she would reply, "Well, I see that is how you feel about me, but it's not my intention to be difficult or annoying. Now, which of the available committee assignments will you take on?" Eventually, the difficult person will learn that belligerent (or tearful) displays are not effective with you, and will settle down to the problem at hand.

With a difficult person who won't admit that he or she is angry with you, Padesky advises, you can act genuinely puzzled about the person's behavior. "You say, 'Look, lately you seem irritated by me. What's going on?' This often disarms an angry person. Listen to them straight through their viewpoint, *even if you disagree with everything they say*, even if they're distorting or exaggerating. Listen attentively, make eye contact, let them express their point of view, and agree with whatever is true." This is easier said than done, because the temptation is to jump in and interrupt as soon as the person says something you disagree with. *Let them finish.* Sometimes, all they want to do is state their case.

Suppose your neighbor accuses you of letting your dog trample her begonias, Padesky says, when you know you keep your dog locked up in the backyard. "You can agree with her feelings, and say, 'It is certainly enraging to come home and find trampled begonias. I'd be angry too. But I'm puzzled, because I keep my dog locked up. Could it be another dog? I'd be glad to help you get to the bottom of this.' "

Another common problem is dealing with the individual who promises to do something and never follows through. "Some people really do forget," says Padesky, "in which case, a few persistent reminders will eventually do the trick. But lots of people will agree with something you want simply to avoid conflict, when in fact they don't agree. They do make life difficult, because you don't know what's going on in their heads."

In such cases, Padesky advises calm assertiveness. "State how you feel—'I'm upset that you didn't do what you promised'—and then turn the tables on them. Instead of your usual accusation, which they will be expecting, ask, 'What prevents you from doing it? What do you recommend that we do?' At this point, shut your mouth and let the other person come up with a solution, since he has obviously been ignoring yours. You might also ask what he suggests you do if he forgets again. Now it's not your problem, but his; and you've asked him to take responsibility for solving the problem."

This all sounds well and good, I said to Padesky, but what happens if the difficult person cannot or will not change, or denies there even is a problem? "You can try to convince the person that it *is* a problem to you," she replied, "that you are upset about it, and that if nothing is done there will be unfortunate consequences for your relationship. If this doesn't work, you must decide either to adapt your thinking and accept this problem as one of the nuisances of life, or to fight it. If you decide to fight, consider the long-term consequences on your blood pressure and on the relationship. If the difficult person is a neighbor, you might be living near that person for years; if it's a co-worker, you might have trouble on your job. How important is the flaw that is making your friend or neighbor so difficult? Are you able to accept the person's good qualities, and overlook the flaws?"

Difficult people, of course, often give off such an angry and hostile air that others ignore or reject them in *anticipation* of their being difficult. This, of course, makes them all the more difficult—and a hostile feedback loop is created. That's why the secret of dealing with difficult people, like the secret of living with difficult spouses, is not to rise to their bait, even if that bait is awfully tempting. "I think that if you're pleasant and cordial, you will, in the long run, wear them down, even get the m to be cordial back," says Padesky. "It's surprising how often they warm up—not always, but often—because so often their hostility masks their own loneliness and insecurity. And in the long run, who benefits most by your being friendly and cordial? You do."

People who follow these basic principles of understanding and problem-solving, Padesky maintains, will find that the pool of "difficult people" will become smaller and smaller. "If you handle people in this way," she says, "they cease to be difficult, because generally you are able to work things out. And if you aren't able to, you won't be as bothered by it. Difficulty, ultimately, is in the eye of the beholder."

THE ANGRY DIVORCE

My husband and I had been married thirty-one years, when he told me that although I had always been a good wife and mother, he wanted to be free for the rest of his life. He wanted, he said, to be "unencumbered by responsibilities." This announcement came completely out of the blue and had a devastating effect on me. In my generation, you signed up for life when you married. I'd done everything right; I'd devoted myself to the family; it was all so *unfair*. For several years afterward I was consumed by anger. I would become enraged at him when *anything* went wrong, even if it was my own fault—if I dropped a glass on the floor, I blamed him. My anger was like having a flu bug that attacks different parts of the body; just when I thought I had recovered, it would strike again.

This woman, whom I will call Lynn Marks, is understandably angry. She feels she is the victim of a colossal miscarriage of justice, that her husband betrayed her, that divorce—for a woman who had done all the right things for so many years—was deeply unfair. Yet the anger of separation and divorce not only strikes women like Lynn Marks. It also strikes women who decide to leave their husbands and women who divorce their husbands by mutual, amicable agreement. It affects men who never have to see their ex-wives again as well as men who must see them often because of the children.

Popular opinion has it that time heals all wounds, that human beings are naturally resilient. But some people do not heal from the wounds of divorce. In 1971, Judith Wallerstein, then working with Joan Kelly, began a study of 131 children and adolescents from sixty families, and their divorcing parents, in Marin County, California. The researchers reinterviewed all family members eighteen months later, again five years after divorce, and again ten and fifteen years after divorce. The parents were upper-middle-class, most white, and had been married anywhere from four to twenty-three years. The children were all developmentally normal, doing well in school, and in good psychological health—until the divorce hit them.

Wallerstein found that even after *ten years*, half of the women and one-third of the men in her study were still intensely angry at their former spouses, and that the consequences of this anger and conflict for their children were often disastrous. Children watched their parents hit, scream at, and abuse one another. Children were often asked to take sides, to snoop on each parent for the edification of the other, and to join one parent's efforts to sabotage the other. "Common sense and clinical wisdom tell us that people should get over being angry at one another, but our study shows that we may be wrong," Wallerstein (and co-author Sandra Blakeslee) write in *Second Chances*. "In the years after divorce, anger can last, anger can intensify, anger can corrupt, anger can be refueled. Anger can also be walled off so it cannot spill into the present. And anger can be resolved."

One of the clearest contributions to lasting anger was that now-familiar factor: the rehearsal of grievances. The angry couples in Wallerstein's study talked incessantly to everyone they knew—their children, friends, lawyers—about the horrible sins of the former spouse. Wallerstein found, along with so many other psychologists, that this chorus of complaints does not diminish anger. On the contrary, she says, "it is refueled with each incantation of sins." As Wallerstein reinterviewed these couples ten years later, she often got the feeling that she was "wandering into the same play, where the same characters are using the same lines to tell the same story with the same intensity of feeling to the same audience. They do not seem to remember telling me—the audience—the same stories many times before. They do not seem to care about audience reaction."

Wallerstein believes, and I concur, that there is a moral as well as a psychological reason for managing anger after divorce and for eventually resolving it: protecting one's children as well as oneself. One child in Wallerstein's study, Dana, had parents who were no less angry at each other than other separating spouses, but they made a point of never physically or verbally attacking one another and *never letting it get out of control.* Dana's mother was furious at her ex-husband and remained so fifteen years later, but she was able, says Wallerstein, to keep her anger within bounds and not use her children as scapegoats or allies. "Among all the things that people can do to protect their children in the wake of divorce, this is one of the hardest and one of the most important," says Wallerstein. "It is, unfortunately, one of the least common."

The first step in controlling the feelings of anger, humiliation, and loss is to understand their origin in the psychology of attachment. "The body does not take kindly to broken attachments, even when we think we want to break them," says Robert Maurer, director of behavioral science at the Family Practice Residency Program at Santa Monica Hospital. "It sets off an alarm reaction—the intense stress symptoms of sleeplessness, pounding heart, inability to concentrate, forgetfulness, digestive problems, fatigue and all the rest." It can take a year or two, or even longer, for the body to readjust, for the alarm mechanism to turn off. This is why, in addition to its emotional wear and tear, separation is *physically* exhausting.

Psychologist Prudence Brown, who wanted to identify the causes of growth or stagnation among women who divorce, interviewed 253 women twice: the first time during a painful and tumultuous stage of divorce (when they registered at a court-related marriage counseling service) and then again four months later. She gave the women a barrage of questions about their attitudes, marriages, and personalities. She asked a number of questions specifically about anger: Did they show it or keep it in? Recover from it quickly or slowly? Feel guilty or good about expressing it? And she measured their self-esteem, overall distress, and amount of improvement over time.

Brown expected that the women who expressed their anger would be in the best psychological shape. To her surprise (but surely no longer to ours), she found that the women who "let anger out" were *not* better off than those who "kept it in." Expressing anger did *not* automatically make a woman feel better, and it did *not* improve a woman's self-esteem. Further, when Brown compared the women whose mental health improved during the four months with those who remained bitter and unhappy, she found that the "growers" had an active social life but did not harp on matters pertaining to the divorce; the "nongrowers" socialized with friends and family just as often but they tended to talk obsessively about the divorce (using choice words, I suspect, about the ex-husband).

Perhaps you think, as I did, that the growers are simply women who were having an easier time of it all around? That they have fewer children, for example, or are younger, employed (and therefore don't have financial worries), and wanted the divorce in the first place? Not at all. Brown found *no differences* between growers and nongrowers in age, number of children, race, ethnic background, working status (employed or housewives), length of marriage, length of separation, whether wife or husband wanted the divorce, or how long each had wanted the divorce.

The difference she did find is, I think, central to the role that anger plays in our social lives. It is that the nongrowers were ambivalent about the divorce: They missed their husbands *and* wanted nothing to do with them, even if they themselves originally wanted the separation. When they quarreled with their husbands, they felt bad about it and blamed themselves, which in turn lowered their self-esteem and increased their sense of guilt and distress.

What keeps people ambivalent and angry, even years after a separation? There is, first of all, little relationship between the degree of anger a person feels and how many reasons he or she has to feel angry. Many people remain vengeful and bitter even though they never have to see Mildred or Joe again in their lives, and many people get over their rage even though they have to see Hilda and Mike frequently because of the children.

Marion Jacobs, a clinical psychologist at UCLA, observes that there is an important difference between appropriate—but occasional—anger and the continuous outrage that feels out of control. "Of course a person should be able to say, 'Boy, I am very angry about this; once again he or she didn't pick up the children on time,' " says Jacobs. "But that's very different from saying 'This whole divorce is such an outrage *that I can't stand it.'* If that kind of rage goes on and on, chances are that the spouses are continually saying things to themselves that are keeping it alive. They are rehearsing a script, playing the part of the wronged wife or misunderstood husband over and over. Now, they may wish to hold on to their righteous sense of having been victimized, but the question they need to consider is: Who is being harmed by all this outrage? Not the ex-spouse. They are paying a much higher price in their own misery."

Jacobs recommends that people who feel overwhelmed by anger begin with some candid self-examination of ways they feed their own rage. "I wish I had a computer printout of two minutes of the thoughts going through my client's heads," she observes. "It's a constant stream of self-critical, hostile thoughts: 'I'm a failure,' 'Nothing is going right,' 'My whole life has been ruined,' 'This is all so unfair,' and so on. Well, yes, it is unfair, but now what? Rehearsing the unfairness will do nothing to make it go away." Jacobs advises clients to write down every negative thought they have in the course of a day. As with Novaco's anger-diary method, they quickly recognize the inner dialogue that contributes to their anger.

The alternative, Jacobs hastens to add, is not to have Pollyanna-ish thoughts that everything is fine and Harry is a swell guy after all. "The point is to be able to take accurate stock of the positive things in one's life," she says. "The heavy, blanket sense of rage and helplessness prevents people from becoming aware of their strengths and opportunities."

People often try to contrast "realistic" anger, say at the ex-spouse's management of money, with "unrealistic" anger, but Maurer thinks this distinction is moot. "I think the real question is whether anger is serving or destroying you," Maurer says. "Is anger moving you forward, propelling you to make a better choice next time, or is it crippling you, offering a reason to hide from the world?"

The crippling kind of anger, Maurer observes, is almost always linked to low self-esteem. "Many women with low self-esteem tried to please their husbands for years," says Maurer. "They sacrificed their own interests and needs in order to be the ideal wife and mother. Anger helps them leave these men or to feel righteously betrayed if they are left, but it doesn't cure their low self-regard. If they didn't hate their spouses they would have to hate themselves, which is intolerable. In their minds, there is no such thing as no-fault divorce: It's all his fault. Anger is more comfortable for such women, because they don't have to face their own self-hatred or insecurity."

Anger has other self-protective uses. Consider the man who has had a friendly divorce, and now finds himself frequently angry at his ex-wife for no apparent reason. Such anger, Maurer suggests, often masks fear. "When the old relationship is no longer in the way of dating," he explains, "many people feel scared. Their self-doubts surface. Anger at the former mate can be a way of holding on to the familiar—'If we hadn't broken up, I wouldn't have all these scary feelings and wouldn't have to go through all of this again.' Instead of facing their fears, many people have learned to get angry."

To overcome rage that doesn't subside, one must first recognize the ambivalence and attachment that contribute to it, and to move toward a sense of closure on the marriage. Anger is often prolonged after divorce because our culture offers no rituals of resolution, no way a community can help its members manage anger as it helps them manage grief. Some churches are instituting "divorce ceremonies" for this reason; some individuals invent their own. (One such end-of-anger ritual was described on page 156.) These rituals need not be angry, but they do need to meet the criteria for catharsis, as illustrated by this woman I interviewed:

On what would have been our thirtieth anniversary, I bought two Waterford goblets and some bread and wine that I knew my husband liked. I sent it all to him with a note, wishing him a happy celebration of his new life. Then I took a boat trip with a friend, threw roses into the water, and officially said good-bye. When I came home, I burned all my cards with my married name, and packed away my wedding dress and photos. When it was over, I felt a lot better. And I felt good at how I had acted toward him, too.

No psychologist can say when or why a person becomes ready to move from righteous rage to closure and forgiveness. But an understanding that one is not alone in one's experience, that anger is a temporary symptom and need not be a way of life, certainly helps. As co-director of the California Self-Help Center at UCLA, Jacobs has studied the benefits of groups that organize around a common concern of their members. She and her associates set up nine groups of divorced women in their forties and fifties, women who were feeling much bitterness, whose self-esteem had been shattered, and who were trying to make sense of the experience.

"If you just keep going round and round the emotional track by yourself," says Jacobs, "it's very hard to get off. Self-help groups allow their members to understand and reinterpret what happened to them. Women begin to see the world more accurately: 'He did this, but I did that,' 'Even if I had done such-and-such, he still would have left.' They become able to evaluate their current problems and future possibilities more realistically. That endless self-critical internal dialogue slows down, along with self-blame and even husband-blame."

In any crisis, Jacobs observes, people turn first to friends and family. Unfortunately, friends and relatives often don't know what to say or do, or, worse, they are critical and disapproving. Many friends try to be supportive for a while, and then lose interest. They start offering pep talks: "Chin up," they say, or "Time heals," or "It's been long enough, time to get on with your life." "Not only are these platitudes unhelpful, they are usually guilt-inducing," says Jacobs. "Now the woman still feels angry at her ex-husband, *and* guilty for feeling angry." A self-help group gives its members a place to share their experiences with others who understand them.

Jacobs and her associates developed a twelve-week program to guide a new group through its formative stages without the presence of a professional. By the end of the program, the divorced women felt less lonely, were less likely to be blaming themselves, and had developed better coping strategies than they had at the start of the sessions. Many studies have shown that people who join self-help groups (to deal with any problem) are typically much better off emotionally and physically than people who try to face their problems alone. It is the sense of being alone that is often so devastating.

Lynn Marks, who went to both a therapist and a self-help group, believes that the self-help group restored her sanity. "The therapist would listen to me and tell me that insomnia and forgetting things were standard stress reactions," she says. "But I can't tell you how reassuring it felt to sit with a group of women and hear them say, 'God, I didn't sleep a wink all night' or 'I forgot six things I had to do today.' The group made me realize I wasn't crazy to have the feelings I have. I learned it wasn't me but the situation I was in that was causing my feelings, and that I would have to expect these emotions."

Ultimately, the best cure for persistent anger is to improve self-regard. "It is hard to convey the message that self-hate is optional, because many women take it as another thing you're blaming them for," Maurer says. "They say, 'I've made all these mistakes, and now here's another thing I'm doing wrong—not liking myself enough.' " And yet, Maurer maintains—echoing the words of the humor therapists and the family-systems therapists—self-love rests on the ability to accept the calamities of life and see one's own role in them. "The despair and rage that often accompany divorce are good motivators to begin learning this lesson," he says. "The problem with holding onto anger is that it has physical costs, in stress to the body, but it also disturbs people's ability to learn from their mistakes, and it inclines them to cling to their victimhood. Anger may be necessary for a while. But it is at best a detour and at worst a destructive diversion from the healing that needs to occur if one is to learn from experience."

One of the women in Jacobs's self-help group illustrates Maurer's point:

> I made mistakes in my marriage, but I did the best I could with the knowledge I had at the time. Finally I'm not somebody's wife and somebody's mother. I am my own person at last. It's OK.

THE AGGRESSIVE CHILD

At the Oregon Social Learning Center, Gerald R. Patterson and his colleagues have been conducting clinical and field studies of aggressive boys in angry families. They have come to the same conclusions that family-systems theorists have: A pattern—a cycle of violence and disobedience—is established early, and quickly spins out of control. "People living in these families are aggressive, angry people," says Patterson. "The parents are turned off, the [child's] peers are turned off, and the child has a very poor self-image as well."

The sequence of events that Patterson has identified looks like this: Parents, under particular stress, become inept at "parenting"—at managing the family in general and disciplining the children in particular. The stress may result from divorce, prolonged unemployment, illness, or drug problems, or other chronic matters; sometimes the parents' problems begin because the boy has an unusually difficult temperament. The parent, unable to control "garden-variety" problems—whining, teasing, yelling, disobedience—permits, even encourages, the child to get away with angry displays. Eventually, the child becomes more and more rebellious, disobedient, and aggressive, which causes other children to reject him, and which causes the parents to reject and dislike him, too. The boy begins to give up at school and develops low self-esteem, which perpetuates the angry disobedience, which perpetuates parental anger and rejection, ad infinitum.

In distressed families, Patterson finds (by close observation of literally thousands of family exchanges), children progress steadily from learning to be disobedient to learning to be physically assaultive. A three-step process may occur *hundreds* of times each day: The child is attacked, or criticized, or yelled at by an exasperated parent or sibling; the child responds aggressively; the child's aggression is rewarded when the attacker withdraws. Thus the child learns to use manipulative and coercive tactics (such as whining, yelling, and temper tantrums) as a substitute social skill. As other family members acquire these same tactics in retaliation, the "coercive chains" become longer. Patterson finds that when such exchanges last longer than eighteen seconds, families are at increased risk of violence. Someone eventually stops talking or even yelling, and starts hitting.

The pattern, as I say, begins with inept discipline. Parents of aggressive boys use a great deal of punishment (shouting, scolding, spanking), yet they fail to make the punishment contingent on the child's behavior. They do not state clear rules, require compliance, praise good behavior, or consistently punish violations. Instead, they threaten, scold, nag, bluster, and "natter" at the child, but, Patterson adds, "they seldom follow through on their threats." So the child continues to misbehave. At infrequent and unpredictable intervals the parents explode and verbally or physically assault the child. This pattern of parental behavior has been repeatedly linked to children's aggressiveness in elementary school.

As the child becomes more skillful at coercion and disobedience, he (or, less often in these studies, she) becomes even more difficult to discipline, so the parents become even more inept. Once the child has become stubbornly disobedient, it is difficult to teach him social skills. "What leads to things getting out of hand may be a relatively simple affair," observes Patterson, "whereas the process itself, once initiated, may be the stuff of which novels are made."

Fortunately, in the last decade several successful programs have been developed to interrupt this process. These programs do not hand out bats to aggressive children and have them hit each other to "release" their feelings. Instead, they teach children how to control anger, how to solve the problems that generate their anger, how to relax and reduce tension, and how to get along with other people so they won't need their anger.

John Lochman, at Duke University Medical Center, set up an anger-coping intervention program with elementary-school boys (one-third of whom were black, the rest white). These boys, who had been referred by their classroom teachers, were highly disruptive, violent, and antisocial. Some were assigned to the anger-coping program; the rest served as a control group, to see if they would simply outgrow their aggressive habits. The researchers also set up a second control group of nonaggressive boys of the same age.

The anger-coping program was remarkably simple. The boys met in groups of four to six, with two co-leaders, once a week during school hours, and the sessions lasted four to five months. There they learned how to speak about their angry feelings (with self-statements, such as "I am feeling . . ." instead of you-statements, such as "You always . . ."). They watched videotaped examples of men modeling anger control and self-management. They set up role-playing situations. They learned problem-solving skills so they could change the problem that was making them angry instead of seething about it. As a group, the boys also created their own videotaped scenarios to dramatize ways of coping with infuriating situations.

Three years later, the boys who had been through the anger-control program were *no different* from the original nonaggressive boys in levels of anger or aggressive behavior, and they were very different from the untreated aggressive boys. The boys in the anger program acquired higher self-esteem, they were better able to solve problems, and they lost many of their antisocial habits. Interestingly, they were also less likely to be using drugs or alcohol. The researchers speculate that the problem-solving training prepared the boys to "make more careful, less impulsive decisions" about drug use.

At Adelphi University, psychologist Eva Feindler and her associates have developed an Art of Self-Control Training Program—which she affectionately refers to as the "Chill-Out" program—for antisocial or delinquent teenagers. It too includes lessons in relaxation and deep breathing, self-monitoring of angry reactions to provocation, problem-solving, and assertiveness. But Feindler also observes that no program will work if it is carried out in a rote and inflexible way, or if the role-playing is done without drama and excitement. You need enthusiasm, playfulness, and the ability to joke, she says, in order for adolescents to listen to you in the first place.

One of the most comprehensive and successful programs for assaultive, hostile adolescents and children is called "Aggression Replacement Training." Developed by Arnold Goldstein, director of the Center for Research on Aggression at Syracuse University, and Barry Glick, a deputy director for social services of the New York State Division for Youth, this program is based on the assumption that anger and aggression are methods of last-resort coping, when a child has not learned to get along with others and solve problems.

Aggression Replacement Training includes anger-control training, based on Novaco's and Feindler's work. But it also includes two additional elements: a "structured learning" program to correct deficiencies in basic social skills, and a "moral education" program to teach moral reasoning skills. Young people may know how to get along with others and know how to control their tempers, Goldstein and Glick observe, but why would they want to? The researchers therefore believe that violent, angry individuals must learn to understand and reason about the moral consequences of their individual actions.

The structured learning program teaches some elementary rules of social life, which most of these antisocial teenagers have never learned: listening, starting a conversation, asking questions, saying thank you. They learn how to deal with feelings: recognizing emotions, expressing affection, coping with fear, understanding the emotions of others. They learn alternatives to aggression: helping others, negotiating, standing up for one's rights, responding to teasing, keeping out of fights. They learn how to deal with stressful provocations: dealing with embarrassment and being left out, responding to failure, sportsmanship after a game, dealing with group pressure, standing up for a friend. And they learn how to plan and solve problems.

Altogether, Aggression Replacement Training offers a remarkable assortment of lessons, which together suggest why simply ordering violent teenagers to "calm down" doesn't work. To date,

Goldstein and his associates have conducted evaluation programs on the effectiveness of Aggression Replacement Training with many groups, including child-abusing parents, young children, police, aggressive adolescents, employees in mental hospitals, and the parents and siblings of chronically violent delinquents. The program has been particularly successful in teaching empathy, negotiation, assertiveness, how to follow instructions, and self-control—all skills that reduce anger.

Parents too can learn the skills of effective discipline, which are best applied before a child has acquired an aggressive, rebellious habit. According to psychologist Diana Baumrind, authoritarian parents exercise too much power and use discipline punitively; permissive parents exercise too little power and fear the use of any discipline at all. As in all things, the middle course is best. "Authoritative" parents know when and how to discipline their children. They neither demand total obedience nor abdicate all rules; they set standards and enforce them firmly, while also explaining the reasons behind their discipline and demands. They use authority when necessary, yet also recognize their children's rights.

How does anyone become an "authoritative" parent? According to a vast number of research studies, the following guidelines are effective ways of raising children who control their aggressive impulses and have high self-esteem:

• Be consistent in enforcing the rules. Do not give in to the child's whining or tantrums, or let the child get away with breaking rules behind your back. Inconsistency—letting the child hit the cat on Tuesday but not on Thursday—encourages the undesirable behavior. A friend of mine realized this when her young child said to her: "Why are you so mad at me today, Mommy? I'm this naughty every day."

• Set high expectations that are appropriate to the child's age, and teach the child how to meet them. Some parents make few demands on their children. They may believe a parent should not "impose" rules on children, or they may simply want to avoid arguments. Others set clear standards, such as requiring children to be polite, help with chores, control their anger, be thoughtful of others, and do well in school. The children of well-meaning parents who make few demands tend to be aggressive, impulsive, and immature. The children of parents who have high demands and expectations tend to be helpful rather than selfish, and above average in competence and self-confidence. Of course, the demands must be appropriate for the child's age, abilities, and temperament. You'll be angry all the time if you expect your two-year-old to read and write, or if you expect your shy five-year-old painter to be a live-wire comedian.

• Establish open communication with your child. Enforce rules and requirements, but talk to your children and explain your reasons. "Because I say so" isn't enough. This doesn't mean you have to argue with a four-year-old about the merits of having measles shots. You can allow children to express their disagreements and feelings, without allowing them to behave violently.

• Notice, approve of, and reward good behavior. Many parents tend to punish the behavior they dislike, a form of attention that may actually be rewarding to the child. But it is much more effective to praise the behavior you do want, which teaches the child what is right.

• Call the child's attention to the effect of his or her actions on others, and how to take another person's point of view. This lesson teaches empathy and consideration for others. Vague orders such as "Don't fight!" are less effective than showing the child how fighting disrupts and hurts others. For boys especially, the greater their ability to empathize, the lower their likelihood of behaving aggressively.

One of the sturdiest findings in developmental psychology is the consistency of aggressiveness between childhood and adulthood. Left to their own devices, bullying children grow into bullying adults; they don't "outgrow" bad habits unless they can replace them with other, more successful ones. Nevertheless, I have found, across the country, an alarming number of official programs for violent delinquents that rest on the outmoded view that you cure aggression by encouraging aggression—you just let these kids "ventilate" by screaming, pounding the walls, or pummeling one another. There is no longer any justification for such a belief or for such programs.

THE VICTIM

The victim who won't forgive will often live in psycho-logical bondage to the victimizer, leading to a kind of paralysis.

—CORETTA SCOTT KING

Had I been able to forgive my mother during her lifetime and tell her so, I might have spared myself years of feeling hagaii *("itchy teeth," Japanese for helpless an-guish tinged with frustration).*

—NORIKO SAWADA, "Memoir of a Japanese Daughter"

When my husband was recovering from a heart attack, now many years ago, his sympathetic doctor, who had read too many psychology books, tried to console him. "You're angry, aren't you?" he said. "You're saying to yourself: 'Why me?' " "No, actually, I'm not," my husband said. "I know *exactly* why me. I've been struggling with a difficult choice, and now I know exactly what to do. My heart has literally made a decision for me that my head was too cowardly to recognize."

Nancy Mairs is a poet, writer, and teacher who is crippled by multiple sclerosis. ("Crippled" is her choice of word; none of this mealy-mouthed "differently abled" stuff, she says.) Mairs has also suffered from chronic fatigue, depression, and agoraphobia. A friend of hers who also has MS asked her one day: "Do you ever say to yourself, 'Why me, Lord?' " Mairs replied: "No, Michael, I don't, because whenever I try, the only response I can think of is 'Why not?' "

Why not, indeed. Yet, as noted in Chapter 9, many Americans persist in the childhood belief that life should be fair, as if it followed the rules of marbles or hopscotch. Nowadays we are witnessing an ever-increasing number of victims of life's unfair-ness. Anyone who has had a bad experience, temporary or long-lasting, may lay claim to the title: anyone who has been sexually abused; who has been through a terrible divorce; who has a serious illness; whose parents were alcoholic or disturbed. People

are being encouraged to respond to these misfortunes with anger—
"Why me? It isn't *fair!*"—and then to find security by wrapping
themselves in the cloak of the victim: "I can't help how I am; look
at all these horrible things that happened to me. I've *earned* my
anger."

By all means, men and women need to identify and acknowledge the origins of their victimization and unhappiness. They
need to understand that bad things can and do happen to good
people, and to stop blaming themselves for "provoking" or
"deserving" the bad things. But while the victim phase may be a
useful part of recovery, it is not sufficient as a *total* approach to
recovery. Too many people end up playing the role of victim to
perfection: "the aggrieved wife," "the rejected lover," the "helpless
patient," and the like. "I didn't deserve this," they complain. "I
was the perfect wife, the most accommodating lover, and I took
my multivitamin every day. How dare this happen to me!"

Of course, there *are* real victims. There really *are* people who
have had a lousy time of it. I don't want to underestimate their
rage, sadness, or humiliation for a minute. But the ultimate issue
is this: The event happened. How can people get beyond the sense
of victimization? The heartening news is that most people do
recover. Most of the people who have suffered even the most
grotesque injustices manage to survive and transcend them.

In their research and clinical work with human resilience,
psychiatrist Frederic Flach and psychologist Julius Segal find that
what survivors have in common, among other things, is that they
do not accept the label or identity of victim. They do not say,
"What happened to me is the worst thing in the world, and I'll
never be free of it!" They say, "What happened to me was pretty
bad, but other people are worse off, and I won't let the bastards
win." They do not wallow around indefinitely, trying to answer
the unanswerable "Why me?" They say, "I haven't the foggiest
idea why me, but at least it wasn't my fault, and maybe I can help
others."

Survivors of tragedy do not blame themselves for bringing on
disaster, but they get on with their lives. Nancy Mairs, who
certainly has plenty to be depressed about, put it best. Ultimately,

she hit bottom and tried to commit suicide. "When I woke from that disagreeable event," she writes, "I recognized for the first time that I was fully and solely responsible for my existence."

None of this means that people must "forgive and forget." Forgiving has nothing to do with memory loss. There is no need to forget injustices and injuries, or pretend they never happened, and some events must never be forgotten. But that is quite different from letting them dominate one's present.

Anger, as I have been arguing, is an informal judiciary, a response to injustice. Prolonged anger is often a way for a person to feel that he or she is righting a wrong, simply by maintaining a punitive emotional state. For people who are using anger as a weapon of retaliation, therefore, the primary "cure" is to find a different symbol of justice.

For example, a common problem that brings couples to psychotherapy is the Dilemma of the Wronged Spouse. One partner has had an affair, or has committed a serious act of betrayal or neglect; the other, feeling helplessly victimized, cannot forgive. Both partners want the relationship to continue. But the Wronged Spouse cannot seem to shake his or her anger and moral outrage, and the Betraying Spouse, having sworn allegiance and apologized until blue in the face, is beginning to feel angry in return. "I just can't shake those images of my husband with another woman," says Wronged. "I feel guilty, I'm trying to make amends, but nothing satisfies her," says Betraying. "How long am I supposed to keep atoning?"

According to psychotherapist Bernie Zilbergeld, the offended partner must recognize that he or she is using anger (a potentially endless emotional state) as retribution for the spouse's behavior (an action that is now in the past), and consider alternatives to anger as punishment. "I ask, 'What would you need to have happen for you to forgive your partner?' " Zilbergeld says. "Often they reply, 'I need to stop feeling so angry.' 'OK, so what would you need to stop feeling so angry?' Now they must come up with some action that the offending spouse can do, which will make their anger unnecessary."

Sometimes, says Zilbergeld, Wronged Spouses demand a huge

behavioral ransom: "He'd have to do everything around the house for the next one hundred years." But eventually they settle down to specifics. And specifics are important. A vague requirement, like "He has to notice me more," will last as long as a New Year's resolution if it is not translated into certain behaviors that the spouse can adhere to ("He has to remember our anniversary and plan a nice evening"; "He has to compliment me at least once a week").

In one case of Zilbergeld's, the wife specified that her husband would have to do three things: clean the bathroom every week (a chore they both hated, which she always ended up doing); make dinner twice a week; and pick up after himself. Moreover, she said, he'd have to do these things *without reminders or hints from her.* She wanted not to have to think about it. At the end of three months, they agreed, they would renegotiate the bathroom rules.

Behavioral agreements like this are usually highly successful, says Zilbergeld. "The guilty spouse comes to therapy cowering and withdrawn, but ready to go into a rage. He's apologized, he's tried to please her, and nothing has calmed her down, so he's ready to try anything. Giving him a specific thing to do suddenly doesn't look so bad, even cleaning the bathroom." This method allows the Wronged Spouse to abandon the need for anger, because everything the partner does is a sign of commitment to the marriage and to the desire to make amends. It helps, though, if the Wronged Spouse also agrees to stop ventilating rage so readily and considers its purpose and effects. If, while making love, she suddenly has an image of her husband with his lover, she can say, "I'm having a bad moment right now; please help me" rather than "How could you, you . . ."

Many people want to know what technique or ritual will resolve, once and for all, their continuing feelings of anger toward a former spouse, a betraying friend, or an unavailable parent. Anyone who knew a simple set of steps for attaining the tranquillity of forgiveness would be deservedly famous. Actually, I think that the steps toward healing are generally known; the problem is that, as with methods for quitting smoking, a person must be ready for them. A person can try to stop smoking for ten years, and suddenly, one day, be ready to let it go. With anger too, the protective feeling of being a self-righteous victim can be hard to abandon. Suddenly, one day, the person is ready to let it go.

Some of the essential elements of letting anger go have been described throughout this book. They include:

• Inventing a healing ritual that marks the restoration of justice and the end of anger. The specific ritual depends on what each person needs to do, drawing on symbols and events that are meaningful.

• Confessing, which *is* good for the soul; not endless expression, but the confession of deepest fears and thoughts in order to gain distance from them and understanding.

• Forming a self-help group with others who have been through the same experience. They know what you are feeling, and together you might come up with solutions. As the self-help research finds, meeting with others in the same boat helps people understand that they are not alone, not to blame, and not crazy to feel as they do.

• Taking action to help others, which puts your own miseries in perspective. At one conference I attended, a woman rose to say that she was enraged and depressed about the killing of her young son by a drunk driver. There was a sympathetic murmur from the audience—until the woman mentioned that the tragedy had happened ten years earlier. Contrast her reaction with that of the women who organized Mothers Against Drunk Drivers, or with that of any number of people who work to change conditions so that others will not suffer what they did.

• Seeking ways of breaking out of your usual perspective. For years you have been rehearsing your "story," the reasons for your anger. Retelling the story from other participants' points of view will help you find routes to empathy, to seeing the world as the target of your anger may have seen it. Family-systems therapists, who study the transmission of family problems across generations, recommend that if, say, you are angry at your father, you become his biographer. Interview members of your family who knew him; write a short story through his eyes. Why was he the way he was?

Noriko Sawada, whom I quoted at the beginning of this section, despised her cruel, paranoid, and controlling mother for many years, and with good reason. Only on her mother's death did her father break his promise of silence to his wife and tell Sawada the truth about her mother's disastrous early life—the baby she had borne in rural Japan as an unmarried girl, the resulting shame and humiliation she had endured, the baby's death, her father's rejection and reproach, her backbreaking field labor for twenty years, her eventual arranged marriage. These revelations allowed Sawada to put her hatred to rest.

I wept for a woman who gamely wore her hair shirt of guilt and who was so perverted by the experience that she could not alter the fatal course of her relationship with her own daughter. I wept for a mother who became grotesque in her daughter's eyes, an object for pity.

I wept for myself.

CONSIDERATIONS

A mother and her three-year-old son argue every night about bedtime. "Won't go!" says the boy. "Yes, you will!" says the mother. This tug-of-war makes bedtime miserable for both of them, but the mother can't see a way out of it. A psychotherapist suggests that she stop quarreling with her son, acknowledge his feelings, and see what happens. The mother tries this. When her son, as usual, digs in his heels and refuses to go to bed, she says: "I can see that bedtime makes you very unhappy."

Long pause. "It's the ghosts," the boy whispers.

"Ghosts? Where are the ghosts?"

"In the tree outside my window."

Well, would *you* want to go to sleep with ghosts outside your window? The mother did not argue with her son (which would have been fruitless; if you know there are ghosts, there are ghosts). Instead, she went to the window, opened it, and ordered the ghosts to get lost. Then she said to her son: "Tell you what. I'll sit here until you fall asleep, and make sure that *not a single ghost* gets in here." The boy went to sleep like a baby, which of course he was.

Far too often, we all get lost in the surface expression of angry feelings, and ignore the ghosts in the trees that are the real concern. Consider all the ghosts behind the problems of anger in this chapter alone: *I'm hurt. I'm worried. I don't know how to express myself effectively. I don't know how to talk to her about my feelings. No one will ever love me again if he leaves me. I don't know how to get my way. No one listens to me. I can't forgive.*

What all successful therapeutic programs share is the ability to teach people to recognize these perceptions, to communicate them without threatening others, and to solve the conflicts that produce them. They teach people that anger is only one tactic, and usually not a very happy one, in solving problems. Anger does not "go underground" when people learn these skills. The less they need to be angry, and the more control they have over their anger, the less often they feel the emotion in the first place.

The fortune-cookie genie who keeps sending me anger advice must think I finally got the message: that the ultimate purpose of thinking twice about anger is to enhance the long-term benefit of the relationship, not the short-term relief of the individual. But both the individual and the relationship benefit. The latest fortune that my fondness for Chinese food has brought me was this:

If you are patient in one moment of anger, you will escape a hundred days of sorrow.

Further Reading

The Notes contain annotations and sources of specific studies and anger programs, which can be found in the full bibliography. But for those who want more general information about anger and its management, I recommend these books:

Aaron T. Beck, *Love Is Never Enough* (Harper & Row, 1988). A cognitive-behavioral approach to improving many of the failures to communicate that cause anger in marriage.

David Burns, *Feeling Good: The New Mood Therapy* (Bantam, 1980) and *The Feeling Good Workbook* (New American Library, 1989). Two helpful books that show readers how to apply principles of cognitive therapy to their own negative emotions.

Harriet Goldhor Lerner, *The Dance of Anger* (Harper & Row, 1985). An excellent description of the family-systems approach.

Michael Schulman and Eva Mekler, *Bringing Up a Moral Child* (Addison-Wesley, 1984). How to teach children to be empathic, ethical, and able to separate anger from aggression.

Julius Segal, *Winning Life's Toughest Battles* (McGraw-Hill, 1986), and Frederic Flach, *Resilience* (Fawcett, 1988). Two constructive approaches to transcending trauma, revenge, and rage.

Robert Solomon, *The Passions* (Doubleday, 1976). A now-classic analysis of the construction and meaning of emotions in human life.

Carol Z. Stearns and Peter Stearns, *Anger: The Struggle for Emotional Control in America's History* (University of Chicago Press, 1986). A provocative exploration of the history of anger rules in America.

Notes

Following are sources, additions, comments, and quotes for the assertions of the text. Published references appear in short form (author's name and year of publication, along with page numbers for specific quotations) and the full citation can be found in the Bibliography. Quotations from interviews that are not cited come from my tape-recorded conversations.

Introduction (pp. 17–25)

19. The importance of "the definition of the situation" was first developed by W. I. Thomas and Florian Znaniecki in their study *The Polish Peasant in Europe and America*, originally published in 1927.

20. The Red Queen's subtraction problem comes from Lewis Carroll's *Through the Looking Glass*, chap. 9 in your favorite edition.

21. Anger as a wild horse seems to have been a popular metaphor, historically. In the *Phaedrus*, Plato compared the soul to a charioteer (the mind) in charge of two horses (appetite and spirit). Spirit is a beautiful horse, white with black eyes, obedient, upright, and noble. Appetite is "a massive jumble of a creature," ugly, hot-blooded, deaf, "hard to control with whip and goad." The job of reason is to control and guide the two horses, which, said Plato, have a tendency to gallop off in the wrong direction.

    In this tripartite concept and the metaphor of the horses, Plato anticipated Freud's ego, id, and superego by some twenty-five hundred years. In *The Ego and the Id*, Freud wrote that the job of the ego (which represents "reason and sanity") is to control the id ("which contains the passions"): "Thus in relation to the id [the ego] is like a man on horseback, who has to hold in check the superior strength of the horse; . . . Often a rider, if he is not to be parted from his horse, is obliged to guide it where it wants to go; so in the same way the ego constantly carries into action the wishes of the id as if they were its own."

And in *Henry VIII* (act I, scene i), Shakespeare gives these beautiful words to Norfolk:

> "Stay, my lord,
> And let your reason with your choler question
> What 'tis you go about. To climb steep hills
> Requires slow pace at first: anger is like
> A full-hot horse, who being allow'd his way,
> Self-mettle tires him."

21. Bowlby's observations about reification are in Bowlby, 1973, p. 320, and appendix 3 of his book.
23. Danesh, 1977, pp. 1109–1112.
23. Rothenberg, 1971, p. 454.

Chapter 1: Rage and Reason (pp. 27–47)

27. The Swami's story is in *Rolling Thunder* by D. Boyd (New York: Random House, 1974), pp. 104–106.
30. Achilles' sulk may be found in Graves, 1959, p. 266.
30. Sören Qvist: in Lewis, 1947, pp. 89–90.
31. Pascal's *Pensées*, chap. 6.
31. That's Hamlet to Horatio, act III, scene ii. Hamlet himself, of course, had his own problems with passion.
31. Seneca, "On Anger," II, 29.
31. Gandhi, 1957, p. 345.
31. Montaigne, 1976, p. 540.
32. Descartes, "Passions of the Soul," CCXII.
33. Darwin, *Descent of Man*, chap. 1.
34. Darwin, *Expression of the Emotions*, p. 237. See esp. chap. 10, "Hatred and Anger," pp. 237–247.
36. On playing angry for effect, see, for example, Berkowitz, 1978.
36. On the universality of facial expressions, see Ekman, 1980; Ekman, Friesen, and Ancoli, 1980; Ekman et al., 1987. In one study that Ekman did with Wallace Friesen, for example, observers in Japan, Brazil, Chile, Argentina, and the United States saw photos of people expressing various emotions—anger, happiness, fear, surprise, dis-

gust, sadness. The majority of people in each country agreed on the emotion being portrayed, but anger fared worse than the others. Only 69 percent of the Americans and 63 percent of the Japanese agreed that the "angry" photo was of anger, whereas there was nearly universal agreement on the facial expression of happiness. Should we be impressed that as many as 63 or 69 percent agreed on the portrayal of anger, or wonder why "only" that many did?

36. On the Japanese, see Lebra, 1976; on the Kiowa example, see LaBarre, 1947, p. 55.

37. Darwin on controlling yourself: in *Expression*, p. 365.

37. On "primitive" brain structures: see Scherer, Abeles, and Fischer, 1975; MacLean, 1963, 1970. Lazarus, Averill, and Opton (1970) observe that "these supposedly phylogenetically old and so-called primitive structures have undergone evolutionary development just as have cortical structures, and they reach their greatest degree of development in man. . . . both phylogenetically and physiologically, there seems to be little reason to draw a sharp distinction between the emotional and the cognitive, and to assign to the former an especially primitive function" (p. 214).

37. Seneca, "On Anger," p. 115.

37. Averill, "Anger," 1979.

38. Solomon, 1976, 1988.

40. "Undischarged drives contribute their energy to the id": Sabini, 1978, p. 344.

40. Freud's comment on metaphor, in *General Introduction to Psychoanalysis*, p. 306.

40. Unhappily . . . what was intended as a temporary concept assumed a life of its own: the same thing occurred with other of Freud's theories. No physiologists have identified a place in the brain where the ego, id, and superego reside, or located the "preconscious" and its "censor." This has not stopped many analysts from writing as if they knew the precise latitude and longitude of each psychological domain. For example, Samuel B. Kutash, a contemporary psychoanalyst, wrote that in some psychiatric disorders, "both the ego-id boundary (inner boundary) and the ego-outer-world boundary (outer boundary) are unevenly cathected or poorly invested with psychological energy, so that there are 'breaks' or 'splits' in both ego boundaries." (Kutash, 1978, p. 25.)

Once we have metaphors separated by metaphorical boundaries with metaphorical breaks, we are in trouble. Freudian language is abstract enough, yet colorful enough, to seem to explain everything while predicting nothing, which is why court psychiatrists so often disagree with one another. But Freud's followers, some in the name of the ego and others carrying the banner of id, established whole schools of therapy on behalf of these figures of speech.

41. The definition of catharsis is in Breuer and Freud (1893), 1982, p. 8.
41. Freud's quotation on living "freely" is in *GIP*, p. 440.
42. The female therapist is Elizabeth Friar Williams, 1977, p. 208.
42. The male therapist is Herb Goldberg, 1976, p. 183, pp. 157–158.
43. Berkowitz on the ventilationists comes from "The Case for Bottling Up Rage," 1973, p. 26.
43. Rubin, 1970, sec. 5, "Taking a Chance on Anger," pp. 203–223.
45. On the effectiveness of cognitive-behavioral and family-systems therapies, see references for Chapter 10.
45. Steinmetz, 1977, p. 24.
46. On the Utku Eskimo, see Briggs, 1970, p. 3.

Chapter 2: Uncivil Rites (pp. 48–69)

48. Hupka's story is from his 1981 article and personal communication.
49. De Rivera, 1977, p. 78.
50. Averill on anger as an informal judiciary, 1979.
50. The story of N!uhka is in Draper, in Montagu, 1978, p. 42.
51. For more on the !Kung, see Draper, 1976, 1978; Thomas, 1959; Lorna Marshall, 1976. Elizabeth Marshall Thomas's quotation on p. 51 comes from Thomas, 1959, p. 22.
51. Draper on the web of !Kung relationships: Draper, 1978, pp. 43–44.
52. Draper's "melodramatic disclaimers": 1978, p. 45.
53. Jake and Basha exchange witticisms in Myerhoff, 1978, p. 156.
54. On the Ifaluk, see Lutz, 1988.
54. On the Siriono, see Holmberg, 1969, esp. p. 154; on "fighting like a white man," p. 156. On the Tahitians, if you cannot go to Tahiti, read Levy, 1973, 1978.
55. The "mad dance" is discussed by Pospisil, 1963; see esp. pp. 67–68.
57. On the Semai and *slniil*, see Dentan, 1968, 1978.
57. On the Arapesh, see Mead, 1949, p. 135.
57. On the Utku Eskimo, see Briggs, 1970, p. 3.
58. On the Temiar, see Roseman, in press; on the Toraja, see Hollan, 1988.

58. On the Mbuti, see Turnbull, 1961, 1978. For the story of what happens to bullies, see 1978, p. 188.
59. The quote from Peter Farb is in *Word Play*, 1975, p. 125. Closer to home, Farb points out, adolescent ghetto blacks play a game (variously called "playing the dozens," "sounding," or "signifying") in which the object is to win a duel with words instead of fists—without losing one's temper. ("Fuck you!" "Man, you ain't even kissed me yet!") See p. 122.
61. Running amok: see Carr and Tan, 1976.
62. "Being a wild pig": see Newman, 1960; also discussed in Averill, 1976, 1982.
64. Seneca, epistle CXVI, "On Self-Control." He adds: "We mortals have been endowed with sufficient strength by nature, if only we use this strength, if only we concentrate our powers and rouse them all to help us or at least not to hinder us. The reason is *unwillingness; the excuse, inability.*" (My emphasis.) For Averill's update, see Averill, 1976, 1979.
65. The Arab-Japanese confrontation comes from an unpublished manuscript by Thomas Sebeok at the University of Indiana. See also Sebeok, 1982.
65. Edward T. Hall, 1976, p. 59.
66. On Japanese restraint dating to the Samurai, see Hall, 1976; Sebeok's manuscript. During the Tokugawa period, Sebeok writes, all demeanor was carefully controlled; indeed, a person was expected to show the opposite of anger or pain. "A common way to show anger, for example, especially anger toward a superior, is not by an angry face and harsh words, but by an effusive flow of excessive politeness while maintaining a neutral expression."
67. Kleinman, 1988.
67. The Arapesh, Mead; the Eskimo, see Farb, Briggs; the Mbuti, Turnbull. As Mead observes, "The child learns that temper tantrums are unbearable and disruptive. As an adult, he joins in punishing the man who provokes another, not the one who, provoked, engages in violence" (1949, p. 136). What a difference to our culture!
68. Solomon, 1978, p. 194.
69. Levy, 1978, p. 226.

Chapter 3: The Anatomy of Anger (pp. 70–100)

70. Quote from *Richard III* on the spleen: "To vent one's spleen" or to be "splenetic" now refer exclusively to anger, peevishness, and

irritation; but the earliest references to it were as likely to associate the spleen with melancholy and mirth as with anger. Shakespeare used *spleen* variously to mean merriment, caprice, high spirits, courage, impetuosity, indignation, surliness, and rage. The historical indecisiveness about which emotion to link with the spleen may have reflected the medical profession's uncertainty about what the spleen was good for. In the late nineteenth century, at about the time that scientists learned that the organ is a reservoir for blood and a Laundromat for old and diseased blood cells, "hot-blooded" anger became the spleen's kindred spirit, at least linguistically.

71. G. Stanley Hall, 1899, p. 529.

71. Hall's report on inanimate objects, p. 565.

72. On aversions such as earrings: p. 543.

72. The quotation is from Hall, p. 538.

73. Bland, 1982, p. 92. The food-allergy question came to the attention of the public with the work of allergist Ben F. Feingold, M.D., who hypothesized from his clinical observations (not controlled experiment) that as many as 50 percent or more of so-called "hyperactive" children can be treated by eliminating additives, synthetic colors and flavors, and certain fruits from their diets. This appears to be unsupported exaggeration. However, Weiss and his colleagues (1979, 1980) tested this idea on twenty-two normal children between the ages of two and a half and seven, none of whom had behavioral problems. Two children, aged three, proved particularly susceptible to the artificial coloring (which they had been given in a double-blind test, so that their experimenters and parents did not know whether they were drinking a placebo or the additive). Their rates of biting, kicking, throwing things, and hitting increased significantly after they had had drinks with additive coloring. See Dorothy Otnow Lewis, 1981.

74. The young woman who nearly killed her mother was described by S. A. Kinnier Wilson in 1940, and is reported in Frank A. Elliott, 1976, p. 54. Steve, the boy who did kill his cousin, is in Woods, 1961, p. 530.

75. The 6- and 14-per-second positive spiking: Gibbs and Gibbs, 1951. The study of thirty violent children: Stehle, 1960; the sample of one thousand children, see Schwade and Geiger, 1960. See also Berman, 1978.

75. Lewis, 1981, and personal communication. Similarly, Alan Berman matched forty-five teenage delinquent boys with forty-five boys of the

same age, race, region, and background who were not in a reform institution, and gave them all a large battery of tests. When the researchers pooled the test results of all the boys, they were able to identify correctly 87 percent of the delinquents and 78 percent of the controls *solely* on the basis of five neuropsychological measures.

77. Two thousand cases of head trauma: in Frank A. Elliott, 1976, p. 53.

77. For an excellent review of the hypoglycemia issue, see Kolata, 1979.

78. *Previously violent* patients become violent: see Scherer, Abeles, and Fischer, 1975, p. 26: "Responses to amygdaloid stimulation seem to be highly individualized and to reflect the patient's personality." In addition, few areas of the brain control only one behavior, even aggressive behavior.

79. New approaches: see Davidson, 1984, 1986; Tucker, 1989; Tucker and Williamson, 1984.

79. Parallel information systems: see Weinberger, in press.

80. On the development and function of facial expressions, see Stenberg and Campos, 1990; Strack, Martin, and Stepper, 1988.

80. Izard, 1988.

81. Freedman's studies of newborn temperament: Freedman, 1979a and 1979b. In the latter see esp. chap. 9, "Biology or Culture?"

82. MAO findings: Sostek and Wyatt, 1981.

83. Buss and Plomin, 1975. If emotionality has a genetic component, they reasoned, then scores on their test of emotional responsiveness should be strongly correlated for identical twins (who have the same genetic makeup) but completely unrelated for fraternal twins (who have no more genes in common than any other pair of siblings). This is exactly what they found.

83. The single-gene notion: The idea that one gene might be responsible for angry impulsiveness became popular in the 1950s, when researchers discovered a chromosomal abnormality, an extra Y chromosome, among some prisoners. The "XYY" Syndrome caught on as an explanation of male violence. However, prisoners who are XYYs turned out not to be in jail usually for violent crimes, but for robbery and the like. "Their overrepresentation among prison populations," reports psychologist Robert A. Baron (1977, p. 223), "seems to stem primarily from their low level of intelligence"—they just got caught more often than violent criminals.

84. Jerome Kagan, 1978, 1984. Kagan also describes a study of 140 white infants who were tested on four occasions for their attentive-

ness, sounds, smiling, tempo of play, and irritability: at four months of age, eight months, thirteen months, and finally at twenty-seven months. There was no relationship between the presence or absence of any of these baby traits across tests: a cranky baby at four months of age might with equal probability still be cranky or perfectly calm at two and a half years. Kagan retested sixty-five of these children when they were ten years old, and found no link between any of their baby qualities and their later personality, IQ, or reading ability. See also Kagan, 1984, for a review of this issue.

85. Individual differences in epinephrine excretion: see Frankenhaeuser, 1975; McGuinness and Pribram, 1980.

85. A child who has a rapid tempo: Sroufe, 1978, p. 56. See also Sroufe, 1979.

86. Ax, 1953. Half of his subjects got the anger scenario first, then fear; the others got the fear scenario first, then anger. The quotes are all actually from the study and described in Ax's report.

87. Problems with Ax's study: see also Buss and Plomin, 1975, pp. 58–59. For some reason, Ax combined data on all forty-three subjects, although only thirty-seven discriminated anger from fear.

88. *The same bodily response occurred in fear as in anger* . . . : The correlations between measures of the two emotions ran from a healthy .26 to an astonishingly high .77, with an average of .53. These are correlations that researchers would kill for, and it seems that Ax merely blinked at them.

88. These heart-rate changes are called "situational stereotypy"; heart rate and skin conductance depend on the stimuli around you and on the tasks you are doing. See Lacey, Kagan, Lacey, and Moss, 1963.

89. Epinephrine is an all-purpose fuel: Frankenhaeuser, 1975.

90. The arousal effects of epinephrine: for a review of new research, see Neiss, 1988.

90. The study of spinal-cord-injured people was conducted by Chwalisz, Diener, and Gallagher, 1988.

91. Your body alone won't tell you: Alfred Kinsey noted the physiological similarity among the emotions in his study of female sexuality: Many of the bodily changes that occur in fear and anger, he wrote, are also present in sexual arousal. Indeed, said Kinsey, *"The closest parallel to the picture of sexual response is found in the known physiology of anger"* (my emphasis). For those parallels, see Kinsey et al., 1953, chap. 17, p. 705.

91. For heat to be transformed into hostility . . . : This is the major

theme of a long line of research, but for general reviews of the argument see Seymour Epstein, 1979; Mandler, 1984; Zillmann, 1979, 1984; Averill, 1982; Frijda, 1986.

92. But if you have someone else to blame: This study of failure, success, and emotion comes from Weiner, Russell, and Lerman, 1979; see also Weiner, 1982, and Weiner and Graham, 1984. You are even more likely to attribute an emotional state to yourself if you have been working on something that is important to you, or if you feel the need to excuse your behavior—remember Seneca. See Averill, DeWitt, and Zimmer, 1978.

92. For the study of how interpretations of a provocation determine anger, see Frodi, 1976.

92. The quote by Arieti: Arieti, 1967, p. 159.

93. The ability to think . . . shapes our emotional experiences: The psychologists who did the most to further this view were Stanley Schachter and Jerome E. Singer, who, in 1962, set up an experiment that rivaled Ax's for its ingenuity of plot and brilliance of its actor-experimenters. "The same state of physiological arousal could be labeled 'joy' or 'fury,' " depending on the situation, they theorized. But if you know why your body is riled up, say because you have just been injected with epinephrine, you won't look to events in your environment to give your body an emotional label. So Schachter and Singer injected some students with epinephrine and told them what they could expect. Other students thought they were getting an injection of vitamins, and had no idea of what symptoms to expect. (Still others, the control group, were injected with a placebo.) Then the students were put in situations in which an ally of the experimenters behaved euphorically or angrily. Schachter and Singer reported that the students who had been injected with epinephrine and who *did not know why* they were physically churned up were particularly susceptible to the mood of persons around them, joining them in happiness or fury. The students who knew they had been given epinephrine were immune to the ally's antics.

This famous study, like Ax's, reported conclusions that didn't quite match the actual results. Schachter and Singer had to pound their data to get them to fit their hypotheses, and no one has been able to duplicate the experiment. Our emotions are not quite as susceptible to the influence of other people as all that. (For excellent criticisms see Marshall and Zimbardo, 1979, and Maslach, 1979.)

For the opposite argument, that feelings precede appraisals, see Zajonc, 1980. In any case it should be made clear that although "appraisals" are part of our cognitive faculties, they aren't necessarily thoughts we are aware of—and they happen very quickly.

93. Polivy, 1981; quote on p. 806.
94. For the study of college students, see Smith and Ellsworth, 1987.
94. For the study of emotional intensity, see Larsen, Diener, and Cropanzano, 1987.
94. For the study of emotional range, see Sommers and Scioli, 1986.
96. On the excuse epidemic in America: see Wilbanks, 1988; Snyder, 1988; Higgins and Snyder, in press.
97. Frank A. Elliott on the dyscontrol syndrome: Elliott, 1976, p. 51.
98. Mackarness was quoted in *Psychology Today*, November 1974, p. 140.
98. I once had a neighbor . . . : Moyer, 1971, p. 9.
99. The wild cat Lynx rufus . . . : Moyer, 1971, p. 7.
99. A hatred of his mother and a lack of regard for his father: Mark, 1978, p. 128. Mark does not recount the sad story of Thomas R., however. Mark and his colleague Frank Ervin, both surgeons, diagnosed Thomas R., an engineer, as having "paranoid delusions" about his wife's infidelity with a neighbor. Her denials, Mark and Ervin said, were enough to set him off into a frenzy of violence. To help Thomas with his outbursts of "violent rage," Mark and Ervin made lesions in both of his amygdalas. According to follow-ups conducted by an independent observer, Thomas R. never recovered. He has been in and out of hospitals ever since, with "paranoid delusions" that two doctors are out to get him. His wife divorced him and married the neighbor.
99. The patient who couldn't get angry: see Moyer, 1971, p. 7. Moyer's doubts about side effects of anger-reducing surgery or drugs, p. 9.
100. The emotional Hydra: de Rivera, 1977, p. 19.

Chapter 4: Stress, Illness, and Your Heart (pp. 101–127)

101. The *Fortune* quote is by Walter Kiechel III, "Facing Up to Executive Anger," *Fortune*, November 16, 1981, p. 208. The second quote is from "Coping with Anger and Frustration," by Maxine Abrams, *Harper's Bazaar*, February 1980, p. 132.
102. J. J. Groen, 1975, p. 738, p. 740.
104. Jackie Barrile, "Confessions of a Closet Eater," *Ladies' Home Journal*, November 1981, p. 56.

105. Bennett and Gurin, 1982, cite the Kaplans' review.
105. Bruch, 1973, pp. 197–98. See esp. the chapter on "thin fat people," pp. 194–211.
106. A physician who wrote a book on ulcers: M. Michael Eisenberg, *Ulcers* (New York: Random House, 1978), p. 52.
107. On ulcers, see Rotter et al., 1979. Once the nearly exclusive preserve of men, ulcers have become much more common among women; thirty years ago, the ratio of male-to-female ulcer patients was 20 to 1, but today it is 2 to 1. It is unlikely that women are suppressing anger any more now than they used to, but they are smoking more—one factor strongly implicated in the onset of ulcers and lung disease.
108. Depression may be the sequel to anger. . . . : On the hopelessness theory, see Alloy et al., 1988. The emotion you feel reflects your subjective estimates of reaching your goal. If you think expressing anger will change the situation or the person who is making you angry, that is what you are likely to do; if your goals are uncertain or vague, you may feel anxiety; if you think you can never reach your goals, you may feel depressed and hopeless.
108. Second, anger and depression may be wholly different . . . : see Hamburg, Hamburg, and Barchas, 1975, and Wender and Klein, 1981, for discussion of the possible biological factors in predispositions to anger or depression.
109. On the simultaneity of anger and depression: Beck, 1976; Wender and Klein, 1981, p. 209, who cite a long-term study by Myrna Weissman and Eugene Paykel, *The Depressed Woman* (Chicago: University of Chicago Press, 1974).
109. Beck, 1976, p. 73. See also Beck, 1988.
110. Brown and Harris, 1978.
111. Leslie Farber, "Merchandising Depression," *Psychology Today*, April 1979, p. 64.
112. Funkenstein, King, and Drolette, 1957.
114. *In two years of testing* . . . : Funkenstein, King, and Drolette, p. 156.
114. Spielberger, 1988; Spielberger, Krasner, and Solomon, 1988.
115. Anger in the three different settings (the Detroit study): Harburg, Blakelock and Roeper, 1978; Harburg et al., 1973; see also Hauenstein, Kasl, and Harburg, 1977.
117. To read the research on hypertension . . . : once again, a study that failed is at the heart of the hypothesis that hypertensives are more emotionally volatile, especially in fear and anger, than normals (see Joseph Schachter, 1957). To get any differences at all

between the two groups, Schachter had to pool the blood-pressure data for three emotional states: fear, anger, and pain. When hypertensives and normals specifically felt angry, there were no significant blood-pressure differences between them. See also Baer et al. (1979) for the comparison of 332 hypertensives and 335 normals; Cochrane's 1973 questionnaire survey; and Julius, Schneider, and Egan, 1985.

117. Twenty-five people . . . take their own blood pressure: This study was conducted by Whitehead et al., 1977; see p. 387 for quoted conclusion.

117. The two emotions were as independent as grapefruit and pickles: Among individuals, the correlations between anxiety and blood pressure ranged from .05 (no relationship) to .79 (a very strong relationship); correlations of anger and blood pressure likewise ranged from the trivial (.01) to the strong (.51). See Whitehead et al., p. 387.

118. None of this need be conscious . . . : Leventhal, 1982.

118. Barry Dworkin et al., "Baroreceptor Activation Reduces Reactivity to Noxious Stimulation: Implications for Hypertension," *Science* (September 21, 1979), pp. 1299–1301; also reported by Gary Schwartz, "Undelivered Warnings," *Psychology Today* (March 1980), p. 116; and Harold M. Schmeck, Jr., "Hypertension: Is It Too Pleasant to Give Up?" in *The New York Times*, September 25, 1979.

118. James and Kleinbaum, 1976, demonstrate that living under conditions of high economic and social stress can produce hypertension.

119. The Western Collaborative Group Study: see, for example, Matthews et al., 1977.

119. On the Framingham study, see Chesney and Rosenman, 1985, and the papers by Suzanne Haynes and her associates. Subsequent research suggests that the "structured-interview" method for assessing Type A does not overlap perfectly with the "questionnaire" method for Type A; different things are measured in person or on paper, which may be one reason for the different findings in the two large studies. See Matthews, 1988.

120. Consider first these anomalies about heart disease: see Berkman and MacLeod, 1979; Rosenman, 1985; Friedman and Booth-Kewley, 1987b.

121. On the notion that social bonds are insurance against illness: for an excellent discussion of this argument, see Syme, 1982.

121. On the concept of *amaeru:* Doi, 1962, 1973.

121. Pascale and Athos, 1981, p. 124. "For the Japanese," they point out, "independence in an organizational context has negative connotations; it implies disregard for others and self-centeredness" (p. 123).

122. Matsumoto is cited in Berkman and MacLeod, 1979.

122. "A rolling stone gathers no moss": see Syme, 1982.

122. And who are the women . . . at risk of heart disease?: In the Framingham analysis of employed women and heart disease, employment per se by women was not related to such illness; indeed, unmarried employed women, who had been employed the greatest number of years, had the lowest rates of coronary heart disease among all women. See Haynes and Feinleib, 1980. (For a review of studies on "housewives' syndrome," see Tavris and Wade, 1984.)

123. At Duke University Medical Center: Williams, 1989; Williams, Barefoot, and Shekelle, 1985. See also Spielberger, 1988.

123. Dembroski and Costa, 1988.

125. On negative emotions and illness, see Friedman and Booth-Kewley, 1987a.

127. Hill, quoted by Barbara Ehrenreich, "How to Let Off Steam," *Ms.,* May 1979, p. 101.

127. Kiechel, 1981, p. 208.

Chapter 5: "Getting It Out of Your System" (pp. 128–160)

128. The John Bradshaw quote is from his essay "Our Families, Ourselves," in the November/December 1988 *Lear's,* pp. 75–76. The comment from the director of the Bio Psychotherapy Institute, Nolan Saltzman, was taken from his letter to the editor of *The New York Times,* January 12, 1989.

129. "There is a widespread belief . . .": John R. Marshall, 1972, p. 786.

131. Plutarch, "On the Control of Anger," in Plutarch's *Moralia,* vol. 6 (London: Heinemann, 1939), p. 103.

132. See Hokanson series, 1961, 1962a, 1962b, 1968, 1970. On "masochism" as catharsis, see Stone and Hokanson, 1969. The hypothesized reactions of male and female subjects are my own interpolations of what people in the study were thinking about.

135. The quote from G. Stanley Hall, 1899, p. 537. On swearing

as a form of catharsis, see Montagu, 1967: "Swearing is a rather more civilized form of behavior that replaces physical violence" (p. 76).

135. The study of prisoners was by psychologist G. Sosa; cited in Quanty, 1976.

136. Feshbach, 1956. When you permit children to play aggressively . . . : see Mallick and McCandless, 1966.

136. The same principles . . . apply to adults: Straus, 1974; Straus, Gelles, and Steinmetz, 1980.

137. Quote is in Berkowitz, 1970.

137. Straus, personal communication.

137. Verbal aggression usually fails . . . : see Fitz and Findley (1979), who put men and women in a competitive task with four possible counter-aggression strategies: pacifism, minimum retaliation, intermediate retaliation, escalation. As Hokanson found previously, men are more likely than women to *escalate* aggression to an opponent's provocation; and they will be pacifistically courteous to women—until the women attack. Fitz and Findley observe that trying to "outdo" an opponent only builds hostility on both sides; those who want to *lower* an opponent's hostility would do well to control their own first.

137. Steinmetz, 1977, p. 66.

138. It's hard on the nervous system: see M. Goldstein, 1988, for a review.

139. Ebbesen, Duncan, and Konečni, 1975.

140. Talking can freeze a hostile disposition . . . . : see Mallick and McCandless, 1966; Kaplan, 1975, whose subjects who expressed their angry feelings became more hostile than those who expressed the opposite of their anger or who took a neutral position. The study of college boys is by Kahn, 1966.

141. Biaggio, 1980; see p. 355.

141. Murray, 1985.

142. On tantrums: see Schimmel, 1979; Buss and Plomin, 1975; Goodenough, 1931.

144. G. Stanley Hall, 1899, p. 563, p. 564.

144. Bowlby, 1973; quote is on p. 56. See esp. pp. 246–257, "Anger: Functional and Dysfunctional." See also Bowlby, 1988. On attachment after divorce, see W. Berman, 1988.

147. Boys Town: see Fixsen et al., 1978, p. 56.

148. The Seif story came from Ellie Seif, "A Young Mother's Story," *Redbook*, June 1979, pp. 49, 165–167.

150. The Siriono story: Holmberg, 1969, p. 205. On the Utku, see Briggs, 1970.

156. For the research on confession, see Pennebaker, 1988; Pennebaker, Hughes, and O'Heeron, 1987; and Pennebaker, Kiecolt-Glaser, and Glaser, 1988. On the paradox of thought suppression—the more you try to not think about something, the more you think about it—see Wegner et al., 1987.

For a good analysis of how social rituals allow people to achieve Pennebaker's ideal benefits of confession—expressing emotions while maintaining some distance from them—see Scheff, 1979.

160. Berkowitz, 1973, p. 31; emphasis in original.

160. Larry Gelbart story: personal communication.

Chapter 6: "Seeing Red" (pp. 161–192)

162. Donnerstein, Donnerstein, and Evans, 1975.

163. If you put a few rats . . . *become* the feeling of anger: For general reviews of this approach to anger, see Sabini, 1978; Baron, 1977.

164. For the original frustration-aggression hypothesis, see Dollard et al., 1939.

165. Bateson on the Balinese, 1941.

165. The once-neat line . . . sags appreciably . . . : see, for example, Peter McKellar (1949), who kept a journal for forty-seven days, noting when and why he got angry and what he did about it. He also asked his adult-education students, ranging in age from seventeen to sixty-six, to describe two incidents of anger in their lives. McKellar found that everyday anger leads to aggression in only the rarest of circumstances, and that "reflex" anger in response to frustration or pain accounts for fewer than half of human angers. The primary provocations for McKellar and his students were insult, attacks to self-esteem, and injustice. See also Sabini, 1978; Buss, 1966; Berkowitz, 1969.

166. Interruptions: see Mandler, 1984.

168. Noise *increases the likelihood* of anger . . . : Donnerstein and Wilson, 1976.

168. Konečni's experiment: Konečni, 1975b.

169. The sheer decibel level . . . noise means to you: studies cited by Cohen, 1981.

169. Babies may seem a far cry . . . : see Frodi and Lamb et al., 1978. The researchers also found that the cry of premature babies produces greater bodily arousal in listeners, and adults say that it sounds worse than the cry of full-term babies.

170. The quote from the child abuser is from Steele, 1978, p. 295.

170. On crowding and control, see Yakov M. Epstein, 1981; Baum and Epstein, 1978; Schmidt and Keating, 1979. On ideas about social distance and cultural rules of crowding, see, for example, Edward T. Hall, 1976.

173. The New Jersey incident: *The New York Times*, November 14, 1988.

173. Statistics on the Car Driving Furies: *The Los Angeles Times*, August 26, 1988 (part V, 1–2).

174. Joe Kaplan's quote: *The Los Angeles Times*, August 26, 1988.

174. Arnold Goldstein quoted in *Science Digest*, August 1985, p. 26.

175. Roger Brown's story is in his 1965 textbook, *Social Psychology* (New York: The Free Press), page 169.

175. Sara Davidson's story of the Santa Monica boardwalk is from her article "Rolling into the Eighties," *Esquire*, February 1980, p. 23.

177. On horn honking and its alternatives, see Baron, 1977.

177. The story of Bob Lemon comes from Tony Kornheiser's article in *The New York Times*, "Lem Is Serene, Hard-Drinking and Loved," April 2, 1979.

178. Researchers who are trying to identify . . . common sense: The study is by Warren and Raynes, 1972; the quote is on p. 986.

179. David M. Rioch's description of the alcoholic's behavior is from Rioch, 1975, p. 689.

179. For Marlatt's fascinating studies of alcohol, see Marlatt and Rohsenow, 1981; Marlatt, Kosturn, and Lang, 1975.

180. Gelles, 1979a, p. 173.

181. On the use of alcohol in colonial America, see Critchlow, 1986.

181. The Johnson-Gossage quarrel occurred in April 1979 (*The New York Times*).

181. On epinephrine and norepinephrine, see Frankenhaeuser, 1975.

182. See Zillmann, 1979, 1984; Zillmann, Johnson, and Day, 1974; and Zillmann and Bryant, 1974.

183. The quotes by Menninger and Storr are cited in Quanty, 1976.

183. Sipes, 1973.

184. On anger and aggression in sports, see *Sports Violence*, edited by J. Goldstein, 1983; especially chapters by Russell, and Bryant and Zillmann.

185. The study of hockey fans is cited in J. Goldstein, 1983, p. 190.

185. There is little doubt . . . : Berkowitz, 1970.

186. "The quest for excitement": cited in Guttmann, 1986.

186. Ziegler is quoted in M. Smith, 1983, p. 37.

187. The *Time* quote on Ciccarelli: September 5, 1988, p. 47.

187. Kurt Neilson's fining of Sadri, *The New York Times*, January 3, 1980.
188. Bjorn Borg's recollections and McEnroe's account of his behavior are quoted by Bud Collins, "Rivals at Flushing Meadows," *The New York Times Magazine*, August 30, 1981, p. 71.
188. Herbert Warren Wind, *The New Yorker*, October 19, 1981, p. 180. (My emphasis.)
189. Jim E. Loehr and Allen Fox are cited in R. Williams, 1988, p. 62.
189. The Pete Rose story is reported by Roger Angell in *Five Seasons* (New York: Popular Library, 1978), pp. 135–136.
190. Joe Torre was quoted in *The New York Times*, October 5, 1981. Dave Righetti was quoted in *Sport*, September 1988, p. 15.
191. On English-American coverage of Wimbledon, see Jane Gross, "Wimbledon's Appeal Engulfs English Life," *The New York Times*, June 29, 1980.
191. On ambiguity, provocation, and interpretation: see Harris and Huang, 1974; Rule and Nesdale, 1976.

Chapter 7: Shouters, Sulkers, Grouches, and Scolds (pp. 193–219)

195. Harriet Lerner, 1977, p. 5; Halas, 1981.
196. Williams, 1977, p. 78.
196. Goldberg, 1976, p. 16; pp. 50–52.
197. Nichols, 1975, pp. 35–36.
199. The sexes differ in expressing other emotions: see, for example, Allen and Haccoun, who found that "the sexes differ most in expressing fear and least in expressing anger" (1976, p. 717).
200. The Buss-Durkee Inventory: See Buss and Plomin, 1975, pp. 166–167.
200. Spielberger, 1988.
201. Deffenbacher, 1988a.
201. This field study was conducted by Frost and Averill, 1978. Although men and women in their study didn't differ in style or likelihood of anger, I found it interesting that men were twice as likely as women to be the *instigators* of anger! Men and women reported more occasions of being angry with men than with women. There's a lesson in here somewhere.
202. Aftermath of anger: Frost and Averill did find that more women than men said they felt ashamed or guilty after expressing anger, as some feminist therapists would predict, but the researchers did not

consider this finding reliable because they were unable to verify it on another sample. And other studies, such as one by Mary K. Biaggio, find (contrary to their assumptions) that men felt guiltier than women about expressing anger; still others find no sex differences in guilt at all.

203. Fitz, 1979a, 1979b.
The public-private difference between sexes . . . wives . . . treat their husbands miserably: This study was done by Fitz et al., 1979.

205. On personality types and anger: Fitz, 1979b.

206. Frodi, Macaulay, and Thome, 1977. In a separate study, Frodi (1977) asked her students what a man or woman would have to do to make them feel angry—physical or verbal aggression, lack of sensitivity, condescending attitude, or lack of efficiency. Men typically felt angry at another man's aggressive action or at a woman's condescending to them, but women were mostly likely to feel angry at condescension by either sex. Pankratz et al. (1976), however, got no significant sex differences in provocations to anger.

206. The national-sample study of violence in families is from Straus, Gelles, and Steinmetz, 1980. (See also chap. 8.)

207. The stereotyped nature of male aggressiveness: see Campbell and Muncer, 1987.

208. Cancian and Gordon, 1988.

210. Bernardez-Bonesatti, 1978, p. 216.

211. Biaggio, 1988.

212. Miller, 1976, p. 92.

212. Miller, p. 101.

213. The typical forms of women's "indirect" anger: in Mueller and Leidig, 1976, p. 2. (Emphasis theirs.)

214. Cline-Naffziger, 1974, p. 55.

215. On the law secretaries and lawyers, see Crosby, 1982.

218. On male-female conversation rules, see Zimmerman and West, 1975; West, 1982; in marriage, Noller, 1980.

Chapter 8: The Marital Onion (pp. 220–250)

221. The quote from David Mace comes from a taped lecture on problems in marriage. See also Mace, 1976.

221. Averill, 1979.

228. Survey of the readers of *Mademoiselle*: "The Love/Work Question-

naire: Who Will You Be Tomorrow?" a survey and report I did for *Mademoiselle*, March 1982; the quote appears on p. 235.

229. Steinmetz's grumbling couples can be found in her book, 1977, p. 77. See also Gelles, 1979a.

230. Straus, Gelles, and Steinmetz, 1980.

231. Straus, 1979, pp. 19–20.

233. Betty Friedan, *The Feminine Mystique* (New York: Dell, 1963).

233. There are working conditions to a housewife's job: see Tavris and Wade, 1984; see also Bernard, 1973.

234. A study by Karyl MacEwen ("Stress, violence in the family of origin and marital aggression"), reported at the American Psychological Association in New York, 1987, examined stress and marital aggression in 275 couples, six and eighteen months after their weddings. There were *no* effects of the family of origin on the likelihood of current violence in the family.

235. *Redbook*, June 1976, "How Satisfying Is Your Marriage?"

237. Wile, 1988, p. 20.

238. Richard Driscoll's anger patterns are from his unpublished manuscript. Driscoll is at Bearden Professional Associates in Knoxville, Tennessee.

239. Lerner, 1985.

242. For Lerner's case study, see Lerner, 1986.

246. Margolin, 1979.

248. The remark of Lynn Fontanne was cited in Harry Stein, "Careless Love," *Esquire*, December 1980, p. 14.

248. Judith Thurman's observation about her father is in "Fear of Fighting," *Ms.*, October 1978, p. 47.

249. Montaigne, 1976, pp. 540 and 544.

Chapter 9: A Rage for Justice (pp. 251–285)

251. Aquinas, *Summa Theologica*, I–II, 46, 47.

252. Watson on Golf: *The New York Times*, May 12, 1979.

253. The Eskimo workmen: Edward T. Hall, 1976, p. 17.

254. "The Totalitarian Ego": Greenwald, 1980.

254. Taylor and Brown, 1988.

254. Melvin J. Lerner, 1980.

256. Frances FitzGerald, "Reporter at Large," *The New Yorker*, May 19, 1981, pp. 53ff.

258. On the religious significance of anger, see Stratton, 1923.

260. Ideas about justice . . . : see Sennett, 1970, 1980; Moore, 1978, p. 60.
261. De Tocqueville and Douglass are cited in Crosby, 1976, p. 85. On relative deprivation and working women, see Crosby, 1982.
262. Mead, 1949, p. 253.
263. Morgan, 1970, p. xv. Malcolm X, 1966, p. 366.
263. Sara Evans, 1979, pp. 227–228.
264. The letter from Johns Hopkins University is accurate; "Louise Friedrichs" kept a copy.
265. The Riverside study comes from Kluegel and Smith, 1979; Wikler, 1973.
265. On women's work since World War II, see Oppenheimer, 1975; also Tavris and Wade, 1984, chap. 7.
266. On the demography of sex ratios, see Guttentag and Secord, 1983.
269. Johnson, 1981, p. 52.
270. An analysis of the autobiographies of Morgan, Bryant, and Stapleton may be found in Dworkin, 1979.
270. Kaplow, 1973, pp. 38–39.
270. Morgan, 1970, p. xv.
271. O'Reilly, 1980, p. xvi.
271. Johnson, 1981, pp. 52–53.
273. John Leonard's "thermostat of sanity," from his column "Private Lives" in *The New York Times*, May 17, 1978.
273. Ernest Harburg's observations: personal communication.
276. O'Reilly, 1980, p. xiv.
279. Sears and Huddy, 1989.
279. Beth Schneider's paper, "Feminist Disclaimers, Stigma, and the Contemporary Women's Movement," is available from Dr. Schneider in the Department of Sociology, University of California at Santa Barbara.
280. Ehrenreich, 1983; Farrell, 1986.
282. Strout's comment was reported in *The New York Times Book Review*, November 11, 1979, p. 7.
284. Bonime, 1976, p. 10.

Chapter 10: Rethinking Anger (pp. 286–319)

287. Deffenbacher, 1988.
289. For Novaco's stress-inoculation program, see Novaco, 1975, 1985.
290. The therapy for bus drivers was reported in *The New York Times*, February 1, 1981.

290. Deffenbacher, 1988. See also Biaggio, 1987.
291. On humor in psychotherapy, see Fry and Salameh, 1987, who have edited an entire handbook of efforts to incorporate humor. (It's not a very funny book, though.) See also Ronald Smith, 1973, who treated a chronically angry woman with "humor therapy." On the backfiring effects of *hostile* humor, see Baron, 1977.
291. The interview with Kundera by Michiko Kakutani: "Milan Kundera: A Man Who Cannot Forget," *The New York Times*, January 18, 1982.
294. Padesky material from personal interview.
294. The Wallerstein study is described at length in Wallerstein and Blakeslee, 1989. "In the years after divorce . . . ," p. 135. The rehearsal of grievances and Wallerstein's feeling of "wandering into the same play . . . ," also p. 135.
300. The example of Dana: Wallerstein and Blakeslee, p. 180.
301. Maurer material from personal interview. On attachment and divorce, see also W. Berman, 1988.
301. On Prudence Brown's research, see Brown, 1976; Brown, Perry, and Harburg, 1977.
303. Jacobs material from personal interview.
307. Patterson, 1985, 1986. His quote on "the stuff of novels" is from his 1986 article, p. 442.
308. Lochman, 1984, 1988.
309. See Feindler, 1989; Feindler and Ecton, 1986.
310. For more information on Aggression Replacement Training, see Arnold Goldstein, 1988; Glick and Goldstein, 1987. The book version of their work is Goldstein and Glick, 1987.
311. The importance of empathy in reducing anger has been amply documented. See, for example, Miller and Eisenberg, 1988; Feshbach, 1983, and Feshbach et al., 1983; Hoffman, 1987.
311. On styles of parental discipline, see Baumrind, 1973.
313. The quote by Coretta King was from her op-ed essay in *The Los Angeles Times*, December 22, 1988. The quotes from Noriko Sawada are in her article, "Memoir of a Japanese Daughter," *Ms.*, April 1980, pp. 68 and 110.
313. Nancy Mairs's comments are in her book *Plaintext* (New York: Harper & Row/Perennial, 1986), p. 20.
314. On resilience, see Flach, 1988, and Segal, 1986.
315. Zilbergeld material from personal interview.
318. "Ghosts in trees" story: personal communication from psychotherapist Mitch Messer.

Bibliography

Allen, Jon G., and Dorothy Haccoun. "Sex Differences in Emotionality." *Human Relations* 29, 1976, 711–722.

Alloy, Lauren, Lyn Abramson, Gerald Metalsky, and Shirley Hartlage. "The Hopelessness Theory of Depression: Attributional Aspects." *British Journal of Clinical Psychology* 27, 1988, 5–21.

Arieti, Silvano. *The Intrapsychic Self.* New York: Basic Books, 1967.

Averill, James R. "Anger." In H. Howe and R. Dienstbier, eds. *Nebraska Symposium on Motivation, 1978*, vol. 26. Lincoln: University of Nebraska Press, 1979.

Averill, James R. *Anger and Aggression.* New York: Springer-Verlag, 1982.

Averill, James R. "Emotion and Anxiety: Sociocultural, Biological, and Psychological Determinants." In M. Zukerman and C. D. Spielberger, eds. *Emotions and Anxiety.* New York: LEA-John Wiley, 1976.

Averill, James R., Gary W. DeWitt, and Michael Zimmer. "The Self-Attribution of Emotion as a Function of Success and Failure." *Journal of Personality* 46, 1978, 323–347.

Averill, James R., Edward M. Opton, Jr., and Richard S. Lazarus. "Cross-Cultural Studies of Psychophysiological Responses During Stress and Emotion." *International Journal of Psychology* 4, 1969, 83–102.

Ax, Albert F. "The Physiological Differentiation Between Fear and Anger in Humans." *Psychosomatic Medicine* 15, 1953, 433–442.

Bach, George R., and Herb Goldberg. *Creative Aggression.* Garden City, N.Y.: Doubleday, 1974.

Baer, Jean. *How to Be an Assertive (Not Aggressive) Woman in Life, in Love, and on the Job.* New York: The New American Library, 1976.

Baer, Paul E., Forrest Collins, Gleb Bourianoff, and Marta Ketchel. "Assessing Personality Factors in Essential Hypertension with a Brief Self-Report Instrument." *Psychosomatic Medicine* 41, 1979, 321–330.

Bandura, Albert. "Learning and Behavioral Theories of Aggression." In I. L. Kutash et al., eds. *Violence*. San Francisco: Jossey-Bass, 1978.

Bandura, Albert, N. E. Adams, and J. Beyer. "Cognitive Processes Mediating Behavior Change." *Journal of Personality and Social Psychology* 35, 1977, 125–139.

Baron, Robert A. *Human Aggression*. New York: Plenum Press, 1977.

Bateson, Gregory. "The Frustration-Aggression Hypothesis and Culture." *Psychological Review* 48, 1941, 350–355.

Baum, Andrew, and Yakov M. Epstein. *Human Response to Crowding*. Hillsdale, N.J.: Erlbaum, 1978.

Baum, Andrew, Jerome E. Singer, and Carlene Baum. "Stress and the Environment." *The Journal of Social Issues* 37, 1981, 4–36.

Baumrind, Diana. "The Development of Instrumental Competence Through Socialization." In A. D. Pick, ed. *Minnesota Symposium on Child Psychology*, vol. 7. Minneapolis: University of Minnesota Press, 1973.

Beck, Aaron T. *Cognitive Therapy and the Emotional Disorders*. New York: International Universities Press, 1976.

Beck, Aaron T. *Love Is Never Enough: How Couples Can Overcome Misunderstandings, Resolve Conflicts, and Solve Relationship Problems through Cognitive Therapy*. New York: Harper & Row, 1988.

Bennett, William, and Joel Gurin. *The Dieter's Dilemma*. New York: Basic Books, 1982.

Berkman, Lisa, and Margo MacLeod. "Coronary Heart Disease: An Epidemiologic Paradox." Paper presented to the American Psychological Association, New York, 1979.

Berkowitz, Leonard. "The Case for Bottling Up Rage." *Psychology Today* 7, July 1973, 24–31.

Berkowitz, Leonard. "Do We Have to Believe We Are Angry with Someone in Order to Display 'Angry' Aggression Toward That Person?" In L. Berkowitz, ed. *Cognitive Theories in Social Psychology*. New York: Academic Press, 1978.

Berkowitz, Leonard. "Experimental Investigations of Hostility Catharsis." *Journal of Consulting and Clinical Psychology* 35, 1970, 1–7.

Berkowitz, Leonard. "The Frustration-Aggression Hypothesis Revisited." In L. Berkowitz, *Roots of Aggression*. New York: Atherton Press, 1969.

Berman, Allan. "Neuropsychological Aspects of Violent Behavior." Paper presented to the American Psychological Association, Toronto, 1978.

Berman, William. "The Role of Attachment in the Post-Divorce

Experience." *Journal of Personality and Social Psychology* 54, 1988, 496–503.

Bernard, Jessie, *The Future of Marriage*. New York: Bantam Books, 1973.

Bernardez-Bonesatti, Teresa. "Women and Anger: Conflicts with Aggression in Contemporary Women." *Journal of the American Medical Women's Association* 33, 1978, 215–219.

Biaggio, Mary Kay. "Anger Arousal and Personality Characteristics." *Journal of Personality and Social Psychology* 39, 1980, 352–356.

Biaggio, Mary Kay. "Clinical Dimensions of Anger Management." *American Journal of Psychotherapy* 41, 1987, 417–427.

Biaggio, Mary Kay. "Sex Differences in Anger: Are They Real?" Paper presented to the American Psychological Association, Atlanta, Georgia, 1988.

Bland, Jeffrey. "The Junk-Food Syndrome." *Psychology Today*, January 1982, p. 92.

Bohart, Arthur C. "Toward a Cognitive Theory of Catharsis." *Psychotherapy: Theory, Research, and Practice* 17, 1980, 192–201.

Bonime, Walter. "Anger as a Basis for a Sense of Self." *Journal of the American Academy of Psychoanalysis* 4, 1976, 7–12.

Bowlby, John. *Attachment and Loss*, vol. 2. New York: Basic Books, 1973.

Bowlby, John. *A Secure Base: Parent-Child Attachment and Healthy Human Development*. New York: Basic Books, 1988.

Brady, Joseph V. "Toward a Behavioral Biology of Emotion." In L. Levi, ed. *Emotions: Their Parameters and Measurement*. New York: Raven Press, 1975.

Breuer, Josef, and Sigmund Freud. *Studies on Hysteria*. Translated by James Strachey. New York: Basic Books, 1982.

Briggs, Jean. *Never in Anger: Portrait of an Eskimo Family*. Cambridge, Mass.: Harvard University Press, 1970.

Brown, George W., and Tirril Harris. *Social Origins of Depression*. Riverside, N.J.: The Free Press, 1978.

Brown, J. S., and C. R. Crowell. "Alcohol and Conflict Resolution: A Theoretical Analysis." *Quarterly Journal of Studies on Alcohol* 35, 1974, 66–85.

Brown, Jonathon D., and Judith M. Siegel. "Attributions for Negative Life Events and Depression: The Role of Perceived Control." *Journal of Personality and Social Psychology* 54, 1988, 316–322.

Brown, Prudence. "Psychological Distress and Personal Growth Among

Women Coping with Marital Dissolution." Ph.D. dissertation, University of Michigan, 1976.

Brown, Prudence, Lorraine Perry, and Ernest Harburg. "Sex Role Attitudes and Psychological Outcomes for Black and White Women Experiencing Marital Dissolution." *Journal of Marriage and the Family*, 1977, 349–561.

Bruch, Hilde. *Eating Disorders*. New York: Basic Books (Harper Colophon), 1973.

Bryant, Jennings, and Dolf Zillmann. "Sports Violence and the Media." In J. Goldstein, ed. *Sports Violence*. New York: Springer-Verlag, 1983.

Burns, David. *Feeling Good: The New Mood Therapy*. New York: Signet, 1980.

Buss, Arnold H. "Aggression Pays." In J. L. Singer, ed. *The Control of Aggression and Violence: Cognitive and Physiological Factors*. New York: Academic Press, 1971.

Buss, Arnold H. "Instrumentality of Aggression Feedback and Frustration as Determinants of Physical Aggression." *Journal of Personality and Social Psychology* 3, 1966, 153–162.

Buss, Arnold H., and Robert A. Plomin. *A Temperament Theory of Personality Development*. London: John Wiley & Sons, 1975.

Campbell, Anne, and Steven Muncer. "Models of Anger and Aggression in the Social Talk of Women and Men." *Journal for the Theory of Social Behaviour* 17, 1987, 489–511.

Cancian, Francesca M., and Steven Gordon. "Changing Emotion Norms in Marriage: Love and Anger in U.S. Women's Magazines Since 1900." *Gender & Society* 2, 1988, 308–342.

Cannon, Walter B. *Bodily Changes in Pain, Hunger, Fear, and Anger*. New York: Appleton, 1915.

Carr, John E., and Eng Kong Tan. "In Search of the True Amok: Amok as Viewed Within Malay Culture." *American Journal of Psychiatry* 133, 1976, 1295–1299.

Chesney, Margaret, and Ray H. Rosenman, eds. *Anger and Hostility in Cardiovascular and Behavioral Disorders*. Washington: Hemisphere, 1985.

Chwalisz, Kathleen, Ed Diener, and Dennis Gallagher. "Autonomic Arousal Feedback and Emotional Experience: Evidence from the Spinal Cord Injured." *Journal of Personality and Social Psychology* 54, 1988, 820–828.

Cline-Naffziger, Claudeen. "Women's Lives and Frustration, Oppression and Anger: Some Alternatives." *Journal of Counseling Psychology* 21, 1974, 51–56.

Cochrane, R. "Hostility and Neuroticism Among Unrelated Essential Hypertensives." *Journal of Psychosomatic Research* 17, 1973, 215–218.

Cohen, Sheldon. "Sound Effects on Behavior." *Psychology Today*, October 1981, 38–50.

Cohen, Sheldon, and Neil Weinstein. "Nonauditory Effects of Noise on Behavior and Health." *The Journal of Social Issues* 37, 1981, 36–71.

Critchlow, Barbara. "The Powers of John Barleycorn: Beliefs about the Effects of Alcohol on Social Behavior." *American Psychologist* 41, 1986, 751–764.

Crosby, Faye. "A Model of Egoistical Relative Deprivation." *Psychological Review* 83, 1976, 85–113.

Crosby, Faye. *Relative Deprivation and Working Women.* New York: Oxford University Press, 1982.

Danesh, Hossain B. "Anger and Fear." *American Journal of Psychiatry* 134, 1977, 1109–1112.

Daniels, David N., Marshall F. Gilula, and Frank M. Ochberg, eds. *Violence and the Struggle for Existence.* Boston: Little, Brown, 1970.

Darwin, Charles. *The Expression of the Emotions in Man and Animals.* 1872: reprinted by the University of Chicago Press, 1965.

Davidson, Richard J. "Affect, Cognition, and Hemispheric Specialization." In C. E. Izard, J. Kagan, and R. B. Zajonc, eds. *Emotions, Cognition, and Behavior.* Cambridge, England: Cambridge University Press, 1984.

Davidson, Richard J. "Thinking About Feeling: Cerebral Asymmetry and the Nature of Emotion." Paper presented to the American Psychological Association, Washington, D.C., 1986.

Deffenbacher, Jerry L. "Cognitive-Behavioral Approaches to Anger Reduction: Some Treatment Considerations," and "A Cognitive-Relaxation Approach to Anger Reduction: A Treatment Outline." Papers presented to the American Psychological Association, Atlanta, Georgia, 1988a.

Deffenbacher, Jerry L. "Cognitive-Relaxation and Social Skills Treatments of Anger: A Year Later." *Journal of Counseling Psychology* 35, 1988b, 234–236.

Dembroski, Theodore M., and Paul T. Costa, Jr. "Assessment of Coronary-Prone Behavior: A Current Overview." *Annals of Behavioral Medicine* 10, 1988, 60–63.

Dentan, Robert Knox. "Notes on Childhood in a Nonviolent Context:

The Semai Case." In A. Montagu, ed. *Learning Non-Aggression.* New York: Oxford University Press paperback, 1978.

Dentan, Robert Knox. *The Semai.* New York: Holt, Rinehart & Winston, 1968.

De Rivera, Joseph. "A Structural Theory of the Emotions." *Psychological Issues* X(4), monograph 40. New York: International University Press, 1977.

Doi, L. T. "Amae: A Key Concept for Understanding Japanese Personality Structure." In R. J. Smith and R. K. Beardsley, eds. *Japanese Culture.* Chicago: Aldine, 1962.

Doi, L. T. *The Anatomy of Dependence.* Tokyo: Kodansha International, 1973.

Dollard, J. R., L. W. Doob, N. E. Miller, and R. S. Sears. *Frustration and Aggression.* New Haven, Conn.: Yale University Press, 1939.

Donnerstein, Edward, M. Donnerstein, and R. Evans. "Erotic Stimuli and Aggression: Facilitation or Inhibition?" *Journal of Personality and Social Psychology* 32, 1975, 237–244.

Donnerstein, Edward, and John Hallam. "Facilitating Effects of Erotica on Aggression Against Women." *Journal of Personality and Social Psychology* 36, 1978, 1270–1277.

Donnerstein, Edward, and David W. Wilson. "Effects of Noise and Perceived Control on Ongoing and Subsequent Aggressive Behavior." *Journal of Personality and Social Psychology* 34, 1976, 744–781.

Donovan, Dennis, and Michael O'Leary. "Comparison of Perceived and Experienced Control among Alcoholics and Nonalcoholics." *Journal of Abnormal Psychology* 84, 1975, 726–728.

Draper, Patricia. "The Learning Environment for Aggression and Anti-Social Behavior among the !Kung." In A. Montagu, ed. *Learning Non-Aggression.* New York: Oxford University Press paperback, 1978.

Draper, Patricia. "Social and Economic Constraints on Child Life among the !Kung." In R. B. Lee and I. DeVore, eds. *Kalahari Hunter-Gatherers: Studies of the !Kung San and Their Neighbors.* Cambridge, Mass.: Harvard University Press, 1976.

Dworkin, Andrea. "Safety, Shelter, Rules, Form, Love: The Promise of the Ultra-Right." *Ms.*, June 1979, 62–64, 69ff.

Ebbesen, Ebbe, Birt Duncan, and Vladimir Konečni. "Effects of Content of Verbal Aggression on Future Verbal Aggression: A Field Experiment." *Journal of Experimental Social Psychology* 11, 1975, 192–204.

Ehrenreich, Barbara. *The Hearts of Men: American Dreams and the*

Flight from Commitment. New York: Anchor Press/Doubleday, 1983.

Ekman, Paul. *The Face of Man.* New York: Garland STPM Press, 1980.

Ekman, Paul, Wallace V. Friesen, and Sonia Ancoli. "Facial Signs of Emotional Experience." *Journal of Personality and Social Psychology* 39, 1980, 1125–1134.

Ekman, Paul, Wallace V. Friesen, Maureen O'Sullivan et al. "Universals and Cultural Differences in the Judgments of Facial Expression of Emotion." *Journal of Personality and Social Psychology* 53, 1987, 712–717.

Elliott, Frank A. "The Neurology of Explosive Rage: The Dyscontrol Syndrome." *The Practitioner* 217, July 1976, 51–60.

Elliott, Robert C. *The Power of Satire.* Princeton, N.J.: Princeton University Press, 1960.

Ellis, Albert. *How to Live With and Without Anger.* New York: Reader's Digest Press, 1977.

Ellis, Albert. "Techniques of Handling Anger in Marriage." *Journal of Marriage and Family Counseling* 2, 1976, 305–315.

Epstein, Seymour. "The Ecological Study of Emotions in Humans." In P. Pliner, K. R. Blankstein, and I. M. Spigel, eds. *Perception of Emotion in Self and Others.* New York: Plenum Press, 1979.

Epstein, Yakov M. "Crowding Stress and Human Behavior." *The Journal of Social Issues* 37, 1981, 126–145.

Evans, D. R., and M. T. Hearn. "Anger and Systematic Desensitization." *Psychological Reports* 32, 1973, 569–570.

Evans, D. R., M. T. Hearn, and D. Saklofske. "Anger, Arousal, and Systematic Desensitization." *Psychological Reports* 32, 1973, 625–626.

Evans, Sara. *Personal Politics: The Roots of Women's Liberation in the Civil Rights Movement and the New Left.* New York: Knopf, 1979.

Farb, Peter. *Word Play: What Happens When People Talk.* New York: Bantam, 1975.

Farrell, Warren. *Why Men Are the Way They Are.* New York: McGraw-Hill, 1986.

Feindler, Eva L. "Adolescent Anger Control: Review and Critique." In M. Hersen, R. M. Eisler, and P. M. Miller, eds. *Progress in Behavior Modification.* Newbury Park, Ca.: Sage, 1989.

Feindler, Eva L., and Randolph B. Ecton. *Adolescent Anger Control: Cognitive-Behavioral Techniques.* Elmsford, N.Y.: Pergamon Press, 1986.

Feshbach, Norma. "Learning to Care: A Positive Approach to Child

Training and Discipline." *Journal of Clinical Child Psychology* 12, 1983, 266–271.

Feshbach, Norma, Seymour Feshbach, Mary Fauvre, and Michael Ballard-Campbell. *Learning to Care: A Curriculum for Affective and Social Development.* Glenview, Ill.: Scott, Foresman, 1983.

Feshbach, Seymour. "The Catharsis Hypothesis and Some Consequences of Interaction with Aggression and Neutral Play Objects." *Journal of Personality* 24, 1956, 449–462.

Fitz, Don. "Anger Expression of Women and Men in Five Natural Locations." Paper presented to the American Psychological Association, New York, 1979a.

Fitz, Don. "Anger of Women and Men: An Interview Study of Behavior in Natural Settings." Paper presented to the American Psychological Association, New York, 1979b.

Fitz, Don, and Maureen Findley. "Anger Between Women and Men: Effects of Four Counteraggression Strategies." Paper presented to the American Psychological Association, New York, 1979.

Fitz, Don, S. Marwit, S. Gerstenzang, and J. Hickman. "Anger Between Intimates: An Experimental Study of Aggression-Reduction Strategies." Paper presented to the Midwestern Psychological Association, Chicago, 1979.

Fixsen, D., E. L. Phillips, R. Baron, D. Coughlin, D. Daly, and P. Daly. "The Boys Town Revolution." *Human Nature* 1, November 1978, 54–61.

Flach, Frederic. *Resilience.* New York: Faucett Columbine, 1988.

Foster, Randall, and Donald F. Lomas. "Anger, Disability and Demands in the Family." *American Journal of Orthopsychiatry* 48, 1978, 228–235.

Frankenhaeuser, Marianne. "Experimental Approaches to the Study of Catecholamines and Emotion." In L. Levi, ed. *Emotions: Their Parameters and Measurement.* New York: Raven Press, 1975.

Frankenhaeuser, Marianne. "Sex Differences in Reactions to Psychosocial Stressors and Psychoactive Drugs." In L. Levi, ed. *Society, Stress and Disease,* vol. 3. New York: Oxford University Press, 1978.

Frankenhaeuser, Marianne, E. Dunne, H. Bjurström, and U. Lundberg. "Counteracting Depressant Effects of Alcohol by Psychological Stress." *Psychopharmacologica* 38, 1974, 271–278.

Freedman, Daniel G. "Ethnic Differences in Babies." *Human Nature* 2, January 1979a, 36–43.

Freedman, Daniel G. *Human Sociobiology.* Riverside, N.J.: The Free Press, 1979b.

Freud, Sigmund. *The Ego and the Id.* Translated by Joan Riviere. New York: W. W. Norton, 1962.

Freud, Sigmund. *A General Introduction to Psychoanalysis.* New York: Washington Square Press, 1961.

Friedman, Howard S., and Stephanie Booth-Kewley. "The 'Disease-Prone Personality': A Meta-Analytic View of the Construct." *American Psychologist* 42, 1987a, 539–555.

Friedman, Howard S., and Stephanie Booth-Kewley. "Personality, Type A Behavior, and Coronary Heart Disease: The Role of Emotional Expression." *Journal of Personality and Social Psychology* 53, 1987b, 783–792.

Frijda, Nico H. *The Emotions.* Cambridge, England: Cambridge University Press, 1986.

Frodi, Ann. "Effects of Varying Explanations Given for a Provocation on Subsequent Hostility." *Psychological Reports* 38, April 1976, 659ff.

Frodi, Ann. "Sex Differences in Perception of a Provocation: A Survey." *Perceptual and Motor Skills* 44, 1977, 113–114.

Frodi, Ann, Michael E. Lamb et al. "Fathers' and Mothers' Responses to the Faces and Cries of Normal and Premature Infants." *Developmental Psychology* 14, 1978, 490–498.

Frodi, Ann, Jacqueline Macaulay, and Pauline Thome. "Are Women Always Less Aggressive Than Men? A Review of the Literature." *Psychological Bulletin* 84, 1977, 634–660.

Frost, Wm. Douglas, and James R. Averill. "Sex Differences in the Everyday Experience of Anger." Paper presented to the Eastern Psychological Association, Washington, D.C., 1978. (See also Averill, 1982.)

Fry, William, Jr., and Waleed Salameh, eds. *Handbook of Humor and Psychotherapy.* Sarasota, Florida: The Professional Resource Exchange, Inc., 1987.

Funkenstein, Daniel H., Stanley H. King, and Margaret E. Drolette. *Mastery of Stress.* Cambridge, Mass.: Harvard University Press, 1957.

Gaines, T., P. Kirwin, and W. Gentry. "The Effect of Descriptive Anger Expression, Insult, and No Feedback on Interpersonal Aggression, Hostility, and Empathy Motivation." *Genetic Psychology Monograph* 95, 1977, 349–367.

Gandhi, Mohandas K. *An Autobiography.* Boston: Beacon Press, 1957.

Gates, G. S. "An Observational Study of Anger." *Journal of Experimental Psychology* 9, 1926, 325–331.

Geen, Russell, David Stonner, and Gary Shope. "The Facilitation of Aggression by Aggression: Evidence Against the Catharsis Hypothesis." *Journal of Personality and Social Psychology* 13, 1975, 721–726.

Gelles, Richard J. *Family Violence*. Beverly Hills, Calif.: Sage, 1979a.

Gelles, Richard J. "The Myth of Battered Husbands." *Ms.*, October 1979b, 65–73.

Gibbs, E. L., and F. A. Gibbs. "Electroencephalographic Evidence of Thalamic and Hypothalamic Epilepsy." *Neurology* 1, 1951, 136–144.

Glick, Barry, and Arnold P. Goldstein. "Aggression Replacement Training." *Journal of Counseling and Development* 65, 1987, 356–362.

Goldberg, Herb. *The Hazards of Being Male*. New York: New American Library, 1976.

Goldstein, Arnold P. "Aggression Reduction: Some Vital Steps." In J. Groebel and R. Hinde, eds. *Aggression and War*. Cambridge, England: Cambridge University Press, 1988.

Goldstein, Arnold P., and Barry Glick. *Aggression Replacement Training*. Champaign, Ill.: Research Press, 1987.

Goldstein, Jeffrey H., ed. *Sports Violence*. New York: Springer-Verlag, 1983.

Goldstein, Michael J. "The Family and Psychopathology." *American Review of Psychology* 39, 1988, 283–299.

Goodenough, Florence L. *Anger in Young Children*. Minneapolis: University of Minnesota Press, 1931.

Gordon, Steven L. "The Sociology of Sentiments and Emotion." In M. K. Rosenberg and R. H. Turner, eds. *Social Psychology: Sociological Perspectives*. New York: Basic Books, 1981.

Graves, Robert, trans. *The Anger of Achilles (Homer's Iliad)*. London: Cassell, 1959.

Greenblat, Cathy S. "Physical Force by Any Other Name . . ." Paper presented to the National Conference for Family Violence, Durham, New Hampshire, 1981.

Greenwald, Anthony G. "The Totalitarian Ego: Fabrication and Revision of Personal History." *American Psychologist* 35, 1980, 603–618.

Greenwell, J., and H. A. Dengerink. "The Role of Perceived Versus Actual Attack in Human Physical Aggression." *Journal of Personality and Social Psychology* 26, 1973, 66–71.

Groen, J. J. "The Measurement of Emotion and Arousal in the Clinical Physiological Laboratory and in Medical Practice." In L. Levi, ed. *Emotions: Their Parameters and Measurement*. New York: Raven Press, 1975.

Guttentag, Marcia, and Paul Secord. *Too Many Women?* Beverly Hills, Ca.: Sage, 1983.

Guttmann, Allen. *Sports Spectators*. New York: Columbia University Press, 1986.

Halas, Celia. *Why Can't a Woman Be More Like a Man?* New York: Macmillan, 1981.

Hall, Edward T. *Beyond Culture.* Garden City, N.Y.: Doubleday, Anchor Press, 1976.

Hall, G. Stanley. "A Study of Anger." *American Journal of Psychology* 10, 1899, 516–591.

Hamburg, David A., Beatrix A. Hamburg, and Jack D. Barchas. "Anger and Depression in Perspective of Behavioral Biology." In L. Levi, *Emotions: Their Parameters and Measurement.* New York: Raven Press, 1975.

Harburg, Ernest, Edwin H. Blakelock, and Peter J. Roeper. "Resentful and Reflective Coping with Arbitrary Authority and Blood Pressure." *Psychosomatic Medicine* 41, 1979, 189–202.

Harburg, Ernest, John Erfurt, and Louise Hauenstein et al. "Socio-Ecological Stress, Suppressed Hostility, Skin Color, and Black-White Male Blood Pressure." *Psychosomatic Medicine* 35, 1973, 276–296.

Harris, M., and L. Huang. "Aggression and the Attribution Process." *Journal of Social Psychology* 92, 1974, 209–216.

Harris, V. A., and E. S. Katkin. "Primary and Secondary Emotional Behavior: An Analysis of the Role of Automatic Feedback on Affect, Arousal, and Attribution." *Psychological Bulletin* 82, 1975, 904–916.

Hauenstein, Louise, Stanislav Kasl, and Ernest Harburg. "Work Status, Work Satisfaction and Blood Pressure among Married Black and White Women." *Psychology of Women Quarterly* 1, 1977, 334–349.

Haynes, Suzanne G., and Manning Feinleib. "Women, Work and Coronary Heart Disease: Prospective Findings from the Framingham Heart Study." *American Journal of Public Health* 70, 1980, 133–141.

Haynes, Suzanne G., Manning Feinleib, and William B. Kannel. "The Relationship of Psychosocial Factors to Coronary Heart Disease in the Framingham Study III: Eight Year Incidence of Coronary Heart Disease." *American Journal of Epidemiology* 1980, 111.

Hearn, M. T., and D. R. Evans. "Anger and Reciprocal Inhibition Therapy." *Psychological Reports* 30, 1972, 943–948.

Higgins, Raymond L., and C. R. Snyder. "Excuses Gone Awry: An Analysis of Self-Defeating Excuses." In R. C. Curtis, ed. *Self-Defeating Behaviors: Experimental Research and Practical Implications.* New York: Plenum, in press.

Hoffman, Martin L. "The Contribution of Empathy to Justice and Moral Judgment." In N. Eisenberg and J. Strayer, eds. *Empathy and Its Development.* New York: Cambridge University Press, 1987.

Hokanson, Jack E. "Psychophysiological Evaluation of the Catharsis

Hypothesis." In E. I. Megargee and J. E. Hokanson, eds. *The Dynamics of Aggression*. New York: Harper & Row, 1970.

Hokanson, Jack E., and Michael Burgess. "The Effects of Status, Type of Frustration and Aggression on Vascular Processes." *Journal of Abnormal and Social Psychology* 65, 1962a, 232–237.

Hokanson, Jack E., and Michael Burgess. "The Effects of Three Types of Aggression on Vascular Processes." *Journal of Abnormal and Social Psychology* 64, 1962b, 446–449.

Hokanson, Jack E., and Sanford Shetler. "The Effect of Overt Aggression on Physiological Arousal Level." *Journal of Abnormal and Social Psychology* 63, 1961, 446–448.

Hokanson, Jack E., K. R. Willers, and Elizabeth Koropsak. "The Modification of Autonomic Responses During Aggressive Interchange." *Journal of Personality* 36, 1968, 386–404.

Hollan, Douglas. "Staying 'Cool' in Toraja: Informal Strategies for the Management of Anger and Hostility in a Nonviolent Society." *Ethos* 16, 1988, 52–72.

Holmberg, Allan R. *Nomads of the Long Bow: The Siriono of Eastern Bolivia*. Garden City, N.Y.: The Natural History Press, 1969.

Holmes, D. P., and J. J. Horan. "Anger Induction in Assertion Training." *Journal of Counseling Psychology* 23, 1976, 108–111.

Hunt, J. McVicker, Marie-Louise Wakeman Cole, and Eva Reis. "Situational Cues Distinguishing Anger, Fear, and Sorrow." *American Journal of Psychology* 71, 1958, 136–151.

Hupka, Ralph. "Cultural Determinants of Jealousy." *Alternative Life Syles* 4, August 1981, 310–356.

Izard, Carroll E. "Emotion-Cognition Relationships and Human Development." In C. E. Izard, J. Kagan, and R. B. Zajonc, eds. *Emotions, Cognition, and Behavior*. Cambridge, England: Cambridge University Press, 1984.

Izard, Carroll E. "The Structure and Functions of Human Emotions." Paper presented to the American Psychological Association, Atlanta, Georgia, 1988.

James, Sherman A., and David G. Kleinbaum. "Socioecologic Stress and Hypertension Related Mortality Rates in North Carolina." *American Journal of Public Health* 66, 1976, 354–358.

Johnson, Sonia. "The Woman Who Talked Back to God." *Ms.*, November 1981, 51–54, ff. Excerpted from her book *From Housewife to Heretic* (New York: Doubleday, 1981).

Julius, Stevo, Robert Schneider, and Brent Egan. "Suppressed Anger in

Hypertension: Facts and Problems." In M. Chesney and R. Rosenman, eds. *Anger and Hostility in Cardiovascular and Behavioral Disorders*. Washington: Hemisphere, 1985.

Kagan, Jerome. "The Baby's Elastic Mind." *Human Nature* 1, January 1978, 66–73.

Kagan, Jerome. *The Nature of the Child*. New York: Basic, 1984.

Kahn, Michael. "The Physiology of Catharsis." *Journal of Personality and Social Psychology* 3, 1966, 278–286.

Kaplan, Robert. "The Cathartic Value of Self-Expression: Testing Catharsis, Dissonance, and Interference Explanations." *Journal of Social Psychology* 97, 1975, 195–208.

Kaplow, Susi. "Getting Angry." In A. Koedt, E. Levine, and A. Rapone, eds. *Radical Feminism*. New York: Quadrangle, 1973.

Kinsey, Alfred, Wardell B. Pomeroy, Clyde E. Martin, and Paul H. Gebhard. *Sexual Behavior in the Human Female*. Philadelphia: W. B. Saunders, 1953.

Kleinman, Arthur. *Rethinking Psychiatry: From Cultural Category to Personal Experience*. New York: The Free Press, 1988.

Kluegel, James R., and Eliot R. Smith. "The Organization of Stratification Beliefs." Paper presented to the American Sociological Association, Boston, 1979.

Koch-Sheras, Phyllis R. "Dealing with Past Hurts in Relationships: Issues in Marital and Family Therapy." Paper presented to the American Psychological Association, Toronto, 1978.

Kolata, Gina B. "The Truth About Hypoglycemia." *Ms.*, November 1979, 26–30.

Konečni, Vladimir. "Annoyance, Type and Duration of Postannoyance Activity, and Aggression: The 'Cathartic Effect.' " *Journal of Experimental Psychology* 104, 1975a, 76–102.

Konečni, Vladimir. "The Mediation of Aggressive Behavior: Arousal Level Versus Anger and Cognitive Labeling." *Journal of Personality and Social Psychology* 32, 1975b, 706–712.

Konečni, Vladimir, and Ebbe B. Ebbesen. "Disinhibition Versus the Cathartic Effect." *Journal of Personality and Social Psychology* 34, 1976, 352–365.

Kutash, Irwin L., Samuel B. Kutash, Louis B. Schlesinger, and associates, eds. *Violence: Perspectives on Murder and Aggression*. San Francisco: Jossey-Bass, 1978.

Kutash, Samuel B. "Psychoanalytic Theories of Aggression." In I. L. Kutash et al., eds. *Violence*. San Francisco: Jossey-Bass, 1978.

LaBarre, Weston. "The Cultural Bases of Emotions and Gestures."
    Journal of Personality 16, 1947, 49–68.
Lacey, J., J. Kagan, B. Lacey, and H. Moss. "The Visceral Level:
    Situational Determinants and Behavioral Correlates of Autonomic
    Response Patterns." In P. Knapp, ed. *Expression of the Emotions in
    Man.* New York: International Universities Press, 1963.
Laird, J. D. "Self-Attribution of Emotion: The Effects of Expressive
    Behavior on the Quality of Emotional Experience." *Journal of
    Personality and Social Psychology* 29, 1974, 475–486.
Larsen, Randy J., Ed Diener, and Russell Cropanzano. "Cognitive
    Operations Associated with Individual Differences in Affect Intensity."
    Journal of Personality and Social Psychology 53, 1987, 767–774.
Lazarus, R. S., J. R. Averill, and E. M. Opton, Jr. "Toward a Cognitive
    Theory of Emotion." In Magda Arnold, ed. *Feelings and Emotions.*
    New York: Academic Press, 1970.
Lazarus, R. S., M. Tomita, E. Opton, Jr., and M. Kodama. "A
    Cross-Cultural Study of Stress-Reaction Patterns in Japan." *Journal of
    Personality and Social Psychology* 4, 1966, 622–633.
Lebra, Takie Sugiyama. *Japanese Patterns of Behavior.* Honolulu: Social
    Science Research Institute (University of Hawaii), 1976.
Lee, Richard B. and Irven DeVore, eds. *Kalahari Hunter-Gatherers:
    Studies of the !Kung-san and Their Neighbors.* Cambridge, Mass.:
    Harvard University Press, 1976.
Lerner, Harriet. "Internal Prohibitions Against Female Anger."
    American Journal of Psychoanalysis 40, 1980, 137–148.
Lerner, Harriet Goldhor. "The Challenge of Change." In C. Tavris, ed.
    EveryWoman's Emotional Well-Being. New York: Doubleday, 1986.
Lerner, Harriet Goldhor. *The Dance of Anger.* New York: Harper &
    Row, 1985.
Lerner, Melvin J. *The Belief in a Just World: A Fundamental Delusion.*
    New York: Plenum Press, 1980.
Leventhal, Howard. "Wrongheaded Ideas about Illness." *Psychology
    Today,* January 1982, 48–55, 73.
Levi, Lennart. *Society, Stress and Disease,* vol. 3. New York: Oxford
    University Press, 1978.
Levy, Robert I. "Tahitian Gentleness and Redundant Controls." In A.
    Montagu, ed. *Learning Non-Aggression.* New York: Oxford University
    Press, 1978.
Levy, Robert I. *Tahitians.* Chicago: University of Chicago Press, 1973.
Lewis, Dorothy Otnow, ed. *Vulnerabilities to Delinquency.* New York:
    Spectrum Medical and Scientific Books, 1981.

Lewis, Janet. *The Trial of Sören Qvist*. Chicago: Swallow Press, 1947.

Lochman, John E. "Cognitive-Behavioral Intervention with Aggressive Boys: Three Year Followup Effects." Paper presented to the American Psychological Association, Atlanta, Georgia, 1988.

Lochman, John E. "Psychological Characteristics and Assessment of Aggressive Adolescents." In C. R. Keith, ed. *The Aggressive Adolescent: Clinical Perspectives*. New York: The Free Press, 1984.

Lorenz, Konrad. *On Aggression*. New York: Bantam Books, 1971.

Lutz, Catherine A. *Unnatural Emotions*. Chicago: University of Chicago Press, 1988.

Lyman, Peter. "The Politics of Anger: On Silence, Ressentiment, and Political Speech." *Socialist Review*, Spring-Summer 1981, 55–74.

Lyman, Stanford M. *The Seven Deadly Sins: Society and Evil*. New York: St. Martin's Press, 1978.

McCarthy, John, and Bryan Kelly. "Aggression, Performance Variables and Anger Self-Report in Ice Hockey Players." *Journal of Psychology* 99, 1978, 97–101.

McGuinness, Diane, and Karl Pribram. "The Neuropsychology of Attention: Emotional and Motivational Controls." In M. C. Wittrock, ed. *The Brain and Psychology*. New York: Academic Press, 1980.

McKellar, Peter. "The Emotion of Anger in the Expression of Human Aggressiveness." *British Journal of Psychology* 39, 1949, 148–155.

McKellar, Peter. "Provocation to Anger and the Development of Attitudes of Hostility." *British Journal of Psychology* 40, 1950, 104–114.

MacLean, Paul D. "The Limbic Brain in Relation to Psychoses," In P. Black, ed. *Physiological Correlates of Emotion*. New York: Academic Press, 1970.

MacLean, Paul D. "Phylogenesis." In P. Knapp, ed. *Expression of the Emotions in Man*. New York: International Universities Press, 1963.

Mace, David. "Marital Intimacy and the Deadly Love-Anger Cycle." *Journal of Marriage and Family Counseling* 2, 1976, 131–137.

Malcolm X. *The Autobiography of Malcolm X*. New York: Grove Press, 1966.

Mallick, Shahbaz Khan, and Boyd R. McCandless. "A Study of Catharsis Aggression." *Journal of Personality and Social Psychology* 4, 1966, 591–596.

Mandler, George. *Mind and Body*. New York: Norton, 1984.

Margolin, Gayla. "Conjoint Marital Therapy to Enhance Anger Management and Reduce Spouse Abuse." *The American Journal of Family Therapy* 7, 1979, 13–23.

Mark, Vernon. "Sociobiological Theories of Abnormal Aggression." In I. L. Kutash et al., eds. *Violence.* San Francisco: Jossey-Bass, 1978.

Marlatt, G. Alan, and Demaris J. Rohsenow. "The Think-Drink Effect." *Psychology Today,* December 1981, 60–69, 93.

Marlatt, G. Alan, Carole Kosturn, and Alan Lang. "Provocation to Anger and Opportunity for Retaliation as Determinants of Alcohol Consumption in Social Drinkers." *Journal of Abnormal Psychology* 84, 1975, 652–659.

Marshall, Gary D., and Philip G. Zimbardo. "Affective Consequences of Inadequately Explained Physiological Arousal." *Journal of Personality and Social Psychology* 37, 1979, 970–989.

Marshall, John R. "The Expression of Feelings." *Archives of General Psychiatry* 27, 1972, 786–790.

Marshall, Lorna. "Sharing, Talking, and Giving: Relief of Social Tensions among the !Kung." In R. B. Lee and I. DeVore, eds. *Kalahari Hunter-Gatherers.* Cambridge, Mass.: Harvard University Press, 1976.

Maslach, Christina. "Negative Emotional Biasing of Unexplained Arousal." *Journal of Personality and Social Psychology* 37, 1979, 953–970.

Matthews, Karen A. "Coronary Heart Disease and Type A Behaviors: Update on and Alternative to the Booth-Kewley and Friedman (1987) Quantitative Review." *Psychological Bulletin* 104, 1988, 373–380.

Matthews, Karen, David Glass, Ray Rosenman, and Rayman Bortner. "Competitive Drive, Pattern-A, and CHD: A Further Analysis of Some Data from the Western Collaborative Group Study." *Journal of Chronic Diseases* 30, 1977, 489–498.

Mead, Margaret. *Male and Female.* New York: Dell, 1949; Laurel edition, 1968.

Miller, Jean Baker. *Toward a New Psychology of Women.* Boston: Beacon Press, 1976.

Miller, Paul A., and Nancy Eisenberg. "The Relation of Empathy to Aggressive and Externalizing/Antisocial Behavior." *Psychological Bulletin* 103, 1988, 324–344.

Montagu, Ashley. *The Anatomy of Swearing.* New York: Collier, 1967.

Montagu, Ashley. *Learning Non-Aggression: The Experience of Non-Literate Societies.* New York: Oxford University Press paperback, 1978.

Montaigne, "On Anger." In Donald M. Frame, trans. *The Complete Essays of Montaigne.* Palo Alto, Calif.: Stanford University Press, 1976.

Moore, Barrington, Jr. *Injustice: The Social Bases of Obedience and Revolt*. White Plains, N.Y.: M. E. Sharpe, 1978.

Morgan, Robin, ed. *Sisterhood Is Powerful*. New York: Random House, 1970.

Moyer, Kenneth E. *The Physiology of Hostility*. Chicago: Markham, 1971.

Mueller, C., and E. Donnerstein. "The Effects of Humor-Induced Arousal upon Aggressive Behavior." *Journal of Research in Personality* 11, 1977, 73–82.

Mueller, Karen, and Margie Leidig. "Women's Anger and Feminist Therapy." Unpublished paper, University of Colorado, 1976.

Murray, Edward. "Coping and Anger." In T. Field, P. McCabe, and N. Schneiderman, eds. *Stress and Coping*. Hillsdale, N.J.: Erlbaum, 1985.

Myerhoff, Barbara. *Number Our Days*. New York: Dutton, 1978.

Neiss, Rob. "Reconceptualizing Arousal: Psychobiological States in Motor Performance." *Psychological Bulletin* 103, 1988, 345–366.

Newman, P. L. " 'Wild Man' Behavior in a New Guinea Highlands Community." *American Anthropologist* 66, 1960, 1–19.

Nichols, Jack. *Men's Liberation*. New York: Penguin, 1975.

Noller, Patricia. "Misunderstandings in Marital Communication: A Study of Couples' Nonverbal Communication." *Journal of Personality and Social Psychology* 39, 1980, 1135–1148.

Novaco, Raymond W. *Anger Control*. Lexington, Mass.: D. C. Heath, Lexington Books, 1975.

Novaco, Raymond W. "Anger and Its Therapeutic Regulation." In M. Chesney and R. Rosenman, eds. *Anger and Hostility in Cardiovascular and Behavioral Disorders*. Washington: Hemisphere, 1985.

Oppenheimer, Valerie. "The Sex Labeling of Jobs." In M. Mednick, S. Tangri, and L. Hoffman, eds. *Women and Achievement*. New York: Halsted, 1975.

O'Reilly, Jane. *The Girl I Left Behind*. New York: Macmillan, 1980.

Pankratz, Loren, Philip Levendusky, and Vincent Glaudin. "The Antecedents of Anger in a Sample of College Students." *Journal of Psychology* 92, 1976, 173–178.

Pascale, Richard, and Anthony G. Athos. *The Art of Japanese Management*. New York: Simon and Schuster, 1981.

Patterson, G[erald] R. "A Microsocial Analysis of Anger and Irritable Behavior." In M. Chesney and R. Rosenman, eds. *Anger and Hostility in Cardiovascular and Behavioral Disorders*. Washington: Hemisphere, 1985.

Patterson, Gerald R. "Performance Models for Aggressive Boys." *American Psychologist* 41, 1986, 432–444.

Pennebaker, James W. "Confiding Traumatic Experiences and Health." In S. Fisher and J. Reason, eds. *Handbook of Life Stress, Cognition and Health*. New York: Wiley, 1988.

Pennebaker, James W., Cheryl F. Hughes, and Robin C. O'Heeron. "The Psychophysiology of Confession: Linking Inhibitory and Psychosomatic Processes." *Journal of Personality and Social Psychology* 52, 1987, 781–793.

Pennebaker, James W., Janice Kiecolt-Glaser, and Ronald Glaser. "Disclosure of Traumas and Immune Function: Health Implications for Psychotherapy." *Journal of Consulting and Clinical Psychology* 56, 1988, 239–245.

Persky, Harold. "Neuro-Endocrine Determinants of Differences in Hostility and Aggression Between Males and Females." In L. Levi, ed. *Society, Stress and Disease*, vol. 3. New York: Oxford University Press, 1978.

Pliner, Patricia, Kirk R. Blankstein, and Irwin M. Spigel, eds. *Perception of Emotion in Self and Others*. New York: Plenum Press, 1979.

Plutchik, Robert. "Evolutionary Bases of Empathy." In N. Eisenberg and J. Strayer, eds. *Empathy and Its Development*. New York: Cambridge University Press, 1987.

Polivy, Janet. "On the Induction of Emotion in the Laboratory: Discrete Moods or Multiple Affect States?" *Journal of Personality and Social Psychology* 41, 1981, 803–817.

Polivy, Janet, Arthur Schueneman, and Kathleen Carlson. "Alcohol and Tension Reduction: Cognitive and Physiological Effects." *Journal of Abnormal Psychology* 85, 1976, 595–600.

Pospisil, Leopold. *The Kapauku Papuans of West New Guinea*. New York: Holt, Rinehart & Winston, 1963.

Quanty, Michael B. "Aggression Catharsis." In R. G. Geen and E. C. O'Neal, eds. *Perspectives on Aggression*. New York: Academic Press, 1976.

Rioch, David M. "Psychological and Pharmacological Manipulations." In L. Levi, ed. *Emotions: Their Parameters and Measurement*. New York: Raven Press, 1975.

Roseman, Marina. "Head, Heart, Odor, and Shadow: The Structure of the Self and the Emotional World." *Ethos*, in press.

Roseman, Marina. *Healing Sounds: Music and Medicine in Temiar Life*. Berkeley, Calif.: University of California Press, to be published 1990.

Rosenbaum, Alan, and K. Daniel O'Leary. "Marital Violence: Characteristics of Abusive Couples." *Journal of Consulting and Clinical Psychology* 49, 1981, 63–71.

Rosenman, Ray H. "Health Consequences of Anger and Implications for Treatment." In M. Chesney and R. Rosenman, eds. *Anger and Hostility in Cardiovascular and Behavioral Disorders*. Washington: Hemisphere, 1985.

Rothenberg, Albert. "On Anger." *American Journal of Psychiatry* 128, 1971, 454–460.

Rotter, J., J. Sones, I. Samloff, C. Richardson et al. "Duodenal-Ulcer Disease Associated with Elevated Serum Pepsinogen I." *New England Journal of Medicine* 300, January 11, 1970, 63–89.

Rubin, Theodore Isaac. *The Angry Book*. New York: Collier, 1970.

Rule, Brendan G., and Lynn S. Hewitt. "Effects of Thwarting on Cardiac Response and Physical Aggression." *Journal of Personality and Social Psychology* 19, 1971, 181–187.

Rule, Brendan G., and Andrew R. Nesdale. "Emotional Arousal and Aggressive Behavior." *Psychological Bulletin* 83, 1976, 851–863.

Rule, Brendan G., Tamara J. Ferguson, and Andrew R. Nesdale. "Emotional Arousal, Anger, and Aggression: The Misattribution Issue." In P. Pliner et al., eds. *Perception of Emotion in Self and Others*. New York: Plenum Press, 1979.

Russell, Gordon W. "Psychological Issues in Sports Aggression." In J. H. Goldstein, ed. *Sports Violence*. New York: Springer-Verlag, 1983.

Russell, James A., and Albert Mehrabian. "Distinguishing Anger and Anxiety in Terms of Emotional Response." *Journal of Consulting and Clinical Psychology* 42, 1974, 79–83.

Russell, James A., and Albert Mehrabian. "The Mediating Role of Emotions in Alcohol Use." *Journal of Studies on Alcohol* 36, 1975, 1508–1536.

Sabini, John. "Aggression in the Laboratory." In I. L. Kutash et al., eds. *Violence*. San Francisco: Jossey-Bass, 1978.

Sanger, Susan Phipps, and Henry A. Alker. "Dimensions of Internal-External Locus of Control and the Women's Liberation Movement." *Journal of Social Issues* 28, 1972, 115–129.

Schachter, Joseph. "Pain, Fear, and Anger in Hypertensives and Normotensives." *Psychosomatic Medicine* 19, 1957, 17–29.

Schachter, Stanley, and Jerome E. Singer. "Cognitive, Social, and Physiological Determinants of Emotional State." *Psychological Review* 69, 1962, 379–399.

Scheff, Thomas. *Catharsis in Healing, Ritual and Drama.* Berkeley: University of California Press, 1979.

Scherer, Klaus, R. P. Abeles, and Claude S. Fischer. *Human Aggression and Conflict.* Englewood Cliffs, N.J.: Prentice-Hall, 1975.

Schimmel, Solomon. "Anger and Its Control in Graeco-Roman and Modern Psychology." *Psychiatry* 42, 1979, 320–337.

Schmidt, Donald E., and John P. Keating. "Human Crowding and Personal Control: An Integration of the Research." *Psychological Bulletin* 86, 1979, 680–700.

Schwade, E. D., and S. G. Geiger. "Severe Behavior Disorders with Abnormal Electroencephalograms." *Diseases of the Nervous System* 21, 1960, 616–620.

Sears, David, and Leonie Huddy. "Women as a Political Interest Group in the Mass Public." In P. Gurin and L. Tilly, eds. *Women in Twentieth Century American Politics.* New York: Russell Sage Foundation, 1989.

Sebeok, Thomas A. *Play of Musement.* Bloomington: University of Indiana Press, 1982.

Segal, Julius. *Winning Life's Toughest Battles.* New York: McGraw-Hill, 1986.

Seneca, Lucius Annaeus. "On Anger." In J. W. Basore, trans. *Moral Essays.* Cambridge, Mass.: Harvard University Press, 1963. (See also "On Self-Control," letter CXVI in *The Letters of Seneca.*)

Sennett, Richard. *Authority.* New York: Knopf, 1980.

Sennett, Richard. *The Uses of Disorder.* New York: Knopf, 1970.

Shott, Susan. "Emotion and Social Life." *American Journal of Sociology* 84, 1979, 1317–1334.

Sipes, Richard G. "War, Sports and Aggression: An Empirical Test of Two Rival Theories." *American Anthropologist* 75, 1973, 64–86.

Smith, Craig A., and Phoebe C. Ellsworth. "Patterns of Appraisal and Emotion Related to Taking an Exam." *Journal of Personality and Social Psychology* 52, 1987, 475–488.

Smith, Michael D. "What Is Sports Violence? A Sociolegal Perspective." In J. H. Goldstein, ed. *Sports Violence.* New York: Springer-Verlag, 1983.

Smith, Robert C., Elizabeth Parker, and Ernest P. Noble. "Alcohol and Affect in Dyadic Social Interaction." *Psychosomatic Medicine* 37, 1975, 25–40.

Smith, Ronald E. "The Use of Humor in the Counterconditioning of Anger Responses: A Case Study." *Behavior Therapy* 4, 1973, 576–580.

Snyder, C. R. "Reality Negotiation: From Excuses to Hope and Beyond." Paper presented to the American Psychological Association, Atlanta, Georgia, 1988.

Solomon, Robert. "Emotions and Anthropology: The Logic of Emotional World Views." *Inquiry* 21, 1978, 181–199.

Solomon, Robert. "On Emotions as Judgments." *American Philosophical Quarterly* 25, 1988, 183–191.

Solomon, Robert. *The Passions.* New York: Doubleday, 1976.

Sommers, Shula, and Anthony Scioli. "Emotional Range and Value Orientation: Toward a Cognitive View of Emotionality." *Journal of Personality and Social Psychology* 51, 1986, 417–422.

Sostek, Andrew J., and Richard S. Wyatt. "The Chemistry of Crankiness." *Psychology Today*, October 1981, 120.

Spielberger, Charles. "State-Trait Anger Expression Inventory: Research Edition." Odessa, Florida: Psychological Assessment Resources, Inc., 1988.

Spielberger, Charles, Susan S. Krasner, and Eldra P. Solomon. "The Experience, Expression and Control of Anger." In M. P. Janisse, ed. *Health Psychology: Individual Differences and Stress.* New York: Springer-Verlag, 1988.

Sroufe, L. Alan. "Attachment and the Roots of Competence." *Human Nature* 1, October 1978, 50–57.

Sroufe, L. Alan. "The Coherence of Individual Development: Early Care, Attachment, and Subsequent Development Issues." *American Psychologist* 34, 1979, 834–841.

Steele, Brandt. "The Child Abuser." In I. Kutash et al., eds. *Violence.* San Francisco: Jossey-Bass, 1978.

Stehle, H. C. "Thalamic Dysfunction Involved in Destructive Aggressive Behavior Directed Against Persons and Property." *EEG Clinical Neurophysiology* 12, 1960, 264.

Steil, Janice, Bruce Tuchman, and Morton Deutsch. "An Exploratory Study of the Meanings of Injustice and Frustration." *Personality and Social Psychology Bulletin* 4, 1978, 393–398.

Steinmetz, Suzanne K. *The Cycle of Violence.* New York: Praeger, 1977.

Stenberg, Craig R., and Joseph Campos. "The Development of Anger Expressions in Infancy." In N. Stein, B. Leventhal, and T. Trabasso, eds. *Psychological and Biological Approaches to Emotion.* Hillsdale, N.J.: Erlbaum, 1990.

Stone, L., and J. E. Hokanson. "Arousal Reduction via Self-Punitive Behavior." *Journal of Personality and Social Psychology* 12, 1969, 72–79.

Strack, Fritz, Leonard L. Martin, and Sabine Stepper. "Inhibiting and Facilitating Conditions of the Human Smile: A Non-Obtrusive Test of the Facial-Feedback Hypothesis." *Journal of Social and Personality Psychology* 54, 1988, 768–777.

Stratton, George Malcolm. *Anger: Its Religious and Moral Significance.* New York: Macmillan, 1923.

Straus, Murray. "Leveling, Civility, and Violence in the Family." *Journal of Marriage and the Family* 36, 1974, 13–29.

Straus, Murray. "A Sociological Perspective on the Causes of Family Violence." Paper presented to the American Association for the Advancement of Science, Houston, Texas, 1979.

Straus, Murray, Richard Gelles, and Suzanne Steinmetz. *Behind Closed Doors: Violence in the American Family.* Garden City, N.Y.: Doubleday, Anchor, 1980.

Syme, S. Leonard. "People Need People." *American Health* 1, July/August 1982.

Tavris, Carol, and Carole Wade. *The Longest War: Sex Differences in Perspective* (2nd ed.). New York: Harcourt Brace Jovanovich, 1984.

Taylor, Shelley E., and Jonathon D. Brown. "Illusion and Well-Being: A Social Psychological Perspective on Mental Health." *Psychological Bulletin* 103, 1988, 193–210.

Taylor, Stuart P., Charles B. Gannon, and Deborah R. Capasso. "Aggression as a Function of the Interaction of Alcohol and Threat." *Journal of Personality and Social Psychology* 34, 1976, 938–941.

Taylor, Stuart P., Gregory Schmutter, and Kenneth E. Leonard. "Physical Aggression as a Function of Alcohol and Frustration." *Bulletin of the Psychonomic Society* 9, 1977, 217–218.

Thomas, Elizabeth Marshall. *The Harmless People.* New York: Random House, 1959.

Tucker, Don M. "Asymmetries of Neural Architecture and the Structure of Emotional Experience." In R. Johnson and W. Roth, eds. *Eighth Event-Related Potentials International Conference.* New York: Oxford Press, 1989.

Tucker, Don M., and Peter A. Williamson. "Asymmetric Neural Control Systems in Human Self-Regulation." *Psychological Review* 91, 1984, 185–215.

Turnbull, Colin M. *The Forest People.* New York: Simon and Schuster, 1961.

Turnbull, Colin M. "The Politics of Non-Aggression." In A. Montagu, ed. *Learning Non-Aggression*. New York: Oxford University Press paperback, 1978.

Vantress, Florence E., and Christene B. Williams. "The Effect of the Presence of the Provocator and the Opportunity to Counteraggress on Systolic Blood Pressure." *Journal of General Psychology* 86, 1972, 63–68.

Wallace, Michael. "The Uses of Violence in American History." *The American Scholar* 40, Winter 1970–71, 81–102.

Warren, Gayle H., and Anthony E. Raynes. "Mood Changes During Three Conditions of Alcohol Intake." *Quarterly Journal of Studies on Alcohol* 33, 1972, 979–989.

Wegner, Daniel M., David Schneider, Samuel Carter, and Teri White. "Paradoxical Effects of Thought Suppression." *Journal of Personality and Social Psychology* 53, 1987, 5–13.

Weinberger, Daniel A. "The Construct Validity of the Repressive Coping Style." In J. L. Singer, ed. *Repression: Defense Mechanism and Personality Style*. Chicago: University of Chicago Press, in press.

Weiner, Bernard. "The Emotional Consequences of Causal Attributions." In M. S. Clark and S. T. Fiske, eds. *Affect and Cognition: The 17th Annual Carnegie Symposium on Cognition*. Hillsdale, N.J.: Erlbaum, 1982.

Weiner, Bernard, and Sandra Graham. "An Attributional Approach to Emotional Development." In C. E. Izard, J. Kagan, and R. B. Zajonc, eds. *Emotions, Cognition, and Behavior*. Cambridge, England: Cambridge University Press, 1984.

Weiner, Bernard, Dan Russell, and David Lerman. "The Cognition-Emotion Process in Achievement-Related Contexts." *Journal of Personality and Social Psychology* 37, 1979, 1211–1220.

Weiss, Bernard, Christopher Cox, Marc Young et al. "Behavioral Epidemiology of Food Additives." *Neurobehavioral Toxicology*, vol. 1, suppl. 1, 1979, 149–155.

Weiss, Bernard, J. Hicks Williams, Sheldon Margen, Barbara Abrams et al. "Behavioral Responses to Artificial Food Colors." *Science* 207, March 28, 1980, 1487–1489.

Weiss, Robert S. "Transition States and Other Stressful Situations." In G. Caplan and M. Killilea, eds. *Support Systems and Mutual Help*. New York: Grune & Stratton, 1976.

Wender, Paul H., and Donald F. Klein. *Mind, Mood, and Medicine: A Guide to the New Biopsychiatry*. New York: Farrar, Straus & Giroux, 1981.

West, Candace. "Why Can't a Woman Be More Like a Man? An Interactional Note on Organizational Game Playing for Managerial Women." *Sociology of Work and Occupations*, February 1982.

Whitehead, William E., Barry Blackwell, Himasiri De Silva, and Ann Robinson. "Anxiety and Anger in Hypertension." *Journal of Psychosomatic Research* 21, 1977, 383–389.

Wikler, Norma. "Vietnam and Veterans' Consciousness: Prepolitical Thinking Among American Soldiers." Ph.D. dissertation, University of California at Berkeley, 1973.

Wilbanks, William Lee. "The New Obscenity: I Can't Help Myself." *Vital Speeches of the Day* LIV, August 15, 1988, 658–664.

Wile, Daniel B. *After the Honeymoon*. New York: Wiley, 1988.

Williams, Elizabeth Friar. *Notes of a Feminist Therapist*. New York: Dell, 1976; Laurel edition, 1977.

Williams, Redford B., Jr. *The Trusting Heart*. New York: Random House, 1989.

Williams, Redford B., Jr., John C. Barefoot, and Richard B. Shekelle. "The Health Consequences of Hostility." In M. Chesney and R. Rosenman, eds. *Anger and Hostility in Cardiovascular and Behavioral Disorders*. Washington: Hemisphere, 1985.

Williams, Roger M. "The U.S. Open Character Test." *Psychology Today*, October 1988, 60–62.

Woods, Sherwyn M. "Adolescent Violence and Homicide: Ego Disruption and the 6 and 14 Dysrhythmia." *Archives of General Psychiatry* 5, 1961, 528–534.

Worchel, Stephen. "The Effect of Three Types of Arbitrary Thwarting on the Instigation to Aggression." *Journal of Personality* 42, 1974, 300–318.

Yarrow, Leon J. "Emotional Development." *American Psychologist* 34, 1979, 951–957.

Zajonc, Robert B. "Feeling and Thinking: Preferences Need No Inferences." *American Psychologist* 35, 1980, 151–175.

Zillmann, Dolf. *Connections Between Sex and Aggression*. Hillsdale, N.J.: Erlbaum, 1984.

Zillmann, Dolf. *Hostility and Aggression*. Hillsdale, N.J.: Erlbaum, 1979.

Zillmann, Dolf, and Jennings Bryant. "Effect of Residual Excitation on the Emotional Response to Provocation and Delayed Aggressive Behavior." *Journal of Personality and Social Psychology* 30, 1974, 782–791.

Zillmann, Dolf, R. C. Johnson, and K. Day. "Attribution of Apparent Arousal and Proficiency of Recovery from Sympathetic Activation Affecting Excitation Transfer to Aggressive Behavior." *Journal of Experimental Social Psychology* 10, 1974, 503–515.

Zimmerman, Don H., and Candace West. "Sex Roles, Interruptions and Silences in Conversation." In B. Thorne and N. Henley, eds. *Language and Sex: Difference and Dominance.* Rowley, Mass.: Newbury House, 1975.

Index

abandonment, 145, 157
abortions, 255
Abraham, Karl, 107
Abrams, Maxine, 330*n*
abusive couples, treatment for,
  246–47
Achilles, 30–31
active pessimism, 69
additives, 97, 326*n*
adolescents:
  and aggression, 140–41
  black, 325*n*
  parents challenged by, 50–51
  repression of rage in, 39
  violent, 74–76, 127, 147–48, 188,
    326*n*–27*n*
adrenal hormones, 89, 166
adrenaline, *see* epinephrine
adrenal medulla, 86
adultery, 48–49, 56–57, 330*n*
Africa, 54
After the Honeymoon (Wile), 237
Agassi, Andre, 189
aggression:
  anger vs., 24, 36–37
  as catharsis, 131–38
  in children, 136, 140–41, 307–12
  displaced, 52, 130, 131, 138,
    163–64, 183–84, 208, 213
  frustration and, 164–67
  passive, 57, 197
  sex and, 44–45
  theories of, 38–41, 164
  therapies for, 310–11
  ventilation by, 131–38
  verbal, 136–38, 177, 207–8,
    288

verbal vs. physical, 136–37
Aggression Replacement Training,
  310–11
aggression training, 196–97
Alaska, Eskimos in, 253
alcohol:
  anger excused by, 163, 177–81
  epinephrine and, 89
  heart rate and, 178
  men and, 179
  women and, 179
Aleichem, Sholom, 53
Allah, 259
Allen, Fred, 286
allergies, 60, 74, 97–98, 106, 143,
  326*n*
amaeru, 121
ambition, 46, 122–23
American Health (Gurin), 104
American Medical Association, 105
amok attacks, 59–64
amygdala, 76, 78–79, 99, 327*n*,
  330*n*
anger:
  ambivalence about, 28–30, 47
  characteristics of, 37–38, 49–50
  chronic, 288–93
  cognitive approaches to, 38, 93,
    109–10, 294–319
  consequences of, 129–30, 202,
    250, 337*n*–38*n*
  dealing with, 286–319
  definitions of, 19–20, 95
  of despair, 145
  economic exchange and, 53–54
  of hope, 145
  "in" vs. "out," 113–14

anger (*cont.*)
  metaphors for, 20–21, 40, 88,
    131, 220, 221, 323*n*–24*n*
  physical response to, 34, 70–71,
    85–91, 328*n*
  policing power of, 49–59, 152–53,
    251–85
  potential of, 25
  punishment for, 58, 62–64,
    147–48, 186–87
  regulation of, 292
  reporting of, 137, 152–60
  repressed vs. suppressed, 103
  research on, 71–85, 86–88, 132–
    35, 136–37, 139–41, 168–69,
    200–208, 249, 329*n*–30*n*
  retrospective, 35
  rewards for, 188
  righteous, 116, 315
  ritual, 52–59, 153, 186
  sex differences in, 193–219
  social, 263–85
  solutions to problems with, 43,
    152–55, 286–87
  targets of, 201
  threshold of, 78–79
anger, causes of:
  circumstantial, 71–73, 89–93,
    115–16, 161–92, 193–95, 201,
    210, 338*n*
  in marriages, 220–37, 248
  in new therapies, 43
  organic, 61, 72–100, 143,
    325*n*–30*n*
anger, suppressed, 24, 31–32, 43,
    101–27
  arthritis and, 126
  asthma and, 126
  blood pressure and, 115–18, 332*n*
  depression and, 23, 101, 102–3,
    107–12
  eating disorders and, 104–7
  expressed vs., 116–17, 201–2, 237,
    242, 248–49
  headaches and, 126
  heart disease and, 113–25, 126
  in men, 196–99
  ulcers and, 102, 103, 106–7, 126

  in women, 67, 116, 125, 195–97,
    334*n*
anger diary, 289–90, 335*n*
anger-intervention therapies, 288–319
  see also specific therapies
Anger of Achilles, The (Graves), 30
anger patterns, breaking of, 238–45
  acceptance in, 241–42
  arthritis and, 126
  bargaining in, 244–45
  fantasies in, 240–41
Angry Book, The (Rubin), 43
anguish, 145, 257
animals:
  brains of, 37
  emotions of, 32–38
anorexia, 104, 105–6
anthropology, 24, 52, 57, 62, 65, 69,
    127, 150, 165, 183–84
antidepressants, 109–10
anxiety, 102, 104, 116, 159, 202
  anger vs., 117–18, 133, 145
  hypertension and, 117–18, 332*n*
  illness and, 125–26
  suppressed anger and, 24
apologies, 68, 177
Aquinas, Saint Thomas, 251
Arab culture, 65, 172
Arapesh tribe, anger as viewed by,
    57, 67
Ardrey, Robert, 32
Arias, Jimmy, 189
Arieti, Silvano, 92
Aristotle, 130
arousability, 83, 85, 90
Art of Japanese Management, The
    (Pascale and Athos), 121
Art of Self-Control Training
    Program, 309
Ashe, Arthur, 188
assassinations, 60
assertiveness training, 65, 204
Attachment and Loss (Bowlby),
    144–45
Australia, aborigine infants in, 82
Averill, James, 37–38, 50, 64, 221,
    337*n*–38*n*
Ax, Albert F., 86–88, 328*n*

Bach, George, 43
Bali, anger as viewed in, 165
Baron, Robert A., 327n
Barrile, Jackie, 104, 105
baseball, 177–78, 181, 184, 186, 189, 190
Bateson, Gregory, 165
Baumrind, Diana, 311
BBC, 191
Beck, Aaron, 109–10
Behind Closed Doors (Straus), 230
Bench, Johnny, 189
Bennett, William, 104–6
Berkman, Lisa, 121
Berkowitz, Leonard, 43, 137, 160, 185–86
Berman, Alan, 326n–27n
Bernardez-Bonesatti, Teresa, 210
Bettelheim, Bruno, 45
Biaggio, Mary K., 141, 211, 338n
Bible, 27, 29–30, 49, 69, 258–59
bickering:
    marital, 45, 51, 220
    as ritual game, 52–59
bicycling, 175–76
binge eating, 105, 125
bioenergetics, 136, 288
biofeedback, 90
biological politics, 95–100, 111
blacks, African:
    infant, 82
    see also individual countries and tribes
blacks, American:
    adolescent, 325n
    anger suppressed by, 67, 127
    blood-pressure levels of, 115, 116, 118
Blake, William, 128–29
Blakeslee, Sandra, 300
Bland, Jeffrey, 74
blood pressure:
    anger and, 73, 86, 88, 89, 288, 332n
    epinephrine and, 89, 90–91
    high, 77, 101, 103, 115–21, 125, 331n–32n
    low, 89
    noise and, 169
    regulation of, 89, 132–35
Bolivia, Siriono tribe in, 54, 150
Bonime, Walter, 284
Booth-Kewley, Stephanie, 125
boredom, 89
Borg, Bjorn, 188
Boudin, Kathy, 262
Bowlby, John, 21, 144–46
bowling, 190
Boyd, D., 322n
Boys Town, 147–48
Bradshaw, John, 128
brain:
    damaged, 74–76
    diseases of, 74–75, 78, 97–99
    emotions controlled by, 37, 76–77, 95
    epinephrine and, 89–90
    hemispheres of, 79–80
    norepinephrine and, 89–90
    "primitive" structures in, 323n
    rage and, 37, 76, 78, 95, 97–100
    surgery on, 98–99
Brazelton, T. Berry, 81
Breuer, Josef, 40
Briggs, Jean, 46, 57–58
Brown, George W., 110
Brown, Jonathon, 254
Brown, Prudence, 301
Brown, Roger, 175
Bruch, Hilde, 105–6
Bryant, Anita, 270
Buddhism, 259
bulimia, 104, 105
bullies, 59, 197, 207
Bushmen, *see* !Kung-san tribe
Buss, Arnold H., 83, 200
Buss-Durkee Inventory, 200

caffeine, 89
Cancian, Francesca, 208–9
Cannon, Walter B., 6
Carroll, Lewis, 321n
catharsis:
    aggression as, 130–38, 288

catharsis (*cont.*)
  defined, 130
  Freudian concept of, 40–41, 131
  optimal conditions for, 137–38,
    272
  as popular notion, 45, 202
  retaliation as, 135, 137–38
  ventilationism vs., 41, 130–38,
    300–301, 302
Caucasians, American, temperament
  of, 81–82
challenge, sense of, 125
Chaplin, Charlie, 292, 293
CHD (coronary heart disease), 120
cheating, 72
chess, 190
Chesterton, G. K., 48
child rearing:
  abuse in, 75–76, 145, 170, 180,
    205–7, 225, 255, 311
  arguments about, 230, 233
  physical punishment of, 45
  self-control in, 45
  ventilation of childhood rage and,
    142–50
children, aggressive, 307–12
  behavioral patterns in, 307–8
  parenting of, 307–8, 311–12
  studies on, 136, 140–41, 307–8
  therapies for, 308–11
  violence of, 73–76
China, cultural rules of, 172
  anger in, 67
Chinese:
  in Malay Archipelago, 61–62
  temperament of, 81–82
cholesterol, 120
Christianity, 259–60
chromosomes, 327n
Ciccarelli, Dino, 187
Cinderella Complex, The (Dowling),
  274–75
circumcision, female, 261
civility, 22, 67–69, 127, 247–50
Cline-Naffziger, Claudeen, 214
coercive chains, 308
cognitive therapy, 38, 45, 109–110,
  294–99

community, as stress buffer, 121–22
competitiveness:
  anger and, 46, 183–84
  in Type A personality, 119–20
complaining, 52–53
condescension, anger at, 72, 210,
  338n
confession, 156–59, 317
"Confessions of a Closet Eater"
  (Barrile), 104
Congress, U.S., 50, 68, 213
Congreve, William, 85
consciousness-raising groups, 271,
  274
conservatives, 255, 270
control, *see* self-control
conversation, rules of, 218–19
convulsions, 75
coronary heart disease (CHD),
  120–22, 123–25, 126
Costa, Paul T., Jr., 123
courtesy, 22, 68, 127, 247–50
crime rate, crowding and, 170–71
Crosby, Faye, 262, 265, 271
crowds, 170–73
  arousal generated by, 163, 171,
    172
crying:
  anger expressed by, 202, 235
  response to, 169–70, 335n
culture:
  emotional expression governed by,
    36, 65–67
  expression of anger determined by,
    48–49, 164–65
  insanity defined by, 59–64
  sex roles in, 216–19
  sports in, 183–84, 191
  values of, 42–43, 59, 172, 176,
    252–53
cursing, 53, 325n
Cycle of Violence, The (Steinmetz),
  45

Dance of Anger, The (Lerner), 239
Danesh, Hossain B., 23
Darwin, Charles, 32–37, 39
Davidson, Sara, 175

"Dear Abby," 294
defense reaction, in infants, 82
Deffenbacher, Jerry, 201, 287, 290–91
deficiencies, nutritional, 74, 98, 106
Dembroski, Theodore, 123
denial, 38–39, 101, 256–57
depression, 57, 107–12
  anger combined with, 102–3
  causes of, 111–12
  after expression of anger, 44, 108, 202, 331*n*
  illness and, 125–26
  as suppressed anger, 23–24, 101, 103, 107–12
  in women, 95, 109, 110–11, 122–23, 195
De Rivera, Joseph, 49, 100
Descartes, René, 32
Descent of Man (Darwin), 33–37
Deuteronomy, 27, 259
diabetes, 77
Diagnostic and Statistical Manual of Mental Disorders, The (DSM), 287
Dieter's Dilemma, The (Bennett and Gurin), 104–6
dieting, 105–6
difficult people, 293–99
  assertiveness and, 298
  defined, 294–95
  management of, 295–99
discrimination:
  racial, anger in response to, 127
  sexual, 265, 268–69, 273
diseases:
  of brain, 74, 76–78, 97–100
  psychosomatic, *see* psychosomatic disorders
displacement, 52, 129–30, 131, 138, 163–64, 184, 208, 213
divorce, 68, 108
  anger in, 299–307
  children of, 300–301
  men in, 304
  women in, 301–4
divorce ceremonies, 156, 304–5
Doi, T., 121
Dollard, John, 164

Donnerstein, Edward and Marcia, 162
Douglass, Frederick, 261
Dowling, Colette, 275–76
Downey, Morton, Jr., 283
Draper, Patricia, 51–53, 57
drinking feasts, 54–55
Driscoll, Richard, 238, 244
driving, aggressive, 78, 173–77
Drolette, Margaret, 112–14
drugs:
  antidepressant, 109–10
  epinephrine and, 89
  psychoactive, 98
  see also specific drugs
drum matches, 59
DSM (Diagnostic and Statistical Manual of Mental Disorders, The), 287
Duncan, Birt, 139–40
Dunning, Eric, 186
duodenal ulcers, 106–7
Dworkin, Barry, 118
dyscontrol syndrome, 97

eating disorders, 104–6
Eating Disorders (Bruch), 105–6
Ebbesen, Ebbe, 139
Ecclesiastes, 27
EEG patterns, 75–76
ego, 32, 253, 321*n*–22*n*
Ego and the Id, The (Freud), 321*n*–22*n*
Ehrenreich, Barbara, 280
Ekman, Paul, 322*n*–23*n*
Elias, Norbert, 186
Elliott, Frank A., 97
embarrassment:
  about fighting, 55, 202
  responses to, 65
  of victims, 269–70
emotionality, 83–85, 327*n*
emotions:
  of animals, 32–38
  brain and, 37, 76–80, 95
  combinations of, 85, 87–88, 91–95, 100, 102, 108–12, 117–18, 125–26

emotions (*cont.*)
  cultural determination of, 36,
    65–67
  differentiation of, 73, 85, 87–88,
    91–95, 100, 102, 113, 117–18
  epinephrine and, 89–91
  expression vs. suppression of, 36,
    40–41, 66–68, 197–99
  negative vs. positive, 64
  reason vs., 31, 32
encephalitis, 74
encounter groups, 43
energy:
  libido as, 40
  output of, 83, 85, 90
England:
  anger as viewed in, 46
  study of depression in, 110–11, 122
Ephesians, 259–60
epilepsy, 74, 76, 77
epinephrine, 85–91, 163, 181–82,
    328n
  alcohol and, 89
  brain and, 89–90
  drugs and, 89
  emotions and, 87–91
  stress and, 85, 89
Equal Rights Amendment, 269, 274
Ervin, Frank, 330n
Eskimos:
  Alaskan, 253
  Ammassalik, 48–49
  anger as viewed by, 46, 57–58
  insanity as viewed by, 59
  sexual practices of, 48–49
  song duels of, 59, 67
  temper as viewed by, 46, 57–58
  Utkuhikhalingmiut, 46, 57–58,
    150
  work schedule of, 253
ethnography, 51
ethology, 32–38, 51
Evans, R., 162
Evans, Sara, 263
excitability, 85
excuses, 96–97, 190
exercise, 89, 181–84
exploitative reciprocity, 260–61

*Expression of the Emotions in Man
  and Animals, The* (Darwin), 34

facial expressions, universality of, 34,
  36, 322n–23n
Falwell, Jerry, 261
family:
  anger patterns in, 238–39, 240–45
  cultural patterns of and responses,
    121–22, 172
  role of, in response to anger, 68,
    231–32, 305
family quarrels, 55–56, 137–38, 180,
    204–6, 234–35, 288
family-systems therapy, 45, 237–47,
    295, 306, 317
Family Violence (Gelles), 180
Farb, Peter, 59
Farber, Leslie, 111–12
Farrell, Warren, 280
fathers:
  abusive, 76, 225, 255
  anger at, 38, 50
  anger of, 225
  crying responded to by, 170
fear:
  anger vs., 87–88, 212–13, 328n
  brain and, 37
  emotionality and, 83–85
  of expressing anger, 29, 51–52, 71,
    194–97
  physical response to, 87–90, 328n
  repression of, 36
  of retaliation, 29, 204
  sex differences and, 199
Feindler, Eva, 309, 310
Feingold, Ben F., 326n
Feminine Mystique, The (Friedan),
    233, 268
feminism, 263–82
  in America, 279, 280
  anger and, 17–18, 98, 261, 277
  connotations of term, 279–80
  as humanism, 278
  "new sexism" in, 280–81
  in Third World, 261
  young women and, 276–80
  see also women's movement

Feshbach, Seymour, 136
fighting:
   disapproval of, 53–54, 58, 59
   embarrassment about, 55
   sexual intercourse after, 44–45
   at sports events, 184–87
   verbal vs. physical, 136–37
Fitz, Don, 203–5, 216
FitzGerald, Frances, 256, 261
Fixsen, Dean, 147–48
Fontanne, Lynn, 248
food allergies, 60, 74, 97–98, 106,
   143, 326n
forgiveness, 305–307, 315–18
Fortune, 101
Fox, Allen, 189
Freedman, Daniel G., 81–82
Freud, Sigmund, 21, 321n–22n
   challengers of, 92–93, 136, 254
   influence of, 32–33, 38–41, 127,
   131
Friedan, Betty, 233, 268, 270
Friedman, Howard S., 125
friendliness, 132–35
friends, role of, 20, 68, 138–40, 300,
   305
Friesen, Wallace, 322n
Frodi, Ann, 206–8, 338n
frustration, 24, 101, 112, 164–67
fundamentalism, 256, 261
Funkenstein, Daniel H., 112–14

Gandhi, Mohandas K., 31
Gelbart, Larry, 160
Gelles, Richard, 180
gender club, 196
Genesis, 69
genetics, 80–85, 107, 118, 163, 327n
Gerulaitis, Vitas, 188
Gestalt therapy, 250
Glick, Barry, 310
Goldberg, Herb, 196–97, 213
Goldstein, Arnold, 174, 310
Goldstein, Jeffrey, 185
golf, 190, 252
Goodenough, Florence, 146–47
Gordon, Steven, 208–9
Gordon, Thomas, 137

Gossage, Goose, 181
gossip, 57, 213
grand mal epilepsy, 76
Graves, Robert, 30
Greenwald, Anthony G., 253
Groen, J. J., 102
guilt:
   anger vs., 275
   eating disorders and, 105
   after expression of anger, 135, 202,
   337n–38n
   necessity of, 41
   suppressed anger and, 24
Gurin, Joel, 104–6
Gururumba tribe, 60, 62–63

habits:
   anger-intensifying, 289
   cooling-off, 289
Haig, Alexander, 6
Halas, Celia, 195–96
Hall, Edward T., 65–66
Hall, G. Stanley, 71–73, 88, 135,
   144
Hamlet (Shakespeare), 31
harangue, 58
Harburg, Ernest, 116, 273
Harper's Bazaar, 101
Harris, Jean, 60, 63–64
Harris, Tirril, 110
Hazards of Being Male, The
   (Goldberg), 196
head injuries, 74–80
healing rituals, 317
heart disease, 101, 103, 119–25,
   333n
heart rate, 73, 162, 163, 178,
   328n
   concentration and, 88, 89–90
Hearts of Men, The (Ehrenreich),
   280
Helmholtz, Hermann von, 40
hemorrhage, 89
Henry IV: Part I (Shakespeare), 193
Henry VIII (Shakespeare), 322n
high blood pressure, 77, 101, 103,
   115–21, 125, 331n–32n
Hill, Anne, 127

Hispanics, 66, 172
hockey, 187
Hokanson, Jack, 132–34
Hollan, Douglas, 58
Holmberg, Allan R., 150
Holocaust, 157, 256
Homer, 30
Horace, 59
hormones, *see specific hormones*
hostility, 202, 291, 334n
    antagonistic, 123–24
    depression and, 109
    humor and, 292
    illness and, 125–26
    neurotic, 123
    self-directed, 107–8, 113–14, 208
    sports and, 129
    suppressed, 22, 105, 113–14, 117–18
    in Type A personality, 119
housekeeping, arguments about, 230
housewives, 110, 122–23, 204, 214,
    233–34, 263–64, 333n
Huddy, Leonie, 279
humor:
    anger dissipated by, 58–59, 67,
        160, 167, 226–27, 284, 291
    hostile, 226, 291
humor therapy, 292, 306, 341n
Huntington's chorea, 74
Hupka, Ralph, 48–49
hyperactivity, 74, 326n
hypertension, 77, 101, 103, 115–21,
    125, 331n–32n
hyperthyroidism, 74
hypocrisy, 69
hypoglycemia, 77, 89
hypotension, 89
hypothalamus, 37, 76
hysteria, 23

id, 32, 40, 321n–22n
idea, as emotional force, 92
Ifaluk tribe, 54
Iliad (Homer), 30–31
Illness as Metaphor (Sontag), 103
immigrants, 121, 171, 231
impatience, 119, 123
impotence, 101, 102

impulsivity, 83
Incredible Hulk, 29
independence, 121–22, 333n
India, Toda tribe in, 49
Indians, *see* Native Americans
indignation, 34–35
individualism:
    anger and, 46, 69
    in Type A personality, 121–22, 123
infants:
    angry, 39, 83–84, 142–43, 145
    crying of, 169–70, 335n
    facial expressions of, 80
    heart rate of, 88
    temperament of, 80–85, 327n–28n
injustice, anger at, 72, 108, 115–16,
    139–40, 152–53, 166, 210,
    252–85
insanity, 59–64
instinct:
    anger as, 24
    displaced, 52
    emotions as, 32, 36
insults:
    anger at, 72, 88, 167, 168–69,
        182, 210
    in Eskimo song duels, 59
    as verbal aggression, 58, 207, 226
internalization, 21–22
interruptions, 166
intimacy, anger and, 221
introversion, 125–26
irritability, 202
    antidepressants and, 109
    dieting and, 106
    of hypertensives, 117
    organic causes of, 74, 76
    test for, 200
Islam, 259
isolation water tanks, 288
Israel, heart disease in, 121
Izard, Carroll, 80

Jacobs, Marion, 303, 305–6, 307
Japan:
    crowding in, 170
    cultural rules of, 36, 46, 65, 67,
        121–22, 253, 318, 325n, 333n

Japanese-Americans, 120–21
jealousy, 48–49, 56
Jefferson, Thomas, 130
Jews:
  ancient, 69
  anger as viewed by, 160
  crowding and, 172–73
  ritual bickering among, 53
jogging, 176, 182–83
Johnson, Cliff, 181
Johnson, Samuel, 251
Johnson, Sonia, 269–70, 271–72
jokes:
  hostile, 226
  in ritual bickering, 52–53, 58–59
*Journal of the American Medical
  Association,* 164
Judeo-Christian tradition, 69
judgment, anger determined by,
  37–38, 91
junk food, 60, 74
justice, 153

Kagan, Jerome, 84, 327n–28n
Kalahari Desert, 50, 51
Kapauku Papuans, 54–55
Kaplan, Harold and Helen Singer,
  104
Kaplan, Joe, 174
Kaplow, Susi, 270
Kelly, Joan, 300
Kettle, Tom, 285
Kiechel, Walter, 127, 330n
King, Coretta Scott, 313
King, Stanley H., 112–14
Kiowa Indians, 36
Klein, Donald F., 98, 109
Kleinman, Arthur, 67
Knoečni, Vladimir, 139, 168–69
Korean War, 184
Kundera, Milan, 291
!Kung-san tribe, anger as viewed by,
  46, 50–53, 57, 68, 232
Kutash, Samuel B., 323n

laughter, 292
  see also humor
Lear's, 128

legal code, 24, 50, 63–64, 97
Lemon, Bob, 177–78
Leonard, John, 273
Lerner, Harriet G., 195, 239,
  241–45, 295
Lerner, Melvin J., 254–55, 257
lethargy, 24
Levy, Robert, 69
Lewis, Dorothy Otnow, 75–76
Lewis, Janet, 30
libido, 40
limbic system, 37, 76, 78, 95, 97
Lochman, John, 308–9
Loehr, Jim E., 189
Lorenz, Konrad, 32
Los Angeles:
  crime rate in, 171
  driving in, 173, 174, 176
losing face, 67, 269
lovers' quarrels, 17–19, 44–45, 60,
  64, 250
Lowen, Alexander, 136
Lunt, Alfred, 248
Luther, Martin, 85
Lutz, Catherine, 54

Macaulay, Jacqueline, 206–8
Mace, David, 221
McEnroe, John, 187–89
Mackarness, Richard, 98
McKellar, Peter, 335n
MacLeod, Margo, 121
"mad dance," 55–56
Mademoiselle, 228
Mairs, Nancy, 313, 314
Malay Archipelago, *pengamok* in, 60,
  61–63
Malaysia, Temiar tribe in, 58
Malcolm X, 263, 268, 270, 272
Mandler, George, 166
Margolin, Gayla, 246–47
marital quarrels, 20, 45, 51, 129–30,
  136, 138, 153, 156, 159, 177,
  180, 204–6, 207, 220–50,
  315–16, 339n
Mark, Vernon, 330n
Marlatt, G. Alan, 179
Marshall, John R., 129

Martin, Billy, 177–78
masochism, 134, 333n
Mason, Geoff, 191
Mastery of Stress (Funkenstein, King, and Drolette), 112–14, 125
Mather, Cotton, 181
Matsumoto, Y., 122
Maurer, Robert, 301, 304, 306–7
Mbuti tribe, 58–59, 67
Mead, Margaret, 57, 262
"Memoir of a Japanese Daughter" (Sawada), 313
men:
    aggression in, 132–34, 334n
    alcohol and, 179
    anger suppressed by, 197–98
    blood-pressure levels of, 115–16, 117
    "manliness" and, 67, 116, 197, 199
    smoking among, 120
    ulcers in, 331n
    women as viewed by, 85, 98–99, 194, 196–97, 213
    see also fathers; sex roles
Menninger, Karl, 183
metabolism, 74
Mexico, sex roles in, 216–17
migraine, 101
Milk, Harvey, 60
Miller, Jean Baker, 212
Mind, Mood, and Medicine (Wender and Klein), 98
Mindess, Harvey, 292
mokhthoditi, 49
money, arguments about, 230–31
monoamine oxidase (MAO), 82
Montagu, Ashley, 334n
Montaigne, Michel Eyquem de, 31–32, 249–50
mood disorders, 287
moodiness, 72, 83, 98
Moore, Barrington, Jr., 260
moral passivity, 159
Morgan, Marabel, 270
Morgan, Robin, 263, 270–71
Mormon Church, 269–70
Morris, Desmond, 32

Moscone, George, 60
mothers:
    abusive, 76
    anger at, 18, 39, 74, 143, 146–47
    angry, 137–38, 167
    crying responded to by, 170
Mothers Against Drunk Drivers, 317
Mourning and Melancholia (Freud), 107
Moyer, Kenneth E., 98–99
Moyers, Bill, 283
murder:
    by adolescents, 74
    excuses for, 24–25, 37, 325n
    guilt for, 30
    temporary insanity as defense for, 59–64
Murray, Edward J., 141
music, 168–69
Myerhoff, Barbara, 53

Nastase, Ilie, 187
National Hockey League, 186, 187
National Institute of Mental Health, 82
National Institutes of Health, 77
National Safety Council, 174
Native Americans:
    Kiowa, 36
    Navaho, 82
    Pawnee, 48
Navaho Indians, 82
NBC, 191
Neilson, Kurt, 187
neocortex, 78, 95
nervousness, 89
Newman, P. L., 62
New Mexico, cultural tension in, 65–66
New Testament, 259
New York City, 167, 284
New Yorker, 188
New York Times, 177–78, 191, 336n–37n
niceness, avoidance of, 42, 46
Nichols, Jack, 197–98
Nick Bollettieri Tennis Academy, 189

nicotine, 89
noise, 163, 167–70
norepinephrine (noradrenaline), 86,
  87–89, 181–82
Novaco, Raymond, 173, 289, 293,
  310
Number Our Days (Myerhoff), 53
nutritional deficiencies, 74, 98,
  106

obscenities, 53, 59, 325*n*, 333*n*–34*n*
obsession, 156–59, 317
Old Testament, 258–59
O'Reilly, Jane, 271, 276
ostracism, 57, 58
overstimulation, *see* stress
overweight, 103, 104–7

Padesky, Christine, 294–99
pancreas, 77
Panza, Sancho, 164
paranoia, 76, 285, 330*n*
Parent Effectiveness Training, 137
Pascal, Blaise, 31
Pascale, Richard, 121
Passions, The (Solomon), 38
passive aggression, 57, 197
passive optimism, 69
Patterson, Gerald R., 307
Pawnee Indians, 48
pedestrians, 175–76
pengamok, 61–63
Pennebaker, James, 156–58
perceptions:
  anger-arousing, 289
  anger-reducing, 289, 293, 317
Perls, Frederick "Fritz," 43
personality:
  aggressive catharsis and, 134–35
  group differences in, 80–85
  hypertensive, 116–18
  sexual differences in, 205, 208–9
  temperament and, 83
  tuberculosis and, 103
  Type A, 119–20, 123–25, 332*n*
  Type B, 119–20, 124
Personal Politics (Evans), 263
Peru, anger as viewed in, 46

Phaedrus (Plato), 321*n*
Phillips, Elery, 147–48
philosophy:
  environment and, 69
  reason praised by, 31
  Stoical, 64
Plato, 21, 31, 32, 95, 130, 161, 321*n*
Plomin, Robert A., 83
Plutarch, 131
Poland, shtetls in, 53
Polivy, Janet, 93
pornography, 162–63
postpartum depression, 95
poverty, 127, 255
"premenstrual syndrome," 95
presenile dementia, 74
Primal Scream, 83, 288
privacy, 51, 172
psychoanalysis:
  anger explained by, 18, 109, 175,
    212–14, 231
  assumptions of, 23–24, 38–39
  current theories of, 40–47
  function of, 41, 138, 140
  see also therapy
psychosomatic disorders, 42, 43,
  101–27, 197
  blood-pressure problems as,
    116–18
  depression as, 107–12
  eating disorders as, 104–7
  heart disease as, 119–25
  tuberculosis as, 103
  ulcers as, 103, 106–7
psychosurgery, 98–99
Puritans, 29, 181

racial differences, 81–83
rage:
  anger vs., 34–35, 78
  brain and, 37, 76–77, 78, 95–100
  brief, 161–92
  defined, 34
  facial expression in, 34
  organic causes of, 73–76
  physiology of, 73
  prolonged, 304–5
  social movements and, 272

rape, 255, 257–58
rationalization, 253–62
rationing and fairness, 166
rats, experiments with, 118, 163, 170
reaction formation, 39
Reagan, Ronald, 255
reappraisal, 290
reconciliation, 292
Redbook, 235
reflection, as anger strategy, 116
reification, 21
relative deprivation, 261
relaxation techniques, 288, 293, 309
religion, 31, 256, 258–60, 261, 270
repression, 57
  defined, 41
  suppression vs., 103
repressors, 79–80
retaliation:
  as catharsis, 135, 137
  fear of, 29
  rage as, 34
  as response to anger, 129–30
retribution, 63
revenge, 63
Richard II (Shakespeare), 220
Richard III (Shakespeare), 70, 325n
ridicule, as punishment, 57, 58–59
Righetti, Dave, 190
Rioch, David M., 179
Rolling Thunder (Boyd), 28
Rose, Pete, 189
Roseman, Marina, 58
Rothenberg, Albert, 23
Rubin, Theodore Isaac, 43–45
running, as sport, 182–83
Russell, Bertrand, 273
Russia, shtetls in, 53

Sabini, John, 40
Sadri, John, 187
salmon, genetic programming in, 83
Saltzman, Nolan, 128
Samurai knights, 66–67
Sawada, Noriko, 313, 317–18
Schachter, Stanley, 329n
Schakowsky, Jan, 263, 264, 266

Scheff, Thomas, 292
Schneider, Beth, 279
Scioli, Anthony, 94
Sears, David, 279
Sebeok, Thomas, 325n
Second Chances (Wallerstein and Blakeslee), 300
Seif, Ellie, 148–49
self-control, 70
  as cultural value, 31–33, 36, 68–69
  rejection of, 45
self-esteem:
  attacks on, 210
  of children, 307, 312
  cognitive therapy for, 110
  after expression of anger, 44, 202, 215–16, 236, 302
  persistent anger and, 306–7
self-help books, 275
self-help groups, 305–6, 317
selfishness, 18, 69
self-punishment, as catharsis, 134
Semai tribe, anger as viewed by, 57
Senate, U.S., 67
Seneca, Marcus Annaeus, 31, 37, 64
sex roles, 132–34, 193–219, 281–82, 337n
  stereotypes of, 214–15
sexuality, sexual intercourse:
  aggression and, 44–45, 157
  alcohol and, 179
  brain and, 37
  id and, 40
  sublimation of, 41
  uncertainty about, 54, 216–18
Shakespeare, William, 21, 31, 70, 193, 220, 321n–22n, 325n–26n
shame, 24, 50, 57, 65, 227n
shtetls, ritual bickering in, 53
siblings, rivalry between, 45, 72, 148–49
sin, 31, 260
Singer, Jerome E., 329n
Sipes, Richard, 183–84
Siriono tribe:
  ritual bickering in, 54–55
  temper tantrums in, 150

situational sterotypy, 328n
skating, skateboarding, 175–76
slavery, 35, 252, 261
Snyder, C. R., 96
sociability, 83
social classes, anger as expressed by,
    35, 251
Social Origins of Depressions (Brown
    and Harris), 110
social sciences, 43, 95, 136–37, 261
sociobiology, 32, 37
sociology, 19, 24
Solomon, Robert, 38, 68
Sommers, Shula, 94
song duels, 59
Sontag, Susan, 103
Sostek, Andrew, 82
South Sulawesi, Indonesia, Toraja
    tribe in, 58
Southwest Pacific, Ifaluk tribe in, 54
spiders, genetic programming in, 83
Spielberger, Charles, 114–15, 200
spleen, 70, 325n
spoilsports, 191
sports:
    anger not displaced by, 129, 131,
        163–64, 183–87
    ventilation in, 187–92
    see also specific sports
Spy, 283
Sroufe, L. Alan, 85
Stapleton, Ruth, 270
State/Trait Anger Expression
    Inventory, 186
Steinmetz, Suzanne K., 45, 137,
    229–30
Stewart, Payne, 190
sticklebacks, instinct in, 34
Stoicism, 64
Storr, Anthony, 183
strangers, aggression toward, 204–5
Straus, Murray, 136–37, 230, 232,
    234
stress, 103, 105, 112–18
    economic, 118, 170
    environmental, 118, 167–73
    epinephrine (adrenaline) and, 85
    social, 118

stroke, 74
Stupid Inanimate Object, 71–72, 95,
    164
stupidity, anger at, 72
sublimation, 41
sugar:
    blood, 77
    rage caused by, 74
sulking, 29, 30, 198
Superman, 29
suppressors, 79
survival:
    anger as threat to, 53–54, 66–67
    cultural rules and, 69
Swami's snake fallacy, 27–28, 37, 47
swearing, 130, 334n
Syme, S. Leonard, 122, 124

taboos, 59, 63
Tahiti, survival in, 54, 69
Taming of the Shrew, The
    (Shakespeare), 193
tantrums, 127, 213, 311
    in children, 127, 142–44, 146–50
    in sports, 188
    as ventilation, 142–50
Taoism, 259
Tarnower, Herman, 60, 64
Taylor, Shelley, 254
Temiar tribe, 58
temper, 20–21, 57, 83, 142–50, 188,
    206, 213
temperament, 80–85, 327n–28n
tempo, 85, 327n
temporal-lobe epilepsy, 74, 76, 77
tennis, 187–89, 191
tension, 112, 122, 132, 291
terror, 35
testosterone, 95, 96
therapy:
    and aggression, 307–12
    aggression training as, 196–97
    as anger business, 23–24, 42–46
    child, 142–43, 307–12
    for chronic anger, 288–93
    cognitive, 38, 45, 109–10, 294–99
    for persistent anger, 299–307
Third World cultures, 261

Thomas, Elizabeth Marshall, 51
Thomas, W. I., 19
Thome, Pauline, 206–8
Through the Looking Glass (Carroll), 20
Thurman, Judith, 248
Tiefer, Leonore, 79
Time, 187
Tocqueville, Alexis de, 261
Toda tribe, 49
Tokyo, crowding in, 170
Toraja tribe, 58
Torre, Joe, 190
totalitarian ego, 254
tranquilizers, 106
Trail of Sören Qvist, The (Lewis), 30–31
Troll, Lillian, 282
tuberculosis, 103
tumors:
  brain, 74
  pancreatic, 77
Twain, Mark, 130
Twinkie defense, 60
Type A personality, 119–20, 123–25
Type B personality, 119–20, 124

ulcers, 101, 102, 106–7, 118, 331n
unconscious, Freudian concept of, 38, 92
understimulation, 89
United States:
  adultery in, 49
  anger as viewed in, 46, 63, 65, 69
  children's anger in, 150
  cultural rules of, 172, 191, 253, 262, 313
  sex roles in, 217–19
  temporary insanity defense in, 63–64
  violence in, 64
  weddings in, 56
urban life:
  heart disease and, 121
  rage and, 161–63, 167, 170–77
Utkuhikhalingmiut Eskimos, anger as viewed by, 46, 57–58, 68, 150

ventilation, ventilationism, 42–46, 68–69, 128–60, 243, 288, 316
  by aggression, 130–38
  catharsis vs., 41, 130–38
  in children, 142–50, 312
  defined, 43
  effects of, 151–52
  optimal conditions for, 152–55
  in sports, 187–91
  talking out as, 138–42
  temper tantrums as, 142–50
verbal dueling, 58–59, 325n
victims, 313–17
Vietnam War, 157, 184, 265, 276
viral encephalitis, 74
Vishnuism, 259

Wade, Carole, 158–59
Wallerstein, Judith, 300–301
Watson, Tom, 252
Way of the World, The (Congreve), 85
Weather Underground, 262
weddings, 55–56
Weinberger, Daniel, 79–80
Weiss, Bernard, 326n
Wender, Paul H., 98, 109
Western Collaborative Group Study, 119
West Malaysia, Semai tribe in, 57
West New Guinea, Kapauku Papuans in, 55
White, Dan, 60, 63–64
White, E. B., 251
Why Men Are the Way They Are (Farrell), 280
wife beating, 180, 207, 252
Wikler, Norma, 265
Wilbanks, William Lee, 96, 97, 190
"wild pigs," 60, 62–63
Wile, Daniel, 237
Williams, Elizabeth Friar, 196
Williams, Redford B., Jr., 123
Wilson, E. O., 32
Wimbledon, 191
Wind, Herbert Warren, 188
witchcraft:
  amok attacks caused by, 62
  punishment by, 57

wolves, instinct in, 34
women:
    alcohol and, 179
    anger suppressed by, 67, 116,
        195–96, 334n
    battered, 180, 207, 252
    depressed, 109, 110, 122–23,
        195
    divorce and, 301–4
    employed, 122–23, 204, 213–15,
        265–69, 273–74
    friendliness of, 132–34
    heart disease in, 122–23
    men's views of, 85, 98–99,
        194–95, 213
    presumed irrationality of, 31,
        98–99, 196–97
    self-esteem of, 302, 304
    smoking among, 120
    Type A, 123
    ulcers in, 331n

    see also housewives; mothers; sex
        roles
women's movement, 133, 265–82
    suburban women in, 266
    young women in, 276–80
    see also feminism
Woods, Sherwyn M., 74
World War II, 184
Wyatt, Richard J., 82

XYY Syndrome, 327n

Yiddish, cursing in, 53
yoga, 90

Zaire, Mbuti tribe in, 58–59
Zajonc, Robert, 330n
Ziegler, John, 186–87
Zilbergeld, Bernie, 211, 247,
    315–16
Zillmann, Dolf, 182

About the Author

Carol Tavris, Ph.D., earned her doctorate in social psychology from the University of Michigan. She was senior editor for several years of a then-new magazine, *Psychology Today*, and went on to develop a career as a teacher, lecturer, and psychology writer. She is coauthor (with Carole Wade) of *The Longest War: Sex Differences in Perspective* and an introductory textbook, *Psychology*. In addition to writing the "Mind Health" column for *Vogue* magazine, she has written many articles and book reviews on diverse issues in psychology for a wide variety of magazines, including *The New York Times, Discover, Science Digest, Human Nature, New York, Harper's, Geo, Ms., Redbook,* and *Woman's Day*. While living in New York, Tavris taught at the Human Relations Center of the New School for Social Research, and in Los Angeles she now teaches from time to time in the department of psychology at UCLA.